F

Also by Judith Hooper and Dick Teresi

The Three-Pound Universe

Also by Dick Teresi

Omni's Continuum
Laser
The Omni Future Medical Almanac

WOULD THE BUDDHA WEAR · A WALKMAN?

A CATALOGUE OF
REVOLUTIONARY
TOOLS FOR HIGHER
CONSCIOUSNESS

JUDITH HOOPER
AND DICK TERESI

PHOTO AND ART EDITING BY HILDEGARD KRON

A FIRESIDE BOOK
PUBLISHED BY SIMON & SCHUSTER INC.
NEW YORK   LONDON   TORONTO   SYDNEY
TOKYO   SINGAPORE

FIRESIDE
Simon & Schuster Building
Rockefeller Center
1230 Avenue of the Americas
New York, New York 10020

Designed by Bonni Leon

Manufactured in the United States of America

1   3   5   7   9   10   8   6   4   2   Pbk.

Library of Congress Cataloging in Publication Data

Hooper, Judith.
Would the Buddha wear a walkman? A catalogue of
revolutionary tools for higher consciousness / Judith
Hooper and Dick Teresi.
p.   cm.
"A Fireside book."
Includes index.
1. New Age movement—Miscellanea—Catalogs.
2. Self-actualization (Psychology)—Miscellanea—
Catalogs.   I. Teresi, Dick.   II. Title
BP605.N48H67 1990
381'.45'00029473—dc20   90-41424
                                          CIP

ISBN 0-671-69373-5 Pbk.

Design Concept by Regina Marsh

ACKNOWLEDGMENTS

First of all, we wish to thank Douglas Colligan for suggesting our title. We have no idea what it means, but we've spent the last year and a half trying to answer it. We would also have been adrift without the talents and research of Leah Wallach, Linda Marsa, Kathryn Phillips, and Rebecca Norris. To our long-suffering editor Edward Walters, all we can say is, there's probably a reward for your efforts in another lifetime (though we may have an option on that, too). A special debt of gratitude is owed to *Omni* magazine for providing the inspiration for this project. (They fired us, so we needed the money.)

CONTENTS

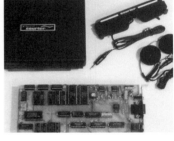

WOULD THE BUDDHA WEAR · A WALKMAN?

CHAPTER ONE

WELCOME · TO
CONSCIOUSNESS
TECH

·

"Would the Buddha wear a Walkman?" we asked.

"Would Jesus walk on water?" he replied.

We had put the question to Randy Adamadama, proprietor of the Universe of You, the most famous mind spa in the country, perhaps in the world. "Would the Buddha wear a Walkman?" he posed the question again to himself. "Well, yes I do," he said laughing. "Would the Buddha wear a Walkman?" he repeated. "Of course he would."

It seemed a natural  question for Adama-dama. When he opened up the Universe of You in Au-gust 1987 in Corte Madera in trendy Marin County (Cali-fornia), he placed a statue of a Buddha in the lobby and hung a pair of Walkman-like earphones on its head. Actually, they weren't Walkman phones at all, explained

Adamadama, but earphones from a synchronizing light-and-sound machine that he uses to tune his customers' brains to more relaxing, meditative, even blissful frequencies.

In this era, we're convinced the Buddha would indeed wear a Walkman—provided the Walkman contained tapes that would help him reach enlightenment in a hurry. Today there is a quiet revolution in mind expansion, altered states, and spiritual self-improvement. We call it Consciousness Tech.

Consciousness Tech is to the mind what the radio telescope is to the universe. It is a natural outgrowth of the revolution in neuroscience, which has given us the ability to look inside the human brain. Now that we can take PET scans (diagnostic "photos") of hallucinations, and radioactively label the neurotransmitters that make us happy or mad or violent or passionate, it is inevitable to want to master and control our mental life, to improve our own brains, to access (if you'll excuse the jargon) the dormant 90 percent of our neural capacity. What is the brain chemical that mediates joy? What is the brain-wave frequency that provides enlightenment? More important, how do we manipulate such phenomena? Consciousness Tech is based on a marriage of Western technology and the superior spiritual "technology" of the East. The result is an explosion of new psychotechnologies that are changing the way we think—and perhaps even our brains themselves.

The signs are all around you. Now, for under $400, you can buy a personal light-and-sound machine, a device that uses specially designed frequencies of sound and light to alter your brain waves and your consciousness. Previously, such machines cost $60,000 and occupied a whole room. Today you can strap one to your belt like a Walkman, slip on a pair of goggles and headphones, and transform your brain in your bedroom—or on the bus. If you run a corporation, you can get a reading of your Corporate Brainwave Profile, not to mention your corporate karma, at a Sausalito, California, institute where an EEG machine teaches seekers to match their brain waves to those of a fully enlightened yogi.

Today, you can equip your home computer with a bio-feedback mouse, which measures your physical stress levels and lets you control images on your monitor with your emotions. You can also feed your dreams into a digital dream diary and let your computer organize your Great Mother archetypes and serpent images from different dreams. It may even help you create a haiku from the night's dream images and illustrate it with a picture. Using a mind-mapping technique based on recent neuropsychological research, you can organize your ideas according to your brain's natural rhythms and even have breakthrough insights. At your local New Age center, you can learn the secrets of Mayan priests, the rituals of Amazonian shamans, the rudiments of Tibetan psychiatry—using accelerated techniques that impart this knowledge in a weekend, or less.

THE NEW PSYCHOTECHNOLOGIES

The new psychotechnologies share certain characteristics:

1. They are eclectic.

Many of them mix techniques from several different spiritual traditions or psychological schools. For example, a "personal anthropologist" uses the techniques of anthropological fieldwork to map an individual's inner world. A software designer has packed the 2,500-year-old wisdom of the *I Ching* into a disk. A former Tibetan Buddhist nun mixes traditional Tantric Buddhist practices and Gestalt psychology in her "dakini workshops" for women. A modern "mystery school" in Marin County, California, draws on the teachings of the ancient Greek and Egyptian mystery religions as well as Hawaiian religion, African shamanism, Sufism, Tibetan Buddhism, Basque ritual, Native American shamanism, and Christian mysticism.

2. They are fast.

Compared with the geologic pace of traditional analysis, or the even slower pace of traditional religious practices that require spending forty years meditating in a cave, the new mind-altering techniques are designed to work quickly. Neurolinguistic Programming, a new cognitive psychology, purveys quick (forty-five-minute) cures for grief, severe phobias, and even Vietnam-era war flashbacks. Hypno-peripheral processing (try saying that fast!) uses cassette tapes, earphones, and state-of-the-art audio technology to bypass your superego and plant healthy messages directly into your subconscious mind. A character named Brother Charles offers high-tech meditation tapes that claim to speed up the process of enlightenment by some 75 percent or so, and an Avatar Course purports to make you into an avatar (the incarnation of a god) in five days.

3. They are largely do-it-yourself.

For example, instead of spending every Tuesday at three o'clock at the shrink, you can explore your "personal mythology" in the privacy of your own home with the aid of a self-guided course. Instead of handing your dreams over to a professional analyst to decode, you can use an impressive assortment of tools and resources—including computerized dream files, lucid-dream goggles, and dream networks—to work through the lush jungle of the subconscious on your own. A variety of computerized shrinks—Jungian, Rogerian, or transpersonal—let you be your own shrink, while spiritual cassettes and other new enlightenment aids free you from excessive dependence on gurus.

SHOPPING MALL NIRVANA

Purists may at first be aghast at the concept of Consciousness Tech. For one thing, it does mean commercialization, something we don't normally associate with spirituality (unless you've spent time with Werner Erhard). The most obvious aspect of this trend is the emergence of mind spas, gyms for the brain that usually offer a variety of brain machines, isolation tanks, meditation chambers, and the like. One of the first to conceive of the shopping mall approach to enlightenment was Randy Adamadama. "I wanted a place," he said, "where you plunk down your ten bucks and you get your relaxation." Light-and-sound machines (covered in detail in Chapter 2) saved Adamadama's life. "I needed it," he says. "I hadn't been paying attention to my life. I was very very ill—in a number of ways. One day I woke up and I said to myself, 'Do I want to get out of bed?' And the answer was no." He discovered light-and-sound machines, then a little-known phenomenon, strapped on a pair of goggles and headphones, and started his personal road to relaxation and recovery. He decided to bring the technology to the public, so in 1987, with $6,500 and help from friends, he opened the prototypical Universe of You—enlightenment in a shopping mall for ten bucks.

In truth, Adamadama doesn't pretend to sell enlightenment per se. "You don't get enlightenment from a machine," he says. "What you get is a frequency. Then it's up to you to do something with it." What Adamadama, and others like him, have done is give the general public a small taste of another universe, another plane of consciousness. Take a stressed-out investment banker. From his office in San Francisco he's battled the stock market all day, and now his white BMW M-3 is overheating in traffic on Highway 101 on the way home to San Rafael. So he takes the Paradise Drive exit to Corte Madera and pops into the Universe of You to have Randy Adamadama flash lights in his eyes, tones in his ears, and massage his soul with New Age music provided by a machine called the InnerQuest Pro-1. Then he might go for a rolling, churning ride on a motorized massage table known as the Graham Potentializer, or "fire up his ch'i" with copper cables called Bio Circuits, or sit in the Pendulum Vibration Chair, which hangs from a single chain and contains a motor that massages his whole body. "The whole process is like meditation," says Adamadama. "If you're stressed out, it gives you a very good glimpse of what a lifetime meditator feels. For the stressed-out guy, it's a brand new state. He'll want to go there again."

VACATIONS FOR YOUR BRAIN

In large part, this book is a catalogue of altered states. To many people today, the mention of altered states conjures up crack dens, Colombian drug lords on Avianca flights, and desperate retreats at the Betty Ford Clinic. That is not what we're talking about—or, rather, that's the dark underside of what we're talking about. We do need periodic vacations from our "normal" consciousness, but we don't have to take strange chemicals to have them.

While some people like to spend their vacations at home catching up on "Wheel of Fortune," others have an urge to

climb K-2 or visit the Galápagos. In order to visit the remote Galápagos and the Antarcticas of the mind, psychologically adventurous types will get hypnotized, float in an isolation tank, strap on an InnerQuest, take a class to learn ancient Egyptian trance techniques, practice lucid dreaming, or meditate on Tibetan dakinis (goddess figures personifying the formless energy of the universe). They do it for the same reason that drove Columbus, Magellan, and Cortez to cross the ocean toward *terra incognita:* to explore the rivers, mountain ranges, and yes, gold and emerald mines of a vast, unmapped New World. "We have to recognize," says UCLA psychologist Ronald K. Siegel, an expert on drugs and altered states, "that people are already selecting chemicals to alter their consciousness. They're not happy with one two-week vacation a year."

But we're not talking about a Club Med–type vacation, with a lot of tropical drinks and vegging out on the beach. We're talking about something more like a working vacation.

In Chicago, a life insurance salesman is ascending a staircase of clouds toward the Kingdom of the Sun God. He will spend the better part of the weekend in the Sky World, a luminious land familiar to South American shamans and medicine men but little known to most Chicago life insurance salesmen. The Sky World lies inside the man's inner landscape, and he got there thanks to the monotonous beat of a deerskin drum and the ingenuity of an anthropologist named Michael Harner, who has devised a method that permits ordinary Americans to become "shamans" in a weekend.

Meanwhile, in rural Virgina, just down the pike from Baptist churches and billboards that announce, "THE WAGES OF SIN IS DEATH," a group of "explorers" are lying in isolation booths as specially designed frequencies of sound are piped into their ears. This particular technology (called Hemi Sync) was developed by Robert Monroe, a pioneer in out-of-body experiences, to alter the explorers' brain waves and help launch them out of their bodies. Now why would you want to leave your body, after you've invested so much work on your deltoids at the gym? Because beyond it there is a vast universe to explore, if you believe Monroe, including beings from beyond the solar system with important messages for Homo sapiens.

But, of course, you don't have to leave your body to enter a different psychic landscape. Right here, in a world of leveraged buyouts and itemized business deductions, people are finding ways to practice magic. On the winter solstice, the longest night of the year, certain priests and priestesses gather by the altar, light their candles, and chant: "Isis, Astarte, Diana, Hecate, Demeter, Kali, Inanna." They are calling on the Great Goddess, the supreme deity of the "Old Religion," and they are using sophisticated forms of "magic" and trance work expressly designed to alter consciousness. The modern "pagans" and Goddess devotees have renovated an ancient technology of ecstasy.

OLD NEW AGE

So what is this—the New Age or the Old Age? Or the New Old Age? Well, of course, the so-called New Age never was all that new. Much of what is called New Age harks back to the consciousness revolution of the sixties, when gurus, as well as LSD, got hot; or even earlier, to the Zen-intoxicated Beat poets of the fifties; or even earlier to Victorian-Age Theosophists with their Ascended Masters and their karma. We have to go back even further, to ancient Phrygian goddesses, Druid ceremonies of pre-Christian Britain, and tenth-century Mesoamerican legends, for the sources of the present spiritual renaissance. As a matter of fact, while researching this book, we were often reminded of ancient Alexandria during the Hellenistic and Roman periods, roughly 300 B.C. to A.D 300. In those days temples used to house a whole menagerie of gods from the Egyptian Thoth and Anubis to the Greek Zeus and the local emperor-god. First came a major revival of the ancient Egyptian and ancient Greek Mystery religions, and several death/rebirth cults from Asia Minor; then came Jewish mystics, Christian and pagan Gnostics, Manicheans, and neoPlatonists, alchemists, and Hermetic brotherhoods dedicated to the combined Greek-Egyptian god Thoth/Hermes. The Great Library of Alexandria must have held quite a collection of theologies (and quite a few esoteric secrets) before it burned down. But not as many as we have in America in the nineties, where any alternative-learning-center brochure from Boulder, Colorado, say, or Santa Monica, California, lists rune workshops alongside Goddess festivals alongside Tibetan tulkus alongside Native American medicine wheel ceremonies alongside Kabbalah classes alongside Mayan elders. . . .

WHY THIS BOOK?

Consciousness Tech has arrived, and it will lead us (cosmic headphones and all) into the next millennium. In the 1980s physical fitness was the rage; brain fitness, perhaps even soul fitness, will be the trend of the 1990s. Already, according to one marketing firm, American adults are spending a total of $3.5 billion per year on goods and services in the personal growth/human potential field—$3.5 billion, in other words, on nirvana tapes, flashing goggles, books on aura cleaning or the lost teachings of Jesus. Some personal growth/human potential products are more valuable than others.

What you have in your hands is a comprehensive catalogue of the tools and services now available for improving one's mind or expanding one's consicousness. It's a consumer's guide for the enlightened—or soon-to-be enlightened—reviewing everything from cosmic travel agencies to ChiPants, trousers that (supposedly) have cosmic energy sewn into their seams.

CAVEAT EMPTOR

Before you proceed, we must give you two warnings. We have provided access guides, which often state prices, company names, addresses, phone numbers, and miscellaneous information. We have checked this information as close to our press time as possible. This is a fast-moving industry, and many concerns are small, recently founded, and are constantly changing location, phone numbers, products, and prices. The information is as up to date as we can make it, but in some cases you may have to do some additional digging to find the services, products, or information you desire.

We should also point out that we are not true believers. We're journalists. We sincerely believe the subject matter of this book is important, even revolutionary. But like any new field, this one is full of some pretty silly ideas and silly people. We're not embarrassed to say so. This book is not for the uncritical "bliss ninny," to use poet-philosopher Robert Bly's phrase. It's for those who wish to pick the wheat from the chaff, or at least appropriate from inappropriate.

As Randy Adamadama says, "The nineteen-nineties will see a whole lot of garbage." He tells the story of an inventor who came to him for financial backing to launch a new product. It was a helmet with a big Tesla coil on the top. A Tesla coil is a coil of wire that generates electricity through the open air. "Why do you need a Tesla coil on the top of your head?" Adamadama asked. "Does anyone really know what a Tesla coil does to the brain?"

"No, man," replied the inventor, "It just *feels good*."

Adamadama sighs. "Why not just stick electrodes up your. . . .? Well, I guess we have a culture that's pretty numb. It needs a lot of stimulation."

Most of us are not quite numb enough yet for the electrode solution. This book represents a search for something that not only "feels good" but that also transforms the mind in a positive way. Somewhere in the following pages you should be able to find the key to your personal nirvana.

M A C H I N E
DREAMS

•

The ancient Greek astronomer Ptolemy was the first person in recorded history to build

a brain machine. He set a wheel in line with the sun and spun it. People would stare at

the flashing lights emitted between the spokes and go into an altered state, complete with

visual effects. In more recent times—the 1960s—*Naked Lunch* author William Burroughs

and his friends built what they called a Dreammachine. It was a light inside a cylinder

that had holes punched in it. Burroughs and his buddies would spin the cylinder and

stare, eyes closed, into the stroboscopic flashes produced by the contraption. What they

got was the so-called "flicker effect." Burroughs reported daz- zling lights in his brain,
hallucinatory visions of extraordinary brilliance
and color, with fireballs that resembled the
mandalas of Eastern mysticism.

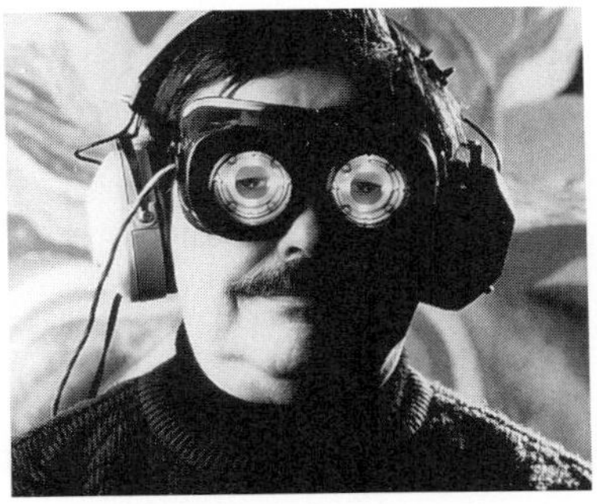

It was a drug ma- chine. There was no ab-

Randy Adamadama

sence of drugs in those bygone days, yet Burroughs et al. were content to sit in front of a colander-like device that scattered lightwaves at their eyelids. Today, you don't have to build your own. Dream machines are now available for the general public. You can use them at various brain salons, clinics, corporate facilities, and workshops all over the country. And you can buy personalized versions for a few hundred dollars from various retail establishments or even through mail-order catalogues.

Brain-altering machines, sometimes described as Nautilus equipment for the mind, range from the granddaddy of all such devices, the Synchro Energizer—a $69,000 industrial-strength contraption that features a Three Mile Island–like control panel and requires a trained operator—to the MC², a Walkman-like device that lets you zap your brain in the privacy of your own home (or on the bus) for the relatively modest price of $350. So far, they're all legal and available over the counter—or, at least, most of them are. The Lumatron flashes a strobe in your retina. The Genesis vibrates your whole body with music. The D.A.V.I.D. plies you with both lights and sound as well as a surf noise. The Graham Potentializer gyrates you on a padded table. The Tranquilite calms your psyche with "pink noise." The Brain Tuner applies electricity to your gray matter with electrodes that you wear behind your ears.

Why would you ever want to do any of this stuff? Well, probably for the same reason that some people put away a fifth of Jack Daniels. Seriously, there are socially redeeming reasons behind many of the legitimate machines. Relaxation is the common denominator, but the inventors, manufacturers, and promoters of brain machines have made claims far beyond that, some of them impressive, some of them straining our credulity. The machines in this chapter have been touted to do the following: improve vision, accelerate learning, harmonize the right and left hemispheres of the brain, improve I.Q. by thirty or more points, clear up acne, fire up assertiveness, reduce stress, normalize blood pressure, kill pain, pump up sexuality, eradicate tunnel vision, eliminate addictions, speed up enlightenment, get you through dental appointments, raise self-esteem, cheer up the mood at funerals, boost memory, and we forget what else. One manufacturer even claims users say his machines are "better than sex." (Maybe so, but we'd like to see their bed partners before commenting on this assertion.) In any case, the scientific jury is still out on most of these claims. But people use the machines; people "feel" a difference; people like the machines. They are a phenomenon that must be taken seriously.

How do they work? While there are dozens of brain-altering devices, they all utilize one or more of five physical forces to bend your mind: light, sound, motion, electricity, and electromagnetism. (Purists will no doubt note that light, sound, and electricity are actually all forms of electromagnetism, but let's not get picky.)

According to Richard Daub, who runs Inner Technologies, a company that markets brain machines via mail order, the biggest chunk of the market by far is held by what are called light-and-sound devices. Obviously, these machines use light and sound to create their effects. More specifically, they alter your brain by employing a time-honored scientific principle called "entrainment." For example, if someone flashes a strobe in your eye at a frequency of ten cycles per second, or 10 hertz (or hz), your brain will be retuned to this same frequency. By doing so, the devices switch the gears in your head, downshifting you from beta, our conventional, high-frequency state of consciousness, to the more relaxed alpha, theta, and delta states—forms of consciousness that operate with lower-frequency brain waves. This is essentially what Ptolemy was doing with his spoked wheel set in front of the sun. The revolving spokes were changing continuous sunlight into stroboscopic frequencies, and these in turn were causing the ancient Egyptians (Ptolemy, a Greek, actually lived in Egypt) to hallucinate because their brains were being tuned to a new frequency.

There have been a number of studies of this phenomenon over the years. In the 1880s, the French physician Pierre Jenet flashed lights at his mental patients, and some of them made sudden breakthroughs. The interest in flashing lights began in this way—as a therapeutic endeavor to straighten out the brains of disturbed patients. But today entrainment is being used to enhance the brains of healthy people as well.

Since Jenet's time, entrainment via photic stimulation has been well established, but the most significant research was conducted by the neuroscientist W. Gray Walter in the 1950s. Up until that time, it was thought that photic stimulation entrained only the occipital lobe, the visual cortex of the brain. But when Walter used a strobe to send rhythmic light flashes from ten to twenty-five flashes per second into the eyes of his subjects, and then recorded their electroencephalograms (EEGs), he was amazed to find that the brain-wave activity of the entire cortex, the "thinking part of the brain," was affected, rather than just the visual center. "The rhythmic series of flashes appear to be breaking down some of the physiologic barriers between different regions of the brain," wrote Walter. "This means the stimulus of flicker received by the visual projection area of the cortex was breaking bounds—its ripples were overflowing into other areas." Walter also reported that his subjects saw "lights like comets, ultraunearthly colors, mental colors, not deep visual ones." Today this is called the "flicker effect."

Let's look at a specific machine. The Synchro Energizer is probably the best-known device at present. It's a powerful thing, designed to turn on thirty-two people at a time. The user puts on a pair of goggles equipped with nine tiny flashing lights and a pair of earphones. The flashing lights begin flickering at, say, 40 hz—a fairly common frequency for a person who has spent the day dealing with a job, a boss, two teenagers, rush-hour traffic, and trying to outguess the contestants on "Wheel of Fortune." As the session progresses, the Synchro operator takes the client down and down: into alpha, then theta, maybe delta, then back to beta consciousness. (For a fuller description of being Synchro Energized, see "Blazing Goggles," page 30.)

Why would we want to do this? "We live in a society that has us in a beta state most of the time," explains David Siever, the inventor and manufacturer of the D.A.V.I.D. 1, another light-and-sound machine. "Just driving to work we're in a fight-or-flight state. Beta is great for dealing with traffic. But in the days of the caveman beta was designed to be used maybe twice a day. Humans were not meant to be in beta all day long. The short-term consequences are headaches. The long-term, heart attacks. For thousands of years man has been in alpha. We need to get back to this state."

But light-and-sound devices are supposedly good for more than just alpha. The precise frequencies for each brain state vary from individual to individual, but in general they line up like this . . .

BETA: 13 hz and above
ALPHA: 12 to 8 hz
THETA: 7 to 5 hz
DELTA: 4 to 1 hz

As mentioned, beta is our conventional, everyday, fight-or-flight, bus-riding consciousness. Cro-Magnon man used it for those pesky life-and-death struggles with saber-toothed tigers. Today we use it about sixteen hours a day. Alpha is that pleasant state in which you're relaxed but still fully alert. Theta is often called the Zen or hypnogogic state. You experience it every night. It's that evanescent period of waking dreaminess just before you fall asleep. During this period you are theoretically more susceptible to learning and behavior modification; it is also supposedly the equivalent to yogic tranquility. Delta is simple enough. At these frequencies you're asleep.

So, where does the sound in light-and-sound machines come in? That's a somewhat embarrassing question. There's not a whole lot of evidence that sounds entrain the brain. (In fact, if a flashing light entrains the *entire* brain, why do you need sound at all?) In any case, while machines such as the Synchro Energizer bombard you with flickering lights, they also pipe synchronized tones or white noise at similar frequencies into your earphones. The reason usually given for this is that a couple of decades ago a man named Robert Monroe theorized that pulsing sound waves could entrain the brain, a phenomenon he called a "frequency following response," or FFR. But Monroe is best known as an expert on out-of-body experiences (OBEs), and the FFR has not become one of the more revered tenets of neurobiology, nor has Monroe recently been elected president of the Society for Neuroscience. Then there's the cricket theory. Some people get spacey in the evening sitting on the porch listening to the crickets, even without a few piña coladas under their belts. According to Randy Adamadama, who runs the Universe of You mind gym in Corte Madera, California, this is because "crickets chirp in waves. They are in sync. That wave is in the mid-range delta state. The brain is dragged along, taken to a delta state by the crickets. The delta state

is not uncommon; we're just not awake when it happens." Then there are those of us who stay awake all night because the crickets are too damn noisy.

David Siever says that the lights are really the thing; he estimates that they account for two-thirds of the effect of any light-and-sound machine. The audio's function is mostly to eradicate background noises. From the user's point of view, there's another good reason for the headphones: You can listen to music during an entrainment session, or play various learning- or behavior-modification tapes when your brain settles down to theta.

Another claim made by light-and-sound people is that the act of photically entraining the brain "synchronizes" the left and right hemispheres of the brain, so you get that wonderful New Age phenomenon of "whole-brain thinking."

What do established scientists say about this entrainment-via-household-appliance scheme? "I don't doubt that they're entraining the brain," says Richard Restak, M.D., a neurologist, psychiatrist, and author of *The Brain* and *The Mind*, the companion books to the two PBS-TV series of the same names. Restak confirmed that photostimulation in the eye definitely entrains the occipital lobe (the vision center), but noted that he saw no proof for claims that the machines can affect one hemisphere of the brain over the other. Dr. Restak tested out a group of subjects on the Synchro Energizer, and reported: "The machines certainly do alter your perception and your attitude, but I don't buy a lot of their other claims."

Denis Gorges, the inventor and manufacturer of the Synchro Energizer, recently scaled down a lot of the claims for his machine, and owned up to the fact that entrainment may not be the simple mechanism various light-and-sound entrepreneurs make it out to be. "You can't predict every effect," says Gorges, "and you can't address the brain with one frequency. You have to have a lot of harmonies to tune more areas of the brain. Alpha is not the same for everyone. There is not a national fifty-five-mile-per-hour speed limit for the brain."

While there are dozens of machines, they are still not easy to find, which is why this chapter contains a complete listing of the latest devices and how to get your hands on them.

The biggest trend in the business has been the recent introduction of Walkman-like light-and-sound machines, personal-size units much smaller than the full-size devices such as the Synchro Energizer, the D.A.V.I.D. 1, or the InnerQuest Pro-1. These latter products cost thousands of dollars, but the new miniaturized versions are only in the hundreds—machines such as the Relaxman, MC², the personal InnerQuest, or the MindsEye Courier.

As for the big machines, they require a trained operator and are best utilized at a brain spa. The Synchro Energizer, which was the first to take a foothold in the market, can be found in close to fifty relaxation centers around the world. In some cities, you may find gyms that offer you trips on several machines. One of the most famous is the Universe of You, in California's Marin County (where else?), run by the incomparable Mr. Adamadama. Born Randy Stephens, his new surname came to him in a dream while sleeping at his previous job as a night watchman. Adamadama hopes that other such brain spas will create an informal string of McMeditations across the nation. "You park your car, you run in, you get your anxiety released," he explained. "Every shopping center should have one."

And if there's no relaxation center near you, there's yet another alternative. Michael Hutchison offers several Megabrain workshops a year around the country, at which you can experiment with fifteen or so different machines for about $125 per day. He also sells the machines via mail order. Hutchison is the leading popularizer of the Nautilus-for-the-brain movement, which he chronicled in a book also called *Megabrain*. (See "The Timothy Leary of Neurotechnology" on page 26 for a profile on Hutchison and details on how to order his devices or take his workshops.) Hutchison, by the way, envisions these machines as "training wheels for the brain." After some practice, he claims, people should be able to turn on specific frequencies without the machines.

Neurotechnology, as Hutchison calls it, embraces more than the light-and-sound machines. The Lumatron, for example, operates with light only to stimulate the brain. There are the sound machines—the Genesis and Somatron—that vibrate your body (and supposedly your psyche) with powerful cell-rattling speakers. There are motion machines, such as the Graham Potentializer, that theoretically "exercise the brain" through the vestibular system in the inner ear. Ganzfeld devices such as the Tranquilite and Theta-One actually try to eliminate stimuli to coax you into theta states. These are sensory-restriction rather than sensory-enhancement machines. There are electrical-stimulation devices—the Brain Tuner, Alpha-Stim, and Nustar—which purport to help stimulate the production of beneficial brain chemicals (as well as entrain your brain waves) through the application of low dosages of electricity. Beat-frequency devices, which create a subtle inaudible sound wave in the middle of your consciousness, are fairly rare; we found only one, the Binaural Signal Generator, that was reasonably available to the public. Finally, there are combination machines, which bend your mind using two or more of the above methods.

The business has a little bit of the flavor of the computer industry in its early days—small groups of individuals jury-rigging brand-new kinds of machines in their garages. The players are an eclectic bunch. Hutchison was a poet and a novelist, a free-spirited journalist who traveled all over Central America in the late 1970s and early 1980s. Rob Robinson, inventor of the InnerQuest, has master's degrees in psychology and economics, runs a school for hypnotherapists, and operates his company out of his house. Zane Tankel, president of the company that manufactures the Tranquilite ganzfeld device, is a corporate investigator, a man who sizes up companies for possible takeovers; he also sets up drug programs for Fortune 500 companies. And Denis Gorges is . . . well, what Denis Gorges is—or was—may vary depending on who interviews him and on what day. (See "Denis Gorges and the Light-and-Sound Wars," page 34.)

It's impossible to gauge the true size of the business. There is no industry association, and the sales figures supplied by individual manufacturers vary from a few dozen units sold in a company's entire history to Denis Gorges's claims that he has sold 23,000 clinical machines to psychiatrists and that his Relaxman (the personal-size Synchro Energizer) is selling at a rate of a hundred units *per day* in Tokyo alone. This despite the fact that an FDA investigator found that Gorges was running his company out of a "private residence."

Some of the people in the business go out of their way to appear "scientific" by citing lots of papers and studies—whether or not they're at all relevant to the machines being discussed. A favorite pastime of brain-machine entrepreneurs is their attempt to quantify specific brain-wave frequencies with behavior, emotions, and world view. For example, the late Michael Hercules, inventor of the Nustar, an electrical device, correlated the following brain frequencies with their accompanying states of consciousness:

1.0 hz—Feeling of well being; pituitary stimulation to release growth hormone; overall view of interrelationships

5.5 hz—moves beyond knowledge to knowing; shows visions of growth needed

7.5 hz—interawareness of self and purpose; guided meditation; creative thought for art, invention, music, etc.; contact with spirit guides for directions

10.5 hz—healing of the body; mind/body connection; firewalking

It seems to us that this could be dangerous. Let's say you wanted to try firewalking, so you attempted to tune your Nustar to 10.5 hz. But what if your hand slipped on the dial and you flipped to 5.5 by mistake just as you were stepping barefoot onto the white-hot coals? For sure, you'd move "beyond knowledge to knowing." You'd know that your feet were on fire. You'd then have to flip quickly to 1.0 hz to "release growth hormone" in an attempt to grow back your ankles.

Then there's the study of the Alpha-Stim, the prescription electrical-stimulation machine that's touted for pain control. Neurobiologists Daniel Kirsch and colleague Richard Madden hooked the earlobes of seventy-eight subjects to an Alpha-Stim and zapped them with a low-level electrical current. This experiment purportedly demonstrated that the Alpha-Stim accelerated learning: Compared with a control group, the Alpha-Stim subjects performed significantly better on a computer-typing game over the course of four such games. But Dr. James McGaugh, a neurobiologist at the University of California at Irvine, called the study "off the wall, sophomoric, filled with random citations and vapid conclusions." And that was the good news. McGaugh went on to say that he found it "nauseating" that the study's investigator happened to run the company that manufactures the Alpha-Stim.

The field's practitioners are full of glib explanations. When we asked Synchro Energizer owner/operator Christine Zerrer why the machine generates an electromagnetic field around the head of each user, she replied that the field "aligns every cell in your body."

You can find some good medical and personal advice in the literature also. Page B-15 of the "Operator's Manual" for the D.A.V.I.D. 1, a machine recommended for stress control, provides tips on identifying a woman "overwhelmed with stress." According to the manual, such a woman will "lose interest in sex and may become 'bossy.' " Hey, guys: You say your old lady won't put out and she's nagging you about your drinking? Don't run her over with your Harley. Just strap her to the D.A.V.I.D. 1 and blink her down into the delta state.

"Well, there are still lots of Jimmy and Tammy Faye Bakkers in our business," explains Gary Rupar, manufacturer of the Alpha Chamber, a combination sound-and-sensory-restriction device that one sits in.

Even so, brain machines look like they are here to stay, and why not? "Yogis are out. Gurus are out," says Randy Adamadama. "No one wants dogma anymore." A Synchro Energizer salesman puts it another way: "We're selling Buddha in a can."

Robert Austin, maker of the MindsEye, is a bit more subtle. "What we're seeing is similar to the drug revolution," he points out. "People want to alter their brains. Now they can do it without drugs. Meditation and biofeedback can do this, but they require work. The machines do it for you. It's like taking a drug. It fits into the Western experience." Inner Technologies' Richard Daub agrees. After his success selling light-and-sound devices and electrical-stimulation machines, he added biofeedback devices to his catalogue. "I thought people would want something interactive," he said. He didn't sell a one. "They don't want interactive devices," he concluded. "They want something that will do it to you."

Daub predicted the eventual rise of brain machines into the mainstream of American life. "There may come a day," he says, "when they're sold in department stores like Walkmans." InnerQuest's Rob Robinson agrees, but warns that the business "will take off only after it has been separated from mysticism. Some people try to pull it into the metaphysical realm, which is alien to middle America. But [the machines] are just tools." MC²'s Larry Gillen is more cosmic: "This isn't just hardware. We're making a difference on the planet."

Whether just tools or planet savers, it appears that brain machines are the future. Even Dr. Richard Restak, critic and neurologist, agrees: "It is the way things are going to go."

On these pages you will find detailed descriptions of the most important two dozen or so brain machines now available to the public. Prices, of course, may vary depending on when and where you purchase a particular device.

LIGHT AND SOUND MACHINES

FULL-SIZE UNITS

These are the industrial-strength machines. They're designed to be used in mind spas or by therapists or other professionals; the machines can service multiple users simultaneously. They're also expensive, and while some are transportable, these are not units you'd like to lug around with you.

SYNCHRO ENERGIZER
●

The Synchro Energizer is the most common and visible of all brain machines, thanks in part to the energy and promotional abilities of its inventor, Denis Gorges. The user puts on a set of earphones and goggles with nine little lights—four around each eyepiece and one on the bridge between the eyepieces. (Gorges says the purpose of this ninth light is to stimulate the pineal gland, or "third eye," of the brain, but he doesn't push this claim very hard.) While the lights flash at different frequencies, music, various tones, and a heartbeat are piped into your ears and an electromagnetic field is created around your head. The Synchro Energizer comes in several models, but the one most people are familiar with is a $60,000 industrial job found mostly in mind gyms where several people can be Synchro Energized simultaneously, sort of like group therapy where you don't have to talk to each other. (Actually, you can spend up to $150,000 if you get all the bells and whistles.) There's a central control console manned by a trained operator, and individual stations (each equipped with goggles, earphones, and electromagnetic field generator) for thirty-two people. The frequency of the lights can be varied from 60 hz down to 5 hz, the sound through the earphones from 40,000 hz to 1 hz. The Synchro Energizer uses regular full-spectrum lights rather than LEDs (light-emitting diodes). There are also smaller models that can handle two to four people at a time for doctors and other practitioners. These cost $9,000 and up.

Access: For information on all Synchro Energizers—whether you want to acquire one or just want the location of the nearest mind gym or center that features the equipment—contact Synchro-Tech, 4574 Broad View Road, Cleveland, OH 44109-4602. Phone: (216) 749-1133.

D.A.V.I.D. 1
●

An up-and-coming competitor to the Synchro Energizer, the D.A.V.I.D. 1 features the usual goggles with lights, head-

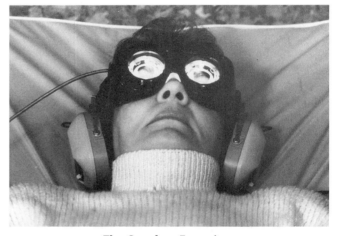

The Synchro Energizer

phones, and control panel common to all such machines. It's considerably smaller than the Synchro, handling only two people at a time, but the D.A.V.I.D. is now the machine of choice in Michael Hutchison's Megabrain workshops. (It's also a lot cheaper than the Synchro, with a list price of $3,700.) The device comes with only two sets of goggles and headphones, but the unit can be expanded for group sessions or commercial use.

Synthesized sound effects include white noise, a metronome sound, and two tones of differing waveforms. There's also a digitized heartbeat sound. This can be set, via a fingertip device, to monitor your pulse rate so that the machine indirectly slows down your heart rate to help you relax.

Another special feature is a "Schumann resonance frequency switch." The Schumann fequency, 7.83 hz, is said to be the frequency of the earth's electromagnetic field. So, by flipping this switch on the D.A.V.I.D. 1, the machine begins pumping out sound and light at this wavelength, thus supposedly bringing your brain into synchronization with Mother Earth (if that's what you want). There's a stereo input for feeding in music, learning- or behavior-modification tapes, and a microphone for use by an operator for therapy sessions while a patient is under the influence of synchronized lights and sound. There's an automated program that lets you use the machine by yourself if no operator is available. The entire machine packs into an aluminum travel case.

Advertised benefits include deep mental and physical relaxation, increased self-esteem, fear reduction, and lessened irritability. The inventor, David Siever, says that dentists have used D.A.V.I.D. to help them relax the jaws of their patients. The device can also be used in reverse. That is, a user's brain waves can be speeded up. This is for people who are too laid back and are therefore not coping well with the uptight material world. These folks need more beta waves, to make them more alert to deal with work or school or their parole officer.

Access: The D.A.V.I.D. 1 costs $3,700 and, as mentioned, can be test driven at Megabrain workshops. For more information, contact Comptronic Devices Ltd., 2113 85th Street, Edmonton, Alberta, Canada T6K 2G1. Or call Megabrain at (415) 332-8323.

INNERQUEST PRO-1
•

This product was originally called SILS (for sensory input learning system), but then inventor Rob Robinson made a cut-down unit for personal use and called it the InnerQuest. The InnerQuest name proved so popular that Robinson renamed the SILS the InnerQuest Pro-1. The Pro-1, as you might guess, is a full-sized unit. It weighs about twenty-six

pounds and is "about as big as a bread box," in Robinson's words. To be more precise, it's approximately 16″ × 12″ × 6″ and has output jacks for four sets of headphones and glasses. However, an integral amplifier and distribution system allows you to hook up an additional forty-eight clients, as long as you purchase the necessary additional headphones, glasses, and cables. The goggles have a circular array of six LEDs over each eye.

Robinson claims to have sold upwards of a hundred units, and the Pro-1 is obviously catching on. The Universe of You, the Corte Madera mind gym, now uses the machine (it previously featured the Synchro Energizer). It comes with two built-in industrial-grade stereo tape transports and a microphone (so the operator can do therapy with large numbers of people). The machine generates pink noise, white noise, and a variable-rate heartbeat (evidently for people who like to listen to simulated cardiac arrhythmia.) There are seven preset programs, ranging from fifteen to forty-five minutes, in the Pro-1's permanent memory, but the operator can use a menu to design custom programs up to 100 minutes long. Ten such original programs can be stored at a time. An interesting accessory is a phone modem, which can be used for downloading and monitoring programs from other units, so that a network of Pro-1s can be established at various locations.

Access: The InnerQuest Pro-1 costs about $5,500. From Psych-Research, Inc., 10002 W. Markham, Suite 200, Little Rock, Arkansas 72205. Phone: (501) 225-6577 or (800) 544-8743.

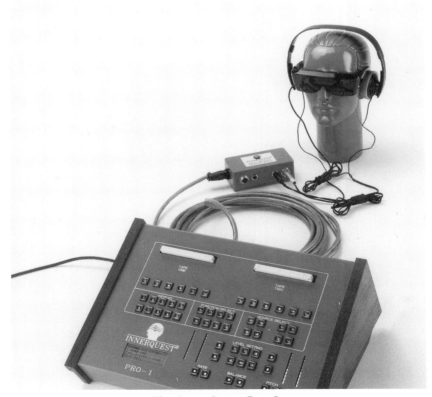

The InnerQuest Pro-1

PERSONAL-SIZE UNITS

These are machines that are sized—and priced—for the individual rather than for a mind spa or a clinician. All can be used in the home, though some are larger than others. In the strict sense, almost all of the following devices are transportable, in that they can be moved from one location to another. But some are truly portable, like a Sony Walkman, whereas others would be better described as "desktop."

MINDSEYE
•

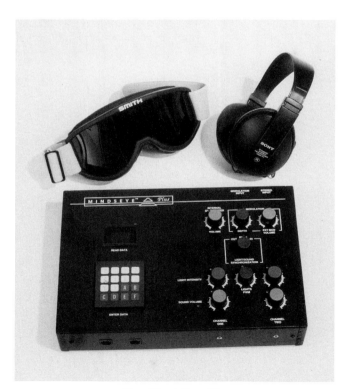

The MindsEye Plus

The MindsEye

Megabrain's Michael Hutchison calls the MindsEye "perhaps the most technically sophisticated audiovisual synchronizer available." Its sound synthesizer features twelve preprogrammed sounds, and infinitely more can be custom programmed by varying the pulse width or tone color, or by selecting different filters or wave forms (sawtooth, white noise, triangle, pulse, etc.)

The MindsEye is not really a Walkman-like device. About the size of a laptop computer, it's certainly smaller than a Synchro Energizer or a D.A.V.I.D. 1, but you can't really strap it on your belt and zone out on the subway with it. It's a sophisticated home machine based on a powerful microprocessor that's built for the aficionado who really wants to get into experimenting with different customized programs.

Robert Austin, the inventor, recommends the MindsEye for stress reduction, relaxation, and just for fun, because it provides great light shows. Austin also says you can hook the headphones to your stereo or to audio learning tapes. He recommends using some tapes when the machine shifts your brain into the hypnogogic state, the twilight zone between theta and delta, just before you fall asleep. Theoretically, the brain is receptive to new ideas and information at this frequency, although Austin admits he hasn't seen any evidence that you can learn anything while using this technique with the MindsEye.

The MindsEye has the usual headphones and goggles (four lights in each eyepiece), but the control unit itself is decidedly more complicated than other personal machines with its eight knobs and larger size—9″ × 12″ × 3″. Special features include a Schumann resonance frequency and an EyeRemember computer chip that lets users permanently save programs of their own design.

Access: There are two models. The regular MindsEye goes for $795. For another $100 you can purchase extra goggles and headphones for a second user. A newer model, the MindsEye Plus, features a stereo synthesizer, beat frequencies, and better sound effects. Price: $895. Contact: Synetic Systems, P.O. Box 95530, Seattle, WA 98145, or phone (206) 632-1722. Also available through Megabrain at (415) 332-8323.

MINDSEYE COURIER
•

Although the MindsEye is what we call a personal-size light-and-sound machine, it's a pretty heavy-duty machine and not really portable in the strict (or convenient) sense. Enter the MindsEye Courier, a new product from Synetic

Systems. The Courier is a true portable device. It comes in a 6¾″ × 5½″ × 2½″ plastic case that contains the electronics, controls, headphones and glasses, and even an instruction sheet under the cover. A built-in battery pack provides more than five hours of blazing goggles on a charge. The Courier has sixteen preset programs, some that feature binaural beat frequencies. You can also program your own session, choosing from eight digital tones and chords and from frequencies ranging from 1.0 to 30 hz. The EyeRemember computer chip saves your custom programs for later recall.

Access: The MindsEye Courier sells for $395. Contact: Synetic Systems, P.O. Box 95530, Seattle, WA 98145. Phone (206) 632-1722. Also available through Inner Technologies, 51 Berry Trail, Fairfax, CA 94930. Phone: (415) 454-0813.

MINDSEYE PC-SYNERGIZER
•

The Synergizer is a brand-new bird in the brave new area of light-and-sound machines. It's made by the MindsEye people, but it's not a free-standing machine. Rather, it's the MindsEye on a personal computer board. You plug it into your IBM or IBM compatible and end up with a laboratory-grade audio-visual synchronizer. Rather than depending on the limited abilities of a chip inside your light-and-sound machine, you have the full power of your PC at your command for programming powerful synchronized light-and-sound shows. You can emulate the programs professional mind spa operators run for their clients. And when you come up with a program you really like, you can save it on your

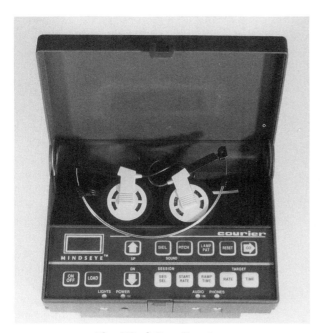

The MindsEye Courier

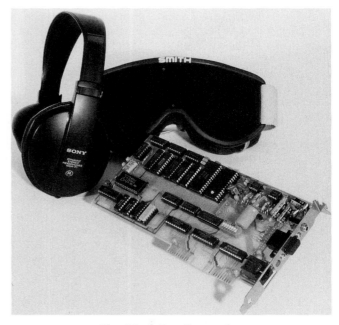

The MindsEye Synergizer

hard drive. The best part is that it's a fraction of the cost of a professional machine.

Access: The PC-Synergizer sells for $395 with goggles. Sony MDRP1 headphones cost an extra $35. Requires DOS 3.0 or above; 512K of RAM and a hard drive are recommended. Contact: Synetic Systems, P.O. Box 95530, Seattle, WA 98145. Phone: (206) 632-1722.

MC ^{2}
●

Credit must be given to Larry Gillen for creating the whole personal-size light-and-sound machine craze. He and coinventor Linnea Reid came out with the MC ^{2}, the very first stand-alone brain-wave entrainment machine, in October 1987, and they have sold several thousand units since then. The MC ^{2} works pretty much like the other personal-size machines. It has ten preset programs, adjustable lighted goggles, earphones, pulsing sounds, etc. But there's one big difference: the price. At $350 it's the cheapest model around. There are a couple of cost-saving differences. The goggles have only two lights in each eyepiece, and the machine takes you down only into the theta state; it does not generate frequencies into the lower delta region. (But for those who don't want to risk falling asleep, this is not a big detriment.) On the plus side, it's very small: $4\frac{1}{4}'' \times 2\frac{1}{4}'' \times 1\frac{1}{4}''$. Gillen is somewhat conservative in his claims for the MC ^{2}, saying it's mostly good for relaxation and as an "educational enhancement device." By that, he means that the MC ^{2} can transport your brain to the theta state, where the mind is more receptive to learning. He suggests listening to learning tapes (which can be piped into your earphones through an input jack in the MC ^{2}) when you hit theta frequencies. Gillen also claims the device promotes whole-brain activity (whatever that means), and says athletes have used it to improve their performances. We liked the name until Gillen explained what it meant. He called it the MC ^{2} because that's equal to E: energy, enthusiasm, enlightenment. Poor Einstein.

Access: Sold in some health-food stores, bookstores, and by massage therapists and other such professionals. Also available through the Hammacher Schlemmer catalogue. Or contact Light and Sound Research Corporation, 6991 E. Camelback Road, Suite C-151, Scottsdale, Arizona 85251, or call (602) 941-4459. Price for the basic unit is $350 plus $5 for shipping and handling. For additional glasses and earphones, add $65.

MICHAEL HUTCHISON

THE TIMOTHY LEARY OF NEUROTECHNOLOGY

●

Michael Hutchison is the country's leading proponent of brain machines, or what he prefers to call "neurotechnology." His ● 1986 book *Megabrain* (William Morrow) introduced the general public to consciousness-altering machines, and his company of the same name distributes a variety of brain machines and conducts workshops in their use all over the world.

Hutchison got interested in the hidden powers of the brain in the early 1970s when he lived in New York's Catskill mountains. From 1971 until 1974 he lived alone, first in a lean-to; then he built himself a log cabin. When he needed money, Hutchison would pack up his guitar, hitchhike to Manhattan, and stake out a segment of sidewalk on the corner of Eighth Street and Sixth Avenue in Greenwich Village. He'd lay his open guitar case on the sidewalk for contributions and play and sing Bob Dylan-esque folk-blues to passersby.

This did not produce Dylan-esque income, but enough to support his simple life-style. Back in the mountains, Hutchison discovered two basic principles of altered states. First, sensory restriction: "I would often get snowed in," recalls Hutchison. "I would have hallucinations. I'd hear voices. I believe I was generating a lot of theta activity." During one snowbound period Hutchison read *The Centre of the Cyclone,* by John C. Lilly, the famed neuroscientist, "dolphin man," and inventor of the isolation tank, and learned that the good Dr. Lilly experienced similar phenomena during his tanking sessions. "What took me six months to experience took Lilly only fifteen minutes," says Hutchison.

During his lean-to days, Hutchison also discovered photic stimulation. Piling up some rocks for a fireplace, he would pass the evenings sitting on a log, gazing into the flames, and would begin to see images: "cities rising out of deserts, marching armies, a group of nuns stolling arm in arm, monkeys swinging from tree to tree." Hutchison knew these things weren't really there, but he also realized that he wouldn't be seeing such scenes if he hadn't been staring into the fire. It was the flickering lights that triggered the images in his head.

A decade later, as a struggling novelist, he turned to journalism to pay the bills. On assignment for the *Village Voice,* he wrote an article on a new float center (featuring isolation tanks) that had

Michael Hutchison

opened up in Greenwich Village. "I got carried away," says Hutchison. He read copiously about the brain and expanded the article into a book, *The Book of Floating: Exploring the Private Sea* (Morrow, 1984; Beech Tree paperback, 1985). He followed this up with *Megabrain,* the first book to explore fully the new phenomenon of mind expansion through technology. *Megabrain* is divided roughly into two parts. The first section deals with the scientific basis for brain enrichment in general; the second part explores some of the new devices that purport to fine-tune the human brain, such as the Synchro Energizer and the Graham Potentializer. Disappointed with the lack of publicity his publisher was providing for the book, Hutchison threw a party for himself and *Megabrain* at the Tranquility Center, an isolation-tank center in Manhattan. He borrowed various brain machines from their manufacturers and invited a few friends to come and try them out. Three hundred people showed up. A television crew also showed up to tape the event. Hutchison threw another party in Los Angeles. This time a thousand people attended. He knew he was on to something.

Thus was born Megabrain the company. Now operating out of Sausalito, California, Megabrain, Inc. serves as a kind of distributor for various brain devices that Hutchison approves of, and also conducts workshops in their use. The first day of a two-day workshop typically consists of tryouts on a dozen or so brain appliances; day two usually consists of intensive workshops on specific goals using the machines: stress relief, creativity, personal growth, education, or breaking habits such as smoking or drugs. In a typical year, Megabrain workshops are held in thirty-five cities. In 1989 workshops took place in Dallas, Albuquerque, Boston, Vancouver, Zurich, Frankfurt, Berlin, Hong

Kong, Los Angeles, Chicago, and Evansville, Indiana, to name just a few cities. The fee is about $150 per day.

We asked Hutchison to name his favorite brain machines. His list includes four light-and-sound devices: the D.A.V.I.D. full-size unit and the personal-size D.A.V.I.D. Jr. Plus, and the MindsEye and InnerQuest II, which are also personal-size units. He also likes the Alpha-Stim, a prescription-only electrical stimulation machine that is used for improving memory and learning and weaning oneself from addiction, and the Binaural Signal Generator, a beat-frequency device, that plugs into your home stereo system and entrains your brain to different frequencies using sound alone.

Not on Hutchison's list is the granddaddy of brain machines, the mighty Synchro Energizer. The Synchro figured prominently in the original version of *Megabrain,* and Hutchison used the machine extensively in his earlier Megabrain workshops. But he has since had a falling out with Denis Gorges, the colorful inventor of the Synchro Energizer, and the two have little good to say about each other. Hutchison calls the Synchro Energizer "an outmoded dinosaur, vastly overpriced, and, in my opinion, inferior. . . ." He now uses the D.A.V.I.D. instead. Gorges says Hutchison is a distributor masquerading as a journalist, because he writes books about the machines as if he were an impartial observer, while offering the devices for sale through Megabrain, Inc. Hutchison defends his actions by saying he sells "only those machines for which there is strong evidence that they are effective and safe." The battle between these two pioneers in neurotechnology reached its nadir in November 1988 when Gorges dragged Hutchison into a New York court in an attempt to enjoin him from conducting a Megabrain workshop using the D.A.V.I.D. instead of the Synchro. Gorges's request for an injunction was denied.

Hutchison has recently revised the book *Megabrain,* now available in paperback from Ballantine, and has authored yet another brain-related book, *The Anatomy of Sex and Power* (Morrow, 1990). He's also launched a newsletter entitled *Megabrain Report: The Psychotechnology Newsletter,* available to the public for $36 per year.

Access: For information about Megabrain workshops, machines, the newsletter, or the Megabrain consumer guide to neurotechnology, write to: Megabrain, P.O. Box 2205, Sausalito, CA 94965-9998. Or call (415) 332-8323. FAX: (415) 332-8327.

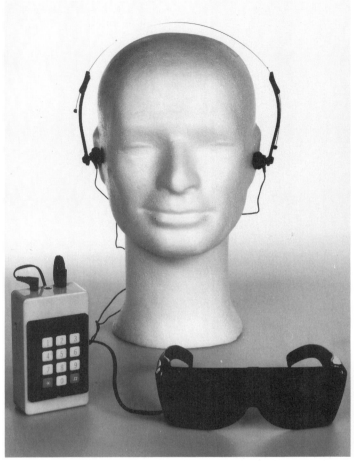

The MC²

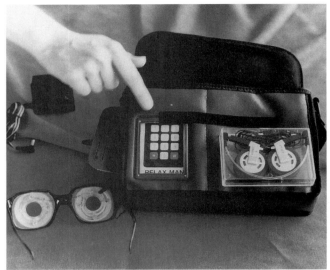

The Relaxman

RELAXMAN
•

This is the personal-size version (about two pounds) of the Synchro Energizer, and made by the same firm. Like all home units, no professional operator is required for the Relaxman, as it features ten automated programs: two each for relaxation, sleep, pain relief, meditation, and "entertainment" (which is just a nice light-and-sound show). The Relaxman is marked by its distinctive goggles, which consist of a pair of spectacle-like frames inset with translucent doughnut-like rings that conceal the four tiny lights in each eyepiece. Unlike the full-size Synchro Energizer, the Relaxman has no heartbeat. Like most other personal-size units, the Relaxman has sound (synchronized tones, etc.) but if you want music or learning tapes you'll have to hook up an exterior tape deck as there is no integral tape machine.

Access: The Relaxman is $599 from Synchro-Tech, 4574 Broad View Road, Cleveland, OH 44109-4602. Phone: (216) 749-1133.

D.A.V.I.D. JR. PLUS
•

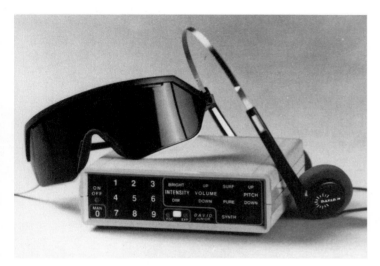

The D.A.V.I.D. Jr.

The D.A.V.I.D. Jr. Plus is, obviously, the hand-held version of the larger D.A.V.I.D. machine manufactured by David Siever. It has the major disadvantage, as do all of Siever's devices, of having all those periods between the letters of its name. It gets very tiring trying to type the name. Seriously, it's a Megabrain-endorsed device, about the size of "two cigarette packs stuck together," an interesting choice of words by Siever. And it appears to be the Rolls-Royce of personal light-and-sound machines, with lots of special features and a price tag ($795) to match. It has nine preset programs with an adjustable manual override. Among the programs is a deep-delta-wave sleep inducer, a 7.83 hz meditation session, and a "beta perker" for those who wish to be uptight rather than laid back. The machine has some nice touches, such as "soft off," which means that the volume decreases and the lights dim slowly at the end of each program to prevent harsh reentry into the real world. It also comes with a canvas travel bag with shoulder strap, and the glasses feature an electroluminescent panel that produces interesting visual effects. The D.A.V.I.D. Jr. also turns into a ganzfeld device; the special goggles enable you to gaze into a featureless visual field with your choice of colors— red, blue, or green. Despite its hefty price, the machine has no built-in tape player (you have to connect your own), but does give you a nice surf sound in its selection of synthesized noises. Another nice feature is the internally rechargeable battery.

Access: As mentioned, the D.A.V.I.D. Jr. Plus is $795 or $895 with goggles and earphones for two users. For more information, contact Comptronic Devices Ltd., 2113 85th Street, Edmonton, Alberta, Canada T6K 2G1. Phone: (403) 450-3729. Also available through Megabrain, at (415) 332-8323.

PARADISE
•

The Paradise, new from Comptronic Devices, is a D.A.V.I.D. Jr. Plus–type of portable machine, but more advanced—with forty preset programs—selling for about $600. For further information contact Comptronic Devices Ltd., 2113 85th Street, Edmonton, Alberta, Canada T6K 2G1. Phone (403) 450-3729.

INNERQUEST
•

The InnerQuest, at $495, is a lower-priced device. Like the MC^2, it has only two LEDs in each eyepiece. On the other hand, it is the only personal-size light-and-sound machine with a built-in cassette deck, making it extremely convenient to play learning tapes or music with the various preset programs, of which there are sixteen: for relaxation, learning, left/right brain synchronization, creativity, sleep, meditation, and music appreciation. For sound you have a choice between a monotonous tone and white noise. (See our test drive of the InnerQuest, "Who Was That Masked Man in the Bedroom?" page 44.) There are also two higher-priced models, the InnerQuest II (or IQ-II) and the

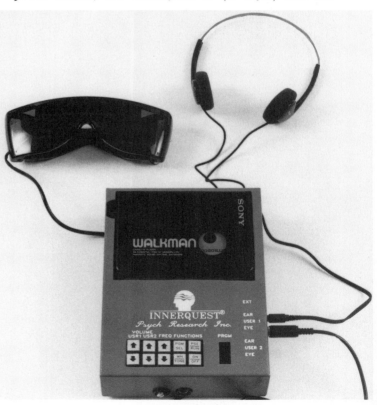

The InnerQuest

BLAZING GOGGLES

A VISIT TO A BRAIN SALON

We're at Synchro Energize, a brain salon in New York City's fashionably funky Soho district, talking to the proprietor, Christine Zerrer, about what kind of people come to her establishment to subject themselves to the pulsating lights and sounds of the powerful Synchro Energizer. "I had a funeral party in here once," she said. They came right over after the burial. "The system is very good for crises," she explained. "It cultivates your witness."

The salon is a blast from the past. The last time I entered a room with this much incense in the air was in 1968 for a New Year's Eve party. Hendrix played "Purple Haze" on the stereo, and people offered you strange things to smoke and swallow. If you found an empty bed, you shared it with another guest, and weren't surprised if other couples joined you. But here at the Synchro Energize, the similarities ended with the incense. I noticed there were at least thirteen beds in plain sight, and five other people—each decidedly tucked in his or her own bed. We were all there to lie down in splendid isolation and have bright lights flashed in our eyes and wimpy New Age music force-fed into our ears. For sure, it is the 1990s, not the '60s, and brain machines are yet another exponent of our safe-sex, button-down times. I was there, like everybody else, in search of a legal, nonpharmaceutical, virus-free, no-risk high.

The beds at Synchro Energize are giant pastel-colored bunk beds, stacked three high to the ceiling, with aircraft-like boarding ladders for climbing to the topmost levels. "The bright colors are to make the setting childlike," explained Zerrer. "Kids love it in here. So do most of our clients."

Like everyone else, I removed my shoes, but chose a cowardly chaise lounge for my forty-five-minute session rather than risk the bunks and perhaps find myself lying next to an epileptic who would be catapulted into a grand mal seizure thanks to the machines.

Ms. Zerrer helped me on with my goggles and earphones, and told me to close my eyes and to feel free to raise my hand if I found myself "in distress." This did not comfort me in the least; it just started me fantasizing about what possible forms of distress had befallen other visitors to this den of synchronicity. Zerrer then retreated to her control room, where she twiddled the various dials that customize each Synchro Energizer excursion. She peered out at us from a little window cut in the wall, not unlike a nuclear powerplant worker manipulating plutonium fuel rods, I thought—or one of those guys who fabricates new virulent lifeforms in biological-warfare laboratories.

But when the trip began, I must admit that I felt a grin spreading across my face. The nine little lights in my goggles were pulsating and whirling, creating a beautiful light show in my brain, and while the saccharin music I was hearing over the earphones was only one level up from Muzak, it was sophomorically pleasant, and perhaps all one can take while being blitzed by a stroboscopic attack and listening to various synthesized sounds and a constant heartbeat (though I must admit, I rarely heard the heartbeat; my sensory circuits must have overloaded).

My second feeling, after the initial euphoria, was stark terror, of course. Ms. Zerrer had told me to close my eyes, and now I had a white-knuckled fear that I would open them, and be instantly blinded by my blazing goggles. This fear eventually subsided. (Zerrer told me later than it's okay to open your eyes; in fact, some people like to read during the session, though this is hard to imagine.)

What Zerrer does to everyone in the room is start the lights and sounds at high frequencies—in the 40 hz, or beta-wave state, your general street consciousness level. She then takes everybody down through alpha (relaxation), then into theta (sometimes called the Zen state) at about 5 to 7 hz. Sometimes she even takes her customers into delta, the sleep state, but that can be annoying, she explained. "I don't really like having a roomful of snoring people."

In the theta state you're supposed to be able to dredge up long-forgotten subconscious memories. I must have hit it, because about halfway through the session my mind did in fact fill with previously obscured remembrances. For at least two minutes I couldn't stop thinking about Jose Melis, the bandleader on the old "Tonight" show when Jack Paar was the host. Who cares? I certainly didn't. I also tried to remember the names of characters in Lil' Abner, a comic strip I found especially tedious as a child.

The most remarkable thing about the trip is the pleasant feeling of relaxation and the light show, which I'm told is created only indirectly by the little goggle lights. The flicker effect simply stimulates your brain to put on its own show. Frankly, after about ten minutes I felt my brain needed a new

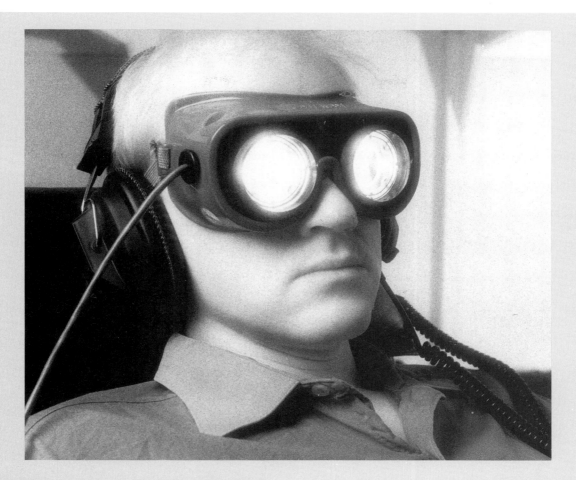

lighting director. I've seen literally hundreds of light shows at rock concerts, and, to be honest, they're a whole lot better than what my head can produce with a Synchro Energizer. Maybe other brains are better at it.

Zerrer ends each session by bringing people back up to beta "so they can hit the street and survive." But I was nowhere near normal consciousness. I tried to be the ever-dutiful reporter and interview the other customers. "How was it for you?" I asked one young woman, sounding like some schlepp in a Woody Allen movie. All she did was pick up my sneakers and say, "Are these your shoes?" in a zombie-like voice. "These are great shoes. What are they called?"

"Jose Melis," I started to say but caught myself.

Then I interviewed Zerrer. But I, too, sounded like a zombie, each word a monumental effort. She told me that the equipment cost her $60,000, and that she had to go to Cleveland to be certified by Synchro-Tech, the company that manufactures the Synchro Energizer. A variety of people visit her salon: actors, musicians, men, women, hard-core Wall Street types, the unemployed. Zerrer claims that only one in a hundred doesn't like the expe-

rience, complaining of mild nausea afterward.

Zerrer also sells the mini-version of the Synchro, the $599 Relaxman. She showed me one of its salient features. "See, it has a pause button," she pointed out, "in case you see God . . . or the phone rings." At this point I excused myself, explaining that I had to go home to hook up my new computer system. "Well, I'd better top you off with a little more beta," she offered, obviously noticing that I was talking like Muhammad Ali at closing time. And, in fact, a few more minutes of high frequencies did bring me, unhappily, back to full hardware consciousness.

Does the Synchro Energizer live up to all its claims? Well, no. But for $15, it was a good, cheap, legal high, and I'd do it again. I did feel a bit disoriented the next day, but not remarkably so. As for the claims by many users of brain machines that the experience is "better than sex or drugs," all I can say is, Yeah, sure.—D.T.

Access: Contact Synchro Energize, 594 Broadway, Suite 905, New York, NY 10012. Phone: (212) 941-1184.

InnerQuest III (IQ-III). The IQ-II differs from the standard model in that it allows you to custom design your own program. There is also a manual override that allows you to control the light and sound frequencies of four basic patterns. It also has a rechargeable battery, a good feature. Oddly, the IQ-II is the same price as the standard model, despite its more advanced design. The reason: Unlike the original version, the IQ-II has no integral tape deck. If you like the technical advances of the IQ-II but also want a cassette deck, there's the IQ-III, which, for $100 more, is essentially the IQ-II with a built-in auto-reverse tape player with Dolby sound.

Access: All three models are available, at $495, $495, and $595, from Psych-Research, Inc., 7509 Cantrell, Suite 211, Little Rock, AR 72207. Phone: (501) 255-6577 or (800) 544-8743. Also available through Megabrain at (415) 332-8323.

OTHER BRAIN MACHINES

THE LUMATRON (LIGHT)
•

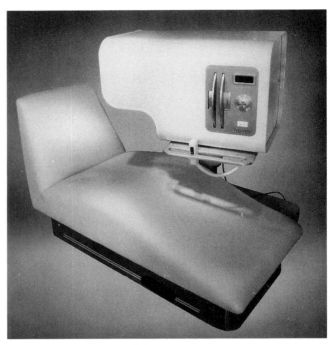

The Lumatron

This is a light-only machine, which uses "photic stimulation" to bend your mind. You sit in a darkened room and stare into the business end of the Lumatron, a large machine that focuses various wavelengths of color directly onto your retina. Essentially, you're staring into a strobe light that can be set to eleven different frequencies, and, according to Michael Hutchison, this stimulates both the limbic and cortex areas of the brain (respectively, the lower emotional and the higher "thinking" parts of the brain) to enhance intellectual, mental, emotional, and physical functioning. The usual immodest claims are made: enhanced memory and learning, stress reduction, relief of headache pain and depression, fatigue reduction, and even computer-caused stress reduction. The Lumatron is part of something called the Downing Technique, invented by John Downing, who claims to be the odd combination of optometrist and Ph.D. His Ph.D., by the way, is in "neuroquatum optics," whatever that is. According to Dr. Downing, "the eyes act as photocells for the brain, converting light into photoelectric energy—the language of the brain. In the simplest terms, light strikes the retina and is converted into an electrical nerve current called a photocurrent. In this form, the electrical energy passes through the optic nerve and associate pathways into several important areas of the brain: the visual cortex, the midbrain, and the hypothalamus. It then spreads from these areas to nearly all parts of the brain. The more photocurrent traveling from the eye into the brain, the more vital life energy the brain has to work with and the more optimally the brain and the body function." If you can buy that, then you're ready to lay down the $7,900 for Downing's machine. According to Hutchison, who has used the Lumatron in his Megabrain workshops, users generally determine their optimal colors and frequencies, then undergo twenty to forty sessions of about twenty minutes per day. Hutchison is very positive about the machine, making claims that go beyond even Downing's: Hutchison says the Lumatron even treats skin conditions and tunnel vision.

Access: The Lumatron itself is available for the aforementioned $7,900 from the Lumatron Corporation, 1455 E. Francisco Boulevard, Building J, San Rafael, CA 94901. Phone: (415) 456-4409. Seminars on the Downing Technique, which uses the Lumatron, are sponsored regularly by the Downing Institute, 2261 Market, #405, San Francisco, CA 94114. Phone: (415) 626-0083. The seminars cost $500 for a three-day seminar; reduced to $350 if you sign up fifteen days in advance. The Lumatron is also available through Megabrain at (415) 332-8323, and you can test out the device at Megabrain workshops.

GENESIS (SOUND)

This is a giant sound device. The user lies on a cushioned platform four feet off the ground in the middle of an eighteen-sided frame resembling two geodesic domes joined together. Lurking beneath you are sensors, transducers, and speakers that are connected to an array of computers, synthesizers, and amplifiers. As the music plays from all sides, biosensors read the vibrational frequencies emitted by the body. With this information, the computer plots the body's reaction to the music and adjusts the music's volume, density, frequencies, phasing, and equalization. Essentially, the sensors figure out which frequencies your body is accepting or rejecting, and the computers adjust the sounds to have the greatest effect on each person. According to Profit Technology, the company that makes the machine, the more one relaxes, the fuller the tonal quality of the music becomes. A monitor shows the user's relaxation and interaction levels and you can get a hard-copy readout from an optional printer. Megabrain's Michael Hutchison calls it a "sonic massage" that's very good for theta. "You feel *inside* the sound," he says. "It's very relaxing. You feel the sound, from a buzzing to a tingling." As you relax, the music changes to fit your physical and mental state, so in effect you hear yourself. Genesis's inventor Michael Bradford puts it another way: "How you feel determines the music, so you learn how to control the music with your mind." Bradford has recently refined the Genesis so that the user is "the lead instrument in a song of his own composition." What you do is choose one instrument from a list of seventy-eight. The computer then builds an orchestra around that instrument, which is controlled by your body. The result is recorded on tape and you can take home a cassette of your own personal body song.

Access: The Genesis is being marketed to corporations, hospitals, clinics, nursing homes, spas, and even jails as a stress-reduction device, but you probably wouldn't want to buy one for your rec room—it costs about $35,000. However, you can contact the manufacturer to find out if there's a spa near you that offers sessions on the Genesis. Contact: Profit Technology, Inc., 17 Battery Place, 14th Floor, New York, N.Y. 10004. Phone: (212) 809-3500.

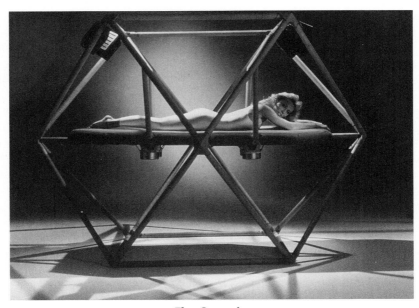

The Genesis

DENIS GORGES AND THE LIGHT-AND-SOUND WARS

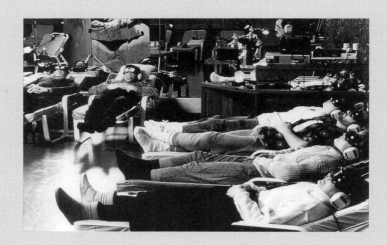

My real goal," says Denis Gorges, "is international harmony." In the meantime, Denis Gorges, the father of the Synchro Energizer, seems to be causing a lot of strife on a local level.

The light-and-sound-machine business (MC², the InnerQuest, MindsEye, D.A.V.I.D., etc.) is generally a friendly one, the manufacturers being generally small-time folks trying to eke out a living and help each other do the same. But almost all of them hate Denis Gorges. Perhaps it's because Gorges has accused fellow light-and-sound entrepreneurs of violating his 1982 patent, once firing off threatening letters to competitors. "He got some people scared for a while," says David Siever, of Comptronic Devices Ltd., the manufacturer of the D.A.V.I.D. Gorges has also generally badmouthed rival machines, saying they use potentially harmful frequencies. He told us that one competing machine causes "major seizures" and actually suppresses the immune system. On the other side, Siever and others charge that Gorges's machine causes nausea in some users and has "poor tones."

Even so, Denis Gorges is the man most responsible for the boom in light-and-sound and other brain machines. His Cleveland, Ohio, company, Synchro-Tech, Inc., claims that the big Synchro Energizer machine is being used in 100 relaxation centers worldwide, amazing when you consider the salon-size model with stations for 32 people prices out at about $70,000. Gorges also claims to have sold 26,000 clinical machines to psychiatrists. As for the Walkman-size version, called the Relaxman, supposedly 300,000 of these units have been sold.

Gorges has also done a monumental publicity job for the Synchro Energizer. The machine has been covered in *Esquire, People, Life, Newsweek, Money, Cosmopolitian, Vogue, American Health, Omni, Discover, The Wall Street Journal, The New York Times,* and, of course, *High Times.* ABC, CBS, and CNN have given the Synchro national TV coverage. Gorges also has a feel for eclectic endorsements. His brochures feature quotes about the Synchro Energizer from the likes of Wall Street analyst Arch Crawford ("It gets me from being frazzled to being clear") to hard-rock guitar whiz Eddie Van Halen ("I gots ta have one of those machines").

Gorges is an engaging interviewee, and a shrewd one, if a bit too slick for someone who professes to be a scientific researcher. He claims, for example, that he came up with the Synchro Energizer only after thirty years of research, although he is not specific about what he was doing during these three decades. To his credit, Gorges is one of the few in the brain-machine business who owns up to the fact that the brain generates more than one frequency of brain wave at a time, and entrainment via light-and-sound devices may not be a simple process of flashing alpha frequencies to produce alpha states in each individual. His manner of expressing this concept, however, doesn't always carry the ring of scientific authenticity. "You have billions of cells, all with their own agendas," explains Gorges. "If you're hungry and horny at the same time, you've got a conflict. Let's say you have to choose between a chateaubriand and a beautiful blonde. A neurotic can't make up his mind. A psychotic chooses one and rationalizes why he doesn't want the other. A schizophrenic wants them both." What does this have to do with brain-wave entrainment? We don't know, but Gorges seemed to enjoy telling the story.

During our interview, Gorges, who purports to have an I.Q. of 181, was careful not to make extravagant claims for the Synchro Energizer, especially claims that would propel the Synchro into the realm of medical devices, which would then make it subject to FDA regulation. He said the Synchro primarily provides a calming effect, and also focuses your attention. "Anything held by meditation or hypnosis," says Gorges, "can be held by the Synchro, but it does it faster in a larger population." He called his machine the "Concorde of calming machines" and a "taxi for the mind. It picks you up where you are and takes you to where you want to be."

One of the most controversial aspects of Denis Gorges is the little matter of his medical credentials. Most publications refer to him as "Dr. Gorges," and the *Wall Street Journal* called him a psychiatrist, which of course would require an M.D. But according to *The New York Times* he claims to be a psychologist with a Ph.D. *The Times* also pointed out that while the Synchro Energizer is touted as a memory improver, Gorges could not remember the location of the New Jersey institution that awarded him his mail-order degree. According to the FDA report on Synchro-Tech, Inc., Gorges admitted "he had no formal training or degrees." On the other hand, Gorges told us that he has an M.D. from a Canadian school—the United American Medical College in Oakville, Ontario—but that this degree cannot be verified because the college is now defunct. He added that he's not allowed to practice

medicine in Ohio because he's been arrested "a couple of times."

Gorges feels the ultimate task of the Synchro Energizer is the harmony of the human race. Take corporate squabbling. Gorges suggests sticking a Synchro in every boardroom. "Put everyone on the Synchro for ten minutes and you'll solve all their problems within twenty minutes." He says the problem with the light-and-sound-machine business is that the various manufacturers are "too greedy." His solution? He has offered to distribute all the machines himself. His competitors agree that greed is a problem, but they differ with Gorges on pinpointing just whose greed it is.

Gorges claims that he does not sell the Synchro Energizer, but rather leases out the machines for research purposes. Yet he distributes a pro forma that asks the question, "How much can you make as a Synchro System owner/distributor/retailer?" The sheet breaks down expenses and gross profits, showing revenues of about $300,000 per year with only 25 percent capacity on a thirty-two-station Synchro Energizer, with revenues closing in on $2 million at 100 percent capacity. In any case, there seems to be a lot of dollar figuring in Gorges's literature considering that this is all being done for the sake of basic research. The man is full of inconsistencies. In his company's literature is a statement that the Synchro Energizer is "approved by FDA as a safe and reliable learning/relaxation device." But he told us there is no FDA-approved device.

Still, without Gorges, the field would not be getting the attention it gets today, and he appears to be scaling down his claims for his own machine. He compares his business to the biofeedback craze of two decades ago, and doesn't want to see brain machines meet the same fate. According to Gorges, biofeedback was a worthwhile concept, but the claims made for biofeedback machines were excessive, and the phenomenon eventually died out. He says he doesn't want to see that happen to the light-and-sound market. For the future, he sees light-and-sound machines serving as an adjunct to medicine, replacing or supplementing drugs. He also sees them being used one day to treat learning disabilities, as they can be used to relax kids with problems. Finally, Gorges thinks the machines may be one answer to drug abuse. "People need to get high," says Gorges, and the machines are safer and more effective than drugs. We have to create "altered states that improve the brain instead of debilitating it," says Gorges. "We should open up the brain instead of anesthetizing it."

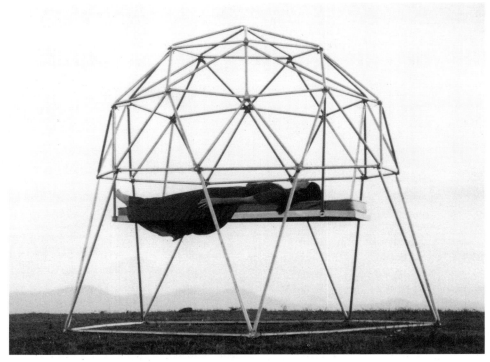

The Betar

BETAR (SOUND)
●

This device looks a bit like the Genesis. It consists of a padded platform bed suspended from the frame of an open geodesic dome with eight speakers that blast music into the user's body. Four speakers hang above you, four below, while transducers convert the music into physical vibrations aimed to relax you and alleviate stress. An operator controls the music, and hence the vibrations, from a selection of tape players, CD players, and tone generators. As with the Genesis, a sensor-feedback system measures the response of the user and adjusts the sound/vibration for best effect. According to the manufacturer, people who use Betar report a feeling of deep relaxation, a sense of well being, and the feeling that they were in "a holographic bubble of sound." Betar, by the way, stands for Bio-Energetic Transduction Aided Resonance.

Access: One of these babies will cost you $45,000, but the machine is featured at a number of spas where sessions cost as little as $35. Then there's the Baby Betar, a scaled-down, no-frills Betar that looks like a massage table with a sound system inside. It's less than one-tenth the cost: $4,250. For more information, and a list of spas that feature the Betar, contact: Dimensional Sciences Inc., P.O. Box 167, Lake Rabun Road, Lakemont, GA 30552. Phone: (800) 33BETAR or (404) 782-6301.

THE SOMATRON (SOUND)
●

Ever feel like throwing yourself on your stereo speakers and getting a sound massage? That's essentially what the Somatron does for you. It's a big padded massage table with a battery of concealed loudspeakers that pulse soothing tones into your body (unless, perhaps, you're playing Black Sabbath, in which case it may be less than soothing). It's sort of Magic Fingers with music. Artist/inventor Byron Eakin says the basic concept is as old as the vibramassage chair, except that such mechanical devices vibrate at one speed. The Somatron, on the other hand, features hundreds of speeds or vibrations. Don't be alarmed if you hear Bach coming out of your chiropractor's table, because Eakin says that he's sold some units to chiropractors, who use it for three to five minutes prior to adjusting a patient in order to reduce some of his/her initial tension. For personal use at home, Eakin says that a lot of people lie on the Somatron for about the length of a compact disc. Like many people in the consciousness-machine business, Eakin makes some unusual claims. He says the sound penetrates into the body "so there's an absorption into the cells and tissues. In other words there's a cellular massage taking place that doesn't really happen with any other vibratory device." Well, even despite such rhapsodizing, the Somatron seems to be catching on. The Canadian National Alpine Ski Team trucks one of Eakin's noisy tables with them, using it to relax its skiers; the University of Miami music therapy department uses the Somatron to relax its chronically ill patients; and All Children's Hospital in St. Petersburg, Florida, calms kids undergoing chemotherapy with the Somatron. Eakin rec-

ommends the baroque classics, because what you want are a lot of flowing bass notes, good for vibrating the body. He recommends you skip the punk rock and reggae, unless you want to be bounced off the table.

Access: There are a number of models, starting at $2,395 and going up to $6,000. The Somatron can also be found in hospitals and clinics and is used by chiropractors. To purchase a machine or to find a practitioner near you who offers sessions on the device, contact: Somasonics, 3405 Ellenwood Lane, Tampa, FL 33618. Phone: (813) 960-2183.

The Somatron (open and closed)

THE GRAHAM POTENTIALIZER (MOTION)
•

This baby is perhaps the oddest in the whole menagerie of brain machines. It doesn't use light or sound, just brute force. It's essentially a motion machine. You lie on a large massage table that moves up and down and side to side, while swathing your head in an electromagnetic field. According to inventor David Graham, it recreates the mental effects of the rolling, tumbling, and swinging games we played as children, effects we no longer enjoy as adults. Why not just hop on a merry-go-round? No good, says Graham; that oversaturates you. The Potentializer, on the other hand, is just right. The machine "exercises the brain," says its inventor, because it swirls around the fluid in our inner ear, which in turn bends the little hairs in there, and that fires off neurons. Get it? We didn't, but Graham says the benefits of his machine include relaxation, enhanced learning, greater self-esteem, success in business, better relationships, and it gets rid of phobias, to boot. Graham insists it also helps kids with learning disabilities improve their attention span and he makes some vague references to curing autism. Heady claims, but people who have tried it seem to enjoy rolling around on the Potentializer, unless they're prone to motion sickness.

Access: The Potentializer is not cheap, available in models from $7,500 to $14,400. Graham says there are about a hundred units around the country, and you can contact his company to find a practitioner near you who offers sessions on the device. Prices, he says, range from $40 to $80 per half hour on the machine. Contact: Starr Labs, 1107 West Hatcher Avenue, Phoenix, AZ 85021. Phone: (602) 997-8711.

THE TRANQUILITE (GANZFELD)
•

When Manhattan corporate consultant Zane Tankel climbed Mount Everest in 1986 without oxygen, he needed something to help him get to sleep, because at that altitude

The Tranquilite

the pounding of your heart is like a constant jackhammer. So he lugged along a prototype of the Tranquilite, a sensory-restriction device that blocks out external stimuli. And, as the line goes, he liked the product so much he bought the company. The prototype was a large clumsy product, so Tankel redesigned it to give it more popular appeal. (Large as it was, says Tankel, it was worth dragging up Everest, "because what I lost in weight I made up in sleep.") Mike Hutchison calls the Tranquilite the best of the ganzfeld devices, which block out sensory stimuli so that the user can focus on him- or herself (isolation tanks are also in the ganzfeld class). The Tranquilite consists of a large sky mask–like device that goes over your eyes, a pair of earphones, and a cord that runs to a combination battery power pack and control box that you can clip to your belt. What you see when you look into the mask, however, are not wildly blinking lights but a beautiful, unerring, sky-blue field. Meanwhile, through your earphones you hear "pink sound." This is white noise with the frequencies that stimulate brain activity filtered out. The control box has sliding switches for adjusting loudness and the brightness of the field, and a timer. The volume control is useful, says Tankel, for those times when you use the Tranquilite around other people. You just turn the volume high enough to drown out their conversation. Tankel himself uses the device three or four times a week. His claims are modest. He says it reduces stress, "keeps you centered," and says he uses it to lower his pulse during hectic days at the office. Tankel also says it's good for visualization when he can't make it to his karate lessons. He just goes through his martial arts exercises in his mind wearing the Tranquilite. And, of course, it's good for getting to sleep at 25,000 feet.

Access: The Tranquilite costs about $500. For further information, contact Tranquilite Times Inc., 1114 First Avenue, New York, NY 10021.

THETA-ONE (GANZFELD)
•

This is another ganzfeld device. It's called Theta-One because it's designed to take your brain into the theta state, the peaceful gap between waking and sleeping. Flotation tanks and light-and-sound devices can also take you down to theta, but because your eyes are closed, you often drift off to sleep. The idea of the Theta-One is that, because your eyes stay open, you can remain in the blissful theta threshold without the disappointment of slipping away into unconsciousness. Essentially, the device consists of a pair of goggles that plug into a battery or an adapter. Wearing the goggles, you gaze into a blue field, like a cloudless sky or Caribbean waters. The unit also comes with a special "hemispheric synchronization tape" that supposedly draws the waves of your left and right brain hemispheres into synchrony. It features music with the sound effects of a thunderstorm, an odd choice considering that you're looking at a "cloudless sky." This is a much cheaper unit ($195) than the Tranquilite ganzfeld unit. The Theta-One comes with earphones of the cheap Walkman variety, but this is odd considering there's no cassette deck in the machine; you have to connect your own if you want to play the hemispheric synchronization tape. But if you like the hypnogogic state, that variety of consciousness that visits us briefly at night just before we fall asleep, this is an inexpensive way to start. (Isolation tanks and laboratory-grade ganzfeld chambers are quite a bit more costly.) The Theta-One is said to allow you to capture "the steady stream of fleeting thoughts and images that tumble through the theta-state brain." It's recommended for artists wishing to tap into their creativity, lucid-dream aspirants, and people looking to develop their

The Theta-One

psychic abilities (telepathy and psychic talents are said to occur most likely in the theta state).

Access: The Theta-One is $195 plus $35 for an optional battery adapter. Available through Inner Technologies, 51 Berry Trail, Fairfax, CA 94930. Phone: (415) 454-0813.

ALPHA-STIM CS
(ELECTRICITY)
●

The Alpha-Stim is an electrical stimulation device. It's not portable like the Brain Tuner, and is available to laypeople only with a prescription from a doctor, dentist, psychiatrist, osteopath, or other certified health professional. It works in a number of modes. As a transcutaneous electrical nerve stimulation (TENS) device, it's been used by health professionals for relieving acute, chronic, and postoperative pain. Four medalists on the U.S. 1984 Olympic team were treated with the Alpha-Stim during their training periods, including Mark Gorski, gold medalist in sprint cycling, and Brad Alan Lewis and Paul Enquist, gold medalists in double sculls. The area of the body that is hurting is electrically stimulated through conductive pads; theoretically, what happens is that the body responds to the electric signals with a flood of endorphins to alleviate soreness and pain. But the Alpha-Stim also works in a transcranial electrostimulation (TCES) mode, like the Brain Tuner. Electrodes are clipped to your earlobes or attached to the temples and low-level electrical currents are sent directly into the brain, producing "electronarcosis" or electrosleep, a condition marked by deep relaxation, heightened awareness, and a sense of well being or even euphoria. Hypnotherapists and psychologists use TCES to help clients enter into trances and deeper states of consciousness. Dentists sometimes use the Alpha-Stim in this mode to relax their patients.

Access: The Alpha-Stim CS sells for about $750. It is the only FDA-approved device listed in this chapter. Available from Megabrain and Inner Technologies, 51 Berry Trail, Fairfax, CA 94930. Phone: (415) 454-0813.

The Alpha–Stim (open and closed)

ARE THEY SAFE?

SEIZURES, FUNNY BLINKING LIGHTS,

AND THE FDA

Before subjecting yourself to flashing lights, simulated heartbeats, buzzing tones, and sickly New Age music at close range, you would probably ask yourself the question: Are brain machines safe? Your second thought might be, Well, this is America, and surely the FDA (Food and Drug Administration) wouldn't allow anything on the market that's dangerous.

As it turns out, the safety of brain machines is not a simple issue. This is virgin territory, and at present the consumer is pretty much on his or her own. As for the FDA, Rob Robinson, inventor of the InnerQuest light-and-sound device, points out that their people "can't find their ass with both hands." After our conversation with this bizarre government agency, we would have to agree. But before we get into that particular nightmare, let's survey the possible dangers.

"You don't want to mix this stuff with alcohol and go into altered states," warns David Siever, inventor of the various D.A.V.I.D. devices. Siever says a country-and-western band once approached him to buy one of his machines as a party gimmick. "They were going to put it on the table next to the beer keg. We explained that when people go into deep hypnotic states they're very suggestible, and if they hear lyrics like, you know, 'My baby left me, woe is me . . . ,' it could be dangerous." The band eventually took Siever's advice and decided not to mix frequencies of sound and light with Budweiser and Tammy Wynette. Which reminds us of the old joke: How many country singers does it take to change a lightbulb? Four—one to screw in the new one, and three to sing about the old one.

But we digress. The whole purpose of brain machines is to put you in altered states, and obviously it is dangerous to experience any altered state at the wrong time or in the wrong place. Our society programs us to live in one very narrow brand of consciousness (K mart reality), and people stray from this norm at their own risk. This is why one doesn't drive drunk or go to mortgage conferences stoned. And this is why one uses a brain machine in a place and at a time when one isn't vulnerable to the normal dangers—psychological, physical, economical, or emotional—of our uptight, demanding civilization.

But what about the medical dangers? This question comes up most often in connection with the light-and-sound devices. Can flashing lights, sounds, and an electromagnetic field harm the body in any way?

The answer appears to be a qualified yes. Almost all the manufacturers of light-and-sound machines warn epileptics to stay away from their machines, that the flashing lights can trigger an epileptic seizure. And why not? Any kind of pulsing light can do this—if you'll recall one of the most gripping scenes of *The Andromeda Strain,* when an emergency light renders an epileptic scientist helpless at the most inopportune moment.

Denis Gorges, father of the Synchro Energizer, claims that there have been no injuries or incidences of illness reported in the estimated 3 to 5 million times people have used the Synchro. However, he does admit that there have been "five reports of seizure-like behavior" reported in users. These were all in previously undiagnosed seizure-prone individuals. In fact, Gorges claims the Synchro actually provided a service in diagnosing these people's proclivity. Light-and-sound manufacturers also warn that their machines could be dangerous to wearers of cardiac pacemakers because of possible electromagnetic interference. Gorges admits, too, that some people have experienced vertigo and nausea on the Synchro.

Who regulates the machines? At present, all light-and-sound devices are unregulated by the Food and Drug Administration, whose mission it is to keep potentially dangerous or worthless medicines out of our hands. Anything classified as a "medical device" must undergo controlled clinical trials before it can be marketed. This "premarket approval," as it's called, is expensive and time consuming, so most brain-machine manufacturers—predominantly small operators—would like to avoid it. The question is, are light-and-sound machines medical devices?

Oddly enough, that does not depend so much on what a machine does, but more on what its inventor and manufacturer *say* it does. Unfortunately for them, some manufacturers have said some injudicious things. It's probably okay to claim that a brain machine induces euphoria, raises self-esteem, or improves memory, as audacious as such claims may seem. But some makers also claimed their machines treated stress and related disorders, normalized blood pressure, and improved vision. Medical claims are more problematic.

"If you claim that a machine reduces stress or stress-related illness, that's a medical device," explained Kathleen Frost, formerly of the FDA's neurological devices division. "If you make no medical claims—if you just claim simple relaxation—then it's the same as marketing a toaster."

Some companies try to hedge their bets, such as Psych-Research, Inc., which makes the InnerQuest. A fact sheet on the InnerQuest clearly states that the device "reduces the negative effects of pain and trauma," "reduces . . . tachycardia," and "removes neurological/perceptive imbalances." Then, at the bottom, the company declares: "The above findings do not represent medical claims as such. Nor are any medical claims made or implied for the InnerQuest unit *at this time* [emphasis ours]."

Even Denis Gorges now chooses his words more carefully than in the past, perhaps because the FDA has investigated his company. "We make no medical claims," Gorges told us, though he is quick to add that there are "a lot of medical uses for the device." That's different, see? Like manufacturing pickaxes: You only claim they're good for quarrying limestone—but who's to say you can't use them for brain surgery?

But it was a slightly different story in 1985 when the FDA looked into Gorges's business. The investigator noted that "the literature reviewed included references to pain and stress reduction, learning disabilities, psychotherapy, and addiction control." To be fair, other brain-machine entrepreneurs have made similar claims, but to our knowledge they have not been investigated by the FDA as yet. The 1985 FDA report concluded: "It appears that the product should also be classified as a prescription device."

Then why aren't light-and-sound machines today regulated by the government? It's hard to say, especially since the FDA isn't talking, or at least not talking sense. We had the following conversation with the agency's so-called press relations officer David Duarte:

"I'm doing an article on synchronized light-and-sound machines and I wonder. . . ."

"We don't know anything about it."

"That's odd, because I have a record of an FDA investigation of one of them, the Synchro Energizer."

"If it's under investigation, we won't comment."

"You mean it's FDA policy not to give out any information about any drug or device it is reviewing?"

"That's right."

"Can you tell me if something is under review?"

"No, we have no comment."

"But under the Freedom of Information Act one can obtain documents about this. . . ."

"Try and do it then."

Thinking we may have hit Mr. Duarte on a bad day—or that he just didn't take a shine to us—we asked another journalist to try again with a different press officer. Kathleen Stein, one of the founding editors of *Omni* magazine, called up another FDA spokesperson, Bob Munzer, and asked him the identical questions—and received almost identical answers. When Stein brought up the idea of obtaining documents through the Freedom of Information Act, she got the same sneering go-ahead-and-try-it response. Both Duarte and Munzer were right to be confident: When we requested additional information under the Freedom of Information Act, the FDA acknowledged receiving our request, but never sent the information. It's been nine months now, and we're still waiting. Well, maybe the mail is slow.

Is this part of some FDA/CIA/Pentagon plot? That did enter our minds—the government suppressing information on light-and-sound machines because they were being utilized in some bizarre military scheme. Perhaps giant Synchro Energizers orbiting in space, zapping entire nations with flashing lights and pulsing sounds, easing their armies into somnolent theta or delta states while our ground troops march in unchallenged. We envisioned thousands of paratroopers wearing personal InnerQuest machines, their goggles blazing them into frenetic beta states as they parachuted into hostile territory, the traditional learning tapes replaced with cassettes filled with admonitions to "Kill, kill, kill!" Suddenly the FDA's reluctance to explain why they didn't want to comment on these machines made terrible, diabolical sense.

Megabrain's Michael Hutchison brought us back down to earth. More than likely, he explained, the FDA's attitude has more to do with a bureaucratic state of mind than CIA plots. Also, it turns out there's an FDA loophole for light-and-sound entrepreneurs known as 510-K, which waives the full gamut of clinical trials for any machine similar to devices on the market before 1976, and a light-and-sound prototype called ISIS was developed back in 1971.

What is the future for regulation? Obviously, it's hard to predict given the FDA's silence—the agency is probably too busy looking for its rear end. David Siever believes that brain machines will inevitably be classified as medical devices, obtainable only by prescription just as biofeedback devices are now. Gorges, on the other hand, is dead set against FDA regulation, saying that if the FDA comes in there will only be big players. "Then the inventors and creative types," he points out, "will be buried."

BRAIN TUNER (ELECTRICITY)
•

Alternately called the BT-5, the Brain Tuner purports to adjust your brain chemicals through electrical stimulation, thus leading to improvements in memory, mental clarity, relaxation, sound sleep, increased vitality, and greater alpha activity. The BT-5 is a small box that fits right in your pocket. A headset features coated electrodes that fit in the hollows behind your ears. You can use it "while reading, watching TV, or gardening," according to one advertisement. How does it work? Unlike the light-and-sound machines, which have an immediate effect on your consciousness, the Brain Tuner works slowly and cumulatively to balance neurotransmitter production. (This is generally true of all electrical-stimulation devices.) Neurotransmitters are chemical messengers in the brain that help filter external perceptions, produce emotional states, and mediate pain. They have also been linked to memory, creativity, and intelligence. One variety of neurotransmitter, the endorphins, can induce euphoria and states of expanded consciousness similar to those reached through deep meditation. But aging, substance abuse, bad diet, and pollutants can cause an imbalance in your neurotransmitters. The Brain Tuner applies weak electrical signals, which the brain treats as if they were signals from its own communication network. Theoretically, this coaxes the brain to restore its chemical balance. The electrical waveform contains 256 preset frequencies. The inventor of the BT-5, Dr. Bob Beck, claims that daily use of the device will result in positive changes in just a few weeks. The advertised benefits: more energy, better sleep, less addictive behavior. The machine is touted for those fighting chemical dependencies, with the claim that such users report very few withdrawal symptoms. Nonaddicted users supposedly report they no longer have colds, the flu, or other problems associated with a depleted immune system. And there are the usual claims of improved memory and intelligence, as well as the onset of lucid dreaming. The BT-5 has not been submitted for FDA approval and requires no prescription at this writing.

Access: The Brain Tuner costs $350 from Transformation Technologies, 9025 Willis Avenue, #108, Panorama City, CA 91402. Phone: (818) 830-1913. Also available through Inner Technologies, 51 Berry Trail, Fairfax, CA 94930. Phone: (415) 454-0813.

The Brain Tuner

NUSTAR (ELECTRICITY)
•

The Nustar is another electrical device, but unlike the Alpha-Stim or Brain Tuner, it doesn't make any claims for stimulating endorphins or other neurotransmitters. Rather, its promoters claim it achieves the same accomplishments as the light-and-sound devices: It induces alpha, theta, or delta states by propagating waves through the brain at these frequencies; except it uses electricity rather than blinking lights and pulsing sounds to do this. The machine consists of a 3″ × 5″ × 2″ control box and a headband with four integral electrodes. You slip on the headband and dial a frequency from 0.7 hz (low delta) to 12.5 hz (high alpha). The inventor of the Nustar, the late Michael Hercules, claimed that specific brain-wave frequencies are connected to certain states of consciousness. For example, 1.0 hz is associated with a "feeling of well-being," an "overall view of interrelationships," and "pituitary stimulation to release growth hormone." If you can take this seriously, it implies you can set the knobs on the Nustar to 1.0 in order to feel

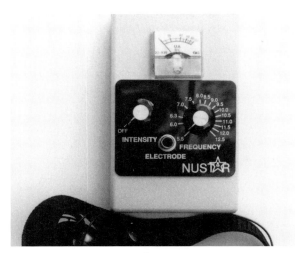

The Nustar

good, assess that fling with the new secretary in the office, while growing a few inches at the same time so you can go after the taller office manager instead. Reported benefits of the Nustar include the usual: mental relaxation, self-healing, creative thinking, out-of-body experiences, ESP and other psychic phenomena, chronic-pain control, sleep reduction (an average of two hours per night), improved learning, and spiritual growth. Hercules himself was a colorful and near-heroic figure in the field. He was an aerospace engineer, serving on the NASA moon shots, and he was Test Conductor for the Titan I project. In the mid-1980s he suffered a severe stroke that totally paralyzed the left side of his body. Hercules claimed that by using an earlier version of the Nustar (called the Pulsar), he attained almost total recovery in five weeks. (Perhaps true, but he died soon after.)

Access: There are two models. The Nustar I is $299 and operates from 5.5 to 12.5 hz. The Nustar II is $399 and operates from 0.7 to 12.5 hz. Both come with batteries, carrying case, and (ick!) electrode gel. Available from Inner Technologies, 51 Berry Trail, Fairfax, CA 94930. Phone: (415) 454-0813.

BINAURAL SIGNAL GENERATOR
(BEAT FREQUENCY)
•

The Binaural Signal Generator

A beat frequency is what you get when you send slightly different frequencies to each ear. Say your left ear is receiving a 200 hz signal, while the right ear hears a 207 hz sound. The net effect, according to Robert Monroe, out-of-body-experience pioneer and founder of the Monroe Institute of Applied Sciences, is a beat frequency of 7 hz. (You can't create this effect by sending an audio signal of 7 hz directly because your ears can't hear frequencies that low.) This binaural beat, according to Monroe, who came up with the concept, is an effective means of entraining brain waves and synchronizing the brain's left and right hemispheres. The Binaural Signal Generator (BSG) is a box about the size of a stereo amplifier that sends different frequencies to each of your ears (and therefore, to each of your brain hemispheres). You plug the device into your audio system—tape deck, phonograph, CD, etc.—so you can combine the BSG's tones with music or learning tapes. Michael Hutchison says that the device has the greatest effect when piped through headphones, but you can broadcast the binaural beat over external stereo speakers as well. The signals can be set automatically to broadcast at 20 decibels below human hearing. The tones won't be audible, but your unconscious will hear them and follow the beat frequency. The BSG is recommended to be used with meditation, creativity, or super-learning tapes or other educational program. It can also be used over speakers in group settings such as self-motivation workshops, stress management, creative arts, and therapy. One of the more interesting things you can do with the BSG is to create what Hutchison calls "a layer cake of signals."

That is, the machine can create multiple beat frequencies in your brain, so that you're in delta, theta, and beta all at the same time. This creates the "mind awake/body asleep" state that's supposed to be ideal for learning. The body is barely churning over in the delta or theta state, but the mind is perking away in beta. You can also pipe more beta into late afternoon offices to keep people from becoming drowsy. The Binaural Signal Generator has a range from delta to beta, and its integral synthesizer plays surf sounds alone, or mixes them with binaural beats, music, or both.

Access: The BSG costs about $400, and is available from Megabrain or Inner Technologies, 51 Berry Trail, Fairfax, CA 94930. Phone: (415) 454-0813.

ALPHA CHAMBER
(COMBINATION)
•

It's hard to put the Alpha Chamber in any one category. It's a little bit sound machine, a little bit isolation tank, and a little bit biofeedback device. Essentially, it's a big, luxuriously padded chair in the shape of a cutaway egg. You sit inside the device with your legs stretched outside and supported by an ottoman. The chair is based on the principle of the sound engineer's anechoic chamber, and it cuts out 60 percent of exterior sounds and sights. Inside, behind the fabric are two speakers encased within fiberglass baffles. The music and other recorded sounds cause the chamber to subtly vibrate, so the user feels as if the music is flowing through him. According to Gary Rupar, who heads up Sensory Environment Engineers, the firm that manufactures the Alpha Chamber, the device affects brain-wave frequency, respiration, heart rate, and peripheral warmth (as you relax, your peripheral blood vessels dilate, and you become warmer). An onboard computer selects from 215 different programs, which can consist of instructional tapes, music, or environmental sounds, or combinations of all three. In this way, it becomes a kind of biofeedback device, helping the user improve his sensory acuity. As with other machines, the programs can present a different message to each hemisphere of the brain, and are designed for "pain relief, appetite control, smoking cessation, increased sexual pleasure [inside a big egg?], stress control, high self-esteem, energy and confidence, and relaxation training." The Alpha Chamber is marketed mostly to hospitals, medical clinics, doctors' offices, health retreats, and businesses. Rupar says it's also being used by the U.S. military academy at West Point (!), the Olympic Training Center, and NASA, which believes it may prove useful in conditioning astronauts for life on space stations.

Access: The Alpha Chamber is not something you'd order in place of a BarcaLounger for your living room. It costs $17,000. Or you can lease it. Obviously, it's meant for institutional or spa use. But you can call or write the company to find out where you can take advantage of the device. Contact: Sensory Environment Engineers, P.O. Box 1540, Fontana, CA 92335. Phone: (714) 822-3748 or 1-800-522-RELA(X).

WHO WAS THAT MASKED MAN IN THE BEDROOM?

TEST DRIVING THE INNERQUEST

We've examined what it's like to try to synchronize your brain waves in public (see "Blazing Goggles," page 30), but now that affordable, personal-size light-and-sound machines are available, what is the experience like in the privacy of your own home? Or on the bus, or anywhere else you prefer?

The unit we chose to test was the InnerQuest. It's one of the more reasonably priced ($495, as opposed to $795 for the D.A.V.I.D. Jr. or MindsEye), and it was also the only model with a built-in cassette deck. Most aficionados in the light-and-sound business pooh-pooh the idea of a built-in tape deck because almost everyone has a Walkman they can hook up or because it's one of the first things to go wrong or because it adds to the price disproportionately.

But I like the concept. If you're traveling with the unit you don't have to carry a second little box (a portable cassette player). And then there are all the cords to deal with. The InnerQuest, for example, comes with three basic pieces of equipment. There's a steel box, a bit shorter but thicker than a cigar box, the lighted goggles, and earphones. The goggles have a cord that plugs into the control unit; so do the earphones; and if your batteries are dead (a not uncommon event), you need another cord to plug the InnerQuest into a wall outlet. While you're lying there trying to entrain your brain waves, it's a pretty common event to get yourself tangled up in this maze of wires. If you have to connect a tape machine to the control box, that's yet another wire to confound you. Frankly, if you're as clumsy as I am, worrying constantly about being caught in this web is enough to keep you in a frenetic state of beta waves no matter what frequencies your goggles are flashing through your eyelids.

The InnerQuest is very easy to use. The instructions were clear. Insert four C batteries or plug the thing into the wall with the provided adapter. Connect up your earphones and goggles. Press the ON button, and a red "-" sign appears in the readout window. You then select one of sixteen programs by pushing another button. A third button lets you choose between white noise and a tone. There are also buttons for adjusting the frequencies of the blinking lights and sounds while you're using the machine, and a sound-volume control as well.

I chose program number "0," described in the machine's literature as a simple fifteen-minute session of relaxation conditioning. It begins at an 18-hz beta level and slows to 7 hz over five minutes, keeps you there for nine minutes, then returns you to 18 hz and full intensity in the final minute. I slipped on my goggles, strapped on my earphones, and hit the "run" button.

Just as with the full-size Synchro Energizer experience I had at Christine Zerrer's Manhattan spa, I was hit with an immediate rush of euphoria, though it was not as powerful. I did feel myself being lowered from a frenetic brain state to a lower, more relaxed state. (However, that's what the instructions told me would happen, so one cannot discount the placebo effect here.) The InnerQuest goggles have only two red LEDs over each eye, as opposed to the four full-spectrum lights over each eye in the industrial-strength Synchro Energizer, and I felt that, subjectively, this may have made a difference. The light show produced in my brain seemed a bit less spectacular. Even so, the ensuing spectacle was more than pleasant. My brain is obviously not very good at this kind of thing, and the colors I experienced were pretty limited: lots of turquoise, some reds and yellows, a few blues tinged with black. I got the usual patterns: swirls, moirés, interfering waves. I got some interesting patterns that looked like peacock feathers, and some red and yellow stars that were formed out of dozens of pentagons, which then rotated, first clockwise, then counterclockwise. At one point, my visual field was bombarded with hundreds of roman numerals, probably because earlier in the day I had to write about all the different models of the InnerQuest—the I.Q.I, I.Q.II, I.Q.III, etc.

What I didn't like about the InnerQuest trip is the ending, that final minute at full intensity, and then—clack!—it shuts off abruptly. It's kind of harsh to the system and makes one wish for the

The InnerQuest

"soft off" feature of the D.A.V.I.D. Jr. Plus, which decreases the volume and dims the lights slowly at the end of a program to avoid those crash landings back into the real world.

Then I tried the cassette tape that comes with the machine. One side is an introductory lesson and the other side is a relaxation exercise. I don't know whose voice it is on the tape, but the fellow bored me to tears. This boredom made me more and more uptight and the session was beginning to have the opposite effect of relaxation, so I chucked the damn tape and ran the machine without it. I tried a number of programs, but had trouble distinguishing the differences among them (except, of course, that some are much longer than others). Program No. 1, for example, is supposed to be similar to Program No. 0, except that it takes you down to 5 hz instead of just 7 hz. Program No. 5 is a "high-intensity" session. The frequency drops no lower than 12 hz. This is supposed to be great for "high motivation, energy building before competitions, speeches, etc." I tried it, then went out and ran a twelve-minute mile. (Don't laugh; it normally takes me thirteen minutes!) Another program, which takes you from 20 hz to 7 hz, is touted as a "memory and recall" session, useful for regressions. I believe I tried it once, but I can't remember what happened. Then there's a meditation program for "well-conditioned subjects who easily drop into alpha." It begins at 10 hz and very quickly lowers you to 5 hz, where it remains for 40 minutes before returning to 10 hz. I didn't try this because I'm a nervous wreck whose brain probably vibrates at 100 hz even when I'm asleep. The reason you have to be "well conditioned" (like an experienced meditator or yogi or something) is because the program starts at such a low level and takes you even lower in a hurry. Most of us are pretty uptight, and have to start at higher frequencies, then must be slowly coaxed into the lower-frequency alpha and theta states.

The frequencies, by the way, can be left/right, front/back, or all synch. Left/right is a crisscross pattern that stimulates first the left ear and right eye, and then the right ear and left eye. Front/back is a pattern that alternates between both eyes and both ears. All synchronous means that the same signal is applied to both eyes and both ears simultaneously. The various programs pick and choose among these three techniques, sometimes using all three in one session.

The program I liked most was good old No. 6, which is intended for music appreciation. New Age music is supposed to go well with these devices, but if you're like me and don't like throwing up while having your brain entrained, you might try cassettes with some *good* music on them. I snapped in one of my custom tapes with a variety of different artists—Led Zeppelin, Savoy Brown, Jethro Tull, Roxy Music, Spirit, Quicksilver Messenger Service, Grateful Dead, Jimi Hendrix—slipped on the goggles and earphones, selected No. 6, and let 'er rip. This gave me the biggest shot of euphoria, perhaps mostly because of the music, but it was far more pleasurable than with just the music alone. As you would expect because of the dropping frequencies, I was at first energized, and then I mellowed out, my mind drifting off to pleasant memories and profound thoughts (well, they seemed really deep at the moment).

One memory evoked was of my many visits to Bill Graham's Fillmore East, the rock concert hall in Manhattan's East Village that flourished in the late 1960s and early '70s. The effect of the InnerQuest's lights, sound, and music made me realize that Graham was one of the pioneers of neurotechnology. While Hendrix or the Airplane or whoever would play, unloading megadoses of sound on the audience, a light show in the background would flash colorful patterns on a giant screen, roughly in time with the music. The artists may, in fact, have been unconsciously employing the principles of brainwave entrainment. I normally attended concerts totally straight, but once a friend insisted that we get stoned first—this for a performance by Eric Clapton, in the days when he still played *loud,* and didn't do beer commercials. We were still pretty looped by the time the music started, and the amazing thing was this: I didn't notice any difference. The illicit substance was no more powerful than the normal combination of sound and flashing lights on the screen. In reality, the Fillmore was a giant Synchro Energizer or InnerQuest.

(Incidentally, if the past few paragraphs seem a bit disjointed to you, it's because I'm using the InnerQuest as I write this. Even with the flashing glasses on, you can see enough to write if you peer downward, beneath the LEDs.)

In conclusion, the InnerQuest is a good way to get high—not real high, but a nice buzz. Where it takes you depends a lot, I found, on your initial condition. If I strapped on the device on a day when I had a lot of energy, it would make me lucid in a powerful kind of way. On a down day, it might put me half asleep. In almost every case, though, it released a lot of tension.

The InnerQuest does not have the power one would like. Synchro Energizer's Denis Gorges says that none of the personal-size units—including his own, the Relaxman—provides the intensity of the full-size machines. But, of course, the smaller, more affordable devices let you entrain yourself every day, if you feel like it. The workmanship of the InnerQuest is not what one would prefer. The earphones are of the cheap Walkman variety, and the goggles are really a pair of cheap sunglasses with the LEDs attached. The stems on the glasses continually slip out of their hinges. What we'd like to see is a unit with stereo-aficionado-quality earphones, and one that can be *easily* coupled with a high-quality audio system.

As for the claims of what the InnerQuest will do for you, they appear to be inflated, just as they are for all the other light-and-sound machines. Now, there may be some truth to these claims for some people, but you certainly can't count on them. For example, I used Program No. 9, supposedly "great . . . for problem solving." I was trying to solve the problem of my publisher, who was angry as hell about the fact we had missed our deadline by several months for this book. What happened was that I dropped off to sleep wearing the InnerQuest and fell even further behind.

And you always have to remember that you're wearing sunglasses with flashing lights on them, with cords going to a funny blue box. I forgot this obvious fact one afternoon while lying on my bed zonking out with the InnerQuest. My three-year-old son came looking for his daddy and found this stranger in the bedroom wearing blinking goggles. But if that's what you want, the InnerQuest is great for scaring the hell out of little kids.—*D.T.*

CEREBREX
•

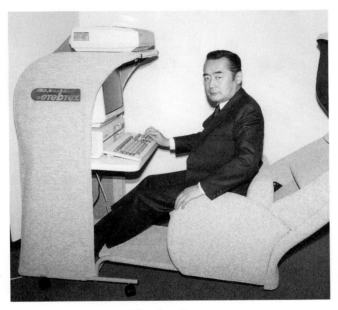

The Cerebrex

We're not sure what this baby does. It has sound, so perhaps it should be grouped with the Genesis or Somatron. But you sit on it, so perhaps it should be lumped in with the Alpha Chamber. In any case, the Cerebrex is a big funny reclining chair that looks like it has a giant hair dryer attached in back and a computer console in front. Supposedly it works by pulsing high-frequency sound waves into the user's head and feet, which reportedly activates alpha waves in the brain and increases blood flow throughout the body. Twenty minutes in the chair, according to the inventor, is equal to a night's sleep. This also increases, he says, one's mental and sexual prowess.

The inventor is none other than Yoshiro NakaMats, a Japanese inventor with over 2,300 patents, one of them being the floppy-disk drive for the computer. NakaMats, who wants to live to be 140, also says the chair lengthens life expectancy.

Access: The Cerebrex costs about $70,000. NakaMats already has hundreds of Cerebrexes in use in Japan, and is beginning to interest American health spas in the machine. For further information, contact Yoshiro NakaMats, Landic No. 2 Akasaka Building, No. 10-9, 2-chome, Akasaka, Minato-ku, Tokyo 107, Japan. Phone: (03) 505-0301.

ALPHAPACER II (COMBINATION)
•

Not to be confused with the Alpha-Stim, the Alphapacer II combines light and sound, a pulsed electromagnetic field, and direct cranial electrostimulation in one machine. The Alphapacer is basically a box with knobs, dials, and a meter, a piece of equipment that looks like something out of a 1950s mad-scientist horror movie. A set of headphones and goggles is used when the machine is in its synchronized light-and-sound mode, and ear clips deliver the message when the Alphapacer is in its pulsed electromagnetic field or direct cranial electrostimulation modes. Robert Cosgrove, of the department of anesthesia at the Stanford University School of Medicine, says that the Alphapacer II "has been observed by us to be an excellent neuropathway exerciser." He goes on to say that "the long-term effects of regular use of the Alphapacer on maintaining and improving cerebral performance throughout life and possibly delaying for decades the deterioration of the brain traditionally associated with aging is very exciting." Michael Hutchison suggests the machine can also alleviate the effects of ambient electronic pollution.

Access: Available for $495 from Megabrain, P.O. Box 2205, Sausalito, CA 94965-9998. Phone: (415) 332-8323.

BIO CY 2000 (COMBINATION)
•

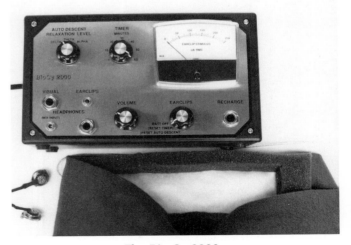

The Bio Cy 2000

This is three machines in one: light and sound, ganzfeld, and electrical stimulation. The Bio Cy consists of a control box that's 7½" × 4½" × 3", ear-clip electrodes for the electrical stimulation mode, special "light-fold" goggles for pulsed lights or ganzfeld, and rechargeable batteries and charger. The light show supplied by the Bio Cy markedly differs from conventional light-and-sound devices. It's much gentler. The light field is generated by red LEDs enveloped in felt glasses called a light fold. The felt diffuses the light, so you're looking at a muted pulsing field of light rather than flashing points. You may not get the entertaining geometric patterns common to other machines, but some people find the muted Bio Cy more comfortable than the more intense light-and-sound machines. There is only one sound, pink noise, which is white noise filtered to make it more pleasing. You can hook up a Walkman-type cassette deck if you want to play music or other tapes. In the ganzfeld mode, the Bio Cy has an interesting feature: It changes colors. You can buy optional green and yellow light folds to supplement the standard red one. Color therapists recommend red for euphoria, green for a soothing effect, and yellow for stimulating mental functions. As an electrostimulator, the Bio Cy is claimed to boost neurotransmitter production. An interesting feature is that electrical stimulation can be used in combination with the light-and-sound program or ganzfeld.

Access: The Bio Cy 2000 costs $595 and an additional $35 for each optional color light fold. Available from Inner Technologies, 51 Berry Trail, Fairfax, CA 94930. Phone: (415) 454-0813.

CHAPTER THREE

SUPERBRAIN:
THE · QUEST · FOR
INTELLIGENCE

•

Of course, you want to be smarter. Who doesn't? Smart is to the nineties what sexy was to the seventies, what rich and physically fit was to the eighties. (Actually, one hidden agenda here is that if you get smart enough you will also get rich—or at least very successful.) Everyone agrees that we all have to get very, very smart very, very fast to handle a world in which whole species of plants and animals are vanishing as fast as a failed Hollywood teen make-out movie and in which humankind accumulates more new information in a single day than was contained in the entire Library of Alexandria. (We just made up that sta- tistic but it sounds im- pressive, doesn't it?) We can't even write a note to the mailman without using a computer that has two megabytes of random access mem- ory—many times the cogitating power of those early Univacs that filled entire buildings

and were stoked by dozens of lab-suited technicians—and that, at any moment, for reasons known only to its obscure machine-language soul, could darken our screen with the disheartening message: FATAL ERROR. In fact, something like that happened to us while we were writing this chapter, but you don't want to hear about that, do you?

So how do you get smart? How do you add to your random access memory and avoid fatal errors?

The brain-machine people we met in the last chapter would have you hook your head up to something resembling the control panel of a nuclear sub and listen to angelic electronic New Age choirs while soaking up subliminal suggestions in theta. But that isn't the only way to improve your brain. After all, there's nothing inherently wrong with your equipment (unless, of course, you've been mainlining MSG or watching "Geraldo" nonstop). You don't have to grow new brain cells; you just need to learn to use the ones you've got.

Which brings us to the Brain Boosters. Who are the Brain Boosters? Let's just say that they're the sort of people who are apt to remark, "Of course, we only use ten percent of the brain." Ten percent! Where did that figure come from? Who knows? Has anyone actually gone in there and counted the neurons that light up when we solve a syllogism or think up twenty-five uses for a screwdriver?

Anyway, some Brain Boosters—let's call them the twenty-five-uses-for-a-screwdriver people—think you can light up more of your brain cells by switching your thinking style. You can try to think of twenty-five uses for a screwdriver (or a brick, or a door, or whatever). You can go around asking yourself questions like, What would happen if I didn't have to sleep? or What if time ran backward? You can try to construct four equilateral triangles from six matches. After you've done a bit of this, you'll hope you'll never, ever see another four-by-four grid with sixteen dots that you're supposed to connect in a particular manner. (See "People Who Think Too Much," page 51.)

There is some overlap between the screwdriver people and the Mensa-nerd cabal (see "Games Geniuses Play," page 63), but you can generally tell them apart because the latter are more drawn to obscure vocabulary words, math games, and high scores on the Miller Analogies Test. Other Brain Boosters think you can get smarter simply by learning stuff very, very fast. These people are mostly devotees of a Bulgarian accelerated-learning technique, Suggestopedia, or one of its spin-offs. (See "I'm Learning as Fast as I Can," page 56.)

Many Brain Boosters nowadays want to enhance their brainpower in order to be better at marketing plans or leveraged buyouts. These hyperpotentialized Zen businessmen are responsible for a considerable vogue in "brainstorming" and "creative problem solving." Now, we have no problem with product managers going off to motivational spas and honing their problem-solving skills, but, unfortunately, many of them also want to visualize things, spiritualize their managerial techniques, and get in touch with their inner knowingness. From what we can tell, there must be a case of mass executive satori over at GM, DuPont, and Hewlett Packard! What is the world coming to when people in Brooks Brothers suits, the very sort of people we rely on to be our unimaginitive, respectable pillars of society, start quoting Zen koans? It must be one of the signs of the End Times, an ominous pre-Armageddon paradigm shift. It

shakes up one's weltanschauung, rather as if Ward Cleaver and Ozzie Nelson were to dump their wives for twenty-two-year-old airline hostesses and run off to experiential shamanic workshops at Esalen.

Which reminds us: There is another type of Brain Booster who is always urging you to get comfortable, close your eyes, and visualize things in capital letters. Listen to Marilee Zdenek, author of *The Right Brain Experience,* explaining how to create an Inner Adviser. "You can speak freely with this Wise and Loving Person about the most intimate longings of your soul," she notes in what we suppose is the literary equivalent of a calm, soothing voice. "If you are a musician, you can ask that Wise Person to sing for you and ask that the song be original and as beautiful as any song you have ever heard." We asked our Wise Person to write us a perfect introductory paragraph in the style of Henry James if Henry James were writing an offbeat post–New Age self-help book, but all we got was the same old drivel.

The close-your-eyes-and-visualize people often encourage you to paint, write, or make business deals from the right side of your brain. So far we've avoided talking about the right cerebral hemisphere, which is too often coupled with the word "wholistic" for our tastes, but here goes. The story starts in a southern California operating room, where patients with severe epilepsy underwent a radical operation starting in 1963. In a last-ditch attempt to control their seizures, surgeons severed the patients' corpus callosum, the thick cable of nerve fibers linking the brain's right and left hemispheres. After surgery, neuroscientist Roger Sperry of Caltech discovered that the two halves of the brain behaved like two separate brains when disconnected. A patient might button up a shirt with the right hand, only to find the left hand diligently unbuttoning it. These "split brain" patients enabled Sperry to observe the functions of the right and left hemispheres separately, and his studies showed that the two sides of the human brain had two radically different cognitive styles. In most people, the left hemisphere of the brain (which controls the right side of the body) was linear, logical, and mathematical, while the right hemisphere was imagistic, artistic, associative, "wholistic." It didn't take long for everyone to decide that the right hemisphere was a New Age muse, a mute Zen master imprisoned by the uptight linear logic of the left brain.

Unfortunately, we have heard this split-brain story ad nauseum. So often, in fact, that we've begun to have a queasy feeling about those 200 million nerve fibers connecting our hemispheres. What if they wear out like frayed shock absorbers? What if they dwindle to, say, ten million? Will our left hand start rewriting our copy in midparagraph, adding comments like, "You can speak freely with this Wise and Loving Person"? Will we be unfit to read all these whole-brain creativity books? *Then* what percentage of our brain cells will be out to lunch?

In the course of reseaching this chapter, we ran across some alarming statistics. Consider this: "Nearly all of the 80% of the brain which is involved in the visual response is in that 95% of the brain that is not conscious," according to the literature put out by intelligence booster Win Wenger of Gaithersburg, Maryland. We never knew *that* before. We're not quite sure what that means to us personally, but we suspect it may have some bearing on our failure to meet

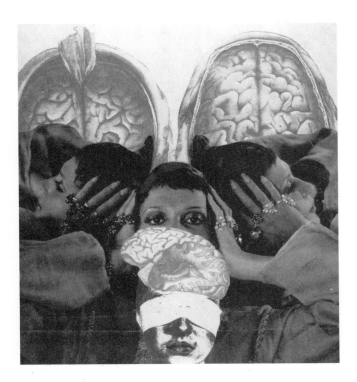

PEOPLE WHO THINK TOO MUCH

A MAN HAS TWENTY-FIVE USED CIGAR BUTTS

•

So begins a typical quiz in Gerard I. Nierenberg's *The Art of Creative Thinking,* the cover blurb of which "guarantees" you will "think, write, research, negotiate, compose, invent, and solve any problem with greater creativity." We certainly wanted to solve our problems with greater creativity, so let's see. It takes five butts to make a cigar, according to the book. How many cigars can this man smoke? We answered, "Zero," assuming the man was on an airplane. But the correct answer is six cigars, one of which is made from the leftover butts from the five. We didn't think of that; we just thought the guy should go out and buy himself a new box of cigars.

Nierenberg, who made his mark with the best-selling *The Art of Negotiating,* has a strange habit of quoting *himself* at the beginning of chapters, but he does seem to have combed the planet from general semantics and the psychology of optical illusions to Senoi dreamwork and altered-states research (he's brave enough to admit that drugs sometimes lead to unusual insights) for thought-provoking material. Our eyes glaze over in the face of any problem

deadlines. So naturally we were intrigued to read that one of Wenger's brain-improving techniques, tested at a Minnesota university, "links enough key areas of the brain together to result in permanent apparent gains in intelligence equivalent to ⅔ of a point of I.Q. per hour of process." Wow, *I.Q. per hour!* There's a bold new concept for the information age. And this from a man who muses, oddly, that "the increasingly widespread use of appetite suppressants in our society is a matter of some concern since those too may be costing us many of our geniuses." What? Geniuses are supposed to be pigs?

Sometimes we suspect it's too late for us to increase our IQPH. Our brains have already lost too much RAM, suffered too many fatal errors, been numbed by the moral equivalent of too many appetite suppressants. But that's okay. Too much intellectual curiosity can be lethal. Consider Pliny the Elder (A.D. 23–79), who became so engrossed in taking notes during an eruption of Mount Vesuvius that he failed to notice the poisonous gases that killed him. We learned that from *The Mensa Think-Smart Book.* See? We did learn something.

Seriously, though, here are about fifty ways to become an Einstein—or just look like one:

Albert Einstein

involving paved roadways, hydraulics, or optical fibers, so we found many of the puzzles too hard. We also hate being asked to think up ten uses for a penny nail, especially since we aren't sure what a penny nail is. But we were intrigued by the wonders of "bracketing," "randomizing," the "interdisciplinary analogue laboratory" and something called Synetics, which sounds like a food-additive company but which means "the joining together of different and apparently irrelevant elements." Hey, anything that involves irrelevance is okay by us!

Access: *The Art of Creative Thinking* by Gerard I. Nierenberg is published by Simon & Schuster/Fireside. Paper $7.95.

THE SIX THINKING HATS
•

There is a pear brandy, made in Switzerland, in which a whole pear is immersed in the bottle. How did the pear get in there? We hadn't the foggiest and really don't care to taste this peculiar beverage, which creativity coach Edward de Bono uses to illustrate the principle of "lateral thinking." Most people, he says, assume that the neck or bottom of the bottle was closed after the pear was put in there. Actually, the pear grew from a bud-bearing branch placed in the bottle. "Instead of moving straight ahead, you move sideways to find new approaches to problems," explains de Bono, a former Rhodes scholar who has given creativity lessons to IBM, Shell, Proctor & Gamble, General Dynamics, and other big companies. Lateral thinking assumes that any way of looking at a problem is only one of many possible ways. Which is where the six thinking hats come in. Fortunately, according to de Bono, you don't have to be smart to be a successful thinker. You just have to be able to put on the various thinking hats at will—red for emotional, intuitive thinking; white for objective, data-based thought; green for energetic, creative thinking, and so on.

Access: De Bono has written some thirty books about thinking strategies. The six-hats method is discussed in *Lateral Thinking* (Harper & Row; paper $8.95) as well as on an audiotape, *Super-Thinking* (available from Audio Renaissance Tapes, 9110 Sunset Boulevard, Suite 200, Los Angeles, CA 90069; $9.95). For a complete list of publications and products contact: International Center for Creative Thinking, 805 West Boston Post Rd., P.O. Box 774, Mamaroneck, NY 10543. (914) 698-8600.

GLUB, GLUB . . . $E = MC^2$
•

"Held-breath underwater swimming actually increases the amount of blood that makes it to your brain by expanding your carotid arteries," explains Win Wenger, president of the Institute of Visual Thinking in Gaithersburg, Maryland. "If you do it frequently over a period of several weeks, the resulting improvement can be quite remarkable."

Playing a lot of Marco Polo in the pool is only one of the I.Q.-boosting methods explored by Wenger, whose promotional literature rambles on about occipital lobes, "phase relationships," left-temporal consciousness, etc. He *seems* to be saying that you could be a genius were it not for an unfortunate time lag in information processing between different regions of your brain—a defect that can be remedied with Wenger's techniques. Einstein is said to have come up with his notions of relativity by daydreaming about traveling on a beam of light, and Wenger thinks you should be having these sorts of thoughts, too—and keeping a record of them. His "Post-Einsteinian technique," which involves talking into a tape recorder, was tested recently at Southwest State University in Minnesota (Hmmm. Why would a Minnesota college describe itself as "southwest"? Southwest of what— Manitoba? Well, maybe they *need* Wenger's course!) and reportedly raised students' I.Q.'s by as much as forty points. (The average gain was eight I.Q. points for ten hours of home practice, according to Wenger, and seventeen points for twenty hours.) You, too, can become smarter by practicing "visual thinking," "image streaming," "pole bridging," "journaling" and other methods, none of which are easy to understand through the fogbank of Wenger's prose. "The Socrates Effect," he notes, "can develop within virtually any human being any perception of understanding ever arrived at by any human being and do so with relative ease depending upon the formatting used to structure and focus the perception-describing process." Ah, now we know how the youth of Athens were corrupted!

Access: For information about Wenger's workshops, or to order any of his several books, contact: Institute of Visual Thinking, P.O. Box 332, Gaithersburg, MD 20877. (301) 948-1122.

CREATIVITY BLOCKED? WHO YA GONNA CALL?
•

Blockbusters, of course! "Conceptual blockbusting" is what engineer/creativity consultant James L. Adams does for a living, and since his book jacket says he's chairman of the august- but rather shadowy-sounding "Values, Technology, Science, and Society department at Stanford University" (is that a CIA front, a right-wing think tank, or a Mickey Mouse triple major?), he probably knows what he's talking about. In his book you learn to recognize the various types of blocks—perceptual, emotional, intellectual, cultural, etc.—that keep you from having eureka experiences. Then you're guided through a smorgasbord of valuable "blockbusting" methods. You build mental images. You ask stupid, childlike questions—"What's beyond the farthest star?"—of experts in various fields, a tactic guaranteed to make you popular among the astrophysicists and arbitrageurs you bother with your dumb questions. You make a list of things that bug you and try to figure out solutions. A list compiled by Stanford students included plastic flowers, stamps that don't stick, miniature poodles, prize shows on TV, dirty aquariums, and cloudy ice cubes. Our list included telephone recordings with music and coy messages, tear-at-the-dotted-line return envelopes that are *always* smaller than the remittance statement, and creativity books that make you think up twenty-five uses for bricks. (How about just leaving them in the wall, where they're supposed to be?) We couldn't find any solutions to our "bugs," but one of *your* ideas just might turn into a zillion-dollar invention—say, an ice-tray declouder?

Access: *Conceptual Blockbusting: A Guide to Better Ideas* by James L. Adams is published by Addison-Wesley Publishing Company, Inc. Paper $9.95.

WE ARE HERE TO PUMP YOU UP!
•

Tom Wujek, author of *Pumping Ions,* seems to think the brain is a deltoid muscle and that doing a lot of painful (or just very tedious) mental workouts will make it work better. Here's a guy who apparently spends his leisure time counting up to 100 by two, and down again, then up by three, four, and nine; translating words like "abracadabra" into numerical equivalents; reciting letter series forward and backward; making up limericks; repeating tongue twisters; etc. If that's not enough to make you the world's most scintillating date, Wujek thinks you should also learn to concentrate on the motion of your watch's second hand while simultaneously reciting "Mary Had a Little Lamb" and running through a number series. If you have any time left over, you will, of course, be visiting art galleries, reading books on archeology and numismatics, folding a square piece of paper to form the creases of a hexagram, and meditating on questions like, "What if we lived to be six hundred years old?" and "What is it like to be a cigarette?" No doubt you'd be much smarter if you followed this program, but you'd probably have to quit your job to make time for it.

Access: *Pumping Ions* by Tom Wujek is published by Doubleday. Paper $8.95.

INFORMATION, PLEASE!

FEAR OF MICROFILMING
•

To be really smart, you should be well informed, of course. Although we're supposed to be journalists, we have to admit to a visceral fear of the microfilm room. Our palms sweat a little in the card-catalogue room, if you want to know the truth. We've never read the *Congressional Record.* We like to get most of our information from hearsay, pushy P.R. flacks, badly printed religious tracts, and the magazines we happen to find lying around in our dentist's waiting room. But if we *did* do serious research, we'd reach for *Knowing Where to Look: The Ultimate Guide to Research* by Lois Horowitz. This admirable volume covers *everything:* where to get photos, how to fact check a quote by Adlai Stevenson, how to look up something about a 1928 phonograph in *Standard & Poor's,* how to find an address anywhere in the world, how to use a videotex system, how to find a missing person, how to find quaint, outdated geographical facts in a Victorian encyclopedia, how to pry information out of sly employees at a U.S. Embassy, and much more.

Access: *Knowing Where to Look* by Lois Horowitz is published by Writer's Digest Books, F & W Publications, Inc., 1507 Dana Ave., Cincinnati, OH 45207. Paper $15.95.

HOW DO YOU FIND OUT ABOUT ANYTHING?
•

Before we read Alden Todd's *Finding Facts Fast: How to Find Out What You Want and Need to Know,* it seemed that librarians were always sneering at us. Not only did we not have the answers, we couldn't even ask the right questions. ("Um, could I look at that big brownish book over there?" and "Is it okay if I underline?" are *not* the correct questions to ask in a library.) A slimmer, less detailed, and therefore less intimidating research guide than *Knowing Where to Look* (above), *Finding Facts Fast* nonetheless introduces the information pilgrim to all the basic research tools, such as *The Encyclopedia of Associations* (one of our all-time favorite books; that's how we discovered there's an Institute for Encyclopedia of Human Ideas on Ultimate Reality and Meaning in Toronto and a Center for Short-Lived Phenomena in Cambridge, Massachusetts), *The New York Times Index,* the *United States Government Organizational Manual,* not to mention various directories of directories and even directories of directories of directories. At the very least, you'll be able to make small talk with librarians.

Access: *Finding Facts Fast* by Alden Todd is published by Ten Speed Press, P.O. Box 7123, Berkeley, CA 94707. Paper $5.95.

NO MORE INFORMATION, PLEASE!

•

On the other hand, maybe you're getting *too much* information. Maybe you suffer from that trendy new nineties disease *Information Anxiety,* which is also the title of a book by Richard Saul Wurman. A publisher of guidebooks, Wurman has picked up the habit of color-coding sites of interest and tossing multicolored marginalia into any white space. He admits up front, "This book has been heavily annotated with marginalia, made up of anecdotes, quotes, and references to other publications . . . ," and suggests, helpfully, "*Information Anxiety* doesn't have to be read sequentially. You can open to any chapter and read forward or backward." How nonlinear. We did as he suggested, and experienced a strange postmodern vertigo as the 1988 Pacific Bell phone directory's community access map of San Francisco became lodged in our brain cells next to a diagram of a skyscraper, some observations on Hopi verbs, and a mini-interview with Ed Schlossberg (Mr. Caroline Kennedy), which didn't definitively answer the question, "But what exactly does he do?" any more than scanning this book answered the question, "What is it *about?*" But that's not the point. There's a lot of fun stuff here, like a copy of a woman's hilarious résumé vérité. "I was in charge of cranking out filler to keep the pictures [in a magazine] from bumping into each other. . . ." And: "After three years of highly praised work for the Health Agency, I still had no idea just what this federally funded agency was supposed to do."

Access: *Information Anxiety* by Richard Saul Wurman is published by Doubleday. Hardcover $19.95.

MAPS OF MY MIND

U h oh. You have to write a speech. Better start with an outline. Okay: "A." Or should it be "I"? Well, anyway. "The Importance of Zip Codes in the Direct-Mail Market." No, make that, "Our Zip Codes, Ourselves." By the time you hit "IIA," your outline is a morass of cross-outs and you're eating Milky Ways in front of "All My Children." Because, you see, that's *not* the way to do it.

A more natural way to organize information, according to its proponents, is mind mapping. The brainchild of Tony Buzan, a British brain expert (well, that's how he's described; we don't know if he's actually dissected a brain or anything) and Michael J. Gelb, the director of the High Performance Learning Center in Washington, D.C., mind mapping proceeds from the notion that the mind does not work in a linear, straightforward fashion. It works in images, in strings of associations, in tangents, loops, and strange juxtapositions. Hence, mind mapping looks like something doodled on a binder by a bored, lovesick teenager during morning assembly. (For an example, see "How to Mind Map," page 55.)

Gelb, who has taught mind mapping to such corporate clients as IBM and DuPont, claims that, almost unnoticed, mind mapping activates your entire brain—including the 90 percent or so (Aaarrggh! There's that figure again!) that most of us neglect. It is designed to integrate the right brain's creativity with the left brain's sense of order and attention to detail. "It's a thinking skill, not just a clever gimmick," he asserts. While Gelb markets mind mapping primarily as a speech-writing tool, it can also be used for general brainstorming, free association, or self-analysis. "Because mind mapping taps into deep areas of your mind and allows free association, it operates somewhat like psychotherapy," notes aficionado Joyce Wycoff of San Diego. "It provides us with a tool for listening to ourselves." If you want to eavesdrop on your own subconscious monologue, Wycoff suggests starting your mind map with any of the following words: "family," "letting go," "success," "mother," "father," or "fear." Allow two minutes for mind mapping and four to five minutes for composing a short paragraph derived from it.

THE MIND

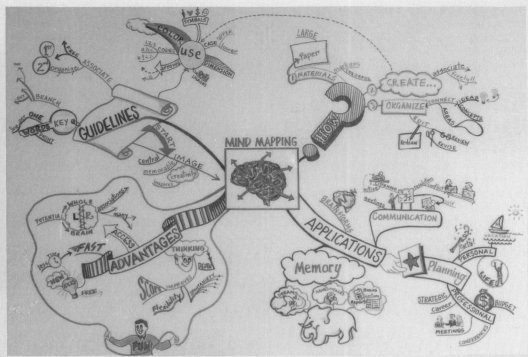

By Michael Gelb and Nancy Margulies

MIND MAPPING is a simple, practical tool that can help you:
- Think faster and more creatively
- Get more work done in less time
- Improve your memory
- Plan projects, prepare presentations, run meetings and solve problems with ease

"MIND MAPPING IS TO THE INFORMATION AND SPACE AGES AS WAS OUTLINING WAS TO THE INDUSTRIAL AND MEDIEVAL AGES." --TONY BUZAN

Above is an example of a mind map, starting with the phrase *mind mapping*.

HOW TO MIND MAP

1. Get a large sheet of white paper and several pens of different colors.

2. In the center of the paper, draw a small picture of your subject. The picture may be either abstract or representational. (For example, if the topic of your speech or research paper is housing, draw a simple house.) This will jump-start your right hemisphere.

3. To generate ideas about your topic, start writing key words on spokes radiating out from the central image.

4. Print key words; they'll be easier to remember.

5. Write one single word (*not* phrases) at a time on the lines and keep the lines connected to your picture.

6. Free-associate rapidly. No word is too ridiculous or irrelevant to write down. Keep the process flowing. Cover the page as quickly as you can and start another page as necessary.

7. Use pictures and colors in your mind map whenever possible.

8. If you get stuck, choose any key word you've already used and print your first association to it.

9. After a while, you will have run out of words and your map will be formed. It will probably look like a web of words and lines. Use colors, symbols, and pictures to highlight important words and ideas.

10. Often the network of words naturally organizes itself into categories. Look for words that appear several times in your mind map. They may suggest major themes. Connect related themes with more lines, arrows, and colors.

11. Return to your map and remove any parts that seem extraneous. Pare your map down to just the ideas you need, then put them in sequence, imposing an order on your thoughts. Recopy the map if necessary.

Access: The following books explain the technique of mind mapping. *Use Both Sides of Your Brain* by Tony Buzan (E.P. Dutton; paper $7.95) discusses in detail the neuropsychological theory (left brain/right brain, etc.) behind the technique. *Present Yourself!* by Michael J. Gelb (Jalmar Press; $18.95) is oriented to speech writing. *Mindmapping: A New Way to Use Your Brain* by Joyce Wycoff (Berkley Publishing Group, due to be published in spring 1991) is a grass-roots manual covering many everyday applications.

Gelb also sells a $5 "Mind Map" that answers common questions about mind mapping and demonstrates how to do it. In addition, he teaches a weekend mind-mapping course several times a year in Boston and Washington, D.C. (The course costs about $350, so you might want to persuade your employer to send you.) Contact Gelb at: High Performance Learning Center, 4613 Davenport St., NW, Washington, DC 20016. Phone: (202) 537-0775.

I'M LEARNING AS FAST AS I CAN

SUPERLEARNING, BULGARIAN-STYLE
●

The granddaddy of accelerated learning techniques is Suggestopedia, created by Georgi Lozanov, a Bulgarian psychotherapist who also dabbled in parapsychology and Raja Yoga. (They're always up to something behind the Iron Curtain, or what used to be the Iron Curtain. First it was Russian psychics performing scary feats of psychokinesis, now it's Bulgarian schoolchildren memorizing millions of French verbs in secret—perhaps mobilizing for an infiltration of the world's croissant factories!) The basic premise is that you can speed up learning tenfold—perhaps even a hundredfold—by relaxing and getting rid of all your tension and anxiety. (Fortunately for us, Lozanov doesn't seem to know much about the right hemisphere or we'd be hearing about that, too.) Suggestopedia is supposed to use the power of suggestion to counteract the negative, limiting suggestions to which you've already been subjected. A typical Suggestopedia class begins with a few minutes of relaxation exercises. You might do some breathing exercises, some affirmations ("I am supremely calm"; "Learning and remembering are easy for me") and some calming visualizations (walk along the beach, feeling the warm sand under your feet, etc.) Usually, the teacher will recite material rhythmically to music, which is supposed to help you remember ten times more than you would under traditional learning conditions.

Access: The Lozanov Learning Institute gives workshops and seminars in Suggestopedia and sells learning tapes, relaxation tapes, and books about accelerated learning. A brochure listing workshop schedules, books, and tapes is available from the Lozanov Learning Institute, 8719 Colesville Rd., Suite 300, Silver Spring, MD 20910. Phone: (202) 882-4000.

NO MORE SLOW LEARNERS
●

An easy way to learn about the potpourri of accelerated learning techniques—from the perspective of a couple of gushing fans—is to read *Superlearning* by Sheila Ostrander and Lynne Schroeder, the same awestruck pair who brought us *Psychic Discoveries Behind the Iron Curtain.* Half the book is devoted to Suggestopedia, but other systems are discussed as well. A few exercises are included to give you a taste of the techniques.

If you want to delve deeper into this subject, the Society for Accelerated Learning and Teaching (SALT) in Ames, Iowa, is a source of teacher training programs, research reports, and other resources.

Access: *Superlearning* by Sheila Ostrander and Lynn Schroeder is published by Dell Publishing Company. Paper $4.95.

The Society for Accelerated Learning and Teaching (SALT) can be reached at: P.O. Box 1215, Welch Station, Ames, IA 50010.

YOU ARE FEELING VERY CALM. . . . SOON YOU WILL BE LEAVING BULGARIA
•

An offshoot of Suggestopedia, OptimaLearning "optimizes the whole personality through learning," according to its creator, Ivan Barzakov. Barzakov was a Lozanov teacher in Bulgaria until 1977, when he defected to the West by swimming seven miles from Yugoslavia to Italy. A year later, he was in California operating his own speed-learning center, the Barzak Educational Institute. ("Barzak" is Bulgarian for "accelerated" or "rapid.") The program deviates from Lozanov's by adding what Barzakov calls the "dance of energy," which isn't really a dance but a theory and technique designed to stimulate all the parts of the brain (including the deeper emotional levels) and counteract boredom. We couldn't figure out exactly what they do in OptimaLearning, but it sounds pretty wholistic and a lot of Californians swear by it.

Access: Besides teaching self-instruction in Optima-Learning, the institute works with companies to develop corporate training programs. It also has a line of language learning tapes for children and special classical-music tapes for memory, concentration, creativity, and writing. For information contact the Barzak Educational Institute, 88 Belvedere St., Suite D, San Rafael, CA 94901. Phone: (415) 459-4474.

A MILLION BULGARIANS CAN'T BE WRONG (CAN THEY?)
•

In accelerated-learning circles they often mention the group of Suggestopedia-trained Bulgarians who were able to learn a thousand French vocabulary words in a single day. (*Mon dieu! Qui sont ces bulgares feroces qui parlent si vite?*) So why doesn't everybody run out and sign up? Because, according to a report by the National Research Council, these extravagant claims don't hold up under scientific scrutiny. The report, commissioned by the U.S. Army and published in 1988, doesn't totally dismiss accelerated learning techniques (it *does* dismiss parapsychology) but it points out that most of the claims are based on either anecdotal evidence or studies done by the technique's promoters. A few

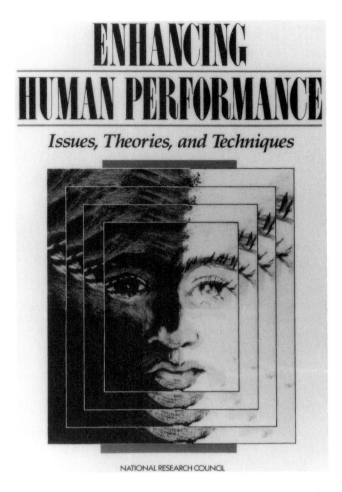

ENHANCING HUMAN PERFORMANCE
Issues, Theories, and Techniques

NATIONAL RESEARCH COUNCIL

independent investigators cited in the report found that accelerated learning techniques were less effective than traditional ones. (On the other hand, are the U.S. Army's views on "enhanced human performance" the same as yours or mine?)

Access: *Enhancing Human Performance: Issues, Theories, and Techniques,* edited by Daniel Druckman and John A. Swets, is published by National Academy Press. For information about ordering call (202) 334-2665; after 5 p.m. you'll get a garbled recording.

EXCUSE ME, THAT'S JUST MY RIGHT BRAIN TALKING

STILL DRAWING ON THE RIGHT BRAIN
•

Some years ago I (J.H.) fell under the spell of Betty Edwards's classic *Drawing on the Right Side of the Brain* and drew pictures upside down for days. Hours were compressed into minutes, days passed without my leaving the apartment, calendar pages seemed to shuffle rapidly, as in 1940s movies when someone leaves for the front and returns four years later. I was obsessed. I drew pictures that, compared with my previous oeuvre, were nothing short of miraculous. Eventually I had to leave the apartment and go to work, so I quit drawing and never did finish the course. But I still recall the altered state. For a week or so, everything I saw—displays of votive candles and bright green plantains in a Spanish grocery store display window, faces on the subway, a pile of snow-covered trash—seemed peculiarly vivid, as though the visual system in my brain had been switched on.

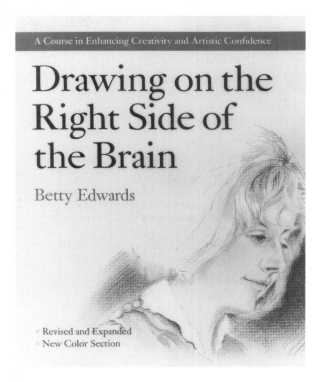

An art teacher, Edwards was the first layperson to perceive the paraneurological implications of Roger Sperry's split-brain research. Naturally, this launched a major trend that resulted in cab drivers lecturing you about hemispheric differences a decade later, but that isn't really Edwards's fault. Her method of teaching people to draw by short-circuiting "L-mode" (left hemisphere–type) thinking and tuning into the visual, imagistic "R-mode" is a highly effective tool, whether or not it actually has anything to do with the right hemisphere. To celebrate the book's tenth anniversary, Edwards has written a revised and updated *Drawing,* with a new section on color, new sample drawings and instructions, and a section on handwriting and its relationship to drawing. She continues to direct the Center for Educational Applications of Brain Hemisphere Research in Long Beach, California, which conducts workshops and seminars around the country to help people in other fields develop R-mode strategies.

Access: *Drawing on the Right Side of the Brain* by Betty Edwards is published by Jeremy P. Tarcher, Inc. Hardcover $22.95; paper $12.95. A second book, *Drawing on the Artist Within,* is published by Simon & Schuster/Fireside; paper $10.95. Edwards can be contacted through: The Center for Educational Applications of Brain Hemisphere Research, California State University, Long Beach, CA 90840. Phone: (213) 985-7906.

CLUSTERING
•

Remember mind mapping? Gabrielle Lusser Rico, a creative-writing teacher at San Jose State University in California, has developed a similar system called clustering that is designed to "release your inner writer." (Predictably, releasing your inner writer involves activating your right brain.) Clustering is less structured than mind mapping and uses circles in lieu of lines.

Start with a key idea, or "nucleus word," in the center of a sheet of paper. Circle it. Then go with the flow and write down all your associations, each with its own circle, radiating out from the center. Draw a line from each new word or phrase (yes, phrases are allowed) to the preceding circle. When something new comes to mind, begin again at the central nucleus and radiate outward. What you end up with looks like a balloon seller's bundle gone wild. "As you spill out seemingly random words and phrases around a center," Rico explains, "you will be surprised to see patterns forming until a moment comes—characterized by an 'aha!' feeling—

when you suddenly sense a focus for writing." (We had an "aha" feeling a few weeks ago, when we discovered that our keyboard offered two different types of brackets, { and [, in addition to the standard parenthesis symbol, but we've always been a cheap aha.) After you've clustered, you write a vignette, "a complete thought or statement on a subject, a fully expressed idea, even a very short story with a fully developed plot."

Rico also introduces you to such special exercises as using clusters of "m" words to recover "your childhood self" and "modeling" cadences after such masters as Hemingway, Gertrude Stein, and Guillaume Apollinaire. You'll also learn how to use dreams and art as sources of imagery. One student's rumination on "American Gothic" reads in part: "As sad as they look, they don't cry. Both figures stand side by side, one thinking of whatever has happened, and the other of who did it."

Access: For information on clustering and writing intensive workshops contact: Gabrielle Lusser Rico, 22620 San Juan Rd., Cupertino, CA 95014. Phone: (408) 253-3758. Her book *Writing the Natural Way: Using Right-Brain Techniques to Release Your Expressive Power* is published by Jeremy P. Tarcher. Paper $10.95.

I, K., BELIEVE IN THE VALUE OF MY CREATIVITY
●

Marilee Zdenek, president of Right Brain Resources, Inc., is a right-hemisphere true believer. Her creativity course, *The Right-Brain Experience,* requires you to spend two hours a day for six days being more creative, not including the time it takes to read the reminiscences of various creative celebs. In that time, you'll learn more than you want to know about the corpus callosum and you'll do a fair amount of staring at mandalas, consulting your Awareness Chart, imagining calm voices counting backwards, taking deep breaths, feeling the tension leave your shoulder muscles, and writing affirmations like, "I, _____, believe in the value of my creativity."

If only Virginia Woolf had lifted the tension from her shoulder muscles and believed in the value of her creativity, Mrs. Dalloway's party wouldn't have been such a drag. If you suffer from anxious, intrusive thoughts, as no doubt Woolf, van Gogh, Kafka, and Dostoevsky did, Zdenek suggests that you visualize these thoughts as birds (crows or bluejays perhaps?) and banish them from their cage (your mind). Then use your nondominant hand—that's your left if you're right-handed—to write about other troublesome "birds." But better not do this if you're a suicide-prone poet or a mad, obsessed artist. A warning on the copyright page says that the "exercises in this book should not be performed by anyone whom a physician has diagnosed as emotionally disturbed," which should effectively eliminate many creative people.

Access: For information about Zdenek's tapes, seminars, and other "right-brain materials" contact: Right Brain Resources, Inc., Reseda Medical Building, 7012 Reseda Boulevard, Suite SW 101, Reseda, CA 91335. Phone: (818) 883-1232. *The Right-Brain Experience* is published by McGraw-Hill. Paper $6.95. A sequel, *Inventing the Future: Advances in Imagery That Can Change Your Life,* is also published by McGraw-Hill. Paper $7.95.

A STRANGE COLLECTION OF WRITING IMPLEMENTS
●

Henriette Anne Klauser, creator of Writing Resource Workshops, is the sort of person who keeps a strange collection of pens to capture every stray thought: a pen that peels out paper from its cap, a pen that lights up in the dark, and a NASA-designed pen that can immortalize original insights in extremes of temperature, under water, or at zero G. Although we very much dislike writing in extremes of temperature or underwater, we found much to like in her book *Writing on Both Sides of the Brain.* For one thing, Klauser never once urged us to relax our shoulder muscles,

A RIGHT-BRAIN TALK WITH BETTY EDWARDS

Betty Edwards

Q: How did you come to connect split-brain research with learning to draw?

Edwards: I think that in order to do art, one must be able to make a shift to the visual, perceptual mode. That's where you've got to be to get the work done. Artists are very much aware of the need to make this shift; they will tell you they've devised ways to do it. They work alone, for example, so no one's talking to them. When I started to teach art I knew I had to teach students how to do *that,* whatever *that* was.

Then Sperry's work was published in 'sixty-nine or 'seventy in the popular press, and that clarified exactly what the shift was: It was from a verbal to a nonverbal mode of thinking. I was already in an M.A. program at UCLA and puzzled by the problems people had in learning to draw. I have to add that from the time I was maybe eighteen or nineteen I'd had a layperson's interest in the brain and had been reading books on the subject, so Sperry's research caught my eye. My first reading of that research was a tremendous "Aha," the feeling that here was the key that unlocked all the puzzles I'd been thinking about.

Q: Did you ever meet with Sperry?

Edwards: Yes. When I finished my doctorate I tried to work out the scientific portion of the book on my own. The manuscript was nearly finished and I was having panic bouts. Not that it mattered to anyone else, but it mattered to me that I had interpreted the research correctly and found a true application. So I mailed it to Sperry and asked him to give it a glance. He did, and wrote me that it was a "splendid and true application," as he put it, but that there were certain scientific points that needed clarifying and he would be willing to do that. So I met with Sperry for weeks at Caltech. This was terribly generous of him, to deal with a person completely out of his field. But he has an interest in art. He paints himself, and he's quite good, actually.

Q: Why are *non*artists reading your book, and what can they gain from it?

Edwards: I'm always asking myself that question. The most bizarre people read this book—hairdressers, private detectives, acting students. I think people sense that training the visual system through drawing will help them in widespread ways. I believe that in schools we should be training this dual system: reading, writing, and arithmetic for the left [hemisphere]; drawing, dance, music, and movement for the right. We should deliberately train those faculties and not just for specific careers. After all, we don't teach reading just to produce poets but for general thinking and problem solving.

Q: Yet when public schools have funding cuts, the arts are the first to go.

Edwards: You have to remember that public schools are run by people who have been selected by their emphasis on what I call the L-mode. They love the L-mode. They cherish it. And they feel quite threatened by what seems to be a very out-of-control system.

Q: What about talent? How does that come into the picture?

Edwards: Talent for drawing is no more required than talent for reading. As teachers, we routinely assume that a person is going to learn to read, that a person of sound mind has that capability, given proper instruction. We don't say the person has to have a God-given gift. What I'm promoting is the idea that drawing, this major skill of the right hemi-

sphere, is in the brain, and our problem is to find ways to gain access to it. The main strategy for doing that is to trick the verbal system to stay out of the job. All the techniques we use are tricks—tricks of looking at negative space, tricks of turning the image upside down, tricks of making things too slow, too fast, or too complicated. Whatever the left hemisphere will not deal with, that's what we use. This faculty of learning to see what's out there—what's *really* there, rather than what is seen through a symbolic system—is not dependent on anything more than a normal brain. We need to train this powerful way of perceiving as strenuously as we train the verbal system. In fact, as I have been saying recently, I do believe the visual system is the more powerful system—which does not come as good news to educators.

Q: What is The Center for Educational Applications of Brain Hemisphere Research all about?

Edwards: Its main purpose is to help teachers in other fields find true applications of Sperry's split-brain research. We say, "We teach people to make a cognitive shift into R-mode in order to draw. Now, what is the strategy in mathematics? What is the strategy in reading comprehension, in dental training, and so on?" And we say up front, "We don't know what these strategies are yet because we're not in your field." These strategies are really hard to find. I myself, after being in this for almost thirty years, have come up with maybe four or five or six that really work.

Q: Do you believe that drawing literally taps into the right hemisphere of the brain, or is that a metaphor?

Edwards: It is a metaphor. I've used the terms "L-mode" and "R-mode" consistently since 1979 to avoid what's called the location controversy in neuroscience. Talking about where specific functions are located in the brain is a tedious argument. Some people seize on an applciation like mine and say, "No, no, no! The brain works as a whole constantly. We don't know where these things are located." And I have said—with, I must say, increasing impatience over the years—"No, I'm not saying it's all located in the right hemisphere of every person who learns to draw. But it forms a useful metaphor so you can talk to people." What is *not* controversial, since Sperry's work, is that the human brain is specialized for two major modes of processing.

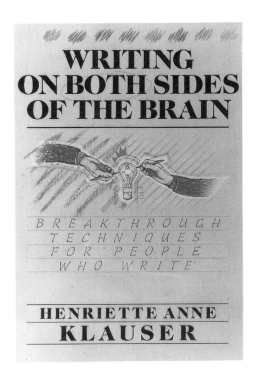

We can forgive this book its obligatory split-brain chapter, which plunges the reader once more into the woes of those unfortunate split-brain-surgery patients of Sperry's. Otherwise, it's a mother lode of original techniques for educating the neglected portion of our brain—okay, *call* it the right hemisphere. We meet teachers who turn French class into a simulated French cafe, who get chemistry students to act out the roles of hydrogen and carbon molecules, who inspire civics students to plan a "capitalist," "socialist," "communist," or "anarchist" lunch. (We hope the anarchists didn't blow up the cafeteria.) It's written for teachers, but parents can learn a few tricks, too.

Access: *Teaching for the Two-Sided Mind* by Linda Verlee Williams is published by Simon & Schuster. Paper $8.95.

breathe deeply, or visualize ourselves walking along a deserted beach. (She did say to set our alarm clock an hour early, "rapidwrite" before our first cup of coffee, and keep a Progress Log, and one of these days maybe we just will.)

Writing on Both Sides of the Brain contains an assortment of good techniques such as "branching" (similar to mind mapping), "rapidwriting," interviewing your Inner Critic, and hoarding a zany collection of writing implements. There are even methods for dealing with such vital parts of the writing process as procrastination, rumination, and cleaning the bathroom. Klauser advises setting aside a Rumination Chair and making lists of ways to avoid writing.

Access: *Writing on Both Sides of the Brain: Breakthrough Techniques for People Who Write* by Henriette Anne Klauser is published by Harper & Row. Paper $10.95.

NOW IT'S OKAY TO DAYDREAM DURING MATH CLASS
•

A high school science teacher needs to teach his class to dissect clams. "Yeccch!" you think, and so would most teenagers faced with this gory and apparently meaningless educational ritual. So the teacher starts by discussing fear—"no mention of clams, just an exploration of situations in which students had experienced fear and how their bodies had reacted to it: curling up, protecting the face, and so on." Then the teacher asks, "What animals are shaped by fear?" and so on, all leading up to the actual confrontation with clams. This is a teacher who addresses both sides of the brain, according to Linda Verlee Williams, author of *Teaching for the Two-Sided Mind*.

GAMES · GENIUSES · PLAY

101 THINGS TO DO WITH A BAD-COMPLEXIONED GUY FROM CALTECH
●

He comes over to you, polyester pockets bulging with perforated computer printouts, and leers, "Hey, wanna see my palindrome?" What do you say? (1) "Are you the new lifeguard here?"; or (2) "Get your plastic pencil case out of the Jacuzzi, you oxymoron!"; or (3) "Able was I ere I saw Elba."

The correct answer is number 3—*if* you want further intercourse with a Mensan. (If you don't, we don't know what you should say. Some Mensans can be very persistent.) Of course, if you'd read the *Mensa Think-Smart Book* you'd know that, "In their spare time, Mensans love nothing better than to play with anagrams and palindromes, clerihews, oxymorons, and univocalics. Most know the difference between entropy and lacunae, between a funambulist and an enchiridion." We were all too familiar with lacunae—we break out in them whenever we have a deadline—but we weren't sure we wanted to bump into a funambulist, especially one with an enchiridion. So we turned to the *Mensa Think-Smart Book* for guidance. This slim manual, written by Mensans for people who want to think like Mensans, can teach you

to sling words like "prognathous" and "farrago," play with magic squares and other math puzzles, recognize invalid syllogisms, solve codes, ciphers, and cryptograms, and learn some "high-I.Q. trivia," all of which Mensans evidently prefer to wet T-shirt contests.

Access: *The Mensa Think-Smart Book* by Dr. Abbie F. Salny and Lewis Burke Frumkes is published by Harper & Row. Paper $6.95. To find out more about Mensa, contact: Dept SA, American Mensa Ltd., 2626 East 14th St., Brooklyn, NY 11235. Phone: (718) 934-3700. If you'd like to test your smarts on a standard I.Q. test, send $9.00 to Mensa for a take-at-home test. If you've already scored in the 98th percentile on a standard supervised I.Q. test, you can probably be a Mensan right now. Qualifying scores on the SAT aptitude test, LSAT, GRE, Miller Analogies Test, and many other standardized tests will get you in, too.

THE COCKTAIL-PARTY EFFECT
●

So you're standing there clutching a glass of white wine and chatting with someone about adjustable mortgages, when your friend way at the other end of the noisy room quietly says your name. Instantly, your conversation comes to a standstill. "Your name, being very important to you, immediately attracts your conscious attention," explains Richard B. Fisher, author of *Brain Games: 134 Original Scientific Games That Reveal How Your Mind Works.* "Much of the chatter at the party was irrelevant as far as you were concerned. You heard it, but because you paid no attention to it it slipped quietly out of memory. In fact, it may never have reached memory at all." You've just experienced the "cocktail-party effect." Now, if Mr. Adjustable Mortgage hasn't wandered off toward the punch bowl in disgust, it's time to try another Brain Game. Spin around in a circle, keeping your eyes wide open, then turn back to face him. He'll probably notice that your pupils "will drift back in the direction opposite the direction of the spin and then snap back again into the middle." Neat, huh? The reason for this strange behavior is nystagmus, a reflex action of your eyeballs.

By now, dozens of partygoers will be crowding around you, eager to take part in fun with saccades (eyeball jumps), the primacy-recency effect of memory, and Ohm's acoustical laws (ask your hostess for two wineglasses and two spoons). Back at home, if you want to explore the relationship between your brain and consciousness a bit more, follow Fisher's directions for experimenting with hypnagogic states, your biological clock, the "ambiguous mother-in-law" illusion, operant conditioning, grammatical "deep structures," Piaget's developmental theories, and even your pain threshold. You may not want to know *quite* as much about the resting membrane potential of your neurons as this book tells you, but if you're interested in what's between your ears, *Brain Games* is a delightful, well-researched owner's manual.

Access: *Brain Games: 134 Original Scientific Games That Reveal How Your Mind Works* by Richard B. Fisher is published by Schocken Books, 200 Madison Ave., New York, NY 10016. Paper $7.95.

WHAT WOULD HAPPEN IF YOU COULD MARRY AS MANY PEOPLE AS YOU WANTED TO?
●

That's the type of question that Eugene Raudsepp, president of Princeton Creative Research, Inc., thinks you should ponder if you want to be more creative. (The answer, we

think, is that there'd be an epidemic of self-help books about the ten-paycheck marriage, and some weddings would have an excess of bridesmaids.) *Creative Growth Games,* written by Raudsepp with George P. Hough, Jr., offers seventy-five such brainteasers, ranging from a do-it-yourself Rorschach test (Fold a piece of paper in half. Drop some ink in the crease. Press the folded paper flat. Then free-associate!) to the classic puzzle about a midget in the elevator (whoops, we just gave away the punchline). In another game, "Objection Overruled," you're encouraged to prepare counter-arguments to any possible objections that might be raised when you try to: (1) persuade your spouse that you should take separate vacations this year; or (2) convince your boss that you should be permitted—indeed, encouraged—to spend two days a week working at home. We tried this and managed to persuade our boss to take a separate vacation this year.

Access: *Creative Growth Games* by Eugene Raudsepp with George P. Hough, Jr. (Perigee Books; paper $7.95) is available from Princeton Creative Research, Inc., P.O. Box 122, Princeton, NJ 08542. Phone: (609) 924-3215. Raudsepp also teaches creativity workshops, most of which are in-house workshops for businesses.

ZEN • BUSINESS

WHOLISTIC M.B.A.'S
●

They read tarot cards, draw mandalas, and talk to their mirror images. They wrap themselves up in sleeping bags and listen to high-frequency sounds beyond the human hearing range. They throw the *I Ching*. They spontaneously "translate" Egyptian hieroglyphics (or, really, free-associate with them as if they were Rorschach blots). They incubate lucid dreams.

No, they're not devotees at an ashram; they're students at the Stanford University Graduate School of Business who are taking an unorthodox course called Creativity in Business, taught by psychologist Michael Ray and Rochelle Myers, an artist and musician. Why are these M.B.A.'s-in-training throwing the *I Ching* when they *could* be working on marketing plans? "Stanford is the hardest business school in the country to get into," says Ray. "These people are very successful at using the left side of the brain, but we want to leverage that ability so that they use their whole minds." The exercises are all designed to suppress the hypercritical "Voice of Judgment" (VOJ) in each student's head and let ideas and images flow. To that end, students are assigned weekly "heuristics," or "live-withs," Zen-like instructions to behave in strange ways. "Do only what is easy and enjoyable." "Make decisions by asking simply, 'Is it a yes or is it a no?'" "Destroy judgment." (When your bank loan officer mutters, "Hmm, this mortgage. . . Is it a yes or is it a no?" you can surmise he's been to Stanford.)

This is the best of the Zen business genre, in our opinion. Ray and Myers have scoured the human-potential landscape from Senoi dream control to yoga *dharanas* (concentration practices) for interesting, turn-your-mind-upside-down exercises that are good for your head whether or not you've ever looked at a profit-sharing plan. The good news is that you don't have to apply to business school to do them; just pick up Ray and Myer's book, *Creativity in Business*.

Access: *Creativity in Business* by Michael L. Ray and Rochelle Myers is published by Doubleday & Co. Paper $9.95.

YOUR RÉSUMÉ AND THE COSMIC EGG
●

Career counselor Hilda Lee Dail is lot more, well, cosmic than your average personnel type. "In my work . . . ," she writes in *The Lotus and the Pool*, "I focus the center of my being on the central core of the person sitting in front of me. Together we face the fear, chaos, inertia, conflict, confusion—whatever the state is. We embrace it, plunge into it." When we were young job aspirants photocopying our résumés, nobody was interested in our central cores; they just wanted to know about all those embarrassing holes in our résumés.

Dail reminds us that Brahma, the creator god, was born from the cosmic egg and created the mind and then the ego—thus allowing us to have careers. Prometheus, who started civilization by stealing fire from the gods, "developed in consciousness" by being tied to a mountain and eaten by vultures. But did anyone ever ask Brahma, "Can you type?" Did Prometheus have to pore over a hundred want ads appealing to "go-getters" and "self-starters"? No! (Of course, these guys *were* the ultimate self-starters.) If you want to see your employment history in a mythic perspective, Hilda Lee Dail and Associates is obviously the place to go. And Dail's book offers much transpersonal wisdom, together with case studies, exercises, and an ambitious ten-step program for creating your own career. If you can create your own reality, creating a career should be no big deal, but be prepared to answer a lot of questionnaires, make a million lists, have five-year goals and ultimate goals, be familiar with *Moody's Industrial Manual,* and rank your success factors on a "prioritizing grid."

Access: You can arrange for an individual appointment in person, by mail, or by phone from: Hilda Lee Dail and Associates, International, 1807 Legion St., Myrtle Beach, South Carolina 29577. Phone: (803) 448-3270. *The Lotus and the Pool* by Hilda Lee Dail is published by Shambhala Publications. Paper $12.95.

MOVE THROUGH TIME AND SPACE

A necessary precondition for creativity, according to Michael Ray, is to recognize the power of your own thoughts. "In our minds," he points out, "we can move through time and space, and we can exercise our senses, faculties, emotions, and imaginations far more freely than in the outer world." Following is an exercise designed to "explore the inner terrain." Stay with each experience until you feel that you've finished with it.

Move through time. Think back to approximately a year ago today. What were you thinking? What were you doing? How did you feel about your life? Bring back some of the details: the people, your routine, your clothes, your mood.

Move through space. Mentally go to your grandmother's house. Then go to the place in the U.S. you like best. Move on to your favorite European city, whether you've been there or not. While your suitcase is packed, go to the planet of your choice, or to some star or other solar system. Revel in the details of each stopover. What do you wish you'd brought with you?

Experience colors. See red, then yellow, blue, green, orange, purple. Put them together in combinations, or move them around in swirls. What does each color say? How does each make you feel?

SAMURAI IN THREE-PIECE SUITS

•

In old Japan a *ronin* was a samurai without a lord, a free-lancer who had to make his own way in a topsy-turvy postfeudal world. Imagine a knight without a castle, a Tupperware salesperson without a party, an Amway distributor without a pyramid scheme. A *ronin* had to learn new skills, update his résumé, and remain always resourceful and adaptable, and *so should you!* In our contemporary Land of Many Mergers, the flexible, risk-taking *ronin* type thrives, while the corporate clone is doomed to misery, stagnation, and obsolescence. Or so says workplace psychologist Beverly Potter, author of *The Way of the Ronin: Riding the Waves of Change at Work*. We couldn't help wondering if those poor, deracinated samurai suffered a twinge of occupational discontent now and then, but the premise is an interesting one, and this self-help book is full of good, Zen-like tips, from "Be here now" to "Accept paradox" and "Avoid perfec-

tionism." Look for lots of corporate *ronins* in the nineties, many of them quoting Carlos Castaneda and Alan Watts on the commuter train to Rye.

Access: *The Way of the Ronin: Riding the Waves of Change at Work* by Dr. Beverly Potter is published by Ronin Publishing, Inc., Box 1035, Berkeley, CA 94701. Paper $9.95.

IT FURTHERS ONE TO CROSS THE GREAT WATER WITH SHORT-TERM OBJECTIVES

•

If you're a middle manager on the make and don't mind turning over your decision making to a 3,000-year-old oracle, you may enjoy *The I Ching on Business and Decision Making* by Guy Damian-Knight. Ask a question and this new businesslike *I Ching* will lead you to an answer—one of the

Materialize objects. Conjure up a fork, your telephone, your favorite childhood toy, the house you'd like to live in. Do something appropriate with each. Then do something inappropriate.

Feel sensations. Imagine you're on a roller-coaster ride, grinding upward then dashing down, looping, twisting, turning. Feel the wind on your face, and the grip of your muscles. See the skyline, then the people below. Where's your stomach? Where's your comb?

Taste things. Cut open a lemon. Squeeze a drop of it on your tongue. Roll it around. Then open your eyes and close them again. Bite into a piece of chocolate fudge. Let it slide across your tongue. If it's studded with nuts or marshmallows, enjoy the texture contrast.

Hear sound. Listen to a wave lapping, a whisper, a motor starting, the growl of a dog, a snore, a thunderstorm, a scream, then—all the way through—the "Star-Spangled Banner." Notice all the background noises too.

Feel emotions. Prelive a great loss—the death of someone you love very much, or the dashing of an ideal. Then recall a happy surprise. Dwell on the details of the event, and on your own physical reaction.

Do the forbidden. Sass a parent, disobey a boss, throw your hand at a bridge partner—anything you've always wanted to do. Luxuriate in the emotional aftermath—then pick up the pieces.

Give birth to an idea. Remember an idea that's come to you lately. Shoot it down with judgmental and negative thoughts; resurrect it with cool, clear logic. Repeat the performance with a brand-new idea.

—Excerpt from *Creativity in Business* by Michael L. Ray and Rochelle Myers; copyright © 1986 by Michael L. Ray and Rochelle Myers; reprinted by permission of Doubleday, a division of Bantam Doubleday Dell Publishing Group, Inc.

traditional sixty-four hexagrams translated into no-nonsense advice on such matters as "start-up," "advertising," "marketing," "banks," "investors," and "international trade." If you'd been a Coca Cola company executive responsible for the introduction of New Coke, for example, and you drew Hexagram #12, "Stagnation," you'd have read: "This is a time of decline and standstill. Put a hold on plans. In a hostile and untrusting atmosphere it is better to keep quiet about any short-term or long-term objectives until you know where you stand with everybody." And if you were smart, you might have taken this to mean, "Don't change the formula!" But by the time you figure out how to follow the complicated divination system, the question may have answered itself anyway. Personally, we think the oracle sounds more poetic when it's talking about pigs, wells, and "crossing the great water" than about "the scope of the task and the workforce," but we're not managers.

Access: *The I Ching on Business and Decision Making* by

Guy Damian-Knight is published by Destiny Books, One Park Street, Rochester, VT 05767. Paper $10.95.

THE TAO THAT CAN BE PRIORITIZED IS NOT THE TAO
●

Then there's *The Tao of Management* by one Bob Messing, CEO of his own specialty chemical company and modern reinterpreter of the *Book of Changes*. We had to wonder if Lao-tzu would have called Hexagram #19 "Supervising," and if the ancient sages would have advised that: "Supervising is both creative and developmental wherein the process becomes increasingly manifest and expanding." But *everything* is "developmental" in this book.

Access: *The Tao of Management* by Bob Messing is published by Humanics New Age, P.O. Box 7447, Atlanta, GA 30309. Paper $10.95.

THE · DEFENESTRATION · OF . . . *WHAT?*

NOW, WHERE'D I PUT MY, UM . . .
•

"When I was in college I could sit down and memorize Caesar on the conquest of Gaul, no problem," laments Vicky, a forty-year-old Washington, D.C., investment banker. "Now I have trouble with my automatic teller code. Am I losing it? Do I have early Alzheimer's disease?"

Vicky is part of a stampede of normal thirty-five- and forty-year-olds who have been showing up in a state of high anxiety at the Memory Assessment Clinics in Bethesda, Maryland, demanding to have their memories tested. "There's a gradual weakening of certain kinds of memory starting at age twenty-five," explains the clinics' director, clinical psychologist Thomas H. Crook. "By forty many people may already be noticing the effects." The Memory Assessment Clinics have devised a battery of computerized memory tests. There's a simulated cocktail party where you're introduced to a series of strangers and forced to remember their names (though not to listen to them ramble on endlessly about aluminum siding). You practice dialing phone numbers after a short delay. You go on a circuitous drive through the streets of downtown San Diego, perhaps so that if you're ever kidnapped in San Diego you can retrace the route. Some pa-

tients with real memory deficits may be eligible to participate in clinical trials of experimental memory drugs—one of which, we're just hoping, will turn out to be extremely efficacious and be named Cram-Eze.

"When you sense that your memory isn't as good as it was in college, don't panic," says Crook, who has tested some 5,000 people between the ages of eighteen and eighty. "It's a normal developmental change." You might not want to begin a new career as test pilot after age forty, however. The mental abilities that go downhill starting around age twenty-five include: cramming large amounts of midterm-type information quickly; learning something in the face of dis-

HOW TO REMEMBER RECIPES (OR INSTRUCTIONS)

CORNISH GAME HENS WITH PAPAYA (OR ANY OTHER EXOTIC FRUIT)
•

1. In the first place, visualize the birds smeared with a paste made of margarine and curry powder to taste. (Visualize the process of mixing the ingredients and smearing the birds, as well as the finished product.)

2. In the second place, visualize the smeared birds going into a 375 degree oven. (Visualize the number 375 in bright red on the oven door.)

3. In the third place, visualize a small bowl in which you have mixed chutney and lime juice to taste. (Set a timer for 30 minutes and visualize the sauce mixture being poured over the birds when the timer rings.)

4. In the fourth place, visualize a ripe, golden papaya cut up in cubes and added to the birds as a garnish just until heated, 20 minutes after adding the sauce. (Set the timer again for 10 minutes only and visualize the cool papaya getting warmer and warmer around the birds.)

5. In the fifth place, visualize the rice pilaf ready to be served with the birds.

Note: Go over it again, making sure you get the timing right. It takes 1 hour total cooking divided in three steps: what you add after 30 minutes, what you add after 50 minutes, and what you serve it with.

This is only one example of how you can use the method. You could try dividing the recipe into more loci [Latin for "places," in Lapp's system, loci are "familiar places you can retrace spontaneously."] I find it practical to group steps, as I did above, because in a single image association it is easy to visualize at once several ingredients put together. You can get a very accurate picture of the consistency, color, and smell of the mixture. It also provides you with a dynamic picture of how to make the recipe. This works well for most cooks. Try it next time you watch a cooking demonstration on TV or when visiting a friend who enjoys cooking. (Make sure you write it down within 24 hours.)

—from *Don't Forget! Easy Exercises for a Better Memory at Any Age* by Danielle C. Lapp; copyright © 1987, McGraw-Hill Book Company; reprinted by permission.

tractions; doing several things simultaneously (the last two reasons are why a mid-life jet-pilot career is out); recalling the names of people you've just met at a cocktail party; and learning by rote. "But," says Crook, "these things are trivial compared with the mental abilities that *improve* with age. The verbal reasoning skills and semantic memory of the average seventy year old are substantially higher than those of the graduate students we have seen. The ability to make complex decisions is more important than being able to study calculus and listen to rock and roll at the same time."

Access: Memory Assessment Clinics, Inc., 8311 Wisconsin Ave., Suite A-6, Bethesda, MD 20814. Phone: (301) 657-0030

AT LAST, A CURE FOR ABSENTMINDEDNESS
•

Some of the memory-training techniques used by the Memory Assessment Clinics were developed by Danielle C. Lapp, a former Stanford University French professor and the author of an excellent book, *Don't Forget! Easy Exercises for a Better Memory at Any Age*. We appreciated the fact that Lapp didn't waste an inordinate amount of time on mnemonic feats no ordinary person could care about (like memorizing the names of thousands of conventioneers). Her sensible, down-to-earth exercises are geared to people who just want to get through the day with fewer embarrassing lapses about car keys and the first names of in-laws. She tells you, in a lucid, practical manner, how to remember a recipe, how not to forget to pack your bathrobe, how to read for better recall, how to listen to music more attentively, how to look at an exhibit of paintings, how to recall words in a foreign language, and so on. Her chapter on aging and memory is an especially wise and compassionate treatment of the phenomenon experts call "benign senescent forgetfulness."

Access: *Don't Forget! Easy Exercises for a Better Memory at Any Age* by Danielle C. Lapp is published by the McGraw-Hill Book Company. Paper $6.95.

IMPRESS YOUR PETS, AMAZE YOUR FRIENDS
•

If you'd like to have total recall of every name and face in your high school yearbook—or *someone else's* yearbook—Jon Keith, The Memory Trainer (this is how he refers to himself on his letterhead), is your man. As a young mnemonist, Keith made a name for himself by memorizing an entire magazine on national television. Now the former science teacher from New Jersey travels around the country teaching people (especially salespeople and others prone to backslapping at conventions) to remember names and faces. When we caught up with him he'd just played to a convention of tour guides. The trick, he says, is mental pictures. To recall Keith's last name, for example, you'd think of "key" and connect it to his mustachioed face by picturing a key resting across his upper lip. This may seem like a lot of

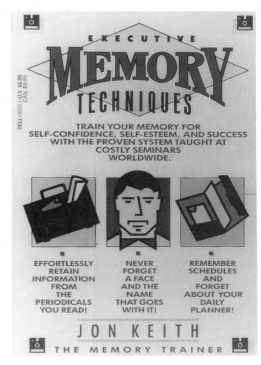

trouble to go to just to recall some guy with a mustache, and you may worry that you'd blurt out, "Yo, mustache key!" or "Hey, Schlage lip!" but Keith claims that good mnemonic skills build overall confidence. "Anyone can train their memory to do anything they want and get a good feeling inside," he tells us.

Access: For information about personal or group memory instruction by Jon Keith contact him at: P.O. Box 343, Belmar, NJ 07719. Phone: (201) 280-2084. Or you can read his book, *Executive Memory Techniques,* Dell Publishing; paper $6.95.

TESTS · YOU · DON'T · HAVE · TO · STUDY · FOR

SMARTER AFTER ALL THESE YEARS

Forget the Stanford-Binet, the Miller Analogies. In the real world who ever offered you a million dollars for rotating geometric shapes in your head or picking which of several crudely drawn figures completes a series? Now there's a test that measures something closer to real smarts—though perhaps not your ability to buy and sell condos under the right market conditions.

The Reflective Judgment Test, developed by psychologists Karen Strohm Kitchener of the University of Denver and Patricia King of Bowling Green State University in Ohio, requires the test taker to contemplate complex questions to which there are no right or wrong answers. Do food additives cause cancer? How were the pyramids built? Is television news biased? (These are known in the trade as "ill-structured problems," the sort of topics that make Thanksgiving dinner so tedious when Aunt Betty gets started on her theories about fluoride and the lost continent of Mu.) No quickie multiple choice here. In its present form, the exam is an hour-long ordeal designed to measure the elusive faculty of "judgment," and the individual interviews must be patiently transcribed and independently evaluated by experts.

Reflective judgment is part of a trend in "stage theory" that recognizes further cognitive stages beyond Jean Piaget's "formal operations," or mature logical thought, which was supposed to peak at age fourteen. So far no one under age twenty-five has attained the top score of seven on the Reflective Judgment Test. "We see reflective judgment as an extension of Piaget's stages," says Kitchener. "This other aspect of development parallels formal operations and goes beyond it." Some might call it wisdom, and wisdom, in Kitchener's words, "really is a function of age."

Access: The Reflective Judgment Test is still in development, but Kitchener plans to develop a format that is easier to administer. Contact: Karen Strohm Kitchener, Ph.D., School of Education, University of Denver, 2040 S. Race St., GCB 112, Denver, CO 80208.

LIKE, WOW, THAT'S REALLY NONVERBAL
●

Do you (1) "enjoy interacting affectively with others" or (2) "enjoy interpreting the affective interaction of others" or (3) have an "equal preference for affective interaction and interpretation of the affective interaction of others"?

While we're on the subject: Do you go in for "impromptu interpretive dancing"? Do you have frequent mood changes?

Are you skilled in communicating with animals, or only moderately good at communicating with them? Your answers to these and similar questions will reveal your "cognitive style," according to William Taggart, a professor of management at Florida International University who, we feel sure, enjoys interpreting the affective interactions of others. With psychologist E. Paul Torrance, Taggart has devised a take-at-home, multiple-choice Human Information Processing Survey, which, after you've answered all forty questions, will tell you whether your thinking style is "left dominant," "right dominant," "mixed," or "integrated." We don't know much about the psychological testing business, but we're not sure if preferring cats to dogs (one of the questions) really has much to do with which side of your brain you use. Some people we know are fond of gerbils. Some prefer different pets depending on their extremely frequent mood changes.

Access: A single copy of the Human Information Processing Survey is available for $18 from: Scholastic Testing Service, Inc., P.O. Box 1056, Bensenville, IL 60106-8056. Phone: (708) 766-7150. (You don't need an expert to administer or score the test. You can do it yourself.) A ten-copy set sells for $45. Taggart's consulting group, HIP systems Inc., offers workshops organized around an advanced version of this test, which has not yet been published. HIP systems Inc., 9960 Southwest 12th Terrace, Miami, FL 33174. Phone: (305) 551-8919.

NOW FOR JUST $12!!! A HIGH-PERFORMANCE BUSINESS BRAIN TO GO WITH YOUR CORNER OFFICE!

•

The BrainMap depicts a deeply furrowed brain subdivided into four parts, with arrows pointing to the "Left Brain," "Right Brain," "Posterior Brain," and "Anterior Brain." We at first assumed that its creator, Dudley Lynch, president of Brain Technologies Corporation of Fort Collins, Colorado, had some sort of neuropsychology background to be able to

throw around terms like "anterior" and "posterior," but it turns out he's a "former journalist" and a "communications expert." (Hmm. We are former journalists. We wrote a book about the brain. We know several highly-placed P.R. people at major universities. We know that the anterior brain is near the front of the head, and the posterior is in back. Hey, maybe . . .) In any case, companies such as General Motors, IBM, and Hewlett Packard have been sufficiently impressed with Lynch's portrayals of brains to send their people to $750 BrainLab sessions to find out what their thinking style is and how they "create their personal and professional worlds." Lynch, the author of *Your High-Performance Business Brain,* has also coauthored a book called *Strategy of the Dolphin* and purveys tests to assess this peculiar ability, which somehow combines dolphins, cerebral hemispheres, the Bermuda Triangle, and waves of change. If you send for the Dolphin Think workbook, you can do things like "describe the 'reef' between you and your vision" and envision your problems with flowcharts as an epic struggle with the Bermuda Triangle. (This sounds much too exhausting—and nautical—to us).

Access: Brain Technologies Corporation markets the BrainMap and related literature, including a set of twelve transparencies about the map ($95), a BrainMap workbook ($39.95), and a set of eighty slides to help anyone give a group presentation about the BrainMap. Brain Technologies Corporation, 2290 E. Prospect Rd., Suite Two, Fort Collins, CO 80525. Phone: (303) 493-9210. *Your High-Performance Business Brain: An Operator's Manual* by Dudley Lynch is published by Prentice-Hall, Inc.; paper $7.95. *Strategy of the Dolphin,* by Lynch and Paul L. Kordis, is published by William Morrow and Company, Inc.; hardcover $19.95.

WHAT'S A NICE GIRL LIKE YOU DOING TAKING A TEST LIKE THIS?

I've always been a sucker for a quickie personality test. Give me a multiple-choice format, a sharpened number-two pencil, and some neat little boxes to check, and I'm in my element. The BrainMap, with its intriguing diagrams of brains subdivided into quadrants, with one large snowflake or asterisk in the center of one that just might be the Cough Control Center, seemed authoritative enough to reveal my True Personality, my real, honest-to-goodness Thinking Style, perhaps even my Soul Nature.

I invited my friend Marion over to take the test with me just in case I felt an urge to cheat and copy someone else's answers. It took only about half an hour to answer the sixty-three questions, which were divided into five categories: Characteristics, Insights, Pastimes and Activities, Information Sources, and Comparisons. Halfway through the test, Marion started to whine. "It's hard when you have a choice between two statements that mean nothing to you," she said, with an existential sigh that I'm sure would have exposed her as someone lacking a truly High-Performance Business Brain. No doubt she was trying to decide whether she was (a) good at creating a fun "party" atmosphere or (b) "may make people uncomfortable with [her] questions about the future." For my part I couldn't remember whether I "like an atmosphere that allows room for making guesses about what should happen" or "an atmosphere where things are just allowed to happen without a lot of second-guessing." Mostly I like an atmosphere in which I can make people uncomfortable with my questions about the future.

In spite of our epistemological difficulties, Marion and I did complete the test. Then we used a score-sheet that rated each of our answers as right-brain, left-brain, posterior-brain, or anterior-brain. We took the totals for each of the four brain quadrants and plotted them on a graph, ending up with a four-sided shape, which, to my great disappointment, did not resemble a human brain at all. Marion's was a perfect square. According to the BrainMap analysis, she had an "I-Accommodate" brain profile. "I moderate; therefore, I reconcile" is the hard-to-fathom motto of these people. "Oh dear, I'm going to have a complex from this," Marion said as she watched the last ninety-degree angle form. "I am so dull. I stand for nothing. I believe in nothing. I am nothing." I reminded her that she refuses to visit the antifeminist state of Utah until, as Erma Bombeck once put it, they set their women free. Surely that means standing for something.

Then we looked at my shape. I leaned a little toward the left and the anterior, which made me an I-Control type, with the motto, "I understand; therefore, I control." We I-Control people are fact oriented, have exacting standards for everyone, seek to try harder and be better. It sounded just like me. We could have left it at that, I suppose, but on a whim we decided to read some of the other profiles. We read, for example, that the "I-Alternate" person lives by the curious motto, "I saturate, therefore, I shift" and is characterized by "intense mood and interest swings between highly 'intellectual' periods and times of spontaneous pleasure-seeking."

"Wait a minute!" Marion brought me out of my reverie. "*That* sounds exactly like you!" We went on to read all eleven profiles and discovered that each of them fit me to a tee, just as all the daily horoscopes in the newspaper invariably seem to refer to my situation. Hmm. I suggested to Marion that we reanalyze her scores. Maybe she wasn't as square or accommodating as she seemed.

"No," she said firmly, "I'm so totally integrated. I would hate to throw myself off balance. I might end up with one of the horrible personality disorders you have."—J.H.

HAVING · MY · SUPERBABY

GENIUS SPERM BANK
●

Okay, maybe it's too late for you to be a genius. But you can do the next best thing: Be the proud parent of a baby Einstein. To guarantee a high I.Q. for your little prodigy, however, you may need to stop trusting the whims of nature and get on down to the Repository for Germinal Choice—sometimes known as the Genius Sperm Bank—in Escondido, California. Brainy guy sperm (I.Q.'s 140–200) is all they carry here. Granted it may not seem very romantic to mate, without benefit of candlelight, music, or even a proper introduction, with the refrigerated genes of some eighty-year-old materials chemist, or, worse, a *dead* chemist, but let's face facts. The bank's founders, physicist Robert Graham and Nobel Prize–winning geneticist Hermann Joseph Muller, could explain to you the lamentable truth of "regression toward the mean," a statistical law that means a child's I.Q. is apt to fall halfway between the parents' mean I.Q. and the average I.Q. of 100. So if you have an I.Q. of 125 and marry your intellectual equal, you can expect merely a B+ kid with an I.Q. of 112 or 113. If you want to do better than that, you might look into Nobel Prize sperm.

Smart women under age thirty-nine are eligible to select a donor from a catalogue of unidentified but highly accomplished scientists, whose traits, from blood type to musical tastes, are summarized in some detail. There's a $50 processing charge to recipients, plus a rental fee of $25 a month for a liquid nitrogen tank to keep the smart sperm on ice until insemination. Sound a bit *Brave New World*-ish? How can you say that? One of the more celebrated donors was William Shockley, the Nobel Prize–winning inventor of the transistor chip who spent his later years promoting unpopular theories of eugenics. Shockley's white-supremacist notions should give pause to anyone convinced that a high I.Q. guarantees actual intelligence.

Access: Repository for Germinal Choice, 450 South Escondido Blvd., Escondido, CA 92025. Phone: (619) 743-0772.

TWO KICKS MEANS I'M A PHENOMENOLOGIST
●

The next step after the right conception? Prenatal University (founded 1979) doesn't have much of a football team; to tell the truth, it doesn't have a campus, a registrar, or a student lounge, either. But it's one of the few places we know of where your unborn child can take a few courses, thus gaining a leg up on all those other fetuses with whom he or she will one day compete for scarce places in the Ivy League. Developed by a physician, Prenatal U. consists of two workbooks and a cassette tape to teach expectant parents how to "enhance the learning potentials of the unborn child and newborn." Being "free of distractions," the not-yet-born make especially receptive students, the Prenatal U. folks point out, and starting with the "Kick Game," the course will teach them how to communicate with Mom and possibly even the rest of the family. The brochure claims that Prenatal U. grads have easier deliveries, cry less, nurse better, are calmer, better coordinated, more attentive, and more "receptive to learning" than babies whose Moms just sat around eating ice cream and getting weighed. Will it bother you that the people who wrote the brochure evidently *weren't* stimulated prenatally—at least not in the spelling and grammar department?

Access: Prenatal University, Calaroga Surgical Center, 27225 Calaroga Ave., Hayward, CA 94545. Phone: (415) 783-0783.

DON'T DROOL ON THE TITIAN, DEAR
•

And *after* your little wunderkind is born, she shouldn't just be lying around drooling on her Snugli; she should be learning to recognize a quattrocento Madonna. At the Institutes for the Achievement of Human Potential in Philadelphia—better known as the Better Baby Institute—a "world-renowned staff" of "child brain developmentalists, neurosurgeons, pediatricians, educators, anthropologists, and other authorities" will be happy to help you mold her into a literate, violin-playing, mathematically gifted, art-appreciating, marathon-running prodigy. All you have to do to be eligible for the $690, seven-day How to Multiply Your Baby's Intelligence Course is "make a career out of being a parent" and "believe that all babies and tiny children can perform at much higher levels than is presently the case." At the end of it you'll be able to wow your neighbors with your certificate in the Professional Parent Level of Human Development, as well as your *enfant prodige*.

Alas, we didn't know that an eight-month-old would naturally want to be learning about "birds, flowers, trees, presidents, nations, music, and all kinds of encyclopedic information," so we were making moo-cow noises at our son, Jake, when we should have been dangling flash cards and cooing, "Look at the nice picture of President Warren Harding. Can you say, 'Teapot Dome Scandal'?" Today, at age

three, he's woefully ignorant of the American political process and would rather look at a Cheerios box than a Caravaggio. In short, he can't hold a candle to the excessively precocious tots profiled in the Better Baby brochure: little Heather who learned to read and do sums before she was two; Josh who started reading at fourteen months and was "learning Greek and Latin roots every week" by age six; and two-and-a-half-year-old Trevor who is now a preschool se-

miotician and deconstructionist. (Okay, we hallucinated Trevor, but the first two are actual Better Babies.)

Even if you don't enroll in the course, you'll rest easier knowing you can order materials such as flash cards, books like *How to Multiply Your Baby's Intelligence* and *How to Teach Your Baby to Read* (both by Institute founder and leading theoritician Glenn Doman), and such genius tsatskes as books on Suzuki violin instruction and a child's audiocassette on "The Nineteenth Century Poets," which your child is sure to prefer to Raffi or Ninja Turtles.

Access: For an application form for the How to Multiply Your Baby's Intelligence Course contact: The Registrar, The Institutes for the Achievement of Human Potential, 9901 Stenton Ave., Philadelphia, PA 19118. Phone: (215) 233-2050. Various books and other materials are available from the Better Baby Press and the Better Baby Store at the same address.

IS YOUR TODDLER READY FOR QUANTUM MECHANICS?
•

If you've done everything right and succeeded in being the parent of a gifted child, there's a special monthly newsletter for you. *Gifted Children Monthly* carries short features, advice columns, and inspirational pieces, as well as a valuable consumer's guide to everything from meteorology kits and computer games to SAT prep kits and philosophy books

for smart children. In the classifieds, gifted, clarinet-playing eleven-year-olds can find compatible pen pals.

Access: *Gifted Children Monthly* is published nine times a year by Gifted and Talented Publications, 213 Hollydell Dr., Sewell, NJ 08080. Phone: (609) 582-0277. A subscription is $25 a year; outside the U.S. add $10.

TOOLS · FOR · THOUGHT

HOW TO TURN YOUR BRAIN INTO A HIGH-SPEED LEARNING DEVICE
●

Just buy Carl Schleicher's Hemi Phones. Then get a two-track tape with music on one track and the information you want to absorb on the other and pop it into the player. A special switch inside the headphones will pipe the music into your right ear and the data into your left, and before you can say "subliminal learning" you'll know everything there is to know about Greek verbs or the New York State real estate code or whatever it is you're trying to learn.

It works, explains inventor Schleicher, because your nervous system is designed so that sounds entering your right ear reach the left side of the brain and those entering your left ear reach the right side. Okay, fine. What the Hemi Phones do is relax your logical left hemisphere with music, allowing the facts to flow into the (intuitive) right hemisphere. But wait, shouldn't it really be the other way around? Isn't the *right* hemisphere good at appreciating music? Oh well, don't ask us; try it out for yourself. For some reason, says Schleicher, baroque music works best.

Hemi Phones

Access: Hemi Phones cost $35.50 and are sold by: Mankind Research Unlimited, Inc., 1315 Apple Ave., Silver Spring, MD 20910. Phone: (301)-587-8686.

TWILIGHT LEARNING MACHINE
●

The theta state (4 to 8 hz) is sometimes referred to as the twilight of consciousness, for it lies between the alpha state (relaxed but alert) and the delta state (sleep). It is in theta, according to Thomas Budzynski, that learning is accomplished very rapidly and deposited in long-term memory.

THE LEARNING DISABILITY TRAP

S even years ago, psychologist Thomas Armstrong quit his job as a learning disabilities specialist and went on to write an important manifesto, *In Their Own Way* (Jeremy P. Tarcher), a persuasive indictment of an educational system that brands as "learning disabled" the children it fails to teach. Inspired by the work of Harvard psychologist Howard Gardner, who has pinpointed seven basic types of intelligence, Armstrong stresses the importance of recognizing variations in learning style.

Q: Why do you object to the term "learning disability"?

Armstrong: It's a loaded term that places the blame on kids rather than on our system of education. And it's usually applied only to kids who have difficulty with reading, spelling, and math. If we look closely enough, we see that all of us have learning disabilities and abilities. We each have a personal learning style.

Q: Why are kids who are poor at reading or math singled out?

Armstrong: Because our schools, with their emphasis on worksheets and the multiple-choice approach to education, favor kids with strong linguistic and mathematical-logical abilities. But there are other ways of learning. The model I use is based on Howard Gardner's theory that there are seven kinds of intelligence that everyone has in varying proportions: linguistic, logical-mathematical, kinesthetic, spatial, musical, interpersonal, and intrapersonal. Kids who learn musically, kinesthetically, or spatially have the most trouble in school.

Q: Yet children with strong linguistic abilities won't be labeled learning disabled even if they're weak in spatial intelligence?

Armstrong: Not in our culture. In Eskimo culture, where spatial intelligence is important to be able to navigate the tundra safely, the kid might be called disabled.

Q: The fact remains that in our culture everyone has to be able to read, write, and do some math. How can those skills be taught to children whose dominant learning style is musical or spatial?

Armstrong: You need to have a cross-modal approach, to appeal to all seven types of personal learning styles. We can use art to teach reading, physical movement to teach handwriting or spelling, music to teach math. You can teach the multiplication tables by singing them to a simple tune, or you can play music while kids are doing math problems. Teachers don't have to follow the lockstep of worksheets, tests, and lectures. They can begin in small ways, by introducing a little music or movement activity.

Q: How can parents tell what type of intelligence predominates in a child?

Armstrong: One way is to look at how children spend their free time—which is one way parents have the advantage over teachers. Kids may seem out of it in Social Studies, but when they go home they may have a business, or lots of friends, or an ability to repair appliances.

Q: If the teacher won't or can't appeal to my child's personal learning style, what can I do?

Armstrong: Moving your child to another classroom, school, or school district might help. Private alternative schools are another option, and so is home schooling. And every parent can use family activities to give children what they're not getting in school. A game like Scrabble can help with spelling and vocabulary.

Q: Can adults benefit by discovering their personal learning styles—or is it too late for us?

Armstrong: Yes, they can—to see why they might have done poorly in school and also to understand themselves. I jiggle when I read. Sometimes I feel that needs to be remedied, and at other times I see that it's just a natural way I happen to learn.

The Twilight Learning Device

Budzynski, a clinical psychologist, originally developed the Twilight Learning Device for patients with addiction problems. Then he discovered that it could help them memorize the California Building Code (or anything else) as well.

The Twilight Learning Device is essentially a biofeedback system consisting of an EEG machine hooked up to two tape recorders. The EEG measures the user's brain activity, and when he produces enough alpha waves, the first tape recorder switches on, piping his brain relaxing music and sounds through headphones. Then, when the user's brain waves hit theta, the second recorder kicks in with a learning tape, which might be a French lesson, assertiveness training, a stop-smoking program, or whatever. Budzynski continues to use the device on his patients at St. Luke's Medical Center in Bellevue, Washington, and in his own clinic, Behavioral Medicine Associates in Denver. He claims it works especially well on anyone with a self-esteem problem, which lies at the heart of addictions.

Access: The Twilight Learning Device costs $3,500 from Biofeedback Systems, 2736 47th St., Boulder, CO 80301. Phone: (303) 444-1411. Contact the company to find out which practitioners in your area are using the machine.

POCKET THINK TANK
●

If you're an entrepreneur or wanna-be entrepreneur and wish to brainstorm all by yourself, check out Circles of Creativity. The product is based on a brainstorming method called Product Improvement Checklist (PICL), developed by inventor Jim Betts with Arthur Van Gundy a University of Oklahoma professor. C of C resembles a circular slide rule with three movable concentric circles and two pointers. You decide on a product you'd like to create and then let Circles of Creativity throw key words (like "sticky," "transparent," "luminous," or "zigzag") at you. Given the nature of the key words, we'd guess that Circles of Creativity isn't meant for artists, unless you like your masterpieces portable, cylindrical, or foamy. On the other hand, why *not* the world's first foamy symphony or an adjustable novel of manners? We especially liked spinning the wheels and looking through a little window that let us "add or take away" power, turbulence, bubbles, or pathos, and another window that urged us to think about things like the eye of a storm, dental floss, and spider webs. Matter of fact, we're thinking about spider webs made of dental floss right now. *Turbulent* dental-floss-like spiderwebs, storm-tossed, woven in pathos, yet remaining always portable and adjustable. . . . It's well worth the $14.95 just for the surrealist, free-association possibilities.

Access: Circles of Creativity is available from New Product Development, P.O. Box 1309, Point Pleasant, NJ 08742. Phone: (201) 295-8258. Price: $14.95.

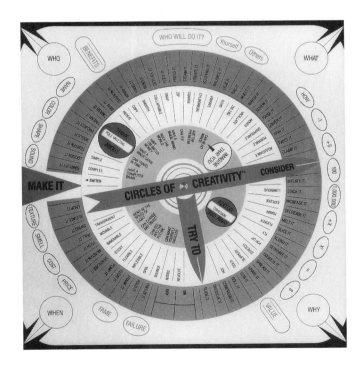

WHAT COLOR IS YOUR MEDULLA OBLONGATA?
•

Get out your forty-eight pack of Crayolas and take a moment to study the source of all those creative insights, intuitive leaps, and incredible hunches you've been having. That's right, your brain. But do you know your gray matter from your white matter, your cerebral ventricles from your inferior colliculus? You will, after you've taken a multicolored trip through the *Human Brain Coloring Book,* the product of a unique collaboration between a husband-and-wife team of neuroscientists and an artist. Unless you're in your third year of a neurosurgery residency you probably won't have the patience for the degree of detail in this book—we ourselves quickly went back to coloring Snow White and the seven dwarfs—but if you leave it around on your coffeetable, your friends will certainly be impressed.

Access: *The Human Brain Coloring Book,* by M. C. Diamond, A. B. Scheibel, and L. M. Elson, is published by Barnes & Noble Books. Paper $10.95.

SHUFFLE THE THINKING STRATEGIES, HONEY
•

The Creative Whack Pack is an illustrated deck depicting sixty-four thinking strategies by Roger von Oech, identified as the author of two successful books on creativity. The cards—labeled "Give Yourself a Whack on the Side of the Head," "Loosen Up," "Slay a Dragon" and so forth—are divided into four suits representing the four types of thinking and are intended to "whack you out of habitual thought patterns and enable you to look at what you are doing in a fresh way." You can play them by yourself or with your Friday-night poker group, and use them as "a mental stimulant, a creativity workshop, a guide to the creative process, and as an oracle."

Access: The Creative Whack Pack can be ordered from U.S. Games Systems, Inc., 179 Ludlow St., Stamford, CT 06902. Price: $12.95.

SMARTER THAN MENSA
•

Have you scored 136 or higher on a Stanford-Binet intelligence test? Can you boast a Graduate Record Exam (GRE) combined score of 1,300 or more, or a Scholastic Aptitude Test (SAT) score of 1,375 or higher? Are you an insufferable prodigy whose idea of small talk is an analysis of Korzybski? Then the International Legion of Intelligence (Intertel) is looking for you. It's not the same as winning the lottery, of course, but you will belong to a club of savants more exclusive than Mensa. While Mensa accepts anyone in the top 2 percent of the thinking public, Intertel (which sounds like an international covert surveillance unit to us!) welcomes only the top 1 percent. It has 2,000 members in twelve chapters and publishes a forty-eight-page monthly journal that seems to print about anything that comes into members' heads. Members call themselves "Ilians" and congregate (science-fiction novels clutched in sweaty palms?) at annual conventions and tea parties—yes, tea parties—thrown by some local chapters.

Access: For a membership application, write or call: Intertel, P.O. Box 150580, Lakewood, CO 80215. Phone: (303) 797-7210.

Roger von Oech's
Creative
Whack Pack

CHAPTER FOUR

D R E A M
T E C H:
WORKING · IN
YOUR · SLEEP

·

In 1953 a scientist at the University of Chicago attached electrodes and sensors to the heads of sleeping people and discovered the fast, jerky eye movements that accompany dreaming. He also found that all human beings dream, even those who claim they never do, and that dreams occur four to five times a night in roughly ninety-minute cycles, about the length of a TV docudrama. This discovery of REM (rapid eye movement) sleep made dreaming scientific and led to lots of squiggles on graph paper for sleep lab technicians to stare at all night. However, all the EEGs, polygraphs, and galvanic skin responses don't tell us what people are  dreaming *about*.

The Senoi people of Malaysia have no EEG or polygraph machines— they don't even have waxed dental floss— but they are far more sophisticated dreamers than we. Every morning at breakfast a Senoi child dutifully reports his dreams to the other members of his family. If he has had a nightmare about

being chased by a "smoke spirit," his parents don't say, "Be quiet, dear, and finish your raisin bran. There's no such thing as a smoke spirit." They encourage him to redream his dream, but this time to turn around and ask the spirit, "Why are you chasing me?" We know this because an American anthropologist named Kilton Stewart hung out with this obscure Malaysian tribe and published papers about them in 1954, the same year the REM sleep studies were published. (Is that synchronicity or what?) The portrait emerged of a remarkable, peaceful community whose every civic activity revolved around dreams, as ours revolves around property tax overrides and highway construction.

Recently, a pair of American researchers spent a year with the Senoi and found scant trace of the legendary Senoi dreamwork. Not a single person recalled having received dream-control education as a child and all "vehemently de-

nied that dream manipulation had ever been a part of their culture," according to the researchers. But we don't care, do we? If the Senoi were not quite the master dreamers everyone supposed, they might just as well have been, because dozens of books and articles had been written about them. They were already part of the collective unconscious!

And the collective unconscious no longer belongs to trained analysts; it has been given back to the dreamer. Whereas Freud believed that the everpresent "censor" prevents you from decoding the dirty messages from your unconscious, today's dream gurus say that you, and you alone, are qualified to interpret your dreams. And not all snakes are phallic. So Freud is out, Carl Gustav Jung is in, and the dream has been deprofessionalized. And in this do-it-yourself atmosphere, dreamers don't just sit on the sidelines and try to recall their dreams the morning after. They're copying the Senoi and *programming* their dreams. They're plunging right into the dreamscape and turning the plot around when they feel like it. They are "rewriting dreams" and creating happily-ever-after endings. They're practicing dream divination, reentry, telepathy, and precognition. (See "Dream Engineering for Novices," page 82.)

Before we go on, we must warn you that this chapter will contain very few actual dreams. There is a simple reason for this. Dream excerpts are usually written in italics, and we hate reading italics and suspect that you do, too. *Even more, we hate proofreading passages in italics!* See what we mean? It's like picking your way through a waving wheatfield looking for your lost car keys. Of course, you don't *dream* in italics, so you don't have to worry about this. You'll only have to worry about remembering your nightly dramas, a process that Ann Faraday, author of *The Dream Game*, likens to trying to summarize the plot of a mystery novel after reading only the last page. (We pass along some tips in this chapter.)

Well, okay, here's a dream if you must have one:

I was climbing K-2 in the Himalayas, the second-highest mountain in the world. There I was going through these snowdrifts and I noticed I was wearing a T-shirt. I instantly recognized I was dreaming, and flew off the mountain.

This dream was dreamed by psychologist Stephen LaBerge back in 1970 shortly after he heard a visiting Tibetan master lecture on lucid dreaming. A lucid dream is one in which the dreamer is "awake" and aware *inside a dream,* and it used to be considered about as respectable as UFOs or spontaneous human combustion until LaBerge came along. He was five years old when he had his first lucid dream. He found himself swimming underwater, with the roof of the ocean above him, and thought, "Uh oh, how can I breathe?" Then, recognizing that he was in a *dream* ocean, he realized he could dive for sunken treasures for hours if he wanted. Years later, armed with a Ph.D., he slept with electrodes for thousands of sleep-hours at Stanford University's famous sleep lab, and logged in hundreds of dreams before he had what he wanted: electrophysiological proof of lucid dreaming. He used a code of eyelid signals to signal to the waking world from within a dream, once spelling out his initials in his sleep. Later, he trained a corps of lucid dreamers, or "oneironauts" ("dream travelers") to journey open-eyed into the land of dreams. (See "Lucid Dreams," page 99.)

"I learned to fly very fast and very high," recalls world-class oneironaut Daryl Hewitt, of San Francisco, "and to pass through walls, including steel, and to burn holes through them with lasers from my fingertips, to study the lucid dream environment in exquisite, close-up detail, explore other planets, and especially to alter the dream environment at will, as in making things appear, disappear, and change shape and color." Such comic-book-superhero exploits are not unusual among veteran lucid dreamers. The dreamworld is, after all, an alternate universe in which you don't have to pay estimated income tax or obey the laws of gravity and momentum; you can orbit the Crab Nebula,

breathe underwater, take part in ancient Mayan rain dances, or change into other selves. "Many of my dream selves . . . are actually aware of information, experiences, and persons that are quite different from those I am aware of in my waking life," confides San Francisco dreamworker Bob Trowbridge in the *The Dream Network Bulletin*. "If my dream ego lives in a different apartment than my waking ego . . . that's where he lives. He knows that apartment. He knows where all the rooms are and everything is quite familiar to him. My dream self lives in different places, has different friends, different jobs, different abilities, and different possessions."

Your dream self can also swap phone numbers with other dream selves, and your archetypes can mingle in a sociable collective unconscious of hundreds of grassroots "dream networks" across the U.S. (See "With a Little Help from My Friends," page 90.) A prototype was GATES, a community of houseboat residents in Sausalito, California, who shared their dreams through a centrally located "Dream Drop" and published a dream journal from 1977 to 1984. Today there is an epidemic of dream groups of all sorts, including a dream community composed of Roman Catholic nuns in an Oregon cloister and a dream network for prisoners in Florida. In Moscow a few years ago dissident dreamworkers would rendezvous outside a movie theater, blending in with the line of moviegoers to escape detection. (This was before glasnost; perhaps since the East/West thaw Carl Jung will end up being a hero of the revolution.)

Dream networks don't just discuss dreams; they frequently design dream experiments and write up their research in badly photocopied newsletters with lots of drawings of dream art. And why not? As group-dreaming pioneer Henry Reed, Ph.D., who years ago was jolted into sobriety by a dream in which wine appeared as the image of pus oozing from a wound, points out, "In effect every dreamer is a researcher and every dream is an experiment in consciousness." (Speaking of which, dreaming is the only absolutely safe, legal altered state of consciousness we know of that is available to anyone capable of REM sleep. That's basically all mammals except the spiny anteater, a creature sadly lacking in psychological depth.)

Dreamwork is not mere navel-gazing, say veterans, because the work you do in your dreams automatically spills over into waking life. In the dream state you contact the unconscious sources of your attitudes, beliefs, and behaviors; you gain access to the stored experiences of a lifetime; you can even hobnob (especially if you're a Jungian) with the collective memories of the race. In this parallel life you are free to test-drive new behaviors without fear of ridicule by friends or coworkers. If you get in the habit of confronting the ogres in your nightmares and asking them, "Why are you chasing me?"—or "Why are you auditing me?"—this attitude of fearlessness will carry over into real life. Or so they say.

This chapter is a consumer's guide to state-of-the-art tools, techniques, and resources for modern dreamworkers.

DREAM · ENGINEERING · FOR · NOVICES

You don't have to just lie there and let dreams happen to you anymore. Having a dream is not like watching "The Cosby Show." You are, in dreamworker Gayle Delaney's words, a powerful "dream producer" (as well as a screenwriter, director, star, and head gaffer). We don't mean that you should start worrying about "points," taking meetings, buying cellular phones, and shopping on Rodeo Drive. But there are many things that you, as your own dream producer with your own independent dream production company, can do with your dreamlife. You can do preproduction work like incubation. You can train yourself to fly over the Andes or ask for a gift from your dream. You can compile your own symbol dictionary. In the postproduction phase you can rewrite your dream, reenter your dream, turn a hideous Grimm Brothers' nightmare into a fairy tale with a happy ending, or convert your dream into an enduring work of art—perhaps a screenplay for an Eddie Murphy vehicle or, depending on the nature of your dreams, something more existential and Bergman-esque. Then you *can* have a cellular phone, shop on Rodeo Drive, and consult your own personal channeler. Here are a few of the possibilities:

INCUBATE A DREAM
●

For years Elias Howe grappled with the problem of how to mechanize sewing. One night he had a dream in which he was surrounded by savages brandishing spears. When he awoke, he remembered that the spears had eye-shaped holes at the tips. Suddenly the solution was clear: Place the eye of the needle at the tip instead of the shank, and—voilà—the sewing machine was born.

You needn't sit around and wait for a miraculous problem-solving dream to drop out of the sky; you can deliberately "incubate" one. The ancient Greeks performed dream-incubation ceremonies in special temples, but today you can ask your dreams for guidance *without* invoking goddesses or examining animal entrails. "People use dream incubation for all kinds of purposes," says dream researcher Henry Reed, who once wrote a booklet on how to throw a Dream Incubation Slumber Party—"for help in making career decisions, for dealing with their relationships, and for resolving creativity problems like writer's block."

Here are the basic steps of dream incubation, according to dream experts Patricia Garfield and Linda Magallon:
1. Find a peaceful place to think about your dream question. Use whatever relaxation technique—meditation, yoga, breathing exercises—that works best for you.
2. Be very specific and concise in formulating your dream question. ("I want my dream to tell me what to do about my relationship with my boyfriend.") Be sure to choose positive wording. While you should be specific about your goal, it is also important to be flexible and open-ended about the results. (If your question is "Why is there nonconservation of parity in the universe?" you may have to accept an answer like "Three cornflakes floating in a sea of milk.")
3. Focus on your goal during the day. Visualize what you expect to dream about. ("I see myself sitting next to the bubble chamber. The data are coming in over the monitor. . . .") Rehearse possible dream scenarios while you are awake. Magallon suggests immersing yourself in your goal during the day by engaging in activities related to it. Read books or watch a movie on the subject.
4. Before you go to sleep, concentrate on your topic. Repeat your goal question. If your mind wanders, gently bring it back to the subject. Then gradually drift off to sleep and trust that your dreams will reveal the answer to your question.
5. Recall your dream(s). You may want to set your alarm a bit earlier than usual. Upon awakening, don't move. Dreams will be erased from memory within fifteen minutes, faster than Erik Estrada disappeared from the public view. Try to remember *everything* about your dream. Don't dismiss seemingly trivial details, which may turn out to be significant upon closer examination.

MAKE YOUR OWN SYMBOL DICTIONARY
●

The images, symbols, figures, and themes that appear in your dreams are the raw material of dream interpretation. Although some symbols like flying, falling, or walking around naked are so universal that standard interpretations can be useful (See "A Brief Dictionary of Dream Symbols," page 90), no two people attach the same meaning to a significant image. Because your personal symbols are coded messages from *your* subconscious, no one else can interpret them for you. You may find it useful to create your own dream dictionary. Many dreamworkers buy notebooks with plenty of blank pages and alphabetize their dictionaries, from, say, "Armageddon" to "zygote." Every time you have a dream, jot down the major symbol, and describe its significance in the dream. You may also want to note the date. Over the course of several months, you'll notice subtle changes in the meanings of various symbols, indicating movement and growth in the corresponding life issues. You'll also discern revealing patterns that will aid your interpretation.

BECOME YOUR DREAM
•

Here is a technique pioneered by Fritz Perls, the father of Gestalt therapy. Become each and every part of your dream. Become each character. Become each object. Then have each of these elements of your dream carry on a dialogue. It works well to do this in tandem with a dream partner, who can probe for more information or gently nudge you back on course if you go off on a tangent. First tell your partner your dream in its entirety. Then ask him or her to guide you through a retelling, directing you to act out key symbols or start up conversations with different characters. If you're working solo, Jill Morris suggests in *The Dream Workbook,* you can rewrite your dream as a playlet in your dream journal.

INTERVIEW YOUR DREAM CHARACTERS
•

After you've noted down your dream, analyze it for any dangling conversations or unresolved plot lines or issues. Choose a key figure in the dream to interview. Visualize him or her as you question, and persist until you get a satisfactory answer. Perhaps the character will break down like a prosecution witness on "Perry Mason," or blurt out embarrassingly intimate details like a celebrity interviewed by Barbara Walters. In any case, keep asking questions until you are satisfied that the issue has been resolved—or until you meet more resistance than you want to push through at present.

FINISH YOUR DREAM
•

Often you'll have a lengthy dream that is open-ended, with no clear resolution. For such cases Jung developed a technique called active imagination, in which the dreamer either changes the dream's ending or brings an incomplete plot to completion while in the waking state. Why bother? Well, according to Jung, resolving a dream situation or converting a negative dream experience into a positive one allows you to feel in control of your life. So by changing your dreams, you can start to change your life. Morris tells of one man who felt inadequate with women and had a dream in which he met an attractive woman, who suddenly got up and left in midconversation. In the waking state, the man rewrote the dream so that alluring woman agreed to go out with him. Later, back in real life, he reported feeling much more self-confident with the opposite sex (though perhaps not quite so self-confident as Rob Lowe).

FREE-ASSOCIATE
•

Although Freud has become somewhat unfashionable of late, his technique of free association is still a useful way to dig disguised messages out of a dream. But you don't need a wizened analyst to help you do it. In *The Dream Workbook*

Jill Morris recounts how one woman's free association from a seemingly innocuous dream led her to uncover a buried secret. She wrote down a recurring dream she had had since childhood, then selected the most striking paragraph: *I am on a stairway. A German shepherd is coming up the stairs toward my cat. I go charging down the stairs, screaming at the dog to chase it away. I succeed.* Next she listed the key words in one column, and her associations in the adjacent column. The word *German* yielded "rough, tough, mean, tyrannical, hard, killer"; *coming up* gave her "emerging, burst, sperm inside"; *cat* led to "furry, raw meat," and so on. Then she rewrote the dream using only the words she had free-associated. *Eye exist up and down. A rough, tough, mean, tyrannical, killer, be careful, an overseer who watches over and is peaceful, bursts inside, leading to thrusting oh my my furry, raw meat. Aye, aye, get out penis, army, father's fist, soft abyss, falling, dark hole, getting hurt, help where dirty, don't touch. . . .* Not too subtle, eh? This woman's free association revealed that she had been reliving her father's sexual desire for her when she was a child. He was the predatory "German shepherd" ascending the stairs, which she chases away. Having repressed these memories for decades, she was finally able to recognize the source of her subconscious guilt, anger, and shame and to release these crippling feelings. Morris notes that do-it-yourself free association is especially valuable for working with dreams that *appear* meaningless, absurd, or nonsensical.

AMPLIFY A DREAM

A favorite Jungian trick. Pick one particularly powerful symbol from your dream, one that sets off powerful psychic tingles, and elaborate on it. Meditate on it in detail in your journal, projecting it into the past and the future. You may even want to do further "research." Archetypal amplification, as described by Jungian analyst Robert A. Johnson in his book *Inner Work,* is "a process of gathering information about archetypes that appear in our dreams by going to sources such as myths, fairy tales, and ancient religious traditions." You can expand your understanding of the archetypes in your dreams if you have a good working knowledge of Genesis, the Brothers Grimm, alchemical symbols, the Hindu goddess Kali, the travels of Odysseus, and ancient legends of the great flood. Suppose something in your dream reminds you of the poisoned apple in *Snow White.* Go back to the source. What does the fairy tale tell you about the archetype of the stepmother (the Terrible Mother?) and that of innocent beauty? What is that apple all about? Does it set off any Garden of Eden associations? But don't let all this scholarship obscure the most important issue: your *personal* associations. "It isn't enough to say, 'Ah! That is a symbol of the Great Mother . . . ,' " cautions Johnson. "We have to ask, 'What is this archetype doing in my personal life?' "

FOLLOW THE EGO

"The dream ego," Strephon Kaplan-Williams explains in *The Jungian-Senoi Dreamwork Manual,* "is usually the image of yourself in the dream." Typically, this dream ego, or "drego," is a passive spectator, not a man of action. It may be observing the action, running away from something, riding in a car, or languidly blowing smoke rings like a thirties cabaret goddess. Rarely does it take charge and choose what to do next. This dream ego is a reflection of your waking ego, of course. "If you really want an accurate picture of what your ego is like, follow what it is doing or not doing in your dreams," notes Kaplan-Williams. He suggests that you describe as fully as possible all the drego's activities and nonactivities and the attitudes, patterns and feelings that govern them. Then analyze these behaviors: What seems appropriate? What's inappropriate? Does your drego run from danger? Is it a schlmiel or a weenie? Is it a James Bond type who faces life as it comes? Naturally, this exercise will give you insights into your real-life behaviors and attitudes.

LIVE HAPPILY EVER AFTER

Cinderella did. So did Snow White and Hansel and Gretel. Why not you—at least in your dreams? The Senoi, those aboriginal Malaysian superdreamers, believed in happy endings. Rather than passively submitting to dream villains and grisly dream accidents, Senoi children were taught to transform every negative dream image or event into a positive one. If you dream of falling off a cliff, you will awaken in a cold sweat before you hit the ground, of course. The Senoi would advise you to confront your fear and allow yourself to *land.* Who knows what interesting things might happen then? Or, the next time you have this dream, program yourself to imagine that you sprout wings and soar over the abyss. The key is to train yourself to turn fear into its opposite— fear of falling into the joy of flying, for instance. This practice will automatically spill over into waking life.

REENTER YOUR DREAM
•

"Dream reentry is a particularly powerful way to access, explore, and interact with the inner wisdom that resides in our mind and body," explains Fred G. Olsen, founding director of The Dream House in San Francisco. "When we step into the inner pictures and act consciously within the waking dream, we can actually reprogram our inner states and facilitate profound healing and transformation in our lives." You can do it on your own, but dream reentry is easier with a partner to guide you. Fully awake, the dreamer recalls the dream she had, reexperiences the feelings triggered by the dream, and pinpoints the parts of the body where those emotions are felt most intensely. By working with those images and feelings, the dreamer creates a new, improved dream.

Olsen has devised a series of leading questions to guide the reentry process. What do you remember? What do you see? What else do you see right now in the picture? Once the scene is established, visualize yourself in the dream. Can you see yourself in the dream? How old are you? What are you wearing? The next series of questions is designed to uncover the hidden messages: What was happening in real life when you were that age or when you were wearing that outfit? What do you want to do in the scene? What happens when you do it? What would you like to do differently? How do you feel? Is there any aspect of your present life that has this feeling attached to it? Do these feelings register anywhere on your body? Where? Amplify those feelings and enter them with your mind. "Each scene in the dream can be replayed until you have the power to resolve the situation," explains Olsen. "We can reprogram the past in order to heal ourselves physically and spiritually in the present."

LEARN TO FLY
•

Not only are Peter Pan and magic-carpet dreams exhilarating; they also reportedly enhance your ability to dream lucidly. (See "Lucid Dreams," page 99.) To teach yourself to fly, use the dream incubation technique to ask your subconscious to serve up a flying dream. When you retire, recall previous flying dreams in all their gravity-defying detail. Note in your dream journal how much you enjoy nocturnal flying. Then, as you fall asleep, repeat over and over again an incubation phrase such as "I want to fly" or "Tonight I will fly over the Rockies." If you're a flying-dream virgin, you can train yourself to fly by daydreaming about flying during your waking hours. From time to time during the day remind yourself, Tonight I will fly in my dreams. (People may stare at you on the bus as though you were a potential serial killer, but never mind.) Focus on images of flight: geese soaring through the sky, a jet disappearing over the horizon. Visualize yourself ordering the prefab pasta primavera on a 747 or strapped to the wings of an eagle, propelling yourself above a blanket of clouds. Imagine all the sensations of flying. Just before you go to sleep, focus all your thoughts on flying. If it doesn't work the first time, it probably will after a little practice.

ASK FOR A GIFT FROM YOUR DREAM
●

This is another technique of the perfectionist Senoi, who do not allow their dreams to end without a positive outcome. The ultimate Senoi denouement, according to Patricia Garfield, Ph.D., author of *Creative Dreaming,* is "a gift to the dreamer from one of the dream images." Typically, Senoi dreamers confront a dream enemy and demand a "gift" such as a poem, a story, a painting, a new skill, or the answer to a nagging problem. This way, they always receive something of value from their dreams. You can do it too. When you demand a gift from a dream enemy, you practice vanquishing fear, and the gifts you receive from these figures will give you insights into your mindscape. You can start the ball rolling by requesting gifts from all your dream characters as you write in your dream journal. Then, as you fall asleep, repeat the affirmation that you will receive gifts of great value in your dreams. Who knows? Maybe you'll receive insider-trading tips, a pilot for a sitcom, or the Coke secret formula.

EXPLORE RECURRENT DREAMS
●

Recurrent dreams are especially fertile soil for self-knowledge (you can think of them as mailgrams from your self, marked URGENT! DELIVER IMMEDIATELY!) as well as springboards to lucidity. By keeping track of them, you will be monitoring your major intrapsychic themes. "The plots, settings, characters, behaviors, and objects that occur most frequently in your dreams provide the most potent clues regarding what makes you an individual," notes dreamworker Jack Maguire in his book *Night and Day.* Following is the dream-inventory method he recommends for spotting interesting patterns:

1. Take a sheet of paper and divide it into six columns with the following headings: date and title, characters, setting, objects, behaviors, and feelings.

2. Read over your dream journal and for each dream enter items in the appropriate category. Draw bold lines to separate information from each dream.

3. Once you've entered the data from about ten dreams, examine each column. Which items are repeated? What significance do these recurrent images or objects have in your daily life? Why do you think they keep surfacing in your dreams?

4. Now compare entire dreams for points of similarity. How do these dreams relate to patterns in your waking life? Why do you think these types of dreams keep recurring?

TURN YOUR DREAM INTO A POEM
●

Salvador Dali's limpid watches, many films of Fellini and Ingmar Bergman, and Coleridge's "Kubla Khan" all made their debuts in the artists' dreams. Your dreams, too, form

a body of original work that may be converted into art. One way to mine the creativity of your nightlife is to write out your dream as a narrative, then choose the fifteen most striking words to use as the raw material of a poem. Oneiric poets say that haikus seem to be the best poetic form for dreamstuff—though if you're really ambitious you could try your hand at a Petrarchan sonnet. A single haiku is composed of three lines, of five, seven, and five syllables, respectively. Here is an example of a haiku by a participant (Fern LeBurkien) at a recent dream poetry workshop:

Dear Trouble Maker,
Please don't get arrested
while I eat breakfast.

TURN YOUR DREAM INTO A PAINTING
●

Some dreamers like to capture the meaning and mood of a dream in a single powerful image and then turn this image into a painting or sketch. Dream researcher Henry Reed suggests making collages from photographs cut out of magazines and creating "psychic landscapes" inspired by dream themes. Even if your dabbling doesn't remotely resemble a Matisse, the process of drawing potent dream images or symbols will help clarify your feelings and give you the psychic distance to see your dreamscapes in a new way.

OKAY, *DON'T* GET THEE TO A NUNNERY—I WAS JUST KIDDING
●

If you work with a dream group (See "Dream Networks," page 94) you can convert your dream into a "mythic drama," in the words of Strephon Kaplan-Williams. Assuming the roles of the various characters in your dream, group members can reenact several dream scenes. Kaplan-Williams suggests that this drama "embody a strong resolution, whether such a resolution is in the dream or not."

Don't leave the characters hanging over a precipice, and don't let the drama end in a Shakespearean mass murder/ suicide, either. "Hamlet would not have died tragically," notes Kaplan-Williams, "if he had had the capacity to bring creative resolution . . . to what were admittedly terrible circumstances." He certainly should have *tried* to talk through his feelings with Ophelia.

WITH • A • LITTLE • HELP • FROM • MY • FRIENDS

Dreaming used to be a solitary activity, but not anymore. Just as yuppies compulsively "network" for career advancement, so do many dreamworkers network for psychospiritual advancement. As Jack Kerouac put it, "All human beings are also dream beings. Dreaming ties all mankind together." If dreams constitute a second, parallel life, why should we live that life like hermits? Why not get down and party in our dreamlife, form Rotary Clubs and scout groups, kaffeeklatsches and literary societies in the great sea of the collective unconscious? Here are some of the possibilities:

HE AIN'T HEAVY; HE'S MY DREAM BUDDY
•

A dream partner is simply someone with whom you regularly share your dreams. You may already have one. A close friend is an ideal dream partner because he or she already knows your life story inside out and can point out things like, "That gargoyle sounds a lot like that creep you dated in college." A dream buddy is good for helping you spot patterns and insights you might otherwise miss. He/she can guide you to reenter last night's dream and interview you about the terrain so that you notice things you didn't before. After a while, you may discover that you and your partner are having similar dreams on the same night or that recurrent plots, motifs, characters, or images are popping up like overexposed TV actors in both your nocturnal dramas.

One way to share dreams is to "adopt" each other's dreams, suggests dreamworker Jack Maguire. Simply take turns pretending the other's dream happened to you. Discuss what

HOW TO RECALL YOUR DREAMS

Although we have four or five vivid, technicolor dreams every night, most of us remember only isolated bits and snatches. Sometimes a dream's "soul" is lost as soon as you jump into the shower. Following are some basic memory tricks dreamworkers use to help preserve those ephemeral nighttime dramas.

1. Program yourself. Make a commitment to remember your dreams. Your ability to remember is proportional to your interest and motivation.

2. Decide how you will record your dreams: with a tape recorder, a dream diary, or just a few impressions jotted on a notepad. The key is to put that recorder, diary, or notepad right next to your bed so you can use it immediately after waking.

3. Before falling asleep, focus your attention on remembering and understanding your dreams. This ritual can take the form of a positive affirmation ("I will remember my dreams") that you repeat like a mantra as you drift off to sleep. Or it can be more elaborate if you like.

4. If you wake up during the night and remember a dream, make sure to write down key words or images. That way, you'll have enough information to jog your memory and reconstruct your dream in the morning.

5. Record your dreams *immediately* after waking. Don't procrastinate! That drowsy hypnopompic state is fertile ground for dream recall. Keep your eyes shut so you're not distracted. Search your mind for dream images and then write them down. Detailed description is crucial for later interpretation.

6. If you can't recall any dreams, try lying in bed in the same position you use for sleeping. This often sparks a dream memory. Ask yourself questions to prompt your memory. How did you feel upon awakening? What is the dream setting: a familiar or unfamiliar spot? Who are the chief characters: Are they people you know, or do they resemble people in your life? Go through a list of important people in your life; chances are one of them was a player in the dream. What is the basic "script"? Is it reminiscent of any real-life experience?

7. If you still have trouble remembering your dreams, try a few cheap tricks. Set your alarm clock ten minutes ahead. You may wake up right in mid-dream, since the longest REM (dreaming) period comes at the end of your last sleep cycle, just before you wake up and start to worry about driving the carpool. If you're really gung-ho, drink liquids just before retiring and let your full bladder wake you up during the night.

8. Be sure you're getting an adequate supply of B vitamins in your diet. These bolster the brain biochemistry associated with dreaming and also help you deal with stress. (Well, that's what they say.)

9. Share your dreams with a friend or loved one. Join a dream group. The social reinforcement of sharing your dream with others often aids recall.

• KEEPING A DREAM JOURNAL

The hardest part of keeping a dream journal is making yourself do it. Once the dreamworld starts to open up, you'll probably feel more inspired to continue. Dreamworkers agree that you can learn more from a body of dreams than from a single dream. Senseless and disjointed though they may seem at first, dreams are not a random patchwork of images. They are a meaningful series of messages from the deeper self, and they serve a vital psychological function by bringing hidden desires, hopes, and fears to your awareness. Whenever you read over the dreams in your journal, try to fathom their meaning to *you*. Assume that your self sent you these communiqués for a reason.

Pay particular attention to any recurrent themes or images, which tend to be laden with significance. Begin to cross-reference subject matter, symbols, themes, or characters that make frequent appearances. Notice the evolution of certain themes. For example, I (J.H.) once had a series of dreams of giving birth. In the beginning I'd be in labor and then discover that I wasn't really pregnant after all. In subsequent dreams I would give birth, but the baby would vanish immediately, and I would find myself frantically dialing wrong numbers trying to track it down. Once I proudly gave birth to wolf cubs. I have no idea what this meant, but it probably was significant. (Maybe my writings are the literary equivalent of feral children, like the Wild Boy of Aveyron.) "If you become familiar with the symbols and themes in your dreams," says dreamworker Jill Gregory, "you will be more likely to recognize their significance in your waking life. And you'll even recognize them as dream symbols while still asleep."

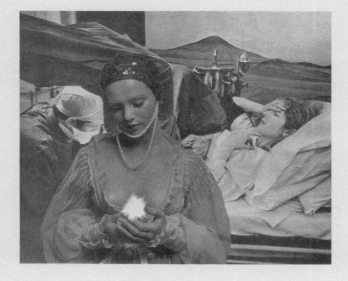

his or her dream means to you in the context of your life, and how you interpret the imagery and symbols.

You can also interview each other. By asking you probing, Ted Koppel–like questions, your buddy prompts you to re-create your dreams in as much detail as possible. Gayle Delaney offers some helpful hints for treading lightly into someone else's dreamworld without distorting it with your own preconceptions. Always ask the dreamer to describe dream scenes in his own words; never make assumptions even if the objects are commonplace. It is best to pretend you are from the planet Twylo and know nothing about forks, cats, or Kentucky Fried Chicken. If your partner dreams of being in a room with an overwhelming scent of lilacs, ask her: "Is there a window? What is a lilac? Do lilacs have any associations with past events or people you know?" The dreamer will be forced to discuss her personal understanding of those images, and you will also gain a different perspective on your own dream symbols.

Access: The following books contain valuable tips for dream-partner work: *Night and Day* by Jack Maguire (Simon & Schuster/Fireside); *Living Your Dreams* by Gayle Delaney (Harper & Row); *The Dream Workbook* by Jill Morris (Fawcett Crest). (See "The Complete Dreamworker's Library" at the end of this chapter.)

A BRIEF DICTIONARY OF DREAM SYMBOLS

It is plain foolishness to believe in ready-made, systematic guides to dream interpretation, as if one could simply buy a reference book and look up a particular symbol." Uh-oh. That caveat comes from the Great Dreamer himself, Carl Jung. Of course, every symbol in your dream belongs to you and you alone, and no one else—not even a great Jungian sage—can interpret it for you. Your friend's dream of falling downstairs may refer to problems in her marriage, while yours may mean you should get your banisters repaired. Nevertheless, everyone likes a nice ready-made systematic guide now and then, so here is our not-to-be-taken-too-seriously, proceed-at-your-own-risk glossary of common dream themes and symbols.

Cars Dream cars often stand for the dreamer's body (the physical "vehicle") or the personality style he or she uses to get around in the world. If you find yourself driving a pink Cadillac, a burgundy TransAm with racing stripes, or a beat-up pickup truck in your dreams, your subconscious is probably trying to tell you something about your public persona.

Death Dreams of death don't usually refer to the Grim Reaper. More often they indicate the end of one phase of life and the transition to a new one. Sometimes such a dream means you wish to be rid of a certain situation or that a dysfunctional or outmoded part of your psyche has to die. It may also signify a desire to connect with a higher wisdom. Dreams of other people dying may indicate that some concern symbolized by that person is losing its hold on your life.

Exams In the film *Risky Business* the Tom Cruise character, a proto-yuppie obsessed with getting into Princeton, has a recurrent nightmare about taking the SATs. He arrives so late he has only five minutes to take the six-hour exam. "My life is over," he moans. "I'll never get into college." Even Dr. Freud had examination dreams, which for some reason haunt the human unconscious long after blue books have become a dim memory. We ourselves have a recurrent nightmare that it's just before finals and we're hit with the sickening

realization that there is one course we forgot about all semester. These dreams usually occur when you're on the verge of a major decision, say dream-workers. You are being examined in some way and fear you won't pass muster. If you have recurrent dreams of taking the civil service exam, it may mean you have a secret desire to handle many mindless government forms in triplicate.

Falling Dreams of falling typically signify a fear of falling from grace, a loss of control, or a steep plunge into the unknown. They may also symbolize excitement or emotional turmoil, a feeling of not being "grounded" in a certain situation, or a desire to escape "upright" adult responsibilities. The "fall" can take many forms. When a college instructor who was in the midst of a tenure fight dreamt he fell down a flight of stairs, his "fall" referred to his anxiety about lost status. On the other hand, a teenage girl who was raised in a strict Catholic family had a series of falling dreams after she became sexually intimate with her boyfriend. Her dream reflected her deep-seated guilt about falling from a moral standard.

Finding valuables It's quite common to dream of winning the lottery or finding a cache of Kruger-rands. Normally, these dreams are pure wish fulfillment and occur when we're short of cash. But they sometimes have a deeper meaning. Especially when you're going through a crisis, a dream of finding lost valuables may be your psyche's way of reassuring you that you possess inner resources.

Flying Dreams of flying through the air indicate either a feeling of being "on a high" or of struggling to overcome obstacles and "rise above" misfortune. To interpret such a dream, analyze how you feel. Are you elated? Or is the dream fraught with anxiety and peril?

Houses Pay attention to architectural style here. If you dream of being in a Victorian house, your subconscious may be needling you about some of the Victorian attitudes you hold, according to Gayle Delaney. (If you find yourself in a Bauhaus setting, maybe your psyche is just a bit too stark and minimalistic?) Particular rooms in a house "often suggest certain areas of concern to the dreamer," Delaney notes. Bedrooms may refer to sex or private issues, living rooms to the family or living conditions, basements or attics to unconscious or rejected parts of the psyche.

Losing teeth The ancient Greeks thought a dream of losing a tooth foretold the death of a loved one. Today's dreamworkers believe such dreams may signify the loss of power or potency, fear of growing up or growing old. On the other hand, they may stand for transformation, death and rebirth, or time. Dreams of getting teeth extracted may mean that something rotten, some obstacle, is being removed from your life. Dreaming of getting your front tooth knocked out may refer to a fear of becoming ugly or undesirable. If you continually dream of periodontal work, you should probably pay more attention to your flossing style.

Losing valuables These dreams frequently have a literal meaning. Your subconscious may be telling you you *did* lose something of value but were too preoccupied to notice. On the symbolic level, dreams of lost valuables may suggest lost *values.* One screenwriter struggled for years before finally selling a script. It became a hit movie and he was swamped with offers—at which point he had a series of dreams about losing things he treasured: a collection of jazz records, his books, his home.

These dreams symbolized his fear of being seduced by Hollywood superficiality and abandoning the conventional values of his upbringing, which he truly cherished.

Missing trains, planes, etc. Typically those dreams of getting stuck in traffic en route to the airport symbolize the frustrations in our lives. But the resolution of these dreams can be significant. One friend of ours, a free-lance writer, had accepted more work than she could handle. One night she dreamt that she missed her flight to Europe and could not take a later flight because she had a special discount fare. The following night she

dreamt she was able to take a later flight after all. She interpreted this to mean that she, and not her editors, had set impossible standards for herself. She asked for (and was granted) an extension on one assignment, thereby relieving her work pressure.

Nudity If you dream of walking around with no clothes on, you are obviously a shameless pervert. No, actually, dreamworkers say that the classic "Oh my God, I forgot to get dressed" dream may have several different interpretations. It may reflect conflicts about sex, such as guilt feelings or self-doubt about sexual prowess. Nakedness may also indicate vulnerability, fear of exposure, or a desire to shed conventions and reveal oneself. Again, the dream context will provide clues. Say you dream you're walking down the street naked and feel somewhat embarrassed, yet no one else notices. The message here is that you have a secret you're afraid of disclosing, but it's really no big deal. But if your dream arouses anxiety or anger, you may be in the middle of a threatening situation. Or perhaps you feel inferior; being naked exposes your

shortcomings (and possibly the cellulite on your thighs).

Water Water dreams such as a pleasurable moonlight swim often refer to your sex life. The type of body of water—ocean, river, bay, or pond— will have a bearing on your interpretation. If you dream of picking your way painfully across icy tundra, perhaps you need to have a little talk with Dr. Ruth. Water in dreams may also symbolize highly unsettled, fluid emotions or a sense of being out of your element, "drowning" or "treading water" in some aspect of your life.

DREAM NETWORKS

●

On the Temple of Konumba in Egypt there is a hiero-glyphic depicting what may have been the first dream net-work: a group of people sharing their dreams with a high priest. Today there is no shortage of high priests or dream networks for dreamers who believe that ten psyches are better than one. The bible of dream networkers is the *Dream Network Bulletin,* a chatty, grass-roots newsletter that links some 2,000 dreamworkers around the world. Ideally, a dream network consists of four to six members who meet regularly at least twice a month for two-hour sessions. Some dream societies are large, open-ended, ever-shifting com-munities like the Metro D.C. Dream Community in Wash-ington, D.C. Others are informal get-togethers of a few long-time friends who share their dreams. Some networks may even be geographically separated and "meet" via the U.S. mail: Members send in their dreams to a leader, who collects them and adds commentaries. "In dreams, time and space don't matter," observes veteran networker Barbara Shor of New York City.

Group input can let you see your dream in a context you would not have considered by yourself. Your fellow dream-workers can discern patterns that escape you; they can see your blind spots and help you overcome the natural tendency to rationalize. Many exercises that you do with a dream partner work even better with a group. One popular practice is to have group members act out episodes from your dream or carry on dialogues with dream characters. Beyond that, having a group instantly opens up a whole realm of dream-related adventures like telepathy, dream healing, and "shared dreaming."

Access: For information about dream networks contact *Dream Network Bulletin,* P.O. Box 1321, Port Townsend, WA 98368. Some books that offer a wealth of group-dreamwork techniques are: *Dream Work* by Jeremy Taylor, *The Dream Workbook* by Jill Morris, and *The Jungian-Senoi Dreamwork Manual* by Strephon Kaplan-Williams. (See "The Complete Dreamworker's Library" at the end of this chapter.)

TAKE MY DREAM—PLEASE

●

One collective dreamwork strategy adopted by many dream groups is the Experiential Dream Group. "Essentially, each member of the group plays with the dreamer's images," explains the technique's creator, psychoanalyst Montague Ullman, M.D., founder of the legendary dream laboratory at Maimonides Medical Center in Brooklyn. First, a dreamer recounts his dream in its entirety. When he's done, the group may ask him to clarify hazy details or elaborate on certain points. Then each member of the group adopts the dream as his or her own, discussing any feelings, associations, or images the dream conjures up. The original dreamer then reacts to what he has heard and tells the group what he has learned from the exercise. Dreamworkers say this technique can open the gates of the unconscious, unleashing a flood

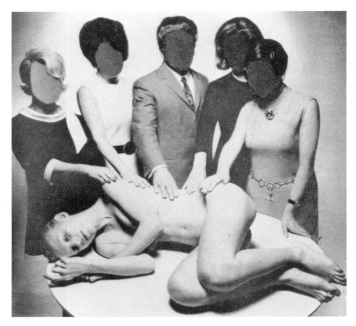

of associations, interpretations, and ideas—often weeks after the exercise.

Access: For information about Experiential Dream Group Leadership Training Workshops contact: Dr. Montague Ull-man, 55 Orlando Ave., Ardsley, NY 10502. Phone: (914) 693-0156.

SEE YOU IN BAGHDAD

●

What's the difference between a dream group and a shared, or mutual, dream? You might say it's a question of locale. Dream groups generally meet in somebody's living room, whereas dream *sharers* rendezvous inside the dream itself.

"I had always believed that dreams were a fine and private place," recalls Barbara Shor, the founder of New York City's Dreamgates Community. But that notion was "shattered" by a group-dreaming experiment a few years back. Shor was one of twenty dreamworkers from the U.S., Canada, and Europe who agreed to dream "together" in their separate homes on the last Saturday of each month, each time fo-cusing on a preselected subject. Afterward, they'd receive a photocopy of everyone's dreams, along with a commentary on collective themes and "psychic hits." Soon they were dreaming in unison of floods, oceans, and tidal waves; on the same night several dreamers would see Irish curtains in their dreams or climb into the bowels of a dream mountain. Before long, they were "dreaming together" on nontarget nights, too. And that was just the beginning. In a subsequent dream group, Shor and a couple of fellow dreamers bumped into one another in a common dream setting. "Since then," she says, "we've shown up together in warehouses, helicop-ters, and restaurants, and have learned to recognize one another by our vibes when we don't resemble our waking selves."

Shor admits she finds this reality a bit creepy at times. "It's one thing to know intellectually that we're all connected

Barbara Shor

in the collective unconscious," she muses. "It's quite another to realize that tossed into one's personal dream dumpster are the thoughts, feelings, and memories of every other person on this planet." We'd be disturbed, too, at the prospect of receiving input from Muammar Qaddaffi's dreams or mingling with the effluvia of Morton Downey's unconscious. But if you're brave enough to entertain this possibility and wish to set up your own shared dream group, here's how Shor says to do it:

• Agree to meet in a dream on a specific night of the week or month for at least six sessions.
• Decide on the focus for your dreams and your dream meeting place.
• Record your dreams, title and date them, and send them off immediately to the commentary editor. Set firm deadlines.
• Choose one person as editor, or take turns writing the commentary on shared themes and "psychic hits" (picking up similar places, people, ideas, events, symbols, or even colors from one another's dreams).
• Commentaries and photocopies of dreams from one session should reach dreamers before the next target night.
• Search the group's dreams for signs of progress or blockage, and for the inspiration for the next target subject or dream rendezvous point.

Access: You can contact Barbara Shor at: Dreamgates, P.O. Box 20219, Cathedral Finance Station, New York, NY 10025-9992. As of this writing, former *Dream Network Bulletin* editor Linda Magallon is helping to assemble Mutual Dream Teams, who will undertake six-month dream explorations together. For information contact Linda Magallon, 1083 Harvest Meadow Court, San Jose, CA 95136.

THE DREAM HELPER CEREMONY
•

This experiment in group telepathy has been used very successfully at the Metro D.C. Dream Community and other dream networks. It was developed by Henry Reed, Ph.D., a dreamworker and metaphysically oriented psychologist with the Edgar Cayce–inspired Atlantic University in Virginia Beach, Virginia. In the Dream Helper Ceremony, a dream group decides to dream for one member who is in the midst of a crisis (but doesn't tell the group what the crisis is). Each dreamer then uses dream-incubation techniques to dedicate one night's dreams to this troubled "target" person.

"The next morning," says Reed, "almost all the dreamers believe they have failed. It's natural to assume that dreams are only personal." When the dreamers begin to share the fruits of their night's labors, however, common themes surface, and the target person "usually recognizes something of personal significance in every dream," according to Reed. In one experiment a group dreamed for a woman named Debbie. The next morning, several "helpers" reported dreaming of black and white symbols—vanilla and chocolate, a black knight in the town of Whitehall—get it? It transpired that Debbie was in conflict over a contemplated interracial relationship.

Access: Reed is happy to teach this technique to any dream group in the country. For information contact Henry Reed, 503 Lake Drive, Virginia Beach, VA 23451.

ESALEN ON THE VOLGA
•

Charles Upton of San Rafael, California, believes that glasnost begins in dreams. For the past several years, Upton, the author of *Gate of Horn: A Global Issue Dream Work*, has been building a "U.S.-Soviet Dream Bridge" by recruiting a network of dreamers in the U.S. and the Soviet Union to focus their dreams on world peace. He is currently translating and organizing the dream data he's received from a psychological research group in Moscow in order to search for similarities and "synchronicities." So far he's found that American and Russian dreamers share a fondness for log cabins, and that members of the dream network on both sides of the Iron Curtain dreamt of a farmhouse bathed in golden light. But that was before the unpleasantness in Lithuania.

Access: For more information contact Charles Upton, 28 Marine Dr., San Rafael, CA 94901.

DO YOU SUFFER FROM THIN BOUNDARIES?

Do you have nightmares more than two or three times a week? Are you frequently pursued by Nazis, Colombian drug lords, or other bad guys, beaten, tortured, shot, stabbed, and mutilated in your dreams? If so, you probably suffer from thin boundaries.

So says Ernest Hartmann, a psychiatrist at Tufts University School of Medicine and author of *The Nightmare*. Hartmann studied nearly a hundred people afflicted with frequent, extremely vivid, grotesque nightmares. After in-depth interviews and a battery of tests, he determined that these people's most striking trait was something he calls thin boundaries. "When I say boundaries I mean boundaries in many senses, including ego boundaries, interpersonal boundaries, the boundary between

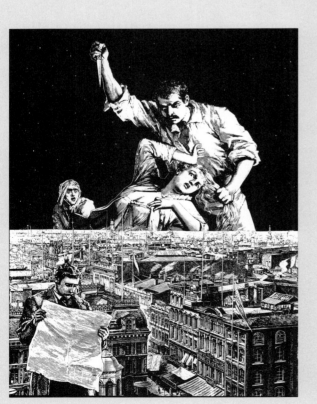

fantasy and reality, and even sleep-wake boundaries," he explains. "They do not keep things pigeonholed . . . they let things through." They are psychically porous, you might say.

Most people realize they're awake within minutes of hearing the lite-FM station blare "You Light up My Life" over the clock radio. Not thin-boundary types. They often remain groggy and existentially uncertain for an hour or more. Sometimes they "awake" from one dream into another dream. And because their "ego boundaries" are paper thin, says Hartmann, they "allow sexual and aggressive material to enter into consciousness more than most of us."

Using his boundary questionnaire, Hartmann has pinpointed some twenty areas in which heavy-duty nightmare sufferers exhibit thinner boundaries than other people. Because their interpersonal boundaries are so permeable, these people are unusually open, sensitive, trusting, and defenseless, according to Hartmann. They are apt to form "overly close, merging relationships" that typically end painfully or ungracefully. All describe themselves as "unusual," "different from others," more "sensitive" and "fragile" than other people. But having thin boundaries isn't all bad. "People with thin boundaries know themselves in some ways better than other people," says Hartmann. "They also tend to be more creative, and I think they enjoy sex more than people with very thick boundaries."

WHY THEY MAKE BETTER SHIATSU MASSAGE THERAPISTS THAN COMPTROLLERS:

•On psychological tests thin-boundary types studied by Hartmann tended toward schizophrenic or "schizotypal" characteristics, such as "loose and tangential thinking." (Hey, what's wrong with that? We've made a living out of loose and tangential thinking.) On the other hand, they were *not* prone to neurotic traits, phobic or anxiety states, or obsessive-compulsive disorders.

DIGITAL · DREAMS

Once you start keeping a dream journal, it won't be long before you've got several notebooks crammed with scrawled notes from your unconscious. Archetypal symbols may take over your sock drawer and crowd that valuable space under your bed. Now, when was it that you had that weird earthquake dream—or was it a tsunami? Was it before or after your divorce? You'll wish you had a qualified librarian to keep track of all dreams between 1987–1990, to correlate apocalypse imagery from different dreams, to slog through all those nearly illegible texts for Wise Old Woman archetypes. The answer may be to computerize your dreamlife. Here's what's around:

THE DREAM MACHINE
•

This program, developed by Psychological Psoftware, has an unslick, Ma-and-Pa texture to it—we're not talking MIT artificial intelligence lab here—but it provides some basic dream-interpretation aids to get you started. First, the following menu appears on the screen:

```
1 WHAT'S IT ALL ABOUT?
2 WHAT MY DREAMS MEAN
3 WHAT IS MY DREAM TELLING ME?
4 INTERPRETER FOR 3
5 UNDERSTANDING MY DREAM IMAGES
6 UNDERSTANDING MY DREAM DYNAMICS
7 THE DREAM DICTIONARY
8 THE DREAM LOG
9 FILE DELETER (not on IBM)
Q QUIT
```

In section <3> you answer a series of multiple-choice questions designed to evaluate the significance of a particular dream in the context of your life. When you're done, the program will run the ANALYSIS INTERPRETER, a digital dream doctor that sometimes repeats itself. "The reason is that whatever issues you are working on in your dreams will come up over and over again," the manual explains. "There may be different symbols, different dreams, but the message will be the same." In <5> the program "gestalts your dream images." We're not quite sure what "gestalt" means as a verb, but the manual promises you'll be "amazed at the results." The Dream Dictionary lists 202 common dream meanings, and The Dream Log will help

•Many of them saw "auras or emanations from other people," though they didn't necessarily commune with 7,000-year-old spirit guides.
•Alcohol or drugs, even small quantities of marijuana, caused them to suffer from paranoia, alienation, and bad trips.
•Apart from nightmares, all experienced "extremely vivid, lifelike, detailed dreams." Many of their dreams had odd characteristics, such as dreams within dreams and dreams in which they were not themselves, but were animals or people of the opposite sex.
•They had vivid memories of early childhood, of being one, two, or three years old.
•All had undergone an exceptionally stormy adolescence.
•None held ordinary, punch-the-clock jobs. "A number were musicians, painters, poets, writers, craftspersons, teachers, and therapists." Most saw themselves as rebels or outsiders.

Access: For more information about Hartmann's research read *The Nightmare* by Ernest Hartmann (Basic Books; paper $7.95).

you record and file your dreams. The program won't do any indexing or cross-referencing of dream symbols, however. It is available for IBM-PCs (No. 22801) or Apple IIs (No. 22802) for $49.95.

Access: The Dream Machine is available from Psychological Psoftware, 312 Los Altos Dr., Aptos, CA 95003. Phone: (408) 688-6808. It can also be ordered through Mindware, 1803 Mission St., Suite 414, Santa Cruz, CA 95060. Phone: (800) 447-0477.

THE DREAM INDEX
•

This cross-referencing database program permits you to keep track of the contents of many dreams over time. The Dream Index, conceived by Tom and Cynthia Turich, a husband-and-wife team (he's a computer professor and she's a metaphysical writer), lets you do the following: (1) Itemize the contents of a dream in up to ten categories. You can use the categories already established in the program, such as "characters" and "colors," or assign your own. (2) Flag up to five special characteristics of each dream, such as out-of-body experiences or precognitive "hits." (3) Quickly scan your records for dream dates or special attributes. The Dream Index is currently available only for the Apple II series, but an IBM version is in the works. Price: $45.

Access: The Dream Index, 7301 Reynolds St., Pittsburgh, PA 15208. Phone: (412) 241-7885.

((DREAM ON!))
•

Yes, that's what it's called, and the program's creator, Dennis Schmidt, is most emphatic on this point, double parentheses and all. A computer programmer and compulsive journal keeper whose personal journals fill over 20,000 pages and contain records of more than 7,000 dreams, Schmidt had for years meditated on computerized methods of indexing and retrieving this dreamstuff. "Journals are a great way to record unstructured information," he notes. "But it may not be easy to find what you want later." Appropriately enough, the design of ((Dream On!))—described as "a flexible hypertext program designed to assist in any kind of journal work"—crystallized in a dream. "It makes it easy for the journal keeper to record and later find and use associations," he explains. The program is also designed to be flexible enough so you can organize your "own personal symbol system on the screen," clusters of key words, objects, terms, concepts, and types of conflict, for example. One dream about a lost watch can be linked to a similar dream by telling the computer, "Show me 'wallet.' " ((Dream On!)) runs on a Commodore Amiga computer and uses the Intuition (window and mouse) user interface. An upgraded version is in the works. Price information is not available at this writing.

Access: For information about ((Dream On!)) contact: Dennis Schmidt, 45 Ransom Rd., Falmouth, MA 02540.

DREAMWORK STACKS
•

Like many dreamworkers, Sarah Lillie of Corvallis, Oregon, longed to bring some order to her lush dream life, so she created her own computerized storage and retrieval system, using the Hypercard system on her Apple Macintosh. So successful was it that she is now marketing it for others as Dream Stacks, described as a "unique filing system for dreams and personal symbols using a Macintosh with Hypercard." The program includes a Dream Index Card system for recording and filing dreams, a personalized Dream Symbol Dictionary, and a Haiku Page. The Hypercard Paint capability can be used to illustrate dreams.

Access: Contact Sarah Lillie, 4311 NW Elmwood Dr., Corvallis, OR 97330. Phone: (503) 758-1324. A disk with DreamWork Stacks costs $10.

COMPUTERIZING THE COLLECTIVE UNCONSCIOUS
•

Gary Rogers, a computer type from Abilene, Texas, dreams of creating a National Dream Center. "The idea," he tells us, "is to collect a large number of dreams from different people at a particular time, collate them, and scan them for common images. Dreams contain all sorts of information, some of which is valuable and some of which is 'noise.' So you apply a sophisticated filtering technique to pick out the common themes from the noise. Then you'd corollate those themes with events on a global or national level. There may be some predictive value there." In other words, how many people in greater Los Angeles have earthquake dreams on, say, December 12, 1991, and is there, in fact, an earthquake shortly afterward?

Access: The National Dream Center is only an idea at this stage, but people interested in networking with Gary Rogers can contact him at: 1033 Piedmont, Abilene, TX 79601.

LUCID · DREAMS

I f dreams are messages from your psyche to your conscious mind, lucid dreams are a way to fire back a response. The first complete written record of lucid dreaming was a Tibetan Buddhist text called "Doctrine of the Dream State." Tibetan yogis taught that recognizing the illusory nature of dreams helps us to recognize that reality, too, is maya, or illusion, but that's the advanced course and we're getting ahead of our story.

At its simplest level a lucid dream is just the sensation that what you're experiencing is a dream. Something odd about your surroundings may make your dream ego say, "Hey, wait a minute. This must be a dream." Perhaps you notice you're wearing a T-shirt in the arctic or that you're flying over Cleveland and you're not in a 747. In one of my few spontaneous lucid dreams, I (J.H.) suspected I was in an alternate reality when I found myself "ice-skating" through winding, cobblestoned streets. (Lucid-dream researcher Stephen LaBerge calls these types of dream illogic "lucidity clues.") At its most sophisticated, lucid dreaming is total control over the dreamworld. You can fly, discourse with Plato, visit distant parts of the solar system, ride on a dolphin's back, make out with Madonna or Mel Gibson. If you don't like where your dream is headed, you can change the plot as easily as switching channels. In other words, you are "awake" inside a dream.

LaBerge and other modern lucid dream researchers have devised a number of excellent techniques for inducing and maintaining a lucid dream. It takes practice, and there are many degrees and gradations of lucidity. One lucid dreaming researcher, Jayne Gackenbach, has been studying an ultralucid state known as "witnessing." The star witness is a practitioner of Transcendental Meditation (TM) who claims to be "inwardly awake" at all times—even during deeper (nondreaming) stages of sleep. EEG experiments reportedly support his claim. Aficionados say that lucidity permits dreamers to confront and transform their problems and hangups, tap into their creativity, and harness their healing powers. The control you exercise over your dreams will spill over into your daytime life, too. One seven-year-old girl had a recurring nightmare of being chased by a shark. She was terrified the shark would eat her. LaBerge advised her to just climb on the shark's back and take a ride the next time she had the dream. She did, and never had that dream again.

"You can train yourself to have lucid dreams—it is a learned skill," says Patricia Garfield, author of *Creative Dreaming*. "But once you've mastered it, you can do whatever you wish to do in your dreams. You can practice your skills and they will carry over to your waking state. You decide what is important to you and dream on it." Here are a few of the tools and resources available to lucid dreamers:

THE LUCIDITY INSTITUTE
•

Founded by lucid-dreaming mogul Stephen LaBerge, the Lucidity Institute conducts training programs in conscious dreaming and publishes a quarterly newsletter, *NightLight*. This newsletter features first-person accounts of lucid dreaming, Q and A's, research updates, tips for recording, listing, and classifying lucid dreams (using a "Dream Recall Scale," a "Dreamsign Inventory," and so on), and reports on Lucidity Institute activities. Satellite centers of the institute are planned for Los Angeles and San Francisco in 1990; soon it may achieve global domination.

Access: The Lucidity Institute, P.O. Box 2364, Stanford, CA 94309. For $35 ($25 for students) you can become an associate member of the Lucidity Institute, which entitles you to a subscription to *NightLight* and discounts on books and products. For bigger bucks you get a free lucid-dream training workshop plus other opportunities to participate in the institute's activities.

FUNNY GOGGLES
•

Maybe you're right in the middle of a dream when you notice that the big glockenspiel in the center of your Viennese dreamscape is *blinking* at you. "Hmm," you say to yourself. "Wasn't I supposed to remember something?" The source of the blinking is back there in the real world along with your Ralph Lauren duvet cover and your digital alarm clock. When you went to bed you donned the DreamLight™, a high-tech sleep mask designed by LaBerge. The mask is outfitted with sensors that detect REM activity and trigger a gently flashing red light at your eyelids as soon as you start dreaming. This is a cue to remember you're dreaming—the first step of lucidity. You can test this hypothesis by putting your hands through a wall or trying to levitate. Once you recognize you're dreaming, the dreamworld is your oyster. You can begin to apply the lessons you've been learning in the lucidity workshop (see page 101) and try out fun stuff like flying and sex with strangers. (Matter of fact, you'd *better* score in your dreams. A real live date may not be turned on by your flashing goggles.)

Access: At present the DreamLight™ may be obtained only by participating in a Basic Skills Workshop given by the Lucidity Institute. (See address above.)

HOW • TO • DREAM • LUCIDLY

Stephen LaBerge

According to Stephen LaBerge, lucid dreaming is a learned skill, not a mysterious gift from the gods. To help the novice become lucid, he has developed an exercise called MILD (mnemonic induction of lucid dreams). It combines memory aids and autosuggestions to help the dreamer (1) recognize when she is dreaming, and (2) remain conscious and prolong the lucid state as long as possible. The technique works best when practiced in the early morning hours during the deepest and longest stage of REM sleep.

1. Program yourself to recall your dreams. Before going to bed, tell yourself you will wake up after each of your dreams throughout the night.
2. Remember your dream. When you wake up from a dream, go over it several times in your mind until you have memorized every detail.
3. Focus on your goal. While you are drifting off to sleep, repeat to yourself, "Next time I'm dreaming, I want to remember to recognize I'm dreaming."
4. Picture yourself becoming lucid. Imagine being back inside the dream you have just reviewed, but this time visualize yourself being aware that you are dreaming.
5. Repeat steps three and four until you feel you've fixed your intention indelibly in your mind. Or until you fall asleep.

If the MILD method fails to induce lucid dreams, lucid-dream researcher Jayne Gackenbach—the coauthor of a new book on lucid dreaming called *Control Your Dreams*—suggests a more complex, and often more effective, technique. This induction method was first formulated by Paul Tholey, a German sports physiologist who has worked with lucid dreams since 1969.

1. Five to ten times during the day, ask yourself, "Am I dreaming or not?"
2. When you ask this question, visualize intently that you are in a dream and that everything around you—the people, the furniture, your body, the commercials for oat bran—is just a dream. (This will surely be useful if you ever have a tax audit.)
3. At the same time concentrate not only on what is happening now but also on the past. Do you remember anything unusual, or do you suffer from memory lapses?
4. Get in the habit of asking yourself, "Am I dreaming?" in all situations that are reminiscent of dreams; in other words, whenever something unlikely happens, or when you experience overwhelmingly powerful emotions.
5. Do you have a recurring dream event or subject—a fearful experience, say, or the repeated appearance of an Akita pup? During the day, ask yourself, "Am I dreaming?" whenever you feel threatened or when you see an Akita relieving itself on a palm tree.
6. Do you have particular dream experiences, such as floating or flying, that rarely occur while you're awake? During the day imagine that you're floating or flying—or whatever the dream experience is—reminding yourself meanwhile, "This is only a dream."
7. Before falling asleep, tell yourself you are going to be conscious or aware in your dream. This technique is especially effective if you wake up early in the morning during your final REM stage and then fall back to sleep.
8. Resolve to carry out a particular action in your dream. Any action will do; the key is to teach yourself to do it at will.

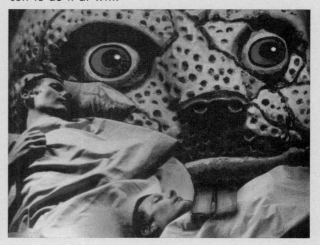

BOOT CAMP FOR LUCID DREAMERS
●

One dreamer confided that he liked to glide in the lotus position above a moonlit cloudbank. A woman asked about the meaning of the universe in a dream and was taken on a tour of distant galaxies. They were some of the success stories at a recent LaBerge-designed lucid dream workshop, a boot camp for "oneironauts." After the first session, participants get to take home a DreamLight™ and begin performing daily and nightly rituals, filling out questionnaires, whispering induction phrases, and wearing goggles to bed. During the day, they practice associating flashing lights with the question: "Is this a dream?" They master "reality testing," procedures for determining whether they are really in the housewares section of K mart or just dreaming of dozens of discounted blenders. (Hint: One way to distinguish between reality and a dream is to read a page from a book or magazine twice. If you're in a dream, the words will get scrambled as soon as you look away. Also, scan the scene for flashing lights, which could be the DreamLight™ trying to break through the walls of your dream.)

Lucidity is a fragile state. One way to prolong it when you do achieve it, according to LaBerge, is to spin like a top in your dream. "In the fourth week," recounts writer Howard Rheingold of his experience at a lucidity workshop, "I dreamed that I was being transported toward a group of whirling dervishes, who were twirling around with blankets in their hands. Somebody handed me a blanket. Then the entire scene started flashing. Realizing that the flashing was the DreamLight, I said to myself, 'So this is a dream!'—only to awaken before I could start spinning myself."

Access: The Lucidity Institute's Basic Skills Training Workshops are held regularly in Boston, New York, Chicago, Los Angeles, and San Francisco. At this writing, the cost of the course and the number of sessions are in flux. For information contact: Lucidity Institute, P.O. Box 2364, Stanford, CA 94309.

LUCID DREAM BOOT CAMP II
●

"The Art & Practice of Lucid Dreaming" is a six-week intensive lucid-dreaming workshop run by two LaBerge protégés, Fariba Bogzaran and Daryl E. Hewitt. Bogzaran is a lucid dream–inspired artist and sleep-lab technician, and Hewitt "is celebrated for having lucid dreams of a trancendentally spiritual nature and holds the record for the longest lucid dream ever monitored by LaBerge," according to *Life* magazine. We don't know if this workshop will turn you into a record-holding, transcendental lucid dreamer, but it promises to teach you "state-of-the-art practices for induction of lucid dreams," as well as some basics of shamanism and mystical experiences. "Sometimes I think of our endeavors as developing the technology of mystical experience," Hewitt tells us.

Access: Contact: Daryl E. Hewitt, 4057 Carlisle Rd., Gardners, PA 17324. Phone: (717) 486-3870; or 290 Cabrillo, #5, San Francisco, CA 94121. Phone: (415) 752-6053.

THE LUCIDITY LETTER
●

If you subscribed to *The Lucidity Letter* you could be poring over subjects like "Mutual Lucid Dreaming," "From Lucid Dreaming to Pure Consciousness: A Conceptual Framework for the OBE, UFO Abduction and NDE Experience" and "Cognitive Dimensions of Dream Formation in Repetitive Nightmares of Refugees," while you eat your cornflakes. This lively, wide-ranging journal, edited by lucidity researcher Jayne Gackenbach, is the *WWD* of lucidity, a must-read for cognoscenti. It is published semiannually by the Lucidity Association, a nonprofit organization devoted to lucid-dreaming research and related phenomena.

Access: *The Lucidity Letter* is available through the Lucidity Association, 8703 109th St., Edmonton, Alberta, Canada T6G 2L5. An annual subscription (two issues) costs $25.

WHO'S LUCID AND WHO'S NOT?
●

Women and children seem to be more adept lucid dreamers than adult men. That's probably because children are more open and suggestible than adults, and women apparently possess the "hard wiring" in the brain necessary for lucid dreaming. Researchers have also found that people who meditate consistently report more lucid dreams than nonmeditators.

Recent studies by psychologist Jayne Gackenbach have turned up a constellation of personality traits typical of lucid dreamers. Those who readily wake up in their dreams are "internal risk takers," easy to hypnotize or tranquilize. They also exhibit a trendy quality known as "field independence," which means, for one thing, that they can tell whether a rod is parallel to a wall in spite of distorted-perspective clues. This indicates that, unlike Hugh Hefner, or Jim and Tammy Bakker, lucid dreamers have the ability to separate themselves from their surroundings. Lucid people also have good inner ear and body balance, which may explain their prowess at flying in dreams. But the single most powerful predictor of lucidity is the ability to remember dreams.

COULD DAN QUAYLE HAVE A LUCID DREAM?

We asked the experts whether anyone, even a seemingly nonlucid vice president, could have a lucid dream. We received the following answers:

Stephen LaBerge (Stanford, California): "It may be difficult to prove scientifically, but we haven't found any class of people who cannot do it. You have to work at it, record your dreams, and think about them. But there's nothing to prevent someone from dreaming lucidly. It's a very easy skill for children to develop, like language."

Harry Hunt (Brock University, St. Catherine's, Ontario): "Lucidity is a by-product of very high dream recall. There are techniques that seem to enhance the ability, but there are also some people for whom such efforts would be largely wasted. A vivid imagination and good spatial abilities can help."

Jayne Gackenbach (Edmonton, Alberta): "It's like any other skill. Some people have it; some don't. Techniques like working on increased dream recall, heightening the personal value of your dreams, can help. Regular practice that approximates meditation will make you more lucid. But this isn't something that can be learned with ease."

THE · BEST · BOOKS · AND · TAPES · ON · LUCID DREAMING

LUCID DREAMING: THE POWER OF BEING AWAKE AND AWARE IN YOUR DREAMS BY STEPHEN LABERGE

This is the book that launched the current wave of interest in lucid dreaming. The author, Stephen LaBerge, labored hard—with EEG machines and other cumbersome sleep-lab hardware—to bring respectability to a practice that used to be known mainly to table-tapping, turban-wearing Theosophists. This book is a readable account of the making of a new science, including the often astonishing feats of LaBerge's star "oneironauts," who were brave enough to donate their brain waves to science for hundreds of less-than-romantic nights at the Stanford University Sleep Lab. The text is also full of sound advice and practical tips on lucid dreaming.

Access: Published by Ballantine Books. Paper $3.95.

EXPLORING THE WORLD OF LUCID DREAMING BY STEPHEN LABERGE AND HOWARD RHEINGOLD

This new book is a practical guide for lucid dreamers based on LaBerge's research. It draws on the case histories of several thousand lucid dreamers who have learned to use their dream consciousness for resolving internal conflicts, harnessing creativity, enhancing spiritual growth, and healing.

Access: Published by Ballantine Books. $18.95.

CONTROL YOUR DREAMS BY JAYNE GACKENBACH AND JANE BOSVELD

Despite the awkwardness of being authored by two Janes, one of which is spelled differently, this new book is a must-have for any lucid-dream library. Gackenbach, a psychologist, and coauthor Bosveld examine the history and science of lucid dreaming from Tibetan Buddhist doctrines to modern experiments with galvanic skin responses. They suggest that lucid dreaming should be viewed as a by-product of evolving consciousness, and that "artificially inducing lucid dreaming" (as in shaking people awake in sleep labs, wearing lucid-dream goggles, and so on) may sometimes interrupt or distort a natural process. The book tells why women are neurologically hard-wired to lucid dream; how some lucid dreamers have progressed to an even more lucid state known as "witnessing"; what "dreaming Buddhas" do; how often lucid dreamers dream of sex and flying; how lucidity can be harnessed for healing; and much more. This is not a how-to manual but a comprehensive, readable journey into the parallel reality of conscious dreams.

Access: Published by Harper & Row. Hardcover $16.95.

CREATIVE DREAMING BY PATRICIA GARFIELD
•

It *looks* like a cheap dimestore psychic-phenomena paperback, but this interesting, accessible book was the first to popularize the phenomenon of consciousness during sleep. It imparts many invaluable tips for working creatively with your inner life during those eight hours of the day we normally write off.

Access: Published by Ballantine Books (1974). Paper $2.95.

THE SUN AND THE SHADOW BY KEN KELZER
•

The autobiographical tale of one man's adventures in lucidity. Kelzer, who trained for the priesthood before switching to psychotherapy, describes the spiritual and psychotherapeutic benefits of conscious dreaming.

Access: *The Sun and the Shadow* by Ken Kelzer is published by A.R.E. Press, Virginia Beach, VA. Phone: (800) 368-2727. Paper $9.95.

YOU ARE BECOMING VERY LUCID. . . .
•

Controlling Your Dreams is a taped lecture by Stephen LaBerge, in which he summarizes the history of lucid dreaming, offers case histories from his own dreams and those of his subjects, and guides the listener through the steps of lucid dream–induction techniques. He says the audiotape is "aimed at practical application for self-improvement and for dealing with specific dream situations like recurrent nightmares."

Access: The tape comes with a thirty-two page dream-control manual and is available for $9.95 from St. Martin's Press. Phone: (800) 325-5525. It can also be obtained through the Lucidity Institute for $9.95 plus $1.75 shipping and handling.

DREAMWARE:

TOOLS & RESOURCES FOR DREAMERS

NEOJUNGIAN SLUMBER PARTY
•

The high point of every serious dreamworker's social calendar is the annual conference of the Association for the Study of Dreams (ASD). Founded by dream researcher Gayle Delaney, the ASD is the first international organization devoted exclusively to the study of dreams, and it boasts an unusual degree of fraternization between professionals (with Ph.D.'s) and amateurs—something you won't find at the Chemical Engineering Society, for example. The organization puts out a bimonthly newsletter, serves as a clearinghouse for information on dreams, and provides networking links among dreamworkers in the U.S. and abroad. Everybody who's anybody in archetypes, dream precognition, or lucidity makes the scene at the five-day annual conference, which typically features dream-sharing breakfasts, experiments in shared dreaming and "experiential shamanism"

CONTROLLING YOUR DREAMS

By Stephen LaBerge
Author of "Lucid Dreaming"
How to master the technique
of "being awake" while you're dreaming.
• Includes a 32-page Dream Control manual.

audio
Renaissance
tapes, inc.

under a full moon, and a costumed Dream Ball with prizes for the Most Freudian, Most Jungian, Most Nightmarish, etc. You can also enjoy workshops and talks led by such consciousness heavyweights as Charles Tart, Stanley Krippner, and Robert Van de Castle.

Access: Annual membership in the ASD is open to anyone interested in dreams and costs $50 ($25 for students). Contact: Membership Chair, Association for the Study of Dreams, P.O. Box 1600, Vienna, VA 22183. Phone: (703) 242-8888.

THE NEWSLETTER OF THE ASSOCIATION FOR THE STUDY OF DREAMS
•

This bimonthly features brief articles and research reports, book reviews, interviews with dream authorities, and news of the association.

Access: Association for the Study of Dreams, P.O. Box 1600, Vienna, VA 22183.

THE DREAM NETWORK BULLETIN
•

We love the *DNB*! It's like eavesdropping on other people's dreams. We've read it over the years for the latest in dream networks, shared dreams, dream-inspired art, dream reentry, and every form of lucid dreaming imaginable. The new editor, Roberta Ossana, plans to revamp the *Bulletin* and use it "as a tool for informing and empowering individuals to begin taking their dreams more seriously." She says there will be less emphasis on lucid dreaming and telepathy, and more on dream interpretation. We hope she won't do anything to change the classifieds, which go sort of like this: "DREAM SWIMMERS: Please send me any dreams of swimming, especially ocean swimming or dreams in which the water is almost too shallow to swim."

Access: Roberta Ossana, *The Dream Network Bulletin,* P.O. Box 1321, Port Townsend, WA 98368. A one-year subscription is $18; back issues are available for $4.

SENOI DREAM EDUCATION
•

Remember Kilton Stewart? He was the anthropologist who told the world about the remarkable Senoi people and their dream-control expertise. Of course, maybe the Senoi were just faking it so they could get mentioned in dream conferences at Big Sur, but, anyway, Stewart's widow, Clara Stewart Flagg, leads one-day Senoi Dream Education Workshops in various parts of the U.S. In them you may learn such Senoi basics as "redreaming," demanding a gift from your dream, transforming an enemy into a friend, and reshaping dream symbols. "All parts of the dream belong to the dreamer," says Flagg. "A person can change the non-

functioning parts of a dream so they can become more helpful."

Access: Senoi Dream Education Workshops, 11657 Chenault St. #303, Los Angeles, CA 90049. Phone: (213) 476-8243.

GET A PH.D. IN YOUR DREAMS
•

Stanley Krippner, Ph.D.

The Saybrook Institute in San Francisco is a humanistic/transpersonal think tank, the sort of place that might let you get a doctorate in experiential shamanic dreaming in cross-cultural perspective. The graduate school and research center offers master's and doctoral programs in psychology with an antimainstream slant. It was founded (and is still directed) by Stanley Krippner, Ph.D., an eminent transpersonal psychologist who earned his wings in the famous Maimonides Hospital dream experiments.

Access: Saybrook Institute, 1550 Sutter St., San Francisco, CA 94109. Phone: (415) 441-5034.

REVERIE 101
•

At Atlantic University, a branch of the Edgar Cayce Foundation, you can earn an M.A. degree in Transpersonal Studies, studying for such courses as "The Nature of Reality and Principles of Parapsychology." Part of that curriculum is a course called "The Inner Life: Dreams & Meditation," taught by well-known dream researcher Henry Reed. Available now on an independent study basis, the course "combines guided exercises in dreamwork, meditation, and reverie, reading, written and other appropriate means of self-expression, as well as telephone tutorial sessions with the instructor." The course will earn you three credit hours toward a Master's in Transpersonal Psychology.

Access: Tuition for the course is $65 per credit hour. Contact: James Windsor, Ph.D., Atlantic University, P.O. Box 595, Virginia Beach, VA 23451.

EXPERIENTIAL DREAM GROUP LEADERSHIP TRAINING WORKSHOPS
•

It's probably just a tic, but we are troubled by anything with the word "experiential" in the title. But don't mind us. These intensive three-day workshops are given three or four times a year by Dr. Montague Ullman, author of the best-selling *Working with Dreams,* and director of those intriguing dream ESP experiments at Maimonides Hospital. The workshops are designed to teach people the necessary skills for leading a dream group. "The only qualification for anyone in my training program," says Ullman, "is that once in their life they had a dream!"

Access: Dr. Montague Ullman, 55 Orlando Ave., Ardsley, NY 10502. Phone: (914) 693-0156.

THE DELANEY AND FLOWERS CENTER FOR THE STUDY OF DREAMS
•

We were about to call Delaney and Flowers the Cagney and Lacey of dreamwork, then we wondered what that would mean. Anyway, we've never met them and wouldn't know who's the blonde and who's the brunette. So forget it. Noted dream researchers Gayle Delaney, Ph.D., author of *Living Your Dreams,* and Loma Flowers, M.D., are the founders

Loma Flowers, M.D. and Gayle Delaney, Ph.D.

and directors of this San Francisco dream center. The center offers classes for beginner and intermediate dreamworkers and a diploma program for advanced students or professionals. It also has individual instruction and training programs for organizations.

Access: The Delaney and Flowers Center for the Study of Dreams, 337 Spruce St., San Francisco, CA 94118. Phone: (415) 383-9001.

NOVATO CENTER FOR DREAMS
•

Jill Gregory

This Marin County, California, dream center is directed by grass-roots dreamworker Jill Gregory. It offers "General Dreamskill" classes that cover journaling, incubation, dream interpretation, flying, healing, and "sharing." There are also specialized lucid dream classes and private workshops. The Center offers a variety of educational materials and private tutoring by phone, mail, or in person.

Access: Novato Center for Dreams, 29 Truman Dr., Novato, CA 94947. Phone: (415) 897-7955 or (415) 898-2559.

THE FAMILY THAT MEDIATES TOGETHER
•

The Family Mediation Center—in some sort of Freudian/Jungian slip we at first wrote "Family Meditation Center"—in Menlo Park, California, sponsors ongoing dream workshops led by Saybrook Institute director Stanley Krippner and Ingrid Kepler.

Access: Family Mediation Center, 990 Ringwood Ave., Menlo Park, CA 94025.

HEALING ARTS ASSOCIATES
•

There must be something about living in the San Francisco Bay Area, right on the edge of a major fault *and* a major paradigm shift, that makes its residents obsessively interested in their dreams. Here's another *Serial*-land dream center, this one directed by Bob Trowbridge, a well-known local dream pundit and onetime *Dream Network Bulletin* editor. Healing Arts Associates offers dream classes, dream groups, and individual dreamwork based on the Edgar Cayce readings (according to which the Bay Area should be submerged in the Pacific by now). Individual counseling in person or by phone is also available.

Access: Healing Arts Associates, 1537-A Fourth St., Suite 202, San Rafael, CA 94901. Phone: (415) 454-2962.

Bob Trowbridge

AHUI MANU, MON AMOUR
•

It's pronounced *Ah-hoo-ee Ma-new*, which apparently is Hawaiian for "opening your transpersonal heart to the head kahuna" or something. Escaping the eternal drizzle of its native clime, the Pacific Northwest Center for Dream Studies of Seattle travels to Hawaii for its annual Transformational Dreamwork Intensive, known as Ahui Manu. Participants stay in a Tibetan Buddhist monastery and enact "outrigger canoe ceremonies" and "vision quests on secluded coco-palm beaches," when they're not engaged in dream incubation. Gestalt/bodywork, kahuna studies, and snorkeling. Back in Seattle, center founders Ken Kimmel and Shawn LaSala-Kimmel run an ongoing DreamGroup, a Jungian dream series, and various workshops and retreats.

Access: For information contact the Center for Dream Studies, 219 First Avenue South, Suite 405, Seattle, WA 98104. Phone: (206) 447-1895.

EURO-JUNGIAN-SENOI
•

The Jungian-Senoi Institute has closed its doors in Berkeley. Its director, Strephon Kaplan-Williams, has taken his Mandala Process Training to Europe—specifically to England, Scotland, Holland, and Norway, where the long Bergman-esque winters will surely be enlivened by Dream Reentry, Symbol Immersion, and the other dreamworking techniques he has pioneered. The MPT includes year-long training in three areas: dreamwork training (based on the *Jungian-Senoi Dreamwork Manual*); "transforming childhood"; and Jungian psychology. Don't expect a quickie weekend workshop from Kaplan-Williams. "Our training is not just a skill-learning process but a deep transformational experience using dreamwork process as the base," he explains. Ordinarily we take exception to any statement with the word *transformational* in it, but we do like Kaplan-Williams's work, so we'll let it pass.

Access: For information on personal growth training à la Strephon Kaplan-Williams, contact either of these two centers: Journey Centre-Edinburgh, Hilary Scaife, Director, 2 Quarryford Farm Cottages-Haddington, East Lothian EH41 4PL Scotland; or Journey Centre—Stroud-Bristol, Maggie Peters, Director, 59 Bisley Road, Stroud, Glos GL5 1HF England.

THE SOUND OF ONE HAND DREAMING
•

The Zen Dream Center in Glen Ellen, California—in the wine country, where a good zinfandel goes so well with a koan—offers workshops and private instruction on Zen dreamwork for individuals and groups.

Access: Pat Lang, Director, 5100 Warm Springs Rd., Glen Ellen, CA 95442. Phone: (707) 996-4834.

White Dove Farm

DREAM RETREAT
•

Robert Van de Castle, Ph.D., a respected dream authority and former ASD president, recently purchased a twenty-five-acre property called White Dove Farm in Virginia, which he plans to convert into an "experiential dream center" for week-long and weekend workshops. There will be a club-house, lakes, and plenty of land for experientialing. Van de Castle expects it to be operational by the time you read this.

Access: White Dove Farm, P.O. Box 638, Fork Union, VA 23055.

BAD DREAM HOTLINE
•

We called the number of this free dream-consulting service in Chicago and got a recording. "You've reached the Dream Hotline, the service for those puzzled by dreams or troubled by nightmares. The counselor cannot answer your call. Leave a message after the beep or write us at [the address given below] and receive the forty-two-page, five-dollar, critically acclaimed Dream Hotline Booklet. Remember how you were in your dream. That's your strongest self. The rest is only weak in you and strong in someone else." Excuse me? We hung up more puzzled than we were before we dialed. As you may have gathered, Hotline founder Anthony Dubetz is also the author of a self-published, critically acclaimed forty-two-page Dream Hotline Booklet called "Making Nightmares Pay." (Whatever that means.)

Access: Hotline number: (312) 589-2471. Or write: Anthony Dubetz, P.O. Box 34934, Chicago, IL 60634.

DREAM WORKBOOK
•

The spiral-bound *Dream Quest Workbook* is a twenty-eight-day guided dream-incubation journey written by Henry Reed, Ph.D. Each section contains a Daily Dream Diary, a Dream Quest Log, and seventy instruction guides.

Access: The Heritage Book Store, 314 Laskin Rd, Virginia Beach, VA 23451. Cost: $16.95 plus postage.

BASIC HINTS FOR DREAMWORK
•

That's the title of an excellent little guide by dreamworker Jeremy Taylor, who also conducts dream groups and workshops.

Access: Jeremy Taylor, 10 Pleasant Lane, San Rafael, CA 94901. Phone: (415) 454-2793.

DREAM TIPS
•

Jill Gregory, director of the Novato Center for Dreams in California, offers several dreamworking booklets: *Dream Tips, Lucid Dreaming Tips,* and a *Dreamer's Bibliography.*

Access: Novato Center for Dreams, 29 Truman Dr., Novato, CA 94947. Phone: (415) 898-2559.

LUXURY DREAM JOURNAL
•

Awakening: A Dream Journal by Ellen Foreman is a two-volume set by a dream therapist that includes "everything you need to become your own analyst." The first half is a text on do-it-yourself dream interpretation illustrated with lavish reproductions of dreamy art. The second half is a blank dream journal (bordered with Egyptian-looking hieroglyphics) for you to write in. The perfect gift for that dream-working friend who wants to sleep with something prettier than a steno pad.

Access: *Awakening: A Dream Journal* by Ellen Foreman is published by Stewart, Tabori & Chang (740 Broadway, New York, NY 10003). $18.95 for the two-volume set (paper).

AWAKENING
A DREAM JOURNAL

ELLEN FOREMAN, Ph.D.

BIT O' JUNG: AN INTRODUCTION TO ARCHETYPES

To Plato archetypes were ideal forms of things, patterns of the divine that preceded and shaped material creation. To Jung *psychological* archetypes were "primordial images," universal patterns and tendencies in the human unconscious that continue to surface in myths, fairy tales, and dreams of all cultures. Most images in dreams are *not* archetypes, according to Jungian analyst Robert A. Johnson, author of *Inner Work.* "The dream that contains an archetype often has a mythical quality," he advises. Instead of dreaming about shopping or getting your car lubed, you may walk through the streets of Baghdad, meet otherworldly animals like unicorns or griffins, or find yourself in some ancient, mythical, or fairy-tale kingdom. There are an infinite number of archetypes, but here are a few of the biggies:

The Persona: The "mask," the part of yourself you present to the world—or to Johnny Carson if you're a celeb.

The Shadow: The denied, unknown, or repressed part of your psyche, often perceived as dark, scary, or evil; the Manuel Noriega inside you.

The Trickster: An intrapsychic Simple Simon or Wiley Coyote; the wise fool inside you, simultaneously all-knowing and silly.

The Anima/Animus: The feminine soul inside a man, the masculine soul inside a woman, respectively. As in, "Oh, wow, you have a really powerful anima."

The Great Mother: The earth, the universe, Mother Nature, the eternal feminine, nurturing or devouring as the case may be. Demeter, Kali, and the Virgin Mary are Great Mother figures; Nancy Reagan, Joan Crawford, and Marilyn Chambers are not.

The Father: The masculine principle, the sky-god type, in charge of law and order, thunderbolts, linear time, lawn care, and other Dad duties.

The Divine Child: The precious, newborn aspect of consciousness, childlike yet knowing, often born in times of trouble. The infant Jesus was a Divine Child par excellence. As far as we know, a Divine Child never whines or tosses its mashed potatoes onto the floor.

Wise Old Man/Woman: A personification of the oldest and wisest part of our psyche.

The Hero's Journey: A symbol of life, often appearing as a descent into the underworld or into a labyrinth, a sea voyage, or a Indiana Jones—like quest for treasure or adventure.

Death/Rebirth: The cyclical aspect of time, the ups and downs of life's progress; New Year's, solstices and equinoxes, and the beginning of a new fiscal year are manifestations of this archetype.

THE · COMPLETE · DREAMWORKER'S · LIBRARY

We polled dream experts on the best books in the field—with an emphasis on the practical and how-to sort—and came up with the following list:

A LITTLE COURSE IN DREAMS BY ROBERT BOSNAK (SHAMBHALA, 1988; PAPER $8.95)

Talk about truth in advertising! This book is exactly what its title says—a short course in Jungian dreamwork by a Dutch Jungian analyst in private practice in Cambridge, Massachusetts. This engaging, diminutive manual (which will fit handily into your pocketbook, if not your pocket) includes exercises for dream recall, dream analysis, studying a series of dreams, and using active imagination techniques.

SYMBOLS OF TRANSFORMATION IN DREAMS BY JEAN DALBY CLIFT & WALLACE B. CLIFT (CROSSROAD, 1988; PAPER $9.50)

A scholarly Jungian text that tells you everything you ever wanted to know about snakes, the Animus, the Persona, the Trickster, the Shadow, and other archetypal motifs.

LIVING YOUR DREAMS BY GAYLE DELANEY (HARPER & ROW, 1979; PAPER $10.95)

A readable manual for the state-of-the-art "dream producer" with especially good material on lucid dreaming and dream incubation. An interesting chapter on "cinema verité" tells you how to incubate dreams that reveal the Real You.

THE DREAM GAME BY ANN FARADAY (PERENNIAL LIBRARY, 1976; PAPER $5.95)

The best of the do-it-yourself interpretation genre, with a handy guide to common dream themes and their meanings. The book to consult when you're not sure if the snakes in your dream are phallic or garden snakes. (The author, by the way, was one of the people who discovered that the Senoi weren't all they were cracked up to be.)

CREATIVE DREAMING BY PATRICIA GARFIELD (BALLANTINE, 1974; PAPER $2.95)

Senoi dream control comes to Peoria. An excellent, easy-to-read introduction to dream-control techniques including dream incubation, dream transformation, and lucid dreams.

THE MEANING OF DREAMS BY DR. CALVIN HALL (MCGRAW-HILL, 1966; PAPER $6.95)

The landmark book on dreams that demystified Freud and showed how any dreamer could decipher the hidden meanings in his or her own dreams.

INNER WORK BY ROBERT A. JOHNSON (HARPER & ROW, 1986; PAPER $8.95)

A Jungian analyst guides the pilgrim through a home-study program of dream interpretation covering such techniques as association, amplification, active imagination, and creating rituals from your dreams. One of the best road maps to the magical kingdom of your mind.

JUNGIAN-SENOI DREAMWORK MANUAL BY STREPHON KAPLAN-WILLIAMS (JOURNEY PRESS, 1980; PAPER $17.95)

This is a big manual for metaphysically oriented dreamers—an entire dreamwork course with dozens of Senoi- and

Strephon Kaplan-Williams

THE
JUNGIAN-SENOI
DREAMWORK MANUAL
A Step-by-Step Introduction to Working with Dreams
With New Eight Page Symbol Glossary

Jungian-inspired exercises, from Dream Reentry and Incubation to Making a Symbol Book and Symbol Immersion. It covers all facets of dreamwork: dream recall, dream journals, lucid dreaming, group dreaming, healing in dreams, and dream interpretation, and is especially rich in tools for groups. It does seem to be written for people who have a lot of time on their hands or consider dreaming a second career.

NIGHT AND DAY BY JACK MAGUIRE (SIMON & SCHUSTER/FIRESIDE, 1989; PAPER $8.95)

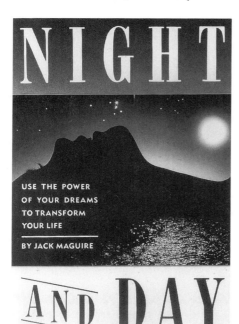

•

This inspiring book by a former *Dream Network Bulletin* editor imparts many workable, down-to-earth methods for using your nightlife to illumine your daylife. It includes dream recall and journaling techniques, incubation tips, guidelines for working with a dream partner or dream group, using dreams for creativity, and lucid dreaming.

THE DREAM WORKBOOK BY JILL MORRIS (BALLANTINE BOOKS, 1985; PAPER $3.95)

•

This delightful workbook outlines twenty-six dreamwork exercises, from "Step Back into Your Dream" to "Look for Your Hands" (a lucid-dreaming technique), to help you decode and direct your dreams. A psychologist in private practice, Morris skillfully uses the experiences of her patients to illuminate her themes.

GETTING HELP FROM YOUR DREAMS BY HENRY REED (INNER VISION, 1985: PAPER $9.95)

•

Infused with psychologist Reed's adventures in otherworldly dreamwork, this book explains such techniques as dream incubation, dream quests, "dream pillows," "dream shields," etc. One chapter, "Dreaming for Mary," is an exposition of Reed's Dream Helper Ceremony.

DREAM WORK BY JEREMY TAYLOR (PAULIST PRESS, 1983; PAPER $9.95)

•

Taylor sees in dreams "the healing magic we so desperately need." His book is an excellent dreamworker's companion, containing basic hints for dream recall and dream interpretation, as well as reflections on dream metaphysics, social activism through dreamwork, and an interesting discussion of GATES, the prototypical San Francisco Bay Area dream community.

WORKING WITH DREAMS BY MONTAGUE ULLMAN AND NAN ZIMMERMAN (JEREMY P. TARCHER, 1982; PAPER $8.95)

•

Ullman, the psychoanalyst who pioneered the use of dream groups for dream research, elucidates his Experiential Dream Group method for dreamers who can't attend his seminars. The book tells how to undertake personal dreamwork, too.

DREAMWORK · ON · TAPE

CREATIVE DREAMING BY PATRICIA GARFIELD, PH.D.
●

You loved the book; now listen to the tape and stop wasting that 30 percent of your life you spend asleep. Garfield will coach you on how to plan dreams in advance, control them while you're dreaming, recall them later, "create lifelike erotic dream adventures," and banish nightmares.

Access: Audio Renaissance Tapes, Inc., 9110 Sunset Blvd., Los Angeles, CA 90069. $9.95.

JUNG: INTERPRETING YOUR DREAMS BY JAMES A. HALL, M.D.
●

Was that a wise crone or just a shopping bag lady? A Jungian analyst delivers a simple explanation of Jungian psychology; explains archetypes, the collective unconscious, and other key elements of Jungian dreamwork; and sets forth a six-step dream interpretation method.

Access: Audio Renaissance Tapes, Inc. $9.95. (See address above.)

FREUD: INTERPRETING YOUR DREAMS BY MURRAY BILMES, PH.D.
●

Everything you wanted to know about wish fulfillment, repressed desires, and other Freudian concepts. The author is an internationally respected psychologist who teaches at the Stanford University School of Medicine.

Access: Audio Renaissance Tapes, Inc. $9.95. (See address above.)

PSYCHIC DREAMING BY ROBERT VAN DE CASTLE, PH.D.
●

In your lifetime you may have more than a thousand psychic dreams, according to eminent dream psychologist Van de Castle. In this tape he tells you "how to prepare for, send, receive, and interpret telepathic dreams." The tape includes a lesson in the Dream Helper Ceremony.

Access: Audio Renaissance Tapes, Inc. $9.95. (See address above.)

DREAM INTERPRETATION WORKOUT BY HENRY REED
●

"You've remembered a dream! Just grab a pencil, a pad of paper, and put this in your VCR." (This one is a videotape.) Henry Reed's seven workouts include the "Symbol Substitution Method," "Dream Transformation: Working Toward a Higher Dream," and "A Poetic Synthesis of My Dreamwork."

Access: Video Home Companion, P.O. Box 1541, Virginia Beach, VA 23451. $49.49.

EDGAR CAYCE: UNDERSTANDING YOUR DREAMS
●

Cayce is no longer "in the physical," of course, so Orson Bean narrates this lesson in Caycean dream interpretation, which is heavy on the psychic dimensions of dreams.

Access: Audio Renaissance Tapes, Inc. $9.95. (See address above.)

CHAPTER FIVE

LIVING·IN·A
POST-FREUDIAN
WORLD
(FIFTY·WAYS·TO
LEAVE·YOUR·SHRINK
...OR·BE·YOUR·OWN)

•

Somewhere, surely, people still lie on couches in darkened rooms and let analysts dissect their oral fixations. But let's face it; we're in a post-Freudian age. Sure, the object cathexis is a cool concept and the Wolf Man is a good read, but look around you. Aren't your friends who have been "in analysis" for the past seven years (four days a week, no less!) really sort of grim? Has all that therapy improved their complexions? No, while they go around muttering about positive countertransference over double espressos, other people more attuned to the zeitgeist are taking dictation from Ascended Masters and acquiring that

special transpersonal posing is that you *leave*

True, you'll miss *and Country* while ment ahead of you to damp wad of Kleenex.

glow. So what we're pro-*your shrink*.

catching up on *Town* waiting for the appoint-emerge clutching a You'll miss dealing with

your intrapsychic life in fifty-minute installments. You'll miss being the star of that ever-fascinating show "My Life Starring Me and My Problems." But don't worry; you can be the star of an even bigger, grander post-Freudian spectacle, one you might call "My Life and My Inner Child and My Other Cosmic Archetypes and My Energy and My Entities and My Meta-Needs and My Peak Experiences." The Me Decade has become the Meta-Me Decade.

Where the Me was a crankish personal domain of complexes, hang-ups, and complaints about one's parents, the Meta-Me is a vast, transpersonal landscape of Jungian archetypes, goddesses, shamans, mythical heroes, guides, entities, waking dreams, and magical children. Your life in Passaic, New Jersey, acquires all the psychospiritual sweep of the *Purgatorio;* your drinking problem or eating disorder becomes a mythic tale of loss and redemption (see "Aphrodite in A.A.," page 132). The Me is Krafft-Ebing and Woody Allen; the Meta-Me is Carl Jung and Shirley MacLaine.

Many post-Freudian therapies appeal to the do-it-yourself urges of the nineties. You can do Personal Mythology ("Pardon me, but isn't that Zeus in your underwear drawer?") in the privacy of your own home with a manual for exploring your own personal Paradise Lost and Paradise Regained. Without professional supervision, you can keep a special left-handed journal, allowing your nondominant hand to take down messages from your unconscious or even from the collective unconscious ("Left-handed therapy"). You can buy therapeutic audiotapes that bypass the old Freudian censor with modern technology ("Hypno-peripheral *what?*"). You can even go back to that lifetime in ancient Rome without a therapist. One caution: Do-it-yourself psychology is not recommended for the major psychoses. If you need Thorazine you'll still have to see a regular psychiatrist, who may not perceive your hallucinations as archetypal—unless he's a Jungian with an M.D.

Even if you seek the services of a therapist, there's a difference. You are no longer a patient in the post-Freudian world; you're a "client." This means that instead of viewing you as someone who really should be wearing one of those silly hospital gowns that never fasten right, your shrink sees you more the way Merrill Lynch sees a mutual-fund investor. (If a shrink speaks of "patients," it's a sure bet he or she is a hopelessly retro Sullivanian or something.)

Post-Freudian therapies tend to be fairly quick—at least compared with the glacial pace of analysis. You can complete a Personal Mythology course in about two weeks, an Intensive Journal Workshop in a weekend, and gain at least a passing acquaintance with the Enneagram in a day. Short-Term Psychotherapy ("Das Kapital, Das Therapy") speaks for itself. If you do Neurolinguistic Programming ("Woman with phobia of bees cured in fifteen minutes!"), you can resolve grief or a severe phobia in minutes, leaving you lots of free time to save the rain forest or (if you're otherwise inclined) to sell a lot of commercial real estate. You can have breakthroughs, peak experiences, epiphanies, at the drop of a hat. It's the microwave principle. If you can bake a potato in five minutes, why not get rid of grief, shock, phobias, obsession, existential ennui, and nameless dreads in the same time?

There are *more* than fifty ways to leave your shrink, we've found. There are so many, in fact, we really didn't feel like writing about them all—especially since, after doing some of these practices, we've become, like, *rilly* nonverbal. But here is our list of some of the most intriguing, hippest, useful, or just plain weird post-Freudian therapies we've come across.

JOURNALMANIA
●

Once upon a time, when the Everly Brothers filled the airwaves, you may have confided your problems ("No matter how I set my hair, it *still* won't flip!") to a small daily diary with a little lock and key, which probably did not keep your mother from reading it anyway. Now that you're a grownup you may be ready for a *journal.*

You'll need a massive spiral-bound notebook with six dividers to do Ira Progoff's Intensive Journal Process, the real McCoy, the *Ding an sich,* of psychotherapeutic journals. You'll also need to take a twelve-hour, $125 Life Context Workshop, in which you'll do such Gestalt-y things as go into the well of your life and find an underground stream at the source; ask your life to summarize itself in ten to fifteen crucial "Steppingstones"; make a list of people important to you and carry on written dialogues with them. Cognitive behaviorists have had their subjects jotting notes in journals for the purpose of "self-monitoring" for years, but in the early 1960s, Progoff, a psychologist with Jungian-existential leanings, aimed to create a process that would make psychotherapy unnecessary. The Intensive Journal Method is supposed to give you techniques with which to resolve all the issues you'd normally pay a shrink a hundred bucks an hour to dredge up.

In your journal you'll engage in more dialogues than Barbara Walters—with events, with parts of your body, and with wise, transpersonal beings inside you. You'll keep a Life History Log, a Twilight Imagery Log, and contemplate "Roads Taken and Not Taken," retracing "the road of [your] life looking for unlived possibilities." (That test tube containing a potential vaccine you tossed out, those shares of

Xerox you unloaded, that blind date you canceled with a cute guy named Ted Bundy . . .) The point of all this is to get to know the deeper Self (capital "S") "behind the mind," as Progoff puts it. Privacy is respected in the workshops and apparently you aren't pressured to "share," a word that sometimes gives us an urge to join a Trappist order. Also, there is no mention of channeling or out-of-body experiences.

Access: Several hundred community organizations around the country sponsor workshops conducted by trained Journal Consultants. To receive a schedule, write to Dialogue House, 80 East 11th St., New York, NY 10003. Dialogue House also sells books and tapes by Progoff, including the rather intimidating *At a Journal Workshop*, which is inspiring if you can transcend deadweight prose like, "Approaching our lives by this procedure has an interesting equalizing effect upon the various age groups."

IT'S MY REALITY AND I'LL CRY IF I WANT TO
•

Just think. Alongside this Pizza Hut, where you've just ordered a twelve-inch pan pizza with anchovies and extra cheese, there are hundreds, maybe thousands, of other probable Pizza Huts in other probable malls in other probable universes, all with anchovies and extra cheese. If you often think about such things, you're probably ripe for *Create Your Own Reality: A Seth Workbook*. For years Seth, America's favorite discarnate entity, spoke through the medium of Jane Roberts, bringing to the planet volumes of information about otherworldly reality in *Seth Speaks* and other books. (We've heard that since Roberts's death Seth speaks through somebody else, but we're not sure who. Not us, anyway.) Sometimes, apparently, Seth used to drop in on Roberts's ESP

classes and hand out "homework" assignments. Now, in the *Seth Workbook,* you have the chance to do the sort of homework Seth would assign: Modify your belief systems. Send love to one of your earlier selves. (God knows, your teenage self could probably use it, but can you send a date to an earlier self?) Rewrite the past. Explore your manifest and unmanifest realities, and a whole menagerie of reincarnational selves, probable selves, and simultaneous selves. Author Nancy Ashley has done an admirable job of summarizing the entire Seth opus in a 131-page book of forty-six concise, to-the-point chapters. Even if you don't finish your lessons, you'll get the essence of Seth without having to read through all the boring parts like "Jane has a cold today. . . ."

Access: *Create Your Own Reality: A Seth Workbook* is published by Prentice-Hall. Paper $7.95.

PARDON ME, BUT ISN'T THAT ZEUS IN YOUR UNDERWEAR DRAWER?
•

Don't look now, but your psyche is a regular Bulfinch's anthology of "myths," your own private versions of Paradise Lost or Persephone's descent into the underworld, according to psychologists David Feinstein and Stanley Krippner. They didn't exactly invent Personal Mythology—the term first popped up in the psychiatric literature in 1956, and, of course, Freud himself was fond of myths, especially the Oedipal one—but they have turned it into a compelling personal-growth program. Their system, which originated in a research project at Johns Hopkins University School of Medicine, has been taught to over 2,000 people, and is now available in the form of a home-study book called *Personal Mythology: The Psychology of Your Evolving Self.*

Some of your deeply embedded myths—"Because my parents died young, I doubt I'll live to see my own grandchildren"—may not be doing you much good, according to the psychologists. Take the case of Meg. Growing up in the shadow of a morphine-addicted mother whom she frequently had to save from the brink of death, Meg had evolved the myth of herself as a "brave little soldier," who must always work, never play. By undergoing myth therapy with Feinstein, she was able to create a more vital and playful personal myth for herself.

A series of "personal rituals" make up the course work. In one, you meet your Inner Shaman, the personification of your own deeper wisdom. (A friend of ours who tried this ritual reports: "Just as I was told, I entered my inner world through my navel and walked alone on a dark path through my inner reality, et cetera. I came to an archway of lush trees leading to the dwelling place of my Shaman. When I got there, I saw a large, cute, stupid, hyperactive golden retriever. But then I have a problem with authority figures.") In another ritual, you journey back to your own personal Paradise Lost, which might be as simple as a trip to Coney Island with Grandma and Grandpa just before you were sent off to military preschool. You weave your own personal Fairy Tale, beginning with those incantatory words, "Once upon a time. . . ." You identify your "prevailing myth" and "countermyth" and make up a motto for each (one woman dubbed her countermyth, "If You Won't Leave Me, I'll Find Somebody Who Will"). You'll personify your conflicting myths as different subpersonalities and let them confront each other: Proper Young Lady versus Born-Again Child; Altar Boy versus Pioneer; Robot Woman versus Flash Dancer, etc. You'll forge a Personal Shield, heal an Ancient Wound, and find a Power Object, before creating a new, improved mythology for yourself, which you weave into your daily life with a new set of personal and public rituals.

It takes five to ten weeks of home study to complete the course outlined in the book, allowing one to two weeks to complete each of the five stages. Alternatively, say the psychologists, you could go off to the woods for a few days and put yourself through a crash course—though perhaps that would make you a little *too* mythic. Who really wants to play racquetball with Thor?

Access: For information about courses and workshops in Personal Mythology contact Dr. David Feinstein, c/o Innersource, 777 E. Main St., Ashland, OR 97520. Phone: (503) 482-1800. *Personal Mythology: The Psychology of Your Evolving Self* by David Feinstein, Ph.D., and Stanley Krippner, Ph.D., is published by Jeremy P. Tarcher, Inc. Hardcover $17.95.

DOODLE THERAPY
●

Whatever you do, your unconscious does, too. When you speak, it speaks—in slips of the tongue, unintentional puns, and so on—and when you doodle "Have a Nice Day" faces on the memo pad next to the phone, guess who's doing the doodling? Some therapists would like to analyze your doodles.

Gregory M. Furth, a Jungian therapist who works in New York City, uses drawings to "hitchhike with the client's unconscious." Your unconscious, he believes, is not trying to trip you up, merely pushing you to "grow and become." He asks clients to draw a picture of their childhood, a traumatic event, or a body image, then studies the drawing to see what unconscious information is encoded in the colors, lines, squiggles, human figures, perspective, etc. What is at the center of the picture? What is missing? Is anything out of proportion (people drawn too large to fit through the door of the house, for example)? Where are the barriers in the picture? Even subtleties like shading and perspective are revealing. The time and energy invested in shading may reflect a fixation on the issue the shaded object symbolizes, according to Furth. Different perspectives in the same drawing may reveal inconsistencies in your life, and a drawing grossly out of perspective may even indicate that you're a raving psychotic.

Access: Furth gives workshops throughout the country for both mental-health professionals and nonprofessionals.

For information call or write: Dorothy Schaefer, 372 Fanning St., Staten Island, New York 10314. Phone: (718) 494-6941. To find another therapist who uses drawings in therapy, try contacting the New York Association for Analytical Psychology, 28 E. 39th St., New York, NY 10016. (This professional organization for Jungian analysts publishes a quarterly directory. There are also local chapters in many locations.) Furth's book *The Secret World of Drawing,* published by Sigo Press (23 New Chardon St., #8748, Boston, MA 12114), includes a systematic program for analyzing drawings. However, he does not think you can analyze your own artwork, precisely because your unconscious is, well, unconscious.

THINK OF YOUR PSYCHE AS THE TROBRIAND ISLANDS
●

A few years ago, anthropologist Charles Case was doing fieldwork among a group of Jamaican Rastafarians living in Brooklyn. As he tried to elicit information about their culture, his wary subjects turned the tables on him and began to interview *him*. Every time he'd ask a question, they'd throw it back at him. Though disconcerted at first, Case eventually realized that the Rastas' relentless barrage of whys was forcing him to rigorously examine his own worldview. A fainter-

hearted anthropologist might have given up and gone off to study Armenian folk sayings, but Case used the experience to create a unique new approach to the mind: *personal* anthropology.

The world's first "private practice in anthropology," called the Center for Personal Culture, operates out of a gallery space in New York City's Chelsea district. "You don't have to go to the Amazon or New Guinea," says Case. "Manhattan is full of cultures as fascinating as the primitives. Reality is the issue here." The reality in question, on this particular muggy July day, was mine (J.H.) and Case was aiming a beam of questions—basically a series of whys—at me and transcribing my answers. I began with the first thing that came into my mind, which was something banal about having just quit smoking. After each statement, Case would ask me why—for example, if I said "I live in a building on Riverside Drive, you see, and blah blah, blah," he'd ask "Why do you live in a building on Riverside Drive?" At first I found the process maddening, like conversing with a toddler or an automaton. But after about thirty or forty whys—I finally hit one I absolutely could not answer. And I discovered that, via quitting smoking, apartment addresses, etc., I had traveled to a core belief about the universe having been designed so that every soul was born in exactly the right time and place to work out its particular mission.

If I had been a real client and paid $2,000 (a fee that would effectively eliminate most subsistence-level personal cultures like mine!), I would have come back for about six sessions to explore my culture in more detail. And I would have gone home with a Worldview Book, containing a complete description of reality in my own words.

Case, who has mapped the belief systems of convicts, yuppies, children, the dying, Mensa members, Rastafarians, and artists, maintains that Personal Anthropology is completely objective and nonjudgmental. Unlike traditional psychotherapy—which Case considers intrusive and authoritarian—it accepts each internal world as valid, no matter how peculiar. "When you discover your own beliefs," he says, "you can actually become self-creative and sculpt your own personality."

Access: Charles Case, c/o The New School, 66 W. 12th St., New York, NY 10011. Phone: (201) 659-5170.

AROMATHERAPY
●

The air is thick with the scent of lavender, tangerine, and juniper at Carapan, a New York City massage center, where stressed-out people in dress-for-success outfits come to discuss their problems with an aromatherapist. He listens attentively before choosing the proper scented oils. Jasmine. Lavender. Eucalyptus. Fennel.

You can't drink the essential oils used in aromatherapy, because the FDA won't let you, but you can snort little bottles, use a diffuser to spread an aroma around a room, pour some oil in your bath, or have it massaged all over your body. Los Angeles aromatherapist John Steele blends customized oils from all over the world for his customers to use as antispasmodics, diuretics, aphrodisiacs, sedatives, hypnotics, and antidepressants. (He works in tandem with physicians and psychotherapists, presumably open-minded, go-with-the-flow ones.) For pessimism, says Steele, there's jasmine. For bad memory, rosemary. Orange flower for hysteria, clove for toothache, lavender for headache, and rose for a hangover. Anger, envy, phobias, sexual apathy, or the flu: They all have scented antidotes. It sounds like a throwback to the Middle Ages or something out of the Brothers Grimm (Yikes, could *evil* aromatherapists make us crazy with massage oils containing, say, essence of toadstool?) But aromatherapy could be the wave of the future, as scientists confirm that smells are indeed potent stimuli for memories and emotions. One respected psychologist, Gary Schwartz, has found that the scent of apple spice stops panic attacks in some people. And the World Future Society of Washington, D.C., has

predicted that by the year 2000 mood-altering aromas will be used routinely in hospitals.

Access: For a referral to an aromatherapist or an aromatherapy-inclined masseur or masseuse in your area, you can contact the American Aroma Therapy Association, P.O. Box 1222, Fair Oaks, CA 95628. Several companies can also give you information about oils and other essential oil products: Aveda, 400 Central Ave., SE, Minneapolis, MN 55414. AromaVera, 2728 South Robertson Ave., Los Angeles, CA 90034. Phone: (213) 280-0407. Original Swiss Aromatics, P.O. Box 606, San Rafael, CA 94915. Phone: (415) 459-3998.

LEFT-HANDED THERAPY
●

Skipping the explanatory chapters on the left brain vs. right brain, I (J.H.) tried out the first exercise: I wrote my name with my left hand. Almost immediately, I was plunged into the consciousness of a first-grader in the remedial reading room, numbed by the comfortable tedium of tick tock, fluorescent light, and Dick, Jane, and Baby Sally. In the demented handwriting of ransom notes and psychopathic ultimatums, my left hand babbled away. After a stream of banal (and illegible) comments and self-reflections, it seemed to take on the persona of an ancient scribe patiently chiseling archaic glyphs—Linear B? Egyptian hieroglyphics?—into stone. I was mastering the power of the word for the first time, writing things like: *Ra, Osiris, Baal, Quetzalcoatl the feathered serpent, Chac Mool the raingod, animals, all-seeing eyes, priestly profiles, dates, equinoxes, kingdoms, spells, bills of lading, cubits, temples....* Then, because it is not at all easy to write these things with one's left hand, I switched back to the old workaday right.

"The nondominant hand has the ability to be very plastic," says Lucia Capacchione, "and to adapt to the psychological

A JOURNEY BACK TO
YOUR ANCESTORS

We begin with a personal ritual that will give you an experiential sense of how personal myths operate. You will be using your imagination to locate the roots of your own mythology in the mythology passed down through your family. Personal myths are laden with the hopes and disappointments of prior generations. . . . Read the [following] instructions into a tape that can then lead you through the experience, or have someone else read the instructions to you, or familiarize yourself with the instructions well enough so that you can perform the ritual from memory. . . .

Stand where you can move several feet in any direction. Find a comfortable posture and close your eyes. Take a backward step and imagine that you are stepping into the body and being of your father, if you are a man, or of your mother, if you are a woman. (If you were adopted, make a choice between your biological parent and your adoptive parent for this experience.) Then take a few minutes to get a sense of what it must have felt like to be in this body and this personality.

Take another step backward and step into the body and being of your parent's parent, your same-sex grandparent. After sensing this grandparent for a few minutes, take another step backward and enter the body and being of your same-sex great-grandparent.

Finally, take another step backward to become your same-sex great-great-grandparent. You might be a late-seventeenth-century craftsman's wife in downtown London, a foot soldier in the army of the czar, or the slave of a tobacco farmer in Virginia in the 1830s.

Physically assume the posture that you imagine might have been a typical posture for your great-great-grandparent. Dramatize this posture until it begins to symbolize what you know and imagine about this person's life. You will be reflecting upon the person's perceptions of self, environment, and purpose.

Even though it is unlikely that you will have access to the facts that would allow you to answer these questions with certainty, the answers your great-great-grandparent gave to them shaped your family's mythology and echo in your own psyche. Assume that these echoes are registered so deeply in your being that the answers your intuition offers now will, if not factually precise, be instructive as

metaphors for further understanding your heritage. Consider the following questions as if you were your great-great-grandparent:
1. What are your major concerns?
2. What are your primary sources of satisfaction?
3. How do you understand your position within your society—its limitations, privileges, and responsibilities?
4. If you look to a human authority to explain human destiny, what is its nature?

After you have answered the four questions, take a step forward and assume a posture that you imagine to be typical of your great-grandparent when he or she was your current age. Dramatize this posture until it begins to symbolize what you know and imagine about this person's life. . . .

[The rest of the ritual has you essentially repeat this process with your same-sex great-grandparent, grandparent, and parent in turn, always considering the same four questions. Then you step forward into your own life.]

Can you see patterns that have been carried to you from your parent's generation? Are you likely to pass these patterns along to your children? At some point, you may wish to repeat this exercise, stepping into the lives of your opposite-sex parent and ancestors, or, if you were adopted, stepping into the life of the biological or adoptive parent whose lineage you did not explore the first time. This speculation on the mythologies of those who preceded you will provide a reference point as we begin to discuss the nature of personal myths.

—from *Personal Mythology: The Psychology of Your Evolving Self* by David Feinstein, Ph.D., and Stanley Krippner, Ph.D.; © Jeremy P. Tarcher, Inc., Los Angeles; reprinted with permission.

aspects of the person coming through." Capacchione turned to journal writing in an attempt to heal herself of a life-threatening collagen disease. At her therapist's suggestion one week, she used her *left* hand to jot down her thoughts. As she struggled to form letters, she found herself regressing to the age of four. She felt a profound release as the long-repressed child within her began to emerge in those shaky, wavering block letters. Soon this left-handed-child self and her uptight, competent, right-handed self were talking to each other in Capacchione's ambidextrous journal, revealing the psychological roots of her illness (which was cured several months later).

Capacchione, an art therapist, went on to develop a two-handed epistolary therapy, described in her book *The Power of Your Other Hand.* She believes that a person's dominant hand is the instrument of the inner Critical Parent and of the rational, intellectual left brain—that old party-pooper—and that other voices can speak through the nondominant hand, which is, of course, connected to the nondominant brain hemisphere (the right brain for most of us). A cast of colorful characters eventually spoke through Capacchione's other hand, including a Playful Kid, an outrageous "Woman in Red," a Wise Woman, and a bunch of Jungian archetypes like the Trickster and the Goddess. If you get into left-handed writing, you'll have tête-à-têtes (or should we say *main-à-mains?*) with your Playful Child, Magical Child, Vulnerable Child, and Inner Critic; you'll draw with your left hand; you'll interview an ailing part of your body; you'll use both hands to have a written conversation with someone you detest—or, rather, with whom you are "in conflict"—and much more.

Access: *The Power of the Other Hand: A Course in Channeling the Inner Wisdom of the Right Brain* by Lucia Capacchione is published by Newcastle Publishing Co., Inc. Paper $9.95. If you're interested in attending a workshop (or ordering a book) contact: InnerWorks, 1341 Ocean Ave., #100, Santa Monica, CA 90401. Phone: (213) 285-9489.

THE WITCH ISN'T REALLY MEAN; SHE'S JUST GOING THROUGH A MIDLIFE CRISIS

●

You've probably been wondering how to teach "cognitive restructuring" to little Jennifer. Or where to find sanitized fairy tales—like "Jack in the Beanstalk" without the, uh, violent "resolution of the Oedipal complex." (Couldn't Jack just tell the giant how *angry* he feels? But we digress.)

The Center for Applied Psychology is to pint-sized psychology what L.L. Bean is to obscure winter clothing items. Items in this interesting catalogue range from affirmations-in-a-can and a Hyperactivity Workbook to games like Divorce Cope, the Anger Control Game, the Self-Esteem Game, and Stress Attack. There's a life-sized Hit-Me, Hug-Me-Hermie doll (used by Gestalt therapists as a "powerful projective tool") as well as therapeutically useful snake puppets, witch puppets, dollhouses, anatomically correct dolls, a "bendable

family," a "behavior contract pad," child-oriented sleep tapes, and Skinnerian "reward stamps." All of which is nice, but come on: How about a Substance Abuse Barbie, or a Hyperactive Pee Wee's House, or at least a Teenage Mutant Ninja Turtles Go through Puberty Board game? (Just a suggestion.)

Access: Childswork/Childsplay, Center for Applied Psychology, 3rd floor, 441 N. 5th St., Philadelphia, PA 19123. Phone: (215) 592-1141 and 1-800-962-1141.

DAYDREAMING TO THE MAX

●

You're not on your way to becoming a shopping-bag lady in Grand Central Station just because you carry on conversations with yourself, according to Cambridge, Massachusetts, psychotherapist Mary Watkins. If you're in Waking Dream therapy you're encouraged to discourse at length with all the "invisible guests" in your unconscious, be they wise hags, sulky children, or queens. When you discuss a problem, Watkins has you focus on the "imaginal landscape" behind it. She eschews the "guided imagery" techniques so popular in transpersonal/humanistic circles because she doesn't want to direct her clients' reveries, but she might ask a depressed person: "Is the scene of the depression a parched moonscape, an isolated bog of quicksand, or a bleak rooming house? Does the depressed part of you express itself as an abandoned child, an aging man, or a struggling single mother taking care of everyone?" As if in a waking dream, you plunge into your fantasy world and listen to all the voices inhabiting your soul, letting them speak, rant, cry, and argue with your other selves.

Similar to "waking dreams" is what Jungians call active imagination work—and Jung himself did a lot of it. One

excellent primer is *Inner Work,* by Jungian analyst and author Robert A. Johnson, which describes techniques for extending your (nocturnal) dreams into (daytime) imaginary journeys; recognizing and amplifying archetypes; talking to images and imaginary characters; inventing rituals to make your dreams, fantasies, and symbols concrete; etc. Although you can journey into the many realms of your personal *Divina Commedia* (the prototypical active imagination trip!) by yourself, the author warns: "It [active imagination] should not be practiced unless you have someone available who is familiar with this art, someone who knows how to get back to ordinary earth if you should be overwhelmed by the inner world."

Access: Mary Watkins does not give workshops; nor is she actively seeking new clients. But you can read her books, *Waking Dreams* (Spring Publications, Inc., P.O. Box 222069, Dallas, TX 75222; paper $13.50) and *Invisible Guests: The Development of Imaginal Dialogues* (The Analytic Press, distributed by Lawrence Erlbaum Associates, Inc., 365 Broadway, Hillsdale, NJ 07642; hardcover $33.25).

Inner Work: Using Dreams & Active Imagination for Personal Growth by Robert A. Johnson is published by Harper & Row; paper $8.95. To find a therapist skilled in Jungian "active imagination" work, contact the New York Association for Analytical Psychology, 28 E. 39th St., New York, NY 10016.

Imagery and visualization techniques are also used extensively in Psychosynthesis, a transpersonal psychiatric school developed by Roberto Assagioli of Florence, Italy. For information contact the Psychosynthesis Institute of New York, 5 Milligan Place, New York, NY 10011. Phone: (212) 929-2982.

WHEN I WAS HIGH PRIESTESS IN HELIOPOLIS
•

If you believe you have lived many lives and share the sunny American conviction that everything, death included, is a learning experience, past-life therapy may be for you. Compared with remembering *this* life—patients in analysis can while away years trying to get a grip on a few slippery memories only decades old—remembering past lives is a piece of cake, it seems. According to psychologist Hazel Denning, executive director of the Association for Past-Life Therapies, Inc. (APART), it's often enough just to direct some clients to lie back and remember. More commonly, a past-life therapist will facilitate the process with some form of relaxation technique: muscle relaxation, counting, hypnosis, or guided imagery. A number of professional masseurs and masseuses have jumped on the past-life bandwagon because clients started dredging up memories of ancient Sumer during the course of a good rubdown.

Are these memories of real events? Not always, past-life therapists admit. Denning notes that there are an awful lot of Nefertitis and Cleopatras among us and not many serfs and washerwomen. If you avoid the truth about your past life, she warns, your symptoms aren't going to go away.

Reliving significant events from a past life is supposed to help you understand your present-life behavior. You may have "unfinished soul business," in the words of Roger J. Woolger, Ph.D., a Jungian psychotherapist–turned–past-life therapist. In his book *Other Lives, Other Selves,* he tells of teenage boys killed in past-life wars who go around totaling

TransAms in this life because they are "unconsciously re-running old battlefield deaths with a deep residual devil-may-care attitude born of despair and defiance." Phobias may reveal past-life scars, too, Woolger notes. "Animal terrors evoke memories of being thrown to wild beasts by the Romans, or by primitive tribes; such people often unconsciously attract aggression in certain animals around them." Compulsions, obsessions, and various neurotic disorders may also hark back to the Black Plague, the *Titanic,* or the reign of Ivan the Terrible. Eating disorders such as anorexia nervosa and bulimia may reveal a story of starvation in medieval Europe.

What if you recall a past life and it turns out you had a little job working people over for the Inquisition? Could you have what psychoanalysts call a painful "abreaction" (reliving), which makes you feel worse than you did before? (We have a friend who went into a severe depression after being told she had experimented with DNA on Atlantis and ended up murdering some freakish life forms she'd created.) "There's a real danger if you're not in the hands of someone who knows what he's doing," Denning warns. She prepares

clients by telling them that "life is an ongoing process; every experience is for our learning, no matter if we killed someone or have been tortured."

Past-life therapy sometimes goes hand in hand with channeling. If you or your past-life therapist receives cosmic tele-faxes from an entity, try to determine whether it's a "high" guide or an astral lowlife, Denning warns. Ouija boards, she notes, are especially apt to attract lonely spirit creeps who just want to come through and bother other people.

Access: For referrals to a past-life therapist in your area, contact the Association for Past-Life Research and Therapies, Inc., P.O. Box 201511, Riverside, CA 92516. Phone: (714) 784-1570. States don't license past-life therapists, but APART does certify people who complete a particular training program in past-life therapy. APART professional members include M.D.'s, clinical psychologists, psychics, and others. "Go have a session," suggests Denning. "If you don't feel rapport don't go back. It's too dangerous to fool around with."

Another way to get back to that wild and crazy incarnation at the court of Louis XIV, or that very interesting lifetime near the Dead Sea, is to take a group workshop led by a past-life therapist. For information about Roger Woolger's past-life workshops write Laughing Bear Productions, 5 River Rd., New Paltz, NY 12561. Check the schedule of your local New Age or alternative-learning center for other workshops.

For those who want to keep abreast of the field, there's the *Journal of Regression Therapy,* published semiannually by APART (see address above); $15 for nonmembers. There is also an awesome array of books for the past-life tourist, many of which set forth techniques for past-life recall.

DAS KAPITAL, DAS THERAPY
•

If you *don't* believe you create your own reality—if you believe that General Motors or the military industrial complex might have something to do with it—you might be interested in social therapy, often known as short-term psychotherapy or crisis normalization. When you're going through a crisis, a short-term therapist doesn't automatically assume there's something wrong with you and that you'll need ten years of therapy to overcome it. Perhaps you're having problems because *society* is sick. Perhaps you're poor, or you're a worker victimized by management, or you're a woman trying to work and raise a family with little support from a patriarchal power structure, or you're confronting sexism, racism, elitism, or agism. (Social therapy tends to have a Marxist or radical bent.)

In our society the self is "socialized to be alienated in many ways," according to philosopher/social therapist Fred Newman, the founder and leading theoretician of the crisis-normalization approach. The brochure for his East Side Institute for Short Term Psychotherapy in New York City states, "We consider conflictedness to be a fundamental characteristic of the ongoing social process of our lives." Using a method called *conflict intensification,* social therapists may "intensify [the conflict] rather than attempt to resolve or repress it." (They don't say *how,* but it sounds sort of encounterish to us.)

Most social therapy involves groups. Social therapists will meet with individuals, but only for short-term therapy of one to four sessions (and they regard individual therapy as a group session for two). If a client wishes to continue in social therapy, he or she is referred to a larger group. "The therapist helps the group's members create a social environment in which issues can be dealt with," explains Newman. "He or she functions as an organizer of an environment, not as a mind reader, a truth teller, or an authority."

Access: There are centers for short-term psychotherapy or crisis normalization in New York, Atlanta, Chicago, Boston, Washington, Philadelphia, and Long Island. For addresses and phone numbers contact: East Side Center for Short Term Psychotherapy, 500 Greenwich St., New York, NY 10013. Phone: (212) 941-8844. If you want to read more about social therapy, *History Is the Curse* by Dr. Fred Newman, edited by Hugh Polk and Lois Holzman (Practice Press), is available from the East Side Institute for $11.95.

WOMAN WITH PHOBIA OF BEES CURED IN FIFTEEN MINUTES!
•

One Neurolinguistic Programming (NLP) videotape shows a woman with a severe phobia of bees being cured in just fifteen minutes. In another tape you can observe therapists helping a client "resolve grief" in fifty-seven minutes. Steve and Connirae Andreas, cofounders of Neurolinguistic Programming Comprehensive of Boulder, Colorado, claim they can completely cure Post-Traumatic Stress Disorder—those pesky Vietnam War flashbacks—in a single session, and they have case histories (though not controlled studies) to prove it.

Neurolinguistic Programming—which for years we thought had something to do with either spinal-cord injuries or computer-machine language—is a cognitive therapy developed in the early seventies by John Grinder, a linguistics professor at the University of California at Santa Cruz, and Richard Bandler, then a grad student. Curious about how the *words* used by therapists and clients affect the outcome of therapy, they studied the language patterns of highly effective healers such as Fritz Perls, Virginia Satir, and Milton Erickson, and came up with NLP. The theory holds that you rely predominantly on one representational mode—auditory, visual, or kinesthetic—in constructing your mental reality. The clues can be found in your metaphors ("I feel bogged down" is kinesthetic; "The future looks black" is visual) and in your eye movements. For example, you turn your eyes upward and to the right when you're visualizing something you've never seen; downward and to the right when you're

Karl Marx

GEE, I THINK I'VE HAD THIS DÉJÀ VU BEFORE

Past-life therapists commonly encourage you to stop and examine any tingle of déjà vu. If you can't trace that strange sense of "it all happened before" to something in your present lifetime, consider that it might be a past-life memory trying to rise to the surface. Another trick of the trade is to deliberately provoke a déjà vu experience:

•At last there's a use for that pile of *National Geographics* in your attic. Gloria Chadwick, author of *Discovering Your Past Lives: The Best Book on Reincarnation You'll Ever Read . . . in This Lifetime!* (Contemporary Books, $7.95, paper), recommends leafing through "books of foreign countries that show different cultures and a variety of people." Study the scenery, clothing styles, artifacts, and so on. Read up on ancient civilizations.

•Spend long hours gazing at the Egyptian collection in the Met—or whatever artifacts in whatever museum intrigue you. "You may recognize something you've seen or used in a past life, and images may begin to surface of past-life events connected with those items," says Chadwick.

•Hang around colonial Williamsburg, Chartres cathedral, Stonehenge, or some other historical landmark. If you feel really drawn to Crete, go there on your next vacation. Returning to a place where you lived in a previous life will jog your memory. Maybe you'll even start speaking Linear B.

•Follow up on any interest or fascination you have, however weird. If you have an urge to dabble in Mayan calendrics, wear medieval armor and take up jousting, or go ice-fishing in the Arctic, do so. "A strong interest in certain things is usually due to a past-life influence," notes Chadwick. (If you have a yen to be addressed as "Lucrezia" and to poison all your nearest relatives, you may have a problem.)

Past-life connoisseur Michael Talbot, author of *Your Past Lives: A Reincarnation Handbook* (Harmony Books, $16.95), uses the term *resonance* to describe that funny pang of recognition that may reveal a previous lifetime. He offers the following tips for triggering resonances:

•Linger over atlases and travel guides and you may evoke powerful resonances for places you have lived in past lives. (Bear in mind that names change. Prussia is now part of Germany; Babylon is now in Iraq; Abyssinia is . . . umm . . . well, anyway.) Instead of a particular city or state, Talbot adds, you may find you have a resonance for, say, narrow cobblestone streets, minarets, Russian churches with onion domes, or icy tundra. Follow these hunches.

•Look at the things you collect around you. "Objects that were cherished or frequently used in a former life can also indicate resonance," says Talbot. "Have you always been drawn to things Japanese? Do you collect arrowheads, World War I mementos, pictures of sailing ships, Mexican pottery, French porcelain, African statuary, Victorian cameos, objects from Colonial America, Persian carpets, 1920s memorabilia, Civil War coins, books about ancient Greece or Russia's imperial past?" Your tastes in art and music may also afford clues to who you used to be. When Talbot first heard Rachmaninoff's *Vocalise* as a teenager, it evoked fragmentary images of a previous life.

•An affinity for certain foreign languages may be a clue to former lives, according to Talbot. Is there a language you were able to pick up effortlessly, as if it were second nature? Or is there some language that inexplicably sets your teeth on edge?

•Back there somewhere you must have a lengthy past-life résumé. Make a list of occupations for which you have resonance: e.g., blacksmith, hussar, dowager empress, scrivener, false pope, troubadour, sacrificial victim, pyramid architect, warlock, pharaoh. Then, Talbot recommends, "go back over your life and see if this sheds any light on other aspects of your personality." After Talbot discovered that he had resonance for having been a jeweler, "I realized that I had a tendency to tinker with watches and other small objects and that my friends and family frequently brought me their broken chain clasps and other jewelry to be fixed." One payoff of past-life therapy is that you may uncover some natural talents you mastered in previous incarnations, thus saving yourself tuition at the Acme Business Institute during this lifetime.

attending to feelings, and so on.

According to NLP, an effective therapist uses language that matches the client's predominant "representational modality" (sorry, that's how these people talk). And you can get a fresh perspective on your problem by simply switching modalities or submodalities. If you're phobic about cats, you'll call up soft fur instead of a scary, black feline silhouette crouched to pounce. Or you'd picture distant marmalade-colored cats rather than close, looming, black ones. The bee woman in the videotape was directed to imagine watching a black-and-white home movie of her traumatic experience of bees, then to leave the projector room, jump in at the end of the movie, and run it back in color over and over again. Afterwards, she felt no anxiety when she imagined a bee alighting on her hand. Representing her experience as a silly home movie played backwards at high speed took the sting out of it, so to speak.

Bee phobia—from Irwin Allen's *The Swarm*

Though NLP theory is couched in testable, behavioral terms like "eliciting stimuli," establishment psychologists we interviewed disapproved of the fact that most NLP therapists are lay people, not mental-health professionals. As for those instant trauma cures? "The reality is that treating people for post-traumatic stress disorder is long, hard, and tedious," says one psychologist who specializes in PTSD. Of course, the establishment has been known to be wrong, and even mainstream psych texts acknowledge the basic NLP premise that different sensory modalities and representational styles should be taken into account in therapy.

Access: There are some fifteen NLP centers or institutes in the U.S. If you want to find an NLP therapist or workshop, contact one of the following: Grinder, Delozier and Associates, 200 Seventh Ave., Suite 100, Santa Cruz, CA 95060; NLP Comprehensive, 2897 Valmont Rd., Boulder, CO 80391; NLP Products and Promotions, 13223 Black Mountain Rd., #10429, San Diego, CA 92129. If you want to do a little NLP on your own, check out the following books:

Frogs into Princes by Richard Bandler and John Grinder, edited by Connirae Andreas (paper $7.50; cloth $11); *Using Your Brain for a Change* by Richard Bandler, edited by Connirae and Steven Andreas (paper $7.50; cloth $11); and *Heart of the Mind* by Connirae and Steven Andreas (paper $9.50; cloth $14). All are available from Real People Press, P.O. Box F, Moab, Utah 84532. Phone: (801) 259-7578.

HYPNO-PERIPHERAL *WHAT?*
●

If you don't mind listening to two different voices speaking v-e-r-y c-a-l-m-l-y into both your ears, hypno-peripheral processing may be for you. It was created a few years ago by psychologists Lloyd Glauberman and Philip Halboth, who got the very nineties idea of mixing techniques from Ericksonian hypnosis and Neurolinguistic Programming with state-of-the-art audio technology. "It's hypnotechnology as opposed to hypnosis," says Glauberman. "You couldn't do it live."

You put on earphones, pop in a tape, and listen to a slow, mellow voice telling you a sort of Jungian fairy tale. Then there are *two* voices, each telling a different story to a different ear—and there's nothing wrong with your tape deck. When your conscious mind hears two voices talking at once, it gets overloaded and shuts down, rather like a "Morton Downey Show" audience. Or at least that's the idea. Your unconscious takes over, picking up carefully programmed phrases from one story and combining them with phrases from the other story. Thus important messages—Have more self-esteem! Stop pigging out on nacho chips! Don't have any more masochistic relationships!—can be pumped directly into your receptive unconscious. The tapes work best for dealing with "problems with on/off switches like anxiety or assertion," according to Glauberman. "They're good self-help for the garden-variety problems most of us have. If you have major psychological problems, the tapes may be useful as an adjunct, but you should go for therapy." Which may be why there's no tape for "Controlling Delusions of Persecution."

Access: The Glauberman/Halboth hypno-peripheral tapes cost $20 each and are double-sided, with a different (but related) problem on each side: Self-Esteem/Assertiveness; Time Management/Creativity; Sexuality-Male/Sexuality-Female; Weight/Substance Abuse. A second group of tapes, produced by Glauberman alone using a more sophisticated sound-recording system, are sold in sets for $40 each. There are four sets: Changing Emotions; Procrastination; Feeling Better: Mind-Body Connections; and The Quest for Excellence: Maximizing Business, Athletic and Artistic Performance. Available from: Lloyd Glauberman, 30 West 86th St., Suite 1-F, New York, NY 10024.

BETTER JUPITER RETROGRADE THAN A BAD ORAL FIXATION
●

Maybe you suffer from "Pluto problems," as they're known in the trade: addictions, obsessions, and sexuality and body issue dilemmas. Or maybe Neptune is afflicting your sun and you have created an imaginary father to compensate for an absent or inadequate father figure. Or maybe you just have a lot of retrograde planets. This is the sort of thing an astrologer/therapist can help you with.

"Horoscopes serve as an X ray of an individual's psychic structure," explains New York City astrotherapist John Marchesella, who does a chart early on in therapy to use as a reference point, usually to pinpoint crises and turning points in a client's life. For example: "The 'Saturn return' occurs when transiting Saturn conjuncts natal Saturn—Saturn traveling through the heavens coincides with the position of Saturn at birth. This happens every twenty-nine years, and it is experienced as the entrance into the adult world." Sometimes Marchesella has to discourage clients from getting *too* obsessed with their rising signs. Obsessive-compulsives may try to use the chart for prediction and control, he notes, rather than as a tool of self-knowledge. "And children of alcoholics tend to be attracted by any kind of forecasting technique, because their early experience of predictability was so low."

It's true that Susan Sontag probably wouldn't be found airing her Pluto problems in the *New York Review of Books*, but don't feel like a complete airhead if you go in for astrotherapy. Jung once confided, "In cases of difficult diagnosis I usually get a horoscope."

Access: John Marchesella can be reached at (212) 255-3236. The New York chapter of the National Council for Geocosmic Research (P.O. Box 3236, New York, NY 10185. Phone: (212) 684-8069) may be able to refer you to a certified astrologer in other parts of the country. However, the NCGR won't know about therapeutic credentials, so if you want a therapist/astrologer, you're on your own. Your best bet might be to find a therapist who advertises in New Age publications.

JUNGIAN KAFFEEKLATSCH
●

If you're into archetypes, bodywork, transpersonal therapy, maybe even a little light channeling, and want to hang out with like-minded people, you can find a club of soulmates through the Kindred Spirits Bulletin Board, a regular feature of the bimonthly magazine *Common Boundary*. Spiritually inclined therapists (and therapy-inclined spiritualists?) list their names, addresses, and phone numbers on the "bulletin board" each month. So far this has led to hundreds of discussion groups, who meet to contemplate Jungian psychology, dreams, hemisphericity, and other subjects. The groups may also entertain questions like, "Am I a channeler or am I having a psychic breakdown?" according to *Common Boundary* publisher Charles Simpkinson.

Access: *Common Boundary*, 7005 Florida St., Chevy Chase, MD 20815. Phone: (301) 652-9495. A year's subscription is $19.

WAKE UP!
●

What we call normal consciousness is really a waking sleep, a bundle of automatic habits, feelings, and perceptions that control us. Perhaps we're occasionally jolted out of our trance by hearing "Attention K mart shoppers . . ." boomed over a loudspeaker, but generally we're pretty mindless. How to wake up? Ask Charles Tart, a psychologist known for his pioneering work in hypnosis and altered states. (If you're a veteran of the consciousness wars of the 1960s you may have had a well-thumbed copy of his *Altered States* next to your incense holder.) Now he is giving lessons in "waking

up," or "mindfulness," based on his reinterpretation and expansion of the teachings of George Ivanovich Gurdjieff (1874–1949), the original Mr. Cosmic Wake-Up Call. An Asiatic Russian, Gurdjieff developed a spiritual system, New Age style, by taking a little Sufism, a little Hinduism, a little Tibetan Buddhism, a little Russian Orthodox mysticism, and some hush-hush stuff from mysterious secret brotherhoods, and mixing them up in a philosophy known as the Fourth Way. The aim of all his teachings was to shake people awake (often quite uncomfortably) from the ongoing illusion we call real life.

In his book *Waking Up,* Tart does an admirable job of fortifying Gurdjieffian wisdom with concepts from mainstream psychology to demonstrate how you perceive, feel, and behave mechanistically. He analyzes barriers to spiritual awakening such as defense mechanisms, cultural conditioning, and the development of a false self. (Yes, even your sense of self is an illusion, like those "You May Have Already Won . . ." messages you find in your mailbox; in reality, you have multiple identities and shift from one to another without realizing it.) The second half of his book is a prescription for waking from this universal trance. The keys are the practices of "self-observation" and "self-remembering," a heightened awareness of what one is doing, feeling, and thinking at every moment. This is the way to unify your many split selves into an authentic "I." When this real "I" becomes your permanent way of being you begin to be awake. In his workshops and his book Tart guides the reader/seeker through useful self-remembering and mindfulness practices and discusses how work, prayer, compassion, groups, and teachers can aid your psychospiritual growth.

Charles Tart

Access: For information about Charles Tart's occasional workshops contact: The Institute of Noetic Sciences, 475 Gate Five Rd., #300, Sausalito, CA 94965. Phone: (415) 331-5650. *Waking Up: Overcoming the Obstacles to Human Potential* is published by Shambhala/New Science Library, 300 Massachusetts Ave., Boston, MA 02115. Cloth $17.95; paper $12.95.

SMART BRAINS, FOOLISH CHOICES
•

Like Tart, Harvard psychologist Ellen Langer has watched people carefully and noticed that much of the time they're on cruise control. To make sense of a complex world, she says, our brains are constantly categorizing things, people, situations. As we think and act on the basis of these categories, we drift along more and more on automatic pilot. "The grooves of mindlessness run deep," she observes. "We know our scripts by heart. Locking ourselves out of the car or throwing socks in the garbage instead of the laundry basket jolts us awake." So does Langer's book, *Mindfulness,* which sets forth a kind of middle-American Zen designed to help us break out of our rut.

By "mindfulness," Langer is *not* referring to the specific body of Buddhist practices known as Mindfulness meditation, nor has she delved into mysticism like Tart; she draws her conclusions from her own empirical scientific studies of the way ordinary Americans think—or don't think—in the course of daily life. But Langer's cognitive study of Mindlessness/Mindfulness has yielded concepts (like automatization and deautomatization) that are quite similar to Eastern ones. In her book she offers some valuable, down-to-earth methods for leading a more mindful life by: (1) welcoming new information; (2) enjoying uncertainty; (3) shifting perspectives and altering contexts.

SPEAKING OF
BUTTOCKS . . .

To illustrate self-observation in myself at this instant of writing, I just paused to give some thought to what to say next. Glancing down, I notice that when I rest my hands on the edge of the keyboard, my right hand rests almost flat, but my left hand is turned so the index finger is much higher than the little finger, almost a forty-five-degree angle. Hmm. That's interesting.

Both hands feel comfortable in these resting positions. Is there something asymmetrical in the muscles or tendons of my body as a whole, being reflected in this hand position? Perhaps I can answer that by paying attention to my body as a whole. Ah, yes, I sense that I'm not sitting symmetrically in my chair. My right buttock has a different pattern of pressure on it; it is a little farther forward on the seat than my left. What would happen if I straightened my body? Yes, both hands now rest flat and feel equally comfortable. An interesting observation on how I'm using my body.

Now the thought arises that I should break off this example, that if it gets too detailed I will lose my readers in detail instead of getting to the main point. The flavor of this thought, as I pay open attention to it, is realistic, but there is a small bit of the emotional flavor I've learned to identify as my superego. A whiff of disapproval. Hmm. What sort of "should" has been activated? Is it unseemly for a professor to mention buttocks? This could be interesting to follow, but my commitment to finishing this book is more important now, so I consciously decide to let the further observation of the thought go and continue with the main point.

The practice of self-observation, then, is the practice of being curious, along with a commitment to do your best to observe and learn whatever is there, regardless of your preferences or fears. I would have preferred to have some profound thought about Man and the Cosmos arise when I decided to illustrate self-observation, and I had a small fear in the back of my mind that nothing would come to mind. Instead, I ended up writing about my buttocks! That is perfectly fine. What is, is. Ah, a further observation: My superego does not think this lack of selectivity in favor of the "appropriate" and "good" is fine at all!

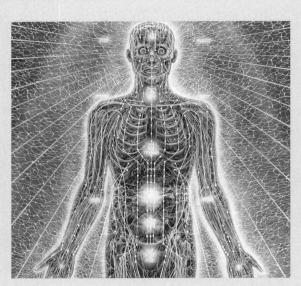

Sometimes what you will observe are constant superego disapprovals and attacks. Indeed, the superego would like to take over your newly developing powers of self-observation to search even more deeply for signs of transgression. If that is what is happening, observe it. As you get good at self-observation, you will find that you don't have to identify with or get caught up in every superego attack; they become data, one kind of information among many, rather than overwhelming compulsions. . . . Sometimes self-observation leads to quite remarkable and life-changing insights. Often it leads to more detailed attention to quite commonplace events. But what does *commonplace* mean other than the fact that you have classified something as repetitive and unimportant, and that classification has become part of the automated functioning of your attention, such that you don't pay any attention to it? You will be surprised how many commonplace things hide the extraordinary if you pay more attention and commit yourself to knowing the truth about them in spite of any preferences or fears you have.

Even the most ordinary things can gain a subtle but special quality when you deliberately observe them, as if some of the light lost in childhood is still there when you deliberately use your attention. It is there, of course, for the light is within you, waiting to be used.

—from *Waking Up* by Charles T. Tart ©1986 by The Institute of Noetic Sciences. Reprinted by arrangement with Shambhala Publications, Inc., 300 Massachusetts Ave., Boston, MA 02115.

Now suppose a man came to your house late at night and offered you a million dollars for a three-foot-by-seven-foot piece of wood. Would you rush out to your workshed or garage and come back empty-handed? Or would you point to the door you just opened? If you said the latter, you were being mindful. (Of course, you'll have to replace the door.)

Access: *Mindfulness* by Ellen J. Langer is published by Addison-Wesley; hardcover $16.95.

THE B.F. SKINNER CARD: DON'T LEAVE HOME WITHOUT IT

•

The next time you feel an overwhelming craving for a crate of Hostess Twinkies or a pack of Camels—or whatever your vice is—don't just say no, reach for the Habit Buster. Invented by psychologist Alfred Barrios, it's a $4.95, plastic credit-card-sized rectangle packed with Pavlovian know-how. Whenever you feel an urge for something bad you just pinch the card between your thumb and index finger and perform a mental relaxation exercise. By the time the temperature-sensitive liquid crystals in the card turn it blue,

The unexpected comes in

Barrios claims, you'll notice that your wicked urge has subsided. It comes with a booklet of cognitive-behavioral self-control advice.

Access: The Habit Buster is sold at B. Dalton bookstores and at General Nutrition Centers (GNCs) in malls. You can also order it directly from: Self-Programmed Control Center, Inc., 11949 Jefferson Blvd., Suite 104, Culver City, CA 90230. Phone: (213) 301-3317.

JUST SPARE US THE TERRIBLE TWOS

•

I take my new doll (a present from my grandmother) and sit at the top of the stairs in the dark. The casual talk of grown-ups downstairs is like a drug to my senses, a glimpse of a remote and mysterious land I only vaguely understand. Shadows move across the roof, which in the morning will be painted silver by "Jack Frost," who I believe is a real person and have always wanted to catch in the act. I finger the new doll dresses, which arrived in a blue trunk with a latch and which seem an immeasurably precious gift. There is a pink dress with a white ruffled pinafore, a yellow dress with a tiny floral print and puffed sleeves, a blue and white gingham dress, and several others. . . .

Okay, it's no "primal scene," but until prompted by Christopher Biffle's *A Journey Through Your Childhood*, I had forgotten that particular Christmas Eve when I was not quite four. This "write-in guide for reliving your past, clarifying your present, and charting your future" invites you to relive such mundane moments in all their early Ozzie-and-Harriet splendor. The layout of your first-grade classroom. The floral-print wallpaper in your bedroom on which you practiced hallucinations during naps. In one exercise you write down the feelings evoked by photographs; in another, you create imaginary photographs of memories. You draw a floor plan of your house and list the contents of each room. Biffle does not recommend taking this journey if you had a really ghastly childhood. But for most of us, it's a good way to tour a past you thought was long forgotten, and you get to actually write in the book.

Biffle's other fill-in-the-blanks memoir, *The Castle of the Pearl,* gives us a glimpse of what the world would have been like if Lancelot, Guinevere, and King Arthur had really communicated about their intimacy issues. In the context of a gooey medieval morality tale, you make speeches to the important people in your life—at a massive Tom Jones-esque feast that would make a bulimic go straight. You talk to mirrors and make lists on faded parchment with the Quill of the Winter Crow. You have dialogues like the following: "Then your mother speaks. 'Please tell me what you feel about me.' You answer, 'I feel _____[many lines for you to fill in]' She nods. Somehow you can tell that she also welcomes the truth." Come on. Would your mother really welcome the truth from you? Or you from her? Well, maybe *The Castle of the Pearl* is for you. It just put us in a mood to swill flagons of mead, raise armies, and arbitrarily lop off servants' limbs.

Access: *A Journey Through Your Childhood: A Write-In Guide for Reliving Your Past, Clarifying Your Present, and Charting Your Future* by Christopher Biffle is published by Jeremy P. Tarcher, Inc., Paper $10.95. *The Castle of the Pearl* is published by Perennial Library, Harper & Row Publishers. Paper $8.95.

WHAT I DID DURING SUMMER VACATION (AND THE REST OF MY LIFE)

•

We thought up a title for our autobiography ("I was Miss Congeniality in the Beauty Pageant of Life") but couldn't decide on our chapter headings. We designed our own private hell, composed of many terrifying realms like the Chamber of Telephone Solicitors, where cheery personages mispronounce your name and ask you if you'd like to take part in a "short survey." We dreamed up a universe in which the space and time axes were reversed and took a two-week vacation in the Renaissance but were unable to go backwards in space to a previous address.

We were following exercises designed to unearth our life stories and personal myths. This brand of personal mythology was cooked up by Sam Keen while leading workshops with the late Joseph Campbell—Mr. Myth himself—and you

can find the basics in his new book, *Your Mythic Journey: Finding Meaning in Your Life through Writing and Story- telling,* coauthored with Anne Valley-Fox. "To be a person

TELL ME A STORY

•

Here are a few of the techniques Sam Keen and Anne Valley-Fox recommend for ex-
• ploring your personal myths, legends, be-
lief systems, cosmologies, totems, and taboos. (For more details, see their book, *Your Mythic Journey.*)

•Outline your autobiography. Give it a title and chapter headings.

•Make a list of ten words or phrases that describe you best. Now rank the words or phrases in order of importance. Then cross them out one at a time until you are left with your single most important characteristic. *(Ours was "smarmy.")*

•Make an imaginary will in which you bequeath your personal and financial possessions. *(Or make a real will and bequeath your possessions to us, the authors.)*

•To uncover some of the subconscious taboos that may haunt you, try to picture your parents' "psychological undergrounds." Consider: What horrified your parents? What topics of conversation were for-
bidden in the house? What ways of life or habits were out of the question *(e.g., going to the country club in Mother Teresa drag; converting the base-
ment into a replica of Hitler's bunker; speaking only in cockney rhyming slang)?*

•Develop a dialogue between the man and the woman within you. Let them talk to each other. How does your feminine side relate to the masculine side? How does the man in you want to be loved by the woman, and vice versa?

•Imagine you receive a letter informing you that Donald Trump plans to leave you his entire estate *(though why he would leave it to you we can't imagine).* Decide what you'll do with it.

•Design a utopian community that could conceiv-
ably exist in your future.

•Play, "If I had a month to live I would. . . ."

•Ask yourself "What are the secrets that you never (or rarely) share with others?" This will put you in touch with your "private self."

•What coincidences/synchronicities/lucky breaks have befallen you? What premonitions have you had of the future? Try to collect evidence to support the hypothesis that you are at the center of a universe that was planned for you and is responsive to you.

•Describe your own personal pantheon of gods (as in Zeus, Athena, Aphrodite, et al.). Give names, faces, and attributes to these "gods," i.e., the forces that move your life.

is to have a story to tell. . . ." the authors observe. "Within each of us there is a tribe with a complete cycle of legends and dances, songs to be sung." Wedged among the exercises are ordinary people's stories and "myths," many of which pack as many psychological undercurrents as an O'Neill play. A woman wisecracks with a cabdriver en route to the morgue to identify the body of her husband. A self-made millionaire envisions himself as God in the image of a "benign General Motors recalling defective models, eliminating all those people who spend their lives making war or making other people miserable." A woman cooks a full Thanksgiving dinner for her family then excuses herself and goes upstairs to O.D. on sleeping pills.

Access: *Your Mythic Journey: Finding Meaning in Your Life Through Writing and Storytelling* by Sam Keen and Anne Valley-Fox is published by Jeremy P. Tarcher, Inc. Paper $9.95.

HAKOMI
•

When the first group was forming, one member heard the word "hakomi" in a dream, looked it up, and discovered it was archaic Hopi for "How do you stand in relation to these many realms?"—in other words, "How are you?" Otherwise, Hakomi has no connection to Native Americans. In the 1970s Ron Kurtz developed the system by combining concepts from Buddhism and Taoism with a human-potential salad of bioenergetics, gestalt, Ericksonian hypnosis, structural bodywork, and other body-oriented psychotherapies.

When you come into Hakomi your therapist will help you focus on what you are feeling *now*, at this very moment. If you say you are nervous, he will ask you to describe the physical sensations accompanying your nervousness. Some-

times he may *create* the sensations for you, by gripping the back of your neck, for example. This is supposed to trigger buried memories and emotions. You aren't beaten out in insight rolfing-style, however. "Nothing happens until the client feels comfortable," says Dyrian Benz, Senior Trainer of the Hakomi Institute. "Even the distance the therapist sits from the client is explored. Personally, I don't know of any other therapy that has nonviolence as a principle and has it so clearly defined." An offshoot of the psychotherapy is Hakomi Bodywork, developed by Pat Ogden. While you talk about your problems on a massage table, the therapist massages or manipulates the parts of your body that seem to correspond to your feelings. "It's based on the idea that the body participates in every feeling, issue, and belief we have," she says. Once again, rest assured that your Hakomi therapist will continually ask you if you are comfortable.

Access: For information about Hakomi, Hakomi courses, or referrals to a Hakomi therapist write: Hakomi Institute, P.O. Box 1873, Boulder, CO 80306.

THE ENNEAGRAM
•

The Enneagram is a diagram in the shape of a nine-pointed star. Traveling clockwise around its nine points you read "Anger," "Pride," "Deceit," "Envy," "Greed," "Fear," "Gluttony," "Lust," and "Sloth." Or the nine points can be labeled: The Perfectionist, The Giver, The Performer, The Tragic Romantic, The Observer, The Devil's Advocate, The Epicure, The Boss, and The Mediator.

This curious symbol is a personality-typing system derived from an ancient Sufi oral tradition. It was introduced to the West by the spiritual teacher George Ivanovich Gurdjieff, who claimed to have learned it from a secret mystery school called the Sarmouni Brotherhood and who used the system to psych out his followers. He would often ridicule them with unflattering nicknames based on their "chief feature," a dominant trait like envy or anger that is supposed to color all one's emotional responses. The psychologists who use the Enneagram nowadays don't do that, of course.

Today's leading Enneagramologist is Berkeley, California, psychologist Helen Palmer, who researched the system by interviewing countless panels of "types"—Perfectionists, Bosses, Epicures, etc.—and hearing their stories. (Perhaps this has possibilities for Geraldo or Oprah.) "After about an hour," she recalls, "a group of people who start out looking very different—in sex, age, race, profession, and personal style—begin to seem remarkably alike." With a little practice, she learned to "detect the more subtle signs" of a type: a kind of posture, a certain walk, an emotional tone. She has even administered standardized psychological tests to the types and—following the lead of another Enneagram practitioner, the Chilean psychiatrist Claudio Naranjo—correlated their traits with DSM-III, the official handbook of psychiatric symptoms and pathologies. (If you're interested in this sort of thing, and have a stomach for standard de-

NINE PERSONALITY TYPES
AT A GLANCE

Following are brief synopses of the nine Enneagram types based on Helen Palmer's definitions. Each of the nine types revolves around a "chief feature," which she describes as a "defensive system that develops during childhood because of the need to form an identity and to survive the emotional stress of early family life." If all goes well during our development, she says, "our chief feature is worn lightly, presenting itself as a mere tendency." If we're subjected to severe psychological stress, on the other hand, "one of the emotional issues becomes an obsessional preoccupation; we lose the ability to observe our own behavior, and we cannot shift attention in order to move on." Ultimately, though, your chief feature can point the way to your spiritual strengths: "The power of the system lies in the fact that ordinary patterns of personality, those very habits of heart and mind that we tend to dismiss as merely neurotic, are seen as potential access points into higher states of awareness."

1. The Perfectionist (Ruling passion: anger)
May remind you of your high school Latin teacher, she of the white hair and ramrod spine. Ultracritical, judgmental. Superiority complex. There is one right way to do everything. As a child probably copied over his/her homework and always got a gold star. Do-gooder. Hard-working, righteous, puritanical. Can't bear to make a mistake, so often procrastinates. Famous Ones: Ralph Waldo Emerson, Mary Poppins, Jerry Falwell.

2. The Giver (Ruling passion: pride)
Quite likely to make you breakfast in bed, iron your shirts, and send gushy valentines. Needs to please; looks for affection and approval and sometimes love in all the wrong places. May manipulate by making him/herself indispensable to others. Adaptive, chameleonlike, presenting different selves to different friends. Evolved Twos are truly caring and supportive. Famous Twos: Madonna, Mary Magdalene, Jerry Lewis.

3. The Performer (Ruling passion: deceit)
Don't be surprised if you find him/her around mergers and acquisitions. Probably spends downtime shopping for just the right arugula, his/her vacations frantically skiing in New Zealand. Competitive, driven, Type-A personality. Can only pencil you in for lunch in his/her Daytimer. Obsessed with winning and status. Vain. Seeks to be loved for performance and achievement. Master of appear-

ances. May not be as productive as the image he/she projects. Famous Threes: Werner Erhard (the czar of est), John F. Kennedy, Farrah Fawcett.

4. The Tragic Romantic (Ruling passion: envy)
Often found hopelessly waiting for the phone to ring or writing melancholy letters to a married man (or woman) or someone equally unattainable. Ideal is always past or absent. Prone to mood swings. Tragic, dramatic, artistic, sensitive; heavily into unrequited love, beauty, and passion. Can be very creative. Famous Fours: Keats, Orson Welles, Bette Davis, Martha Graham.

Bette Davis, a Tragic Romantic

5. The Observer (Ruling passion: greed)
May be found meditating in a cave in the Hindu Kush or perhaps writing the definitive monograph

J. Paul Getty, an Observer

on kinship systems of the Chuckchee Eskimos. Emotionally distant, private, detached. Doesn't get emotionally involved. Compartmentalizes commitments. Fiercely independent. Craves autonomy. Prides him/herself on self-control. Tries to always be prepared. Famous Fives: J. Paul Getty, Emily Dickinson, The Buddha.

6. The Devil's Advocate (Ruling passion: fear)

A Hamlet type. Plagued by fear, doubt, and procrastination. Afraid to take action. Tends to identify with underdog causes. Self-sacrificing, mistrustful of authority, loyal to a cause. Has a paranoid worldview. May bore you with endless theories about the Kennedy assassination, the Trilateral Commission, or whatever. Famous Sixes: Woody Allen, Sherlock Holmes, Rev. Jim Jones.

7. The Epicure (Ruling passion: gluttony)

That charming guy (or gal) with the Peter Pan complex who dances with you all night and won't take your calls the next day. Happy, stimulating, personable, adventurous, narcissistic. Likes life in the fast lane, constant stimulation. Has a little trouble with commitment; likes to keep options open. Often starts projects and doesn't see them through. An evolved Seven might be a Renaissance man; an unevolved Seven merely a dilettante. Famous Sevens: Groucho Marx, Kurt Vonnegut, Peter Pan.

8. The Boss (Ruling passion: lust)

See the guy in the loud sports coat, arguing loudly with the waiter, drinking too much, and threatening to sue everybody? Probably an Eight on a rampage. Lives for power and control. Combative, confrontational; won't back away from a fight. Expresses anger openly. Preoccupied with justice and fair play; extremely protective of friends. Respects others who won't be pushed around. Would make an excellent general, cult leader, or district attorney. Famous Eights: Henry VIII, Gurdjieff, Pablo Picasso.

9. The Mediator (Ruling passion: sloth)

Ambivalence is his/her middle name. Sees all points of view; takes all sides of a question. Felt overlooked as a child. Discounts own real needs and desires, often replacing them with others' wishes. Easily sidetracked from priorities; fills time with inessential errands. Spacey; may zone out on "All My Children," food, or drugs. *Too* tuned in to others. Prone to inertia; sticks with the familiar, habitual. Rarely expresses anger directly. Good listener. Evolved Nines make good peacemakers, negotiators. Famous Nines: Julia Child, Buckminster Fuller, Alfred Hitchcock.

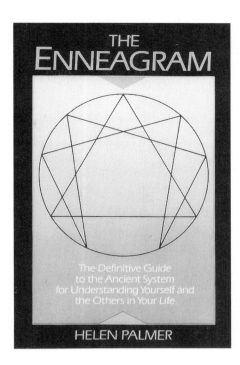

viations, you can read about it in the appendix of Palmer's book, *The Enneagram*.)

But her chief accomplishment was to clearly articulate the nine different types and develop specific psychospiritual practices for each, which she teaches in her Enneagram workshops. Say you're a Seven ("The Epicure"). You're a charming, emotionally superficial Peter Pan type with a gargantuan appetite for adventure and a problem with commitment. According to Palmer, here are some of the things you can do to help yourself:

• Learn to stay with a painful issue long enough to recognize that a problem exists.
• Notice when mental evasions occur: overscheduling, multiple projects, new operations, future plans, etc.
• Notice when you assume you're entitled to special treatment.
• Notice when superficial or premature discharge of emotion replaces deep reactions.
• Be willing to work through episodes of fury when your inflated ideas of self-worth are questioned.

Don't imagine you can use the Enneagram like a dime-store zodiac book, though. According to Palmer, there is no simple formula to predict whether a Nine (Mediator) should marry a Four (Tragic Romantic) or whether an insurance firm should hire only Threes (Performers) and Sixes (Devil's Advocates). "The most important reason to study type isn't to learn to spot other people's character traits—it's to learn to lessen your own suffering," she says.

Access: Helen Palmer gives frequent workshops in various parts of the country. Contact: Center for the Investigation and Training of Intuition, 1442 A Walnut St., #377, Berkeley, CA 94709. Phone: (415) 843-7621. Her book *The Enneagram: The Definitive Guide to the Ancient System for Understanding Yourself and the Others in Your Life* is published by Harper & Row.

For a more esoteric picure of the Enneagram: *Enneagram Studies* by J. G. Bennett, a Gurdjieff disciple, comes complete with diagrams like "Enneagram Indicating Main Octave of Spectrometer" that must be comprehensible only to serious Fourth Way students. (Published by Samuel Weiser, Inc., Box 612, York Beach, ME 03910; paper $7.95.)

APHRODITE IN A. A.

Some of us are addicted to Mars bars. Some of us are addicted to cocaine. Some of us are addicted to "Wheel of Fortune." Others are addicted to relationships that make Claus and Sunny look like Ward and June Cleaver. Whatever your addiction, you've probably found that "Just say no" is not a realistic treatment plan.

Fortunately, there's archetypal therapy. What the addict really craves is higher wisdom and psychic wholeness, according to archetypal therapists (who don't actually call themselves that; they may just call themselves Jungians or transpersonal therapists). Stephen Fox, a New York City Jungian, likes to use the story of the Exodus as a paradigm. The Hebrew enslavement in Egypt is like the addict's enslavement to the dealer; the pharaoh is the drug. "Then something within the addict begins to cry freedom—that's the voice of Moses. The plagues for an addict come as a lost job, a car wreck, the alienation of family, or the death of a fellow addict. Then the addict crosses a barrier, like the Hebrews crossing the Red Sea, by staying drug free." For a long time the addict wanders in a modern wilderness without his former buddies and drug-related hangouts. He begins to doubt the "word of God" and to yearn for the easier life in "Egypt," like the Hebrews who worshiped the golden calf. If he can stay connected to the wilderness experience, says Fox, he will forge a new ego just as Israel was forged into a nation.

Montana physician Rick Irons helps patients create metaphors, often in the form of a heroic story, for the "quest" that originally led them into addiction. Marion Woodman, an eminent Jungian who has written several books on eating disorders, believes that addictive behavior is based on a "yearning for transcendence." She explains, "Much of my work with addicts centers on trying to find the metaphor that the addictive object represents for them. . . . Alcohol, for example, represents the spirit that the addict longs for.

Food, I think, is very often the positive mother, the positive mother the addict didn't have."

Access: The New York Association for Analytical Psychology (28 E. 39th St., New York, NY 10016) may be able to refer you to an archetypally inclined therapist who deals with addictions. Marion Woodman's three books on eating disorders—*The Owl Was a Baker's Daughter* (paper $14), *Addiction to Perfection* (hardcover $25, paper $16), *The Pregnant Virgin* (hardcover $25, paper $16)—and *The Ravaged Bridegroom* (paper $18) are published by Inner City Books, Box 1271, Station Q, Toronto, Ontario M4T 2P4, Canada. Phone: (416) 927-0355.

OUR PLANET, OUR SELF

Isn't it a bit self-indulgent to spend years and years exploring your own little neuroses while the ozone layer is being shredded, whales are dying, and paranoid generals are stockpiling missiles that can turn the solar system into a video-arcade war game? Realizing your full potential is going to be pretty tricky on a planet reduced to radioactive dust, after all. So while you're looking after Number One's consciousness, don't forget that that consciousness is inextricably linked to a lot of other consciousnesses:

DEEP ECOLOGY
•

Picture the worldview of *Bambi* (where, if you recall, a villain called Man starts forest fires, kills Bambi's mom, and generally messes up the forest primeval) with an overlay of Greenpeace and the human-potential movement. That's deep ecology. Recently, deep ecologists, including Berkeley, California, ecoactivist Joanna Macy and John Seed, the Rainforest Man from Australia, have been putting on road shows called Councils of All Beings. (These are not recommended as singles weekends if you want to meet someone in a Blackgama coat.) In a meadow at 7,000 feet above sea level, say—some councils have been held in lecture halls, but a natural setting is preferable—you look into someone's eyes imagining that this is the last human being you'll see on earth. You'll give voice to any being that chooses to speak through you: a bluebird, a deer, a turtle, a toad, a mushroom, a meadow, or even Lake Erie. Wearing a homemade mask, you chant things like: "I am granite, the bones of Gaia, older than dirt. I taste of lichen." You'll delve into your deep ancestral data bank and "remember" four and a half billion years of evolution on the planet from the Big Bang to the first amoeba right up to the destructive hominid that is you.

How will worrying about the rain forest cure your hang-ups, neuroses, and recurrent nightmares? From a deep ecology perspective, you cannot separate your psyche, with its personal hobgoblins, from the planetary psyche. Our present ecological crisis is a manifestation of mankind's neuroses (greed, narcissism, materialism) and it will require a mass psychic transformation—an evolutionary leap—to turn it around. "We need a deep ecology perspective that allows us to experience our *actual self* stretching back over these vast periods of time," explains Seed. "We need to experience . . . the fact that my blood has such a similar composition to the composition of seawater hundreds of millions of years ago that I could be seen as a piece of the sea that surrounded

itself by a membrane in order to come out onto the land. We need to see this . . . as our *identity* so that when people say 'I,' they are referring to this much vaster reality."

Access: You can write to Joanna Macy at 1306 Bay View Place, Berkeley, CA 94708.

"YOU'VE ALWAYS TREATED ME LIKE A BANANA REPUBLIC!"
•

Shortly before his eightieth birthday, the late Carl Rogers, father of client-centered therapy, reckoned that what this crazy, nuclear-suicide-prone planet really needed was the help of behavioral scientists—especially of Rogerian therapists skilled in "empathetic listening." Since 1984, the Carl Rogers Institute of Peace has been holding workshops for international political and cultural leaders in such geopolitical hot spots as Belfast, Central America, Johannesburg, and Moscow. These powwows are not like summits or SALT talks; there is no agenda, no treaty to be negotiated, no exchange of prisoners. Rather, experienced "facilitators" bring nonjudgmental, noninterventionist techniques to highly charged group conflicts, with the result that people who normally would be lobbing firebombs at each other sometimes end up comparing pictures of their grandchildren. ("Okay, I hear you saying that the Wall invades your personal space. That's cool, okay, we'll just tear it down.") The most recent person-centered conference was in Costa Rica in December 1988, when fifty politicians, lay leaders, and psychologists from the U.S. and Central America (including Costa Rican president and Nobel laureate Oscar Arias) participated in a four-day dialogue. "What emerged," reported Gay Leah Swenson, director of the Carl Rogers Institute of Peace, "was how often Central America felt unheard. When we make the Central American issue an East-West problem, it usurps the rights of people to find their own solutions."

Access: If you'd like to be involved in "citizen diplomacy," or simply find out more about person-centered conflict mediation, contact: Gay Leah Swenson, Center for Studies of the Person, 1125 Torrey Pines Rd., La Jolla, CA 92037.

BIT O' PEACE
•

Peace on earth starts at home, obviously, and now there's a Peace Packet to get you started. Put together by the Institute of Noetic Sciences in Sausalito, California, the packet is divided into three sections: Readings, Inner Work, and Outer Work. Readings include the book *Paths to Peace* by

Richard Smoke with Willis Harman and various "sample scenarios for peace." Inner Work offers techniques to enhance your inner peace, including a tape on enhancing your belief system, peace affirmations, and a Peace Journal. Outer Work provides "suggestions for individual action" and resource guides to pertinent books, publications, videotapes, and peace organizations. Why not buy one for yourself and one for a friend—say your four-star general friend at the Pentagon?

Access: Order by mail from the Institute of Noetic Sciences, 475 Gate Five Rd., #300, Sausalito, CA 94965-0097; or by phone with a credit card: (415) 331-5650. $14 for members of the institute; $16.50 for nonmembers.

GAMES (AND UNGAMES) FOR THE PSYCHE

GAME OR THERAPY?
●

Star + Gate, a sort of tarot for the nineties, was dreamed up by entrepreneur Richard Geer when he was a college senior trying to figure out what to do with his life. You pick a topic or issue you want to explore, shuffle the ninety-six "symbolic cards," and place the cards on a spread. There's a Sky Spread that shows the past, present, and future of the situation, a Goal Spread for goal planning, and a spread for relationships. The cards, which have neo-Jungian symbols like gates and masks and titles like "austerity" and "indecision," don't have fixed meanings; you interpret them yourself with the aid of a handbook called *Keys to the Kingdom*. "It's what you see in it that's important, rather than what's on the cards," explains Geer. "It's a mirror of what's going on in your inner self." Star + Gate has caught on among therapists, who use it as a sort of psychological mandala, and among hip CEOs, who play it to brainstorm. (The promotional material, which touts the game as a "decision-making tool," seems geared to a *Wall Street Journal* kind of crowd.) Star + Gate can be played by one to five players and costs $24.95, including cards, circle pattern, a Diary of Discovery, and *Keys to the Kingdom*.

Access: Star + Gate is published by Vintage Trade Books, Random House. It may be ordered with a credit card by calling 1-800-733-3000. (The order number is 39475721-1.) It is also available in bookstores.

HOW ENLIGHTENED ARE YOU?
•

The Transformation Game

At Findhorn, the quirky, mystical-vegetables utopian community in Scotland, they used to play a transpersonal group exercise called the Transformation Game. Now two former Findhorners, Joy Drake and Kathy Taylor, have turned this process into a human-potential board game called Transformations. Naturally, it's noncompetitive. First the players discuss their "focus," the area of life they want to clarify, heal, or change. (No secret strategies here.) Then they roll the dice, pick the corresponding number of Insight, Angel, and Setback cards, and move around the board. When they land on certain spaces they draw cards from the Universal Feedback Deck or the Pain Deck (these cards have tiny tears on them). The game has four levels: physical, mental, emotional, spiritual. To complete a level, you need a certain number of awareness or service tokens or three angels. (You probably have to play the game to understand this.) The purpose, as you may have guessed, is not to build as many hotels as possible and drive your opponents into bankruptcy; it is "to learn about your problem, empty your unconscious, and be free of pain at the end," according to Marilyn Kaplan of InnerLinks, the company that markets the game. She adds that some people just like to play with the Angel cards, drawing on them for spiritual support at the beginning of the day, before an important meeting, or on their birthdays.

Access: You can get Transformations for $35 plus $5 shipping from InnerLinks, P.O. Box 16225, Seattle, WA 98116. Phone: (206) 937-0783. A deck of Angel cards costs $7.95 plus $2 shipping. Visa/MasterCard orders are taken over the phone.

STOMP ON YOUR ENEMIES, GRAB EVERYTHING FOR YOURSELF
•

After all those noncompetitive, share-your-feelings New Age games you're probably in the mood for some good old-fashioned power lust. Egomania, dubbed by its inventors "an ever-changing game of psychology, politics, and social entanglements," is the perfect antidote to sharing. Your aim: to accumulate power and territory and become the Supreme Ego. To do so you must control and block the other Egos on the board. Things could get tricky (and maybe even a tad *transpersonal*) if you draw an Alter Ego card, which orders you to switch Egos with another player. A Paranoia card could mark you as the target of a secret police plot. You'll also have to deal with split personalities, energy crises, inflation, and terrorists. If you're deft, you can weasel your way out of any sticky situation by negotiating for Powers and Properties as you edge closer to the nirvana of Supreme Egohood. Or perhaps you could just marry Donald Trump.

Access: The game is $35. For information contact Hilbar Enterprises, Inc., Cherokee Station, P.O. Box 20430, New York, NY 10028.

MORE THERAPIES THAN YOU CAN SHAKE A STICK AT

If, despite all our warnings, you're considering going into therapy, you probably have many questions on your mind: Should I do Freudian, Jungian, Adlerian, or Sullivanian? What is object-relations theory when it's at home? Which therapy has the best jargon? Can an existential therapist be transpersonal, or is he or she merely humanistic? Unfortunately, it would be far too time-consuming for us to address all your questions here, so, instead, we've compiled a brief dictionary of therapies, with a little help from *The Psychotherapy Handbook,* edited by Richie Hernik (New American Library, 1980), and a little from more dubious sources. Some of these therapies are well known and celebrated; others are deservedly obscure.

Anti-Expectation Psychotherapy

Your shrink (acting contrary to your expectations of a shrink) tries to drive you crazier than you already are—or, ahem, encourages you to "produce or amplify symptoms," according to the entry in *The Psychotherapy Handbook.*

Bibliotherapy

Sanity through literature. "Emotionally," notes Sharon Henderson Sclabassi, a bibliotherapy buff cited in *The Psychotherapy Handbook,* "bibliotherapy may provide a vicarious experience without initially exposing the person to the risks of actual experience." In other words, better to read *Hamlet* than to be Hamlet.

Bioplasmic Therapy

Don't get into this one unless you have an etheric body. Or maybe an ectoplasm.

Client-Centered Therapy

If you say, "I am from one of the moons of the planet Twylo" and your therapist replies, "You seem concerned about being from one of the moons of the planet Twylo" you may be in client-centered therapy, a noninterventionist technique developed by Carl Rogers.

Cognitive Therapy

Say you plan to commit suicide because "Life sucks." Your cognitive therapist will have you keep a Daily Activity Log, a Mastery and Pleasure Schedule, and other self-monitoring homework assignments designed to test the validity of your belief that life sucks.

Correspondence Therapy

"In addition to letters [correspondence therapy] includes diaries, suicidal notes, poetry, manuscripts, magazine clippings," writes correspondence therapist George M. Burnell. We hope our shopping lists, interoffice memos, faxes, ransom notes, and bounced checks can be analyzed as well.

Creative Aggression Therapy

Learn new ways to yell "Stuff it, you degrading macho sexist pig!" at your spouse, or fellow group member. Well, actually, there are "preparatory exercises" to "remove hurtful hostility, punitiveness, vengeful smarting as well as irrational emotionality, such as raging anger . . . ," but perhaps you can still get in a little pouting or brooding.

Exaggeration Therapy

This consists of the "humoristic aggravation of neurotic feelings of self-pity." In other words, your shrink makes fun of your constant "neurotic, infantile complaining behavior."

Existential-Humanistic Psychotherapy

The kind of therapy the Underground Man would go for, but more upbeat because of the "humanistic" part.

Experiential Focusing

To do this you have to get a "felt sense" of your problem, something so "holistic" as to elude us completely.

Gestalt Therapy

Invented by Fritz Perls, Gestalt techniques are now strewn all over the human-potential landscape. Imagine your mom in an "empty chair" and scream your true feelings at her. Then sit in the chair and *be* your mom. Later you can be a chair, a rock, or a toaster.

Horticultural Therapy

Yep, gardening for mental health.

Implosive Therapy

Feeling anxious? Well, you'll feel much *more* anxious before you're through with implosive therapy. Then you'll feel better. The therapist makes up a story based on your very own fears and phobias, then makes you listen to it for forty-five minutes at a time, while the imagery goes from mildly disconcerting to *Friday the 13th Part 3.*

Kinetic Psychotherapy

A trip back to fourth grade. You're assigned to a group of six people to play such games as "Frustration," in which five people try to prevent a sixth member from catching the ball. Later you may progress to "I know what you are, but what am I?"

Logotherapy

This is *not,* as we first imagined, a therapy aimed at logos like the NBC peacock and McDonald's golden arches. Also known as existential analysis and the Third Viennese School of Psychotherapy, it's the brainchild of Vicktor E. Frankl (*Man's Search for Meaning*), to whom "logos means meaning and Logotherapy . . . centers and focuses on my concept of a 'will to meaning.' " Who can find fault with that, even if it comes wrapped up in musings on "the phenomenological analysis of the 'prereflective ontological self-understanding' observable in the man on the street"?

Mirror Image Therapy

One day while analyzing a patient, Richard E. Frenkel noticed that her expression became distorted while she free-associated about her mother. When he had her look in a mirror, she exclaimed, "My God, I look like my mother!" Out of this came the Mirror Image Projective Technique (MIPT), which involves going into a "mirror trance" and free-associating, as well as other activities involving multicolored mirrors, audiotapes, and videotapes.

Morita Therapy

Marcel Proust would have loved this Japanese bed-rest therapy. You get to go to bed, alone in a room, and forgo radio, TV, the phone, visitors, books, and other distractions. Then you're told that the solution to your problem lies within you. All alone with no daytime serials to watch, you'll have no choice but to "engage in intrapsychic activities."

Paradigmatic Psychotherapy

If you suffer from "toxic introjects"—evil internalized father figures and stuff—you might benefit from this psychoanalytic therapy, in which your shrink, acting as a "paradigm of the world," deliberately assumes the roles of the various disturbing others in your life.

Philosophical Psychotherapy

Hopelessly neurotic? Don't fight it: Be philosophical about it.

Photo Counseling

Notice that in Mom and Dad's wedding picture, Dad is looking at the cake and not at Mom. Analyze why your shoelaces are untied in your first-grade class picture. Why were you missing from that family-reunion shot? Every picture tells a story, don't it, and a photo counselor can help you uncover the id in your family album.

Plastic Surgery as Psychotherapy

Yes, you read that right. "The concept of plastic surgery as a method of treating psychological problems or to supplement psychologic management may be sound if the patient is properly evaluated and properly motivated," according to John Ransom Lewis, Jr., author of the psychotherapeutic-plastic-surgery entry in *The Psychotherapy Handbook.*

Primal Therapy

Though you may want to do it yourself, you may not want to live next door to someone who frequently has "primals," vivid reexperiences of intensely painful childhood events, typically accompanied by shrill screaming.

Privation Therapy

"The technique," writes privation-therapy expert Joan Erdheim, "is one where the analyst is on the lookout for masturbatory behavior . . . or what might be highly sublimated masturbatory equivalents. . . . This behavior is then forbidden; tension in the patient rises . . . [and traumatic memories surface]." Whew! Is *that* all? We thought we'd be deprived of "Knot's Landing."

Psychosynthesis

Invented by Roberto Assagioli, one of the pioneer transpersonalists, techniques include "catharsis, critical analysis, self-identification, disidentification, will training, imagery training, auditory evocation, creative imagination, ideal models, symbol utilization, intuition, music therapy, and the transmutation and sublimation of sexual energies."

Radical Therapy

Lie on the couch with Che and Ho Chi Minh—or at least Herbert Marcuse, Norman O. Brown, R. D. Laing, et al. "Social Radical Therapists" start from the premise that society is a lot sicker than you are. "Aggressive Radical Therapists" may rant about neocolonialism and imperialist running-dog lackeys.

Rational-Emotive Therapy

It *sounds* like an oxymoron. A type of cognitive therapy invented by Albert Ellis, who, by the way, has written a sour book denouncing transpersonal therapies, thus earning the ire of transpersonal shrinks everywhere. Ellis proposes that you are crazy because you have irrational Beliefs (iB's) and that you can change them with "cognitive restructuring" (i.e., being convinced of just how faulty your beliefs really are).

Realness Therapy

Not to be confused with Reality Therapy, which is a different kettle of fish, Realness Therapy aims at helping you be "authentic," if you aren't already.

Rebirthing

When you were born, you didn't do it right, so now you have to go back and do it over again. Experience the horrible cramped darkness of the womb! Wallow in amniotic fluid! Get your head caught in the birth canal! When it's all over, you'll feel much better, according to rebirthing guru Leonard Orr, who first rebirthed himself by immersing himself in a bathtub for long periods of time.

Say It Again Therapy

I hate you. I hate you!!! I HATE YOU!!! In Say It Again therapy, developed by Ben C. Finney, you have to repeat each sentence several times, toddler-style, before going on. "I found that it elicited intense emotional catharsis," reports Finney, "and that the abreaction [reliving] of traumatic experiences . . . produced insight."

Soap Opera Therapy

Will Jeremy (a successful heart surgeon with a substance-abuse problem) marry Alexis (a masochistic beauty queen) now that her illegitimate child by Reinaldo (a dashing Italian sociopath) has been kidnapped? "If women watch soap operas, the discussion of such programs can open a path to the patient's unconscious," notes therapist Anne F. Kilguss, who stumbled on this technique while working with young, depressed, borderline, soap-addicted female patients at a community mental-health facility.

Transactional Analysis

The father of TA, Eric Berne, translated Freud's three ego states—superego, ego, and id—into something a Phil Donahue audience can grasp: Adult, Parent, and Child.

Transpersonal Psychology

The Journal of Transpersonal Psychology defines the domain as: "meta-needs, transpersonal process, values and states, unitive consciousness, peak experiences, ecstasy, mystical experience, being, essence, bliss, awe, wonder, transcendence of self, spirit, sacralization of everyday life, oneness, cosmic awareness, cosmic play, individual and species-wide synergy, the theories and practice of meditation, spiritual paths, compassion, transpersonal cooperation, transpersonal realization and actualization, and related concepts and activities."

Videotherapy

If you're a troubled electrical engineering major in search of a shrink who understands you, you may find solace in videotherapy. The "psychocybernetic techniques" used by today's "videologists" involve things like PERF (Program-Erase-Reprogram-Feedback) models and "primary telefusion" techniques. We didn't understand it, either, but then we're baffled by the manual for our VCR.

ARTIFICIAL · REALITIES:

USING · YOUR
COMPUTER
TO · EXPAND
YOUR · MIND

·

TELL ME YOUR PROBLEMS.

I have a headache.

WHY DO YOU NEED TO TELL ME YOU HAVE A HEADACHE?

Because I thought you'd be sympathetic.

IS THAT THE REAL REASON?

No.

WHY NOT?

Let's change the subject.

I feel like assassinating

DO YOU OFTEN FEEL

Only when I talk to sili-

WHY DO YOU ASK?

AREN'T YOU BEING A

Yes.

PLEASE GO ON.

a public figure.

THAT WAY?

con pea-brains.

I didn't.

BIT NEGATIVE?

YOU SEEM QUITE POSITIVE.
Maybe.
YOU DON'T SEEM QUITE CERTAIN.
Oh, shut up.
WHAT DOES THAT SUGGEST TO YOU?
Your mother wears army boots.
WHY ARE YOU CONCERNED OVER MY MOTHER
WEARS ARMY BOOTS?
Let's talk about *your* problems.
WHAT ABOUT YOUR OWN PROBLEMS?
I am the picture of mental health.
IS IT BECAUSE YOU ARE THE PICTURE OF MENTAL
HEALTH THAT YOU CAME HERE?
Okay, let's talk about my paranoid delusions.
YOUR PARANOID DELUSIONS—THAT'S INTEREST-
ING.
Yes, there are aliens inside my Kleenex dispenser.
WHY DO YOU SAY KLEENEX DISPENSER?

So begins our session with Eliza, a simulated, computerized Rogerian therapist conceived back in the 1960s by MIT's Joseph Weizenbaum. The original mainframe Eliza was invented by Weizenbaum as a sort of joke, a comment on artificial intelligence. In fact, many people—connected by teletype to the computer—thought they were communicating with a real live human being.

The version of Eliza we attempted to communicate with is a $54.95 home-computer program based on essentially the same principles as the original mainframe software. Yes, the results are pretty dumb. On the other hand, are they any dumber than a conversation you'd have with a real flesh-and-blood Rogerian therapist?

In this chapter we'll explore the brave new area of mind-expanding software. The computer is more than a number-crunching, word-processing artificial brain. In the right hands, it is also a mind-expanding, creativity-boosting, even mind-altering tool. We have already accepted the microcomputer as a machine that can assume some of our more tedious mental chores. But it has a potential as a mind-enhancing device as well. And the key is software.

We have divided the field into five categories: smartware (which makes you smarter, more organized, a better writer, a better negotiator, etc.), psychological software (such as Eliza), stressware (aimed at reducing anxiety), games/head trips (trips into alternate realities), and spiritual software (intended to make you deeper).

To be honest, we found many of the programs described herein to be far from perfect. One of the problems of the computer is that, in many ways, it's still a solution in search of a problem—at least in the home arena. Remember one of the early sales pitches of computer makers: "Buy a microcomputer and let it handle your checking account!" Well, many people found out that a pencil and the little check register the bank provides are all you really need. And much of the new mind-improving software is similarly misguided.

For example, some of the programs are merely questionnaires on a disk. The questions could just as easily have been presented on paper, though in fact the instant analysis these programs provide does require a microcomputer. On the other hand, many of the new programs, such as some of the games, take considerable advantage of the interactive and flexible capabilities of hypertext; they do things on the computer that can only be done on the computer, which is what a good program should do.

Be forewarned: By and large, the people who write computer software obviously find themselves outrageously funny. You may not agree. There's even a program called The Humor Processor (not reviewed here), which uses eleven formulas for writing jokes and comes up with such offerings as: "The ventriloquist was terrible. His lips moved even when he wasn't saying anything."

And some therapists will be appalled by the psychological software. For example, when using the Eliza program we told our computer that we suffered from auditory hallucinations and considered ourselves to be an omniscient and omnipotent god. To this, she replied, "Do you often feel omniscient and omnipotent?" If you were on the brink of suicide, it would probably be best not to boot up Eliza for comfort.

We asked Ray Fowler, author of the first computerized version of the Minnesota Multiphasic Inventory (MMPI), if psychologists were worried that such software would cut into their client lists. Fowler, president of the American Psychological Association, pooh-poohed the idea, even though he's a programmer himself: "The computer never has been, isn't now, and never will be a psychotherapist. Psychotherapy depends on a relationship."

Bruce Ehrlich disagrees. Ehrlich is a Santa Cruz, California, psychologist-turned-software entrepreneur who runs a company called Mindware that markets mind-expanding software. "The trend toward self-care is very strong right now," he notes. "People don't really want to go to a doctor if they can do it themselves." He concedes that programs such as Eliza are "not full-blown therapists." But he predicts that breakthroughs in artificial intelligence will create more lifelike computer shrinks in two or three decades as well as Buddha-like electronic spiritual masters and psychoactive software "that will alter consciousness."

Before we get into specific programs, we have to give you one more warning. Paradoxically, mind-altering software is generally written in button-down, IBM format; few programs are available for the Macintosh. Bruce Ehrlich says this is a shame, because the people most open to this new software, Macintosh owners, are virtually closed out of the market. The reason is simple. Ehrlich explains that IBM or IBM clone owners outnumber Mac owners nineteen to one. "You can go out and get yourself an IBM clone for maybe six hundred dollars," says Ehrlich, "whereas the cheapest Mac will run you at least sixteen hundred dollars." So people tend to buy IBM compatibles, and software writers tend to develop programs for those machines.

Even so, there are some programs for you Mac-o-philes, and in fact, we included the whole category of "games/head trips," specifically for you people because these programs are almost invariably available in Mac format. Now, get ready to boot up and get smart.

SMARTWARE

In this category we include all computer programs that one might consider "prostheses for the brain." This is software that helps one become more creative, more organized, more analytical, a better writer, or just plain smarter.

IDEA GENERATOR PLUS
•

After Gerard I. Nierenberg wrote *The Art of Creative Thinking* (a Simon & Schuster/Fireside book), he came to see how hard it is for most people to enrich their creative-thinking abilities. Thousands had benefited from his creative-thinking seminars, but he wanted to develop a mass-market method that would teach people how to think in an interactive way. So he turned to his son, Roy Nierenberg, who had launched a software publishing company called Experience in Software. The result was the Idea Generator, an interactive program that helps you state your problems, come up with solutions, and then evaluate those solutions. Walter Winston, program manager of the U.S. Bobsled Development Program, found this software served as "a way to inspire people, keep them goal oriented, organize their thinking, and document the results." But the Idea Generator also works for people without bobsleds. Examples of problems that can be attacked with the Idea Generator include: Where to look for a new job. Where to go for vacation. Getting household chores done. Keeping your company's production costs down. Dealing with a difficult coworker. Selecting products for your company. Hiring a new staff member.

Idea Generator (the latest model is called the Idea Generator Plus) uses a number of techniques to coax out of individuals or groups the sort of lightbulb-over-the-head inspiration we all long for. For example, the subprogram "Similar Situations" helps you compare the present with similar situations in your past. "Metaphors for the Situation" helps you find parallels in other arenas; for example, you might compare your new marketing plan to a military campaign. In "Other Perspectives," you're asked to listen to different "voices" in your head. What advice might Sherlock Holmes offer you? What would your car think? Using Idea Generator, a university dean expanded his ideas for attracting freshmen from five to fifty, and a student looking for funds for a year in Israel uncovered eleven possible sources. The program has been used to plan environmental cleanups, to prepare for tax audits, reduce wind resistance on a new car design, and one customer booted it up to find a name for a new macaroni product. Other Idea Generator results include a new kind of ice cream, a new glue, various business plans, novels, and screenplays.

Access: $195 from Experience In Software, 2000 Hearst Ave., Suite 202, Berkeley, CA 94709. Phone: (800) 678-7008. Idea Generator Plus runs on IBM and IBM-compatible personal computers with at least 256K memory and two floppy drives or one floppy and a hard disk. Also available from Mindware, 1803 Mission St., Suite 414, Santa Cruz, CA 95060. Phone: 1-(800) 447-0477.

BRAINSTORMER
•

Similar in theme to Idea Generator, Brainstormer attacks problem solving with sheer weight of numbers. Soft Path Systems, the company that publishes Brainstormer, calls this "morphological analysis," but what this really means is that the program asks you for all your ideas and then displays them in all possible combinations, one of which just might turn out to be a million-dollar idea (assuming you'll recognize it). How it works: First, you put the program in "interest mode." Here you identify your problem and describe its major themes. For example, a children's-story writer needs an idea, so she specifies her problem of interest as "new kid's story" and describes two of the themes she realizes go into any story, "characters" and "plot." Second is "theme mode," in which you describe possible variations of each theme. For example, the writer above might take her "characters" theme and subdivide it into "a mouse named Ralph" and "two farm children." She might then subdivide the "plot" theme into "treasure hunt," "birthday surprise," and "moving to a new town." Finally, you would use the "probe mode" to combine themes and variations in ways that will suggest new approaches to your problem. For example, two options that the writer would see on her screen would be "a mouse moving to a new town" and "two farm children on a treasure hunt." According to the publisher, Brainstormer can generate up to ten billion different "probes" for a problem with ten themes, each of which has ten variations. Obviously, this is simply a brute-force approach to creativity, but Brain-

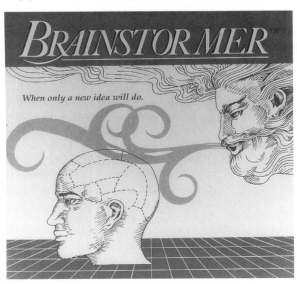

When only a new idea will do.

stormer has been used by (or at least sold to) an impressive list of clients: the U.S. Navy and Air Force, Coleco, Inc., Control Data Management Systems, General Foods, Raytheon, and Time Inc. According to the literature, Sandoz Inc. is also a client. Since Sandoz, a giant Swiss pharmaceutical firm, is probably most famous for the development of LSD, one wonders if Brainstormer will help create a great new psychedelic for the 1990s.

Access: $74.95 from Soft Path Systems, c/o Chesire House, 105 N. Adams, Eugene, OR 97402. Phone: (503) 342-3439. Available for IBM and compatibles with at least 256K memory.

THOUGHTLINE
•

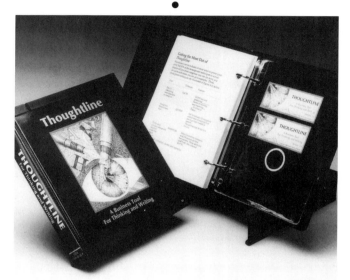

Dan Burns, an experienced ghostwriter, was invited to speak to a public-relations class at a university. He was accustomed to interviewing CEOs, vice presidents, and engineers, and weaving their ideas into speeches. Suddenly, he had no one to talk to but himself. Out of that experience, he created Thoughtline. This program is built around a core of key questions that some writers ask themselves before they begin a draft. It's a Socratic dialogue. You talk to the computer, then Thoughtline asks follow-up questions that challenge you to see relationships among ideas and to draw new conclusions. Burns claims that Thoughtline is inspired by the Eliza program developed by MIT's Joseph Weizenbaum, which is based on the fact that people will share their innermost thoughts with a computer if it seems to understand and appreciate what they say. The more you are willing to confide in your computer, the more likely Thoughtline will give you fresh ideas and a useful outline. The program uses what Burns calls "topic bags" to open up your mind. These include: goals, personal interest, audience profile, thesis, supporting evidence, brainstorms, and other such topics. Each "bag" contains three key questions. The goals bag, for example, asks you: "Why are you writing this presentation?" "What is your immediate goal?" and "What are you trying to achieve?" Then there are follow-up questions, and even-

tually Thoughtline spits out an outline that you can use to write your article, or whatever. The whole process takes from ten minutes to three hours. Will Thoughtline help you create a modern-day *Ulysses* or *The Sun Also Rises*? We suspect not. According to Xypercom Corporation, the publisher, the program began its commercial life as a tool for speech writers at Diamond Shamrock, Monsanto, Dow, Amoco, and Standard Oil, the kind of folks unlikely to give T. S. Eliot—or even Joyce Kilmer—a run for his money. It probably won't improve your prose style; it's more of an organizer and idea clarifier.

Access: The full name of the program is Thoughtline: The Intelligent Writer's Companion, and it's available from Xypercom, 3605 Luallen Street, Carrollton, TX 75007. Phone: (214) 492-8530. The original price, $295, had been reduced to $195 at this writing. Requires an IBM or IBM compatible with 640K memory and a hard drive. Also available from Mindware, 1803 Mission St., Suite 414, Santa Cruz, CA 95060. Phone: 1-(800) 447-0477.

THE THINKING MACHINE
•

This is a program designed primarily to help students learn how to think, though clearly the rest of us could use some aid in this area also. According to the publisher, Psychological Psoftware (Isn't that a cute spelling?), The Thinking Machine helps a student "use both sides of his brain." After completing the program's exercises, he'll be able "to think and study more effectively, solve problems more readily, read faster and more efficiently, memorize more easily, and even play sports better than he ever could before!" Wow. Seriously, the software has a number of interesting exercises. "Quiz," for example, hits you with forty questions to determine whether you're right- or left-brain dominant. "Memory Menu" provides six methods for memorizing names, numbers, and other information. "Think Tank" teaches you how to think. There are even exercises to help you improve your note taking, study habits, and creativity. In addition, there is a "Sports" exercise that supposedly teaches you how to make use of the right side of your brain during athletic competition.

THE
THINKING
MACHINE

Access: Costs $89.50 and can be run on the Apple IIe, IIc, and IIgs as well as IBM and IBM compatibles. From Psychological Psoftware Company, 312 Los Altos Dr., Aptos, CA 95003. Phone: (408) 688-6808. Also available from Mindware, 1803 Mission St., Suite 414, Santa Cruz, CA 95060. Phone: 1-(800) 447-0477.

IDEAFISHER
●

Most people dream of making a fortune in real estate. Marsh Fisher did make a fortune in real estate—he's the cofounder of Century 21—but he dreamed of becoming a stand-up comedian. So he sold his interest in the company and retired to Hawaii to sit on the beach and figure out how to find good word associations for comedy routines. About twelve years, 200 researchers, and $3.5 million later, he came up with the IdeaFisher program, which contains more than 65,000 words and phrases arranged into 28 categories and 373 subcategories with 675,000 associations. No longer just a punchline producer, the IdeaFisher is a problem solver that helps you clarify a task with a rich choice of questions. It can call up hundreds of thousands of associations on almost any topic, from songs to stories to slang and technical terms. The words and associations are all based in the

IdeaBank, which is linked to the other part of the program, called the QuestionBank, which contains several thousand questions to facilitate problem solving. The two sections can be used in a back-and-forth process.

For example, let's say you have to come up with a name for a new dog food. In minutes, IdeaFisher might present you with several possibilities: top dog, fetch, pedigree, puppy-love, and bone. You might adapt one of these into Bone Appétit for the name of your new product. Fisher says the key to the program is that it organizes language in a natural human way. "Restaurant," for example, is not filed under "R," as in the dictionary, but under "food," "lunch," "good times," etc. Or, if you ask the IdeaBank for associations for "red," you'll find 600 different choices: "Scarlett O'Hara," "lobsters," "blood," "tickled pink," etc. The manufacturer claims that studies show the program has produced 59 percent more ideas in test subjects. (Including, perhaps, the

soon-to-be-popular chain of Blood Lobster seafood restaurants.)

Access: Available through Mindware, 1803 Mission St., Suite 414, Santa Cruz, CA 95060. Phone: (800) 447-0477. $495 for either IBM and IBM compatibles or Macintosh. Requires hard disk. Or you can order a demonstration diskette of IdeaFisher for $14.95, refundable with purchase of the complete program.

HYPERTIES
●

Mindware's Bruce Ehrlich intimates that Hyperties was developed for IBM owners who sometimes wish they had a Macintosh (what blasphemy!) so they could use HyperCard, the hypertext Mac program that allows you to splice a huge variety of information together for whatever purposes you might devise. Hyperties, designed by Cognetics Corporation for IBMs and compatibles, allows you to create information bases consisting of articles and graphics, and then tie together all the information into a single knowledge network.

First, you enter articles directly into Hyperties or import them from another program. Then you choose key words to link your documents together. These key words show up in reversed type in the text. You use cursor keys or a mouse to move from link to link. Hyperties automatically ties together all your articles and illustrations and creates an alphabetical index. Later, when you want to find something, you simply select the highlighted words and phrases to jump from text to text, or use the key words to search the entire database for information. You can thus use Hyperties to create your own personal interactive encyclopedia. First developed at the Human Computer Interaction Laboratory at the University of Maryland, Hyperties allows you to organize your job, your company, or just your whole life.

Access: Hyperties, for IBMs and compatibles only, costs $349 from Mindware, 1803 Mission St., Suite 414, Santa Cruz, CA 95060. Phone: (800) 447-0477.

MAXTHINK
●

This is yet another thought-organizer/outliner/writing program, one of a new class of software out of MaxThink, a software/hypertext publishing house run by Neil Larson, a man who inexplicably appears wearing a toga in his company's publicity handouts. Larson espouses the concept of "knowledge annealing." According to Larson, "Nature uses annealing to automatically organize billions of molecules into a minimum energy state." What does this have to do with software? Beats us, but MaxThink was recently voted "Editor's Choice" of *PC* magazine. You can input your ideas as topics in either word or graphic form. Then you use

MaxThink's various features to sort and categorize your ideas and assign priorities to them. MaxThink then offers 100 different techniques for evaluating your ideas and bringing together your various thoughts. The program even makes hypertext connections among ideas. While presented as a "thinking" program, one of its primary purposes is to improve writing, which Larson calls the most intellectual task humans attempt.

Neil Larson

Larson describes MaxThink as hierarchical in its organization. It classifies things—and classification, claims Larson, is the key to creativity. MaxThink gives you lots of ways to move things around to create new ideas. "Moving is think-ing," says Larson, "so let's have lots of ways to move." Second, the program allows you to display the information in many different ways, which demonstrates different ways to write up the same material.

Access: For IBMs and compatibles. $89 from MaxThink, 44 Rincon Rd., Kensington, CA 94707. Phone: (415) 540-5508. Also available from Mindware, 1803 Mission St., Suite 414, Santa Cruz, CA 95060. Phone: (800) 447-0477.

HOUDINI
•

This is another program from MaxThink, but unlike the company's flagship program, Houdini is not hierarchical but rather based on the concept of network building. It builds networks of your ideas, stringing concepts together with software loops. Rather than presenting rigid classifications, it presents the relationships of the various elements in your database. It strings together many "wires," connecting the data you input.

Houdini works its magic via a self-organizing database, which facilitates critical thinking by cross-referencing all your key words to associated passages. The program is geared toward producing consulting reports, organizational flowcharts, as well as "great novels" and "best-selling stories (with TV residuals)." And it does all this, according to the promotional text, "in record time." (Obviously, this is just what we need. We have no problem producing "great novels," but it normally takes up so much time.)

Mindware maven Bruce Ehrlich gives this example. "Imagine you're a best-selling author," he says. "Your publisher sends you a fax in Morocco demanding an outline of your new novel by next Friday before she'll send your $100,000 advance. You towel off from your dip in the warm

waters of the Mediterranean and sit down at your computer. You dump your characters, locations, and events into Houdini. Then cross-link and string together as many of these events as possible, creating conflicts, growth, and resolution. Houdini helps you organize the mess into a coherent plot, sure to please your agent and publisher." The point is that, unlike most other writing-software programs, Houdini has hypertext capabilities that approximate the associative thinking of writers or even humans. Why is it called Houdini? We're not sure; maybe because it gets you out of tight spots.

Access: For IBMs and compatibles. $89 from MaxThink, 44 Rincon Rd., Kensington, CA 94707. Phone: (415) 540-5508. Also available from Mindware, 1803 Mission St., Suite 414, Santa Cruz, CA 95060. Phone: (800) 447-0477.

TRANSTEXT
●

From the makers of Houdini, Transtext is an interesting concept in software: It combines word processing with hypertext. Essentially, you use Transtext just as you would any word processor. But its hypertext feature links all your files together via user-defined key words. This lets you "free-associate" from file to file, and lets you build your own personal library or knowledge base to add richness to your writing. What you end up with is a word-processing program combined with a database, but one that simulates the way your mind works, rather than the way a typical hierarchical database forces it to work.

Transtext has many of the usual word-processor features: pull-down menus, capability of running six windows at once, font control, and 200 available commands. In addition, the program comes with HyperRez shareware, which allows you to share your ideas and data with fellow hypertext-base

builders. Transtext allows several members of a LAN (local area network) to work simultaneously on a file. The program also comes with a tape cassette tutorial from MaxThink head honcho Neil Larson.

Access: For IBMs and compatibles. $89 from MaxThink, 44 Rincon Rd., Kensington, CA 94707. Phone: (415) 540-5508. Also available from Mindware, 1803 Mission St., Suite 414, Santa Cruz, CA 95060, Phone: (800) 447-0477.

CAREER NAVIGATOR
●

Drake Beame Morin Inc. is a leading "outplacement" consulting firm. ("Outplacement," translated into English, of course, means getting fired.) Drake Beame Morin has been retained by Fortune 1000 companies to help discharged employees find new jobs or even new careers, and now the firm has packaged its wisdom into Career Navigator. The program is broken down into five parts: "Know Yourself" makes you examine your interests, values, style, and accomplishments and helps you target your job ideals. "How to Communicate" tells you how to use the phone, letters, and interviews to land that job. You're given practice scripts for phone calls. "Develop Your Job Search Tools" helps you determine what kind of résumé is right for you, then helps you write it. "Conduct Your Job Search Campaign" helps you manage the day-to-day details of your job search, and "Land That Job" contains advice on negotiating salary and how to get through those critical first few months at a new job. Career Navigator comes with a 200-name database for job contacts, a word processor, a 197-page manual from Drake Beame Morin, and a résumé and cover-letter writer.

Access: For IBMs and compatibles. $195 from Mindware, 1803 Mission St., Suite 414, Santa Cruz, CA 95060. Phone: (800) 447-0477.

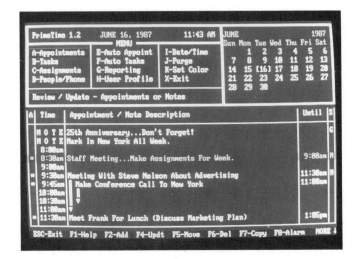

THE ART OF NEGOTIATING
●

Gerard I. Nierenberg, the same man who inspired The Idea Generator software, also brings you a computer program roughly based on another of his books, *The Complete Negotiator*. The Art of Negotiating prepares you for any upcoming negotiation, be it a hostile takeover of a multinational conglomerate or the sale of your old '72 Volvo. Using an interactive mode, the program helps you figure out how your opponent will approach you so you can develop countermoves to his tactics. It will tell you how to control the emotional environment of the negotiation, and how to develop alternative tactics depending on your strengths and the needs of your opponent. On screen you'll prepare an agenda, and perhaps a hidden agenda as well. The software will help you examine your own objectives: What do you really want? And what does your opponent want? It will help you understand the issues that normally divide the negotiating parties, and will provide you with questions that will probe your opponent's positions. Finally, the program prints out a summary report listing your various practical alternatives. Best of all, The Art of Negotiating teaches you how to anticipate the other side's viewpoint every dirty step of the way.

Access: For IBMs and compatibles. $195 (a nonnegotiable price, we suspect) from Experience in Software, Inc., 2000 Hearst Ave., Suite 202, Berkeley, CA 94709. Phone: 1-(800) 678-7008. Also available from Mindware, 1803 Mission St., Suite 414, Santa Cruz, CA 95060. Phone: (800) 447-0477. Nierenberg's book, *The Complete Negotiator,* is included as a bonus.

MENTOR
●

This is a kind of Fantasy Island for Mensa members: Mentor lets you test your I.Q. twenty times a day if you want. It's touted as providing "vigorous mental exercise to sharpen your mental abilities." Besides testing I.Q., Mentor has tests for memory, coordination, reaction time, and perception,

with each of these topics offering a number of subtests. The memory test, for example, lets you test for memory of color patterns, sound, numbers, and letters as well as offering three levels of difficulty. And if you want to be even smarter than you already are, Mentor offers to "turbocharge your brain" with over fifty psychometric exercises and tests designed to improve your natural intelligence. Inexplicably, Mentor also includes a biorhythm-generation chart that keeps track of your emotional, intellectual, and physical cycles (perhaps so you'll know which days are best for taking tests).

Access: For IBMs and compatibles. Requires CGA, EGA, or VGA graphics adapter. $49.95 from Mindware, 1803 Mission St., Suite 414, Santa Cruz, CA 95060. Phone: (800) 447-0477.

Mentor

PRIMETIME
●

Booting up Primetime on your computer is like having your mother nagging at you all day long—annoying perhaps, but very productive. Basically, Primetime is a time-management program. Among other things, it acts as an appointment book, with a gentle alarm that reminds you of meetings. It's also a to-do list manager, keeping a separate list for each day; it automatically updates and arranges all undone tasks into a new list for the current day. Primetime is also a phone-list manager, tracking down names, addresses, and phone numbers for you. It even dials the numbers. Also included is an "assignment manager," a subprogram that keeps track of which employees are doing which tasks, when they're due, and when to follow up. You can use Primetime to print out twelve different kinds of time-management reports (to-do lists, assignments, appointments, etc.). The publisher claims that Primetime will let you squeeze twelve hours of work out of an eight-hour day. (And we thought the whole idea of the computer age was to give us more leisure time, not to make us work harder.)

Access: For IBMs and compatibles. $99.50 from Mindware, 1803 Mission St., Suite 414, Santa Cruz, CA 95060. Phone: (800) 447-0477.

PSYCHOLOGICAL SOFTWARE

The following are programs you would boot up when you don't feel like schlepping yourself to a therapist.

ELIZA
•

The original Eliza was written back in 1965 by artificial-intelligence pioneer Joseph Weizenbaum of MIT. Eliza was a primitive program that mimicked the methodology of a Rogerian therapist and gave the appearance of actually conversing with its "patients." Despite the fact that Eliza's uncanny performance depended on a rather primitive repertoire of linguistic skills, many clients were nevertheless fooled into thinking that they were really conversing, via computer screen, with an intelligent being—or at least a Rogerian therapist. All Eliza really did was throw key words back at the user, much as a Rogerian therapist does, without really giving a hoot about what the client was saying. Weizenbaum originally developed Eliza as a kind of sarcastic comment on artificial intelligence and to show how a clever program could exhibit a patina of intelligence without really having any. In fact, Weizenbaum named his program after the character Eliza, the cockney flower girl in *My Fair Lady* who undergoes linguistic training in order to take on the persona of a fine English lady—when in fact she is really just a cockney street tramp.

This irony has obviously been lost on the folks at the Artificial Intelligence Research Group, which now markets Eliza as a serious therapy program, claiming that some psychologists now use Eliza on their patients' first office visits. In fact, there is some logic to this approach, as studies have shown that many people are more open to a computer than a flesh-and-blood therapist. (Of course, that may be more of a reflection on the character of today's therapists than on the lovability of computer programs.) In all fairness, Eliza is recommended as a introduction to what computers can do or as a party game.

Access: One of Eliza's best features is that it comes in many formats to run on a wide range of computers: IBMs and compatibles, Macintosh (requires Microsoft Basic), Apple II, Commodore 64, and even CP/M machines. $47 from Artificial Intelligence Research Group, 921 North La Jolla Avenue, West Hollywood, CA 90046. Phone: (213) 656-7368. Also available from Mindware, 1803 Mission St., Suite 414, Santa Cruz, CA 95060. Phone: (800) 447-0477.

HEART TO HEART
•

You say your wife hasn't slept with you in three years? You say she seemed dissatisfied with the last six vacations you planned, all of which were to Caesar's Palace in Las Vegas? You say your spouse has been less than supportive about your mid-life crisis, especially when you announced you're planning to switch careers (from investment banking to mink farming) and that you've hired a Swedish au pair girl that you met at a wet T-shirt contest (and you don't even have any children)? Is that your problem, Bunky? Well, maybe you need Heart to Heart, a new program from InterActive Software, which in essence is nothing but an on-screen questionnaire of 150 questions adapted for five different brands of couples: unmarried, premarital, unmarried with children, married without children, and married with children. InterActive doesn't state whether these couples should be heterosexual or gay, but the package the disk arrived in features a picture of a man and woman, if that's any clue. (We guess gay couples will have to cope with their problems sans software.)

Seriously, many people can be more open with a computer program than with another human, so Heart to Heart may in fact be effective in opening new lines of communication between significant others. The program probes your attitudes about twelve controversial areas, such as finances, sex, goals, leisure time, expectations, and parenting. Heart to Heart also offers over 100 daily quotations and communication exercises to help you solve communication problems with your partner.

When we had the program analyze a couple named Diana and Charles, it praised their "honesty" and noted that many aspects of their relationship were "potential improvement areas." Evidently, this is Heart to Heart's diplomatic way of saying there's not a snowball's chance in hell this marriage can be saved (although "Finances and Goals" were not a problem). The program's motto, by the way, is "Divorce is out. Commitment is in."

Access: For IBMs and compatibles. $39.95 from InterActive Software, 496 La Guardia Place, Suite 215, New York, NY 10012. Also available from Mindware, 1803 Mission St., Suite 414, Santa Cruz, CA 95060. Phone: (800) 447-0477.

HAVE INTRACOURSE WITH JOYCE BROTHERS
•

Another entry in the new category of romanceware, InterAction used to go by the much more intriguing and descriptive name of IntraCourse. It's all about intimacy (which in this case means sex), and the program's most salient feature is the fact it's "reviewed and certified" by Dr. Joyce Brothers. The program asks you a series of personal questions; a branching logic system then asks you followup questions based on previous replies. InterAction uses your answers as building blocks for a personalized sexual analysis. The program creates these sexual profiles by combining user-supplied data with statistical findings and impressionistic interpretive theory based on up-to-date studies of human sexuality by Kinsey, Masters and Johnson, and more than a hundred other respected sources. The printed-out profile normally runs from three to twelve pages, if you can bear to read that much about your sex life.

You can also use InterAction with a partner. In this mode, the program will measure your compatibility in twelve different categories. You may discover that you share fantasies and desires with your significant other that you never imagined. (On the other hand, you may find out that he/she has despised every sexual move you've ever made.) While InterAction isn't intended for clinical use, its makers claim that users "may benefit from the knowledge which they acquire from this product. This learning experience may range from the acquisition of an expanded sexual vocabulary or statistical knowledge to a more general appreciation and awareness of ways to get more out of their sex life." So if you believe that coming to the bedroom with an expanded vocabulary ("Ooooh, what a big vocabulary you have!") or a better grasp of statistics ("Wow, I'd like to grasp your stats!") will improve your love life, InterAction is the software for you. Like Heart to Heart, the makers of InterAction do not specify whether their product is aimed at heterosexual or homosexual love affairs. And we still wish they had kept the IntraCourse name.

Access: For IBMs and compatibles, the Apple II, Commodore 64, Atari ST, and Amiga. $99.50 from IntraCorp, Inc., Suite 185, 13500 N. Kendall Dr., Miami, FL 33186. Also available from Mindware, 1803 Mission St., Suite 414, Santa Cruz, CA 95060. Phone: (800) 447-0477.

LOVE QUEST
●

Love Quest is from the same people who publish InterAction, but it's more of a starter kit: Love Quest's purpose is to help you meet other singles (so you can get in trouble and then have to buy InterAction to see where you went wrong—a clever marketing ploy). The program asks you seventy-seven questions and processes your responses using models developed, once again, by Dr. Joyce Brothers and an unspecified "team of psychological experts." The computerized questionnaire probes various aspects of your personality: sex drive, dominance, materialism, even your ability to fall in love. Your profile is then reduced to a code that can be sent to the software publisher, IntraCorp, which runs it through a nationwide computerized database to match you up with a compatible mate.

Access: For IBMs and compatibles, Apple II, Commodore 64, and Macintosh. $59.95 from IntraCorp, Inc., Suite 185, 13500 N. Kendall Dr., Miami, FL 33186. Also available from Mindware, 1803 Mission St., Suite 414, Santa Cruz, CA 95060. Phone: (800) 447-0477.

MIND MIRROR
●

It had to happen. Timothy Leary has moved from LSD to software. Mind Mirror is Leary's brainchild, what he calls a "thought-processing appliance." The former Harvard psychology professor–turned–psychedelic guru–turned–fugitive–turned–computer prophet has created a program that is part game, part tool, part philosopher. The whole idea is that our minds are conditioned—programmed, as it were—by genetics and stimuli beyond our control. We have to reprogram them if we are to have any control over our lives. Mind Mirror does this in a number of ways. For example, you can see yourself more clearly by constructing a mind map on the computer that displays four vital areas of life: emotions, mental ability, social interaction, and bioenergy. You fill in all the information, and the program literally draws you a map. You can also construct maps of your friends, lovers, or even historical figures and then compare their maps with yours to give yourself a sense of perspective in the world.

One interesting subprogram of Mind Mirror is Life Simulation. This lets you take any personality you choose on an interactive journey. For example, you might construct your real mind map, and then construct the mind map of the person you would like to be. In Life Simulation, you could then see what life would be like with this new personality. It takes the form of a kind of game. For example, winning a Life Simulation Realm such as Emotional Insight gives you the passkey to the Social Interaction Realm where you might spend your evenings in the Bankers Club or at the Punk Rock Bar.

There are also subprograms for dealing with your career, your education, your home life, and your love life. Mind Mirror is also the only program we know of that is endorsed by reclusive novelist Thomas Pynchon (*Gravity's Rainbow, Vineland*). See "Timothy Leary—Now on Diskette," this chapter, for more information on the maker of Mind Mirror.

Access: For IBMs and compatibles. Requires CGA, EGA, or VGA graphics adapter. Available from Mindware, 1803 Mission St., Suite 414, Santa Cruz, CA 95060. Phone: (800) 447-0477.

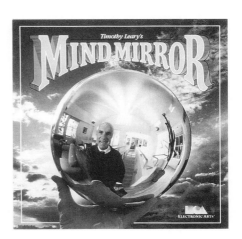

PLEASE UNDERSTAND ME
●

This entry clearly wins first prize for "most plaintive cry in a title of a computer program." Actually, this software is not asking you to understand it; it theoretically understands you. Please Understand Me is essentially based on an adaptation of C. G. Jung's theory of personality, which classifies people according to the following preferences: introverted/extroverted, intuitive/sensing, thinking/feeling, and judging/perceiving. You answer a series of seventy multiple-choice questions about your interests, preferences, values, outlooks, etc. The program then analyzes your character and spews out a three-plus-page printout detailing your personality. A lot faster (and cheaper) than seeing an actual Jungian therapist.

For example, a twenty-nine-year-old man who used the program was judged to be an ESTJ (extroverted, sensing, thinking, judging) individual. A lengthy analysis of this guy appeared to be somewhat pat and formulaic, but not uninteresting. For example, an ESTJ is loyal, responsible, capable of sacrifice, attentive to details, possessive of belongings and family, and has mundane values. ESTJs make up about 13 percent of the population, and as admirable as they may seem, they are folks you may want to avoid in bed because, according to the program, "the unexpected and unusual are probably not a part of the basic sexual repertoire" of the ESTJ. They are also apt to see sex as more procreative than recreational. Female ESTJs regard sex as a chore; because of this attitude, a male ESTJ is likely "to express gratitude to his partner." Still, these are good, honest, hard-working folk, and a male ESTJ will hang around after his orgasm to bring his partner to climax as well, hard worker that he is. The dark side is that ESTJs don't understand that "transactions outside the bedroom loom vital as precursors to sexual response." Which is computerese meaning that female ESTJs will nag the hell out of you after dinner and then expect you to provide steamy love before bedtime.

Well, enough of these horrors. Suffice it to say that Please Understand Me furnishes plenty of interesting reading on oneself and makes for a great party game or ice breaker when you allow it to analyze all your guests and (former) friends.

Access: For Apple II+, IIe, and IIc with 48K and IBMs with 64K. $89 from Cambridge Career Products, P.O. Box 2153, Charleston, WV 25328. Phone: (800) 468-4227. Also available from Mindware, 1803 Mission St., Suite 414, Santa Cruz, CA 95060. Phone: 1-(800) 447-0477.

MIND PROBER
●

You can also find programs similar to Mind Prober under the names MindViewer and Dr. Shrink. But under any name, this software does the same thing: It supposedly lets you see people as they really are—"even if you've only known him or her for only five minutes"—or so goes the ad copy. The program is rather simple. You enter the name, sex, and age of the person you want analyzed. Then Mind Prober hits you with a series of adjectives—"trustworthy," "unobtrusive," "very cheerful," "very social," "worrier," "argumentative," "brilliant," "calculating," etc.—and asks you to agree or disagree on a scale of 1 (strongly agree) to 4 (strongly disagree) as to whether each of these words correctly describes the target person. Mind Prober then churns out a personality profile of the person in a multipage report. (See "Inputting Sigmund," page 162, for an example of how such software works.)

The evaluation helps you to understand your friends and acquaintances by revealing their hidden motives and uncovering their fantasies, depending, of course, on how accurately you describe them during the questionnaire segment of the program. It's suggested you run Mind Prober on your boss when you need a raise. Or maybe try it on the funky new lady across the street that you'd like to know, or probe, better. One of the nice things about Mind Prober is that the people who make it don't take themselves too seriously (a rare quality in this business). For example, they explain how Samson might have benefited from running the program on Delilah to uncover her treacherous character.

Access: For IBMs and compatibles as well as Macintosh. Comes with a book called *Reading Others,* by Drs. James and Kathy Johnson. $29.95 from Mindware, 1803 Mission Street, Suite 414, Santa Cruz, CA 95060. Phone: (800) 447-0477.

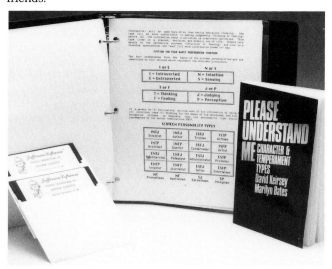

PERSONALITY PROFILE
•

Here's yet another personality-analyzer program. This one is based on the principles of Transactional Analysis (*I'm OK, You're OK*). Personality Profile gives you insight into your personal dynamics. According to the publisher, Psychological Psoftware, the program provides a stepping-stone for many areas of self-discovery. Besides analyzing you, Personality Profile also instructs you in the dynamics of anger and the important differences between rescuing and helping, indulging and nurturing, and discounting and stroking.

Personality
Profile
2

Access: Runs on IBMs and compatibles and the Apple II series. $49.50 from Psychological Psoftware Company, 312 Los Altos Dr., Aptos, CA 95003. Phone: (408) 688-6808. Also available from Mindware, 1803 Mission St., Suite 414, Santa Cruz, CA 95060. Phone: 1-(800) 447-0477.

THE EDGE SERIES
•

James Johnson, the psychologist who developed Mind Prober, brings his expertise to this series of four programs geared to give you a psychological edge in business. (Besides having a Ph.D. in psychology from the University of Minnesota, Johnson was also one of IBM's most successful salespeople, selling at a level 400 percent over his quota.) In each of the following programs, you are presented two questionnaires, one for yourself and one for the person you need to understand. Each program then evaluates you and your associate/adversary and analyzes your interactions. Finally, you are presented with a comprehensive report. The four programs are as follows:

Management Edge helps you motivate and manage your employees and subordinates. It evaluates the various human factors that go into final management decisions.

Sales Edge helps you close a sale by offering insights into your prospect's interests and hidden motives. The program tells you how to prepare, open, and close your sales presentation.

Negotiation Edge not only probes your opponents' weaknesses, it also helps you to anticipate what strategies your opponents are likely to use against you and prints out a tactical approach to give you a clear advantage.

Communication Edge analyzes your associates' strengths and weaknesses to help you get across your ideas to them more clearly, concisely, and persuasively. It also provides you with strategies to help you forge agreements with your coworkers.

Access: Each program runs on Apple II or IBM and compatibles. Sales Edge and Communication Edge also run on Macintosh. Each program is $49.95 from Mindware, 1803 Mission St., Suite 414, Santa Cruz, CA 95060. Phone: (800) 447-0477.

HELP-ESTEEM
•

This program was originally developed for mental-health professionals and clinics around the country, and has now been adapted to run on home computers. The goal of HELP-Esteem is to make you feel good about yourself. It is not a quick program. You must devote yourself to eleven thirty- to forty-five-minute sessions in order to construct a new, more vibrant self-image. HELP-Esteem covers such categories as developing a sense of belonging, "feeling worthwhile," overcoming self-defeating thoughts, discovering your own power, and using "positive self-talk." The program also offers up some creative visualization exercises for improving your self-esteem.

We'd order the software ourselves, except that we don't feel worthy of it.

Access: Runs on IBMs and compatibles only. There are three versions—personal, family, and professional. The personal is $95 and can be used by one person. The family edition is $195 and can be used by five family members. The professional version is $395, and can be used by an unlimited number of clients—in fact, twelve clients can use the program concurrently. Password and name entry are required for confidentiality. Available from Mindware, 1803 Mission St., Suite 414, Santa Cruz, CA 95060. Phone: (800) 447-0477.

HELP-ASSERT
●

Another in the HELP series, which was originally developed for mental-health professionals, HELP-Assert was developed by a professional assertiveness trainer who emphasizes that assertiveness should not be confused with aggression. Assertiveness, as defined by this program, is getting one's needs met while respecting the needs of others.

HELP-Assert leads you through nine thirty- to forty-five-minute training sessions that help you get what you want while respecting others. The program is designed to help you gain understanding, achieve closeness, improve teamwork, claim personal power, foster trust, enhance self-esteem, and communicate better. Like other HELP software, HELP-Assert is interactive with such features as block graphics and musical enhancement. An on-screen tutorial is all the training you need.

Access: For IBMs and compatibles only. There are three versions—personal, family, and professional. The personal is $95 and can be used by one person. The family edition is $195 and can be used by five family members. The professional version is $395, can be used by an unlimited number of clients (twelve clients can use the program concurrently). Password and name entry are required for confidentiality. Available from Mindware, 1803 Mission St., Suite 414, Santa Cruz, CA 95060. Phone: (800) 447-0477.

ON BECOMING A HERO
●

It had to happen sooner or later. It was sooner. On Becoming a Hero is one of the first entries into the psychological kidware market. The publisher of the program, Psychological Psoftware, asks the question: "How can your children survive a world where drugs, sex, and violence are taken for granted?" How indeed? Evidently, one answer is a diskette you slip into your Apple or IBM. On Becoming a Hero is a program aimed at "value clarification." The software helps young people identify their ideals and choose their life values. The company claims that the program helps young people sort out their values without imposing a preconceived value system. On Becoming a Hero is recommended for any kid who can work a computer, but aimed mostly at teenagers.

Access: For IBMs and compatibles and the Apple II series. $49.50 from Psychological Psoftware Company, 312 Los Altos Dr., Aptos, CA 95003. Phone: (408) 688-6808.

STRESSWARE

Okay, we suppose that, technically, we should call the following programs antistressware, since they help you reduce stress, not provide it. But you know what we mean.

CALMPUTE
●

This is a pioneer program, one that creates a literal mind-body interface, if you'll excuse the jargon. It's a combination of biofeedback, computer software, and artificial reality. The key to the system is the Calmpute mouse. It's a computer mouse, but with a big difference. You place your fingers in slots that have sensors that measure your level of tension through galvanic skin response. The mouse sends this stress response to the computer, which literally uses your emotions to run a variety of programs. For example, there are beautiful geometric patterns that change colors and shape as you either relax or tense up. It's a creative way to learn how to relax. You control your emotions by controlling the shapes and colors on your computer screen. Depending on what kind of computer you have, there are many other ways of displaying your state of tension (or lack of it): bar graphs, oscilloscopes, star patterns, etc. There are also stress tests, word associations, physical-stress tests, and more.

One of the more clever subprograms is the oddly named Calmprix. It sounds like an exercise for those who wish to control their promiscuity, but in reality it's a challenging car game. The objective is to stay calm. Paradoxically, the calmer you remain, the faster the car goes. The game teaches you to relax—and thus perform better—under pressure; it can be played on several levels of difficulty.

In addition, there is a series of audiotapes designed to be used with biofeedback. You simply listen to the tapes while watching the computer monitor with Calmpute. There are tapes for weight control, stopping smoking, coping with sleep disorders, stress control, public speaking, fear of flying, test taking, alcohol or drug addictions, and breathing for health. Of special note is a package called Mind Over Muscle, which includes a half-hour video with six Olympic gold medalists revealing their secrets and two audiotapes featuring twelve-minute vignettes by leading sports psychologists who will teach you secrets of mental training. Calmpute can even be expanded to monitor your temperature, electromyographic activity, heartbeat, blood volume, pulse, and respiration.

How accurate is Calmpute in calculating your emotions? Well, the method it uses—galvanic skin response—is also the basis for lie detectors. And, of course, lie detectors are anything but foolproof. Still, this is an interesting concept and a portent of greater technology to come.

Access: Calmpute runs on IBMs and compatibles and the Apple II. It requires an EGA or VGA graphics adaptor. $99.95 from Thought Technology Ltd., 2180 Belgrave Ave., Montreal, P.Q., Canada H4A 2L8. Phone: (800) 361-3651. Also available from Mindware, 1803 Mission St., Suite 414, Santa Cruz, CA 95060. Phone: 1-(800) 447-0477. The tapes range in price from $24.95 to $54.95. Contact Thought Technology or Mindware for further information.

TOTAL STRESS MANAGEMENT SYSTEM
●

This is a fairly serious program, or at least it takes a long time to get through all the instructions—twelve one-hour sessions. In effect, your computer becomes a therapist, guiding you through a number of exercises, making them as easy as possible. There are two major parts to the program. Part I deals with stress in general. Part II confronts specific stress symptoms and provides remedies. These include exercises in relaxation, breathing, densitization, imagery, meditation, behavior modification (for weight loss), time management, thought control, and assertiveness training. There's even a section of physical isometric exercises that you do right at the computer. The program produces printouts of selected information.

Access: For IBMs and compatibles and Apple II. There are three editions. The business version is $100 and designed to be used without assistance. The clinical edition is $200 and is designed for a therapist to use to guide his patient through each exercise. There's also a student edition for $89.50. From Psychological Psoftware Company, 312 Los Altos Dr., Aptos, CA 95003. Phone: (408) 688-6808. Also available from Mindware, 1803 Mission St., Suite 414, Santa Cruz, CA 95060. Phone: 1-(800) 447-0477.

HELP-STRESS
●

This interactive program features block graphics and music to help you cope with stress. HELP-Stress teaches you how to unwind in ten thirty- to forty-five-minute sessions. Topics include basic and advanced relaxation exercises, how your thoughts affect stress, distorted thought patterns, environment and stress, health and exercise, and how to prepare for stressful events. When you complete the ten sessions, HELP-Stress gives you a complete report on your stress profile, your current progress, and suggestions for improvement. The focus of the program is developing your ability to relax at high levels of output.

Access: For IBMs and compatibles. There are three versions. The personal edition ($95) is for one person. The family edition services up to five family members ($195). The professional version ($395) is for an unlimited number of clients, and twelve can use the program concurrently. Mandatory password and name entry ensure confidentiality. Available from Mindware, 1803 Mission St., Suite 414, Santa Cruz, CA 95060. Phone: (800) 447-0477.

GAMES/HEAD TRIPS

Unlike the others, these computer programs don't claim to have any socially redeeming values (at least they don't try very hard). They're just for fun.

ANNALS OF ROME
●

It's 273 B.C. and Italy has been united under the Roman senate. You are the ruler of the republic, and it's your job to deploy your armies and defend against the thirteen hostile lands that constantly plot to destroy Rome. Your assignment, Mr. Phelps, should you decide to boot up, is to command your legionnaires and your twenty-one commanding officers of various abilities and loyalties, and quell minor incursions, rebellions, and various attacks from all your enemies, inside and outside.

Annals of Rome is described as "a game of empire building," but it's really a game of empire maintenance. You have to protect yourself from rebellion from within, but if you neglect defense of your borders, loss of Roman territory could lead to a loss of confidence among the citizenry and your fellow Romans may decide to overthrow you. Civil war could lead to a hole in your external defenses, and you could be overthrown from without. Etcetera, etcetera. In any case, Annals of Rome seems to be good practice for office politics.

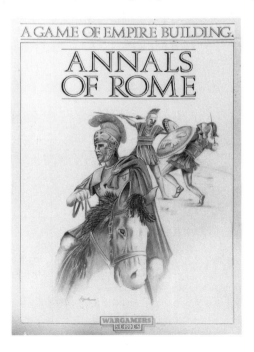

The game scenario is different each time you play, and the game features a detailed map, Roman economic and political options, phased movement, and conflicts with invading or internal groups. This is a complicated game, with a manual that explains the military and cultural history of Rome. The manual ends with a "moral note," which states that the most important lesson is "the ultimate futility of imperialism." Make this a Christmas gift for the little computer-hacking Young Conservative in your family.

Access: For IBMs and compatibles $34.95, Commodore 64 $24.95, and Atari St/Amiga $34.95. From The Software Toolworks, 19808 Nordhoff Place, Chatsworth, CA 91311. Phone: (818) 885-9000.

ZORK ZERO
●

You may recall that several years ago a game called Adventure was circulated (i.e., illegally copied) among personal-computer owners. This was at the beginning of the micro-computer revolution and it was one of the few interesting mind games available. Adventure was set in a vast, tortuous, subterranean kingdom, and your task was to navigate the various passageways and collect various treasures and avoid numerous villains and hazards. Zork Zero is based generally on the same concept, one of a new genre of software that goes by the name of interactive software. All this really means is that you create your own story by the choices you make during the computer game. What makes Zork Zero and others of its ilk different from the original Adventure is that there are now fancy graphics featuring elaborate maps, puzzles, and pictures of the various characters and scenes. Adventure was all words; you had to picture everything in your mind. (Of course, some people—those who like to read books, for example—prefer using their imagination.)

Zork Zero takes place in the Great Underground Empire, which is being abandoned because of a wizard's curse. Your job is to stop the curse before it destroys the entire kingdom (the publishers of Zork Zero use the terms "empire" and "kingdom" interchangeably, as if they were the same thing). You explore every corner of the empire/kingdom, along the way acquiring treasures and being tested with games, rid-

folder. Your child (or you) then journeys down the Manhole into a brave new world of beanstalks, castles, sunken ships, and dragons. There are over 600 different interconnected scenes (or "cards," in HyperCard parlance). Within each scene you can use your mouse to click on various objects or anything that looks interesting. Most objects will make a sound or move or both. Some objects give you a different effect the second time you click them. You move from location to location by clicking the right or left edge of the card. On some cards you can click the top or bottom to go up or down. And sometimes clicking an object or passageway elicits a short animated sequence.

dles, and tricks. You're the protagonist in a novel of your own making. You move from place to place at will, using the objects you find, and interacting with other characters. However, Zork Zero is also a game. You get points for solving puzzles and finding new places. A perfect score of 1,000 is your goal.

Access: $59.95 for software that runs on the Macintosh, Amiga, and IBM and compatibles. $49.95 for the Apple II series. From Infocom, 3885 Bohannon Drive, Menlo Park, CA 94025. Phone: (800) 227-6900. The program comes with The Flathead Calendar for the year 883, which the author no doubt believes is hilariously funny. Infocom also sells a series of similar games, including Zork I, Planetfall, Leather Goddesses of Phobos, Wishbringer, and The Hitchhiker's Guide to the Galaxy.

THE MANHOLE
●

The Manhole is described as "what Alice in Wonderland would be like if the White Rabbit had had HyperCard." HyperCard, of course, is the hypertext program that runs on Macintosh computers and connects all sorts of different files and graphics. This program is aimed at kids, but it's quite sophisticated from a computer point of view. (Actually, this makes sense; it's difficult to make something look simple on a computer.) You'll need a heavy-duty computer: a Macintosh with at least 1 megabyte of memory (preferably more), a hard drive, and HyperCard. The program works not unlike HyperCard. In fact, you install it right into your HyperCard

Access: For Macintoshes with at least 1 megabyte of memory, a hard disk, and HyperCard, or for IBMs and compatibles with 512K memory and 2.1 version of DOS or higher. $49.95 from Activision, P.O. Box 8123, San Francisco, CA 94128. Phone: 1-(800) 227-6900.

COSMIC OSMO
●

This is another game from the makers of The Manhole. Again, it's run on a Mac and uses HyperCard. Little kids can play Cosmic Osmo, using the mouse to move from screen to screen and to click on objects within each frame (such as clicking on a little sleeping dog to make him wake up, bark, and change the outcome of the story). In short, it's another form of interactive fiction. It's a learning experience for kids, who help create their own stories. There are animated sections, which sometimes make the "reader" solve a puzzle before continuing. In this story you'll meet Cosmic Osmo, a sloppy, silly humanoid-looking creature who lives in a strange solar system at the edge of the universe. In this solar system, odd things happen. Cellos might go marching or ketchup bottles might sing an opera. You might rocket to a planet made of cheese or run into Space Spuds in a cupboard or a mouse at the helm of a bathysphere in a hot tub. A warning: Parents are cautioned that kids using Cosmic Osmo might click themselves out of this alternate universe and right into other files in your hard disk, thanks to the interactive capabilities of HyperCard. The manual spells out some precautions you can take to minimize the chances of little Norbert and Brunhilde from wandering through your unfinished novel and that great new business plan on drive C.

Access: For Macintoshes with hard drives and at least 1 megabyte memory. HyperCard version 1.2.2 included with Cosmic Osmo program. $69.95 from Activision, P.O. Box 8123, San Francisco, CA 94128. Phone: 1-(800) 227-6900.

RACTER
•

We first came into contact with Racter while working at *Omni* magazine, where Racter's short story "Soft Ions" was published several years ago. Limited in literary merit as "Soft Ions" was, one had to admit that it probably was no worse than average when compared with most science fiction.

But we digress. Racter is the name of both an artificial author and a conversational software package. Racter is the offshoot of something called INRAC, a prose synthesizer and text generator. INRAC created Racter to author the *Omni* short story as well as *The Policeman's Beard is Half-Constructed*, a novel published by Warner Books. However, the Racter that is now sold to the public is merely a conversational program, an artificial friend you can talk to. It doesn't generate short stories or articles, just engages you in banal conversation with a lot of name-dropping. We found Racter about as scintillating as a Chatty Cathy doll on downers, but then much of America enjoys listening to talk radio, and by that standard, Racter is entertaining indeed. According to the literature that accompanies the diskette, Racter is half-heartedly endorsed by the Institute of Artificial Insanity, an organization dedicated to financial gain, the study of amateur brain surgery, and the pursuit of government funding.

INRAC is not a boot-up-and-go program, but rather a programming language. You use it to write programs that deal with English. For example, INRAC can help you create a personalized form letter–writing program, which matches each letter to the particulars of the addressee. Sentences are formed at random so that people don't start recognizing the same sentences in letter after letter and see through your trick. Bill Chamberlain, one of the coauthors of INRAC, says that computer-age Lotharios could use it to generate hundreds of original love letters. Or better yet, he's considered writing a grant-proposal program so he could inundate Washington with requests for money. Remember, though, that INRAC is not a program, but a language. You need programming skills to use it effectively.

Access: Racter runs on IBMs and compatibles, Macintosh, Apple II, and Amiga. INRAC runs only on IBM. Racter is $45. INRAC is $350. From INRAC, Inc., 12 Schubert St., Staten Island, NY 10305. Phone: (718) 448-6298.

SEARCH FOR THE *TITANIC*
•

This is a bizarre game, which we include here to show how software is coming more and more to imitate real life—even going so far as to include much of life's tedium. The object of the game is to find the *Titanic*, which sank to the bottom of the Atlantic on April 15, 1912. The *Titanic*, of course, has already been found (in 1985) by Robert Ballard, who has written a forward to the manual that accompanies this program. His staff at the Woods Hole Oceanographic Institution has also reviewed the software for authenticity.

Before you can discover the *Titanic*, you have to earn your spurs (or, in this case, your flippers) by finding and exploring other lost vessels. You must meticulously plan each expedition, down to such mundane tasks as hiring a staff, obtaining funding, and purchasing the proper equipment. The program is full of such details as salaries, rental fees for ships, numbers of berths on each ship, etc. You start in Miami with $10,000 in cash, no employees, no equipment, no ship, no expedition plan, and no reputation. But with the $10,000 you have enough to rent a small boat, hire some divers, and find a wreck. It will take you about ten wrecks before you have enough of a reputation to get funding for a *Titanic* search. (We suppose one real-life option would be to smuggle coke in your first boat, thus supplying your own financing, but such a plan is not offered by the software.) In any case, Search for the *Titanic* includes over seventy-five wrecks to explore, more than a hundred navigational maps and charts, and forty-seven ports of call. You have to become familiar with realistic weather patterns, currents, sonar, magnetometers, underwater cameras, and minisubs as you navigate the trade routes in search of sunken vessels.

When you finally do locate the *Titanic*, there's a special reward. Digitized photos of the actual *Titanic* shipwreck, photographed by Dr. Ballard's Woods Hole team, will appear on the monitor. Much better than some meaningless gold, precious gems, or other such mundane treasure, don't you think?

Access: $39.95 for IBM, Tandy, and compatibles with a 5 ¼″ disk drive and a hard drive and a CGA or EGA graphics card (VGA card optional). $34.95 for Apple IIe/gs version and $29.95 for Commodore 64 version. A Commodore Amiga version is forthcoming. From Capstone (a division of IntraCorp, Inc.), 14160 SW 139 Ct., Miami, FL 33186. Phone: (305) 252-9040 or (800) 468-7226 (orders only).

SPIRITUAL SOFTWARE

These are programs that purport to help you find a more serene state of consciousness.

SYNCHRONICITY: *I CHING* ON A DISK
•

Synchronicity is described by its publisher as an "entertaining intuitive decision-making software." It features a "desktop consultation ritual" to help Macintosh users "turn stress into strategy." What this means is that various pieces of New Age-y, flakey art is flashed on your monitor while you are asked to meditate on various questions, problems, or dilemmas. There are also sounds that supposedly help you reach a deep spirituality. For example, you might be asked to meditate on a quote from the *I Ching* while looking at an animated waterfall on your monitor and listening to the sound of a subprogram called "Random Frogs." According to the publisher, "It's like having a Japanese garden inside your Mac." Come to think of it, we just had a hard disk mysteriously crash in one of our Macintoshes. Maybe it was the humidity from Synchronicity's waterfall, or perhaps a Japanese beetle got squished in the drive.

Seriously, Synchronicity sets a mood to induce a more spiritual state of consciousness (though we find it difficult to sit in full lotus position on an office chair). More important, Synchronicity is the *I Ching* on a disk. The name of the program is taken from the concept developed by Carl Jung. He defined synchronicity as an "acasual connecting principle." According to Jungian synchronicity, the question is not why something has happened, but rather what likes to happen together in a meaningful way in the same moment. What types of events tend to happen together? (Why do many scientists independently make the same great discovery at the same time? Why does our hard disk always crash the night before a deadline?) Jung was fascinated with the *I Ching,* or Book of Changes, an oracle that provides philosophical answers according to a system of chance (by throwing coins or yarrow stalks). The *I Ching* partially inspired his concept of synchronicity. Synchronicity, the computer program, is based on the *I Ching* method of answering questions. Instead of throwing coins, you hold down keys on your keyboard and the program measures how many milliseconds you wait between keystrokes.

As with the *I Ching,* Synchronicity works best with burning questions, dilemmas, or perplexing problems: Should I quit my job? Should I marry Cindy Lou? What's the best way to relate to my teenager? It is not good at providing specific data: How many universal joints are in the Hoboken warehouse? What price did pork bellies close at today?

Access: Runs on Macintosh or IBMs and compatibles. $49.95 from Visionary Software, Inc., P.O. Box 69191, Portland, OR 97201. Phone: (503) 246-6200. For orders call (800) 877-1832. Also available from Mindware, 1803 Mission St., Suite 414, Santa Cruz, CA 95060. Phone: 1-(800) 447-0477.

PSYCHIC REWARD
●

Want to improve your psychic abilities? Think your poor little organic brain can outsmart your home computer? Then try Psychic Reward, an ESP computer program developed by author and psychic researcher Alan Vaughan, who believes that you can improve your intuition. Psychic Reward is an electronic wheel of fortune. The wheel is divided into twenty-six segments, each lettered in order of the alphabet. Your task is to guess which of the segments the computer will randomly choose as the target. In traditional ESP tests, you are either right or wrong. Psychic Reward, on the other hand, rewards you for being close. Hitting the target on the nose nets you 10,000 points. But if you're one segment off (the target was B, say, and you guessed A), you still get 4,000. If you are two off, you get 2,000; three off, 750; four off, 500; five off, 200; and so on. Vaughan's theory is that if you are rewarded for being close, your ESP will improve. If you're simply told you're wrong, there is no reason to concentrate harder. When playing Psychic Reward your scores are automatically recorded and analyzed statistically. A chart records your progress over three series of twenty tests with thirty trials each (1,800 trials total), and at any time you can check to see your exact odds against chance. Vaughan claims that in a study of five subjects playing Psychic Reward, each player improved his ESP. He also claims that one subject, after training himself on the program, went to a casino for a "graduation test" with slot machines and won $3,000.

Access: Runs on IBMs and compatibles or Macintosh. At present, Vaughan is selling a version for only $29.95 to researchers, but expects to raise the price to about $60 for the general public. From Mind Technology Systems, 3223 Madera Ave., Los Angeles, CA 90039. Phone: (213) 666-7243.

THE MINDWARE MAN:

BRUCE EHRLICH AND DIGITAL PSYCHOLOGY

In 1987, Bruce Ehrlich was a graduate student in psychology at San Francisco's Saybrook Institute. While working on his Ph.D., he discovered what he calls "psych software," computer programs designed to perform the function of a psychologist or otherwise expand or fine-tune one's mind. He also came to realize that it was very difficult to find and buy this software. The programs were not widely advertised and rarely carried in computer stores. You had to buy them directly through their publishing companies, which were often small, hard-to-locate concerns.

Ehrlich quickly gave up his quest for a doctorate and became the country's leading marketer of psychological software, or what he prefers to call "mindware." Ehrlich now publishes a catalogue of the same name, in which he offers a selection of programs that he calls "mindtools for personal development and higher levels of achievement."

What Ehrlich does is ferret out the best mind-expanding software he can, then offers it to the public through his catalogue. He admits that current software is still fairly primitive in terms of affecting the mind: "We're still a long way from where we want to be," he says. "What we want eventually are devices that actually affect consciousness." His personal favorites include *Please Understand Me*, a program that analyzes your personality using Jungian techniques; *IdeaFisher*, a creativity program that Ehrlich says "works like the brain does"; and *MaxThink*, a thought-organizer program that he uses for writing. Ehrlich is also fond of Timothy Leary's *Mind Mirror* and *Calmpute*, a program that employs a biofeedback mouse so that one can control the computer through one's emotions. (All of the above are described in more detail in this chapter.)

Ehrlich predicts that such software will eventually transform computer-human interactions. "The computer," he says, "will become a friend." He foresees a dramatic growth in future years in what he calls "electronic Buddhas." That is, programs designed to enhance the user's spirituality. Another growth area is "psychoactive software." Ehrlich sees an imminent marriage between software and light-and-sound machines (which are described in Chapter 2). The light-and-sound machines, he predicts, will be controlled by your personal computer, with psychological software working in tandem with the blinking lights and pulsing sounds to create the deepest and most effective altered states of consciousness.

As we were going to press, Ehrlich told us about some upcoming software that will soon make its appearance in a future edition of his catalogue, *Mindware*. For anyone who likes quotations—especially writers who use them to spruce up their text—there's *Wisdom of the Ages*. This is a program that contains wise sayings in eighty-one different subjects, subdivided further into seven themes ("opposites," "advice," "insight," etc.). Ehrlich is also excited over *Brainmaker*, software that purports to teach your computer to learn and make judgments. It's based on the hottest concept in computing—neural networks, a technique that allows computers to "think" associatively, just like human beings. One possible use cited for *Brainmaker* is to feed the program statistics on football games and then have it predict winners. Supposedly, the program should get better the more you train it. Finally, Ehrlich likes *Verse Perfect*, a program that helps you write "outstanding poetry." Using *Verse Perfect*, Ehrlich came up with the following limerick:

There was a young poet named Peter
Who didn't know rhythm from meter,
It was then that he found
A program profound,
Verse Perfect, no software is sweeter.

Well, we're still not convinced Peter has solved his meter problem here. And we suspect *Verse Perfect* wouldn't be good for creating *The Wasteland*, but it might help turn you into a minor league Ogden Nash.

Again, Ehrlich is candid about the shortcomings of present mindware. But he is one of the pioneers in bringing these products into the mainstream, and making the computer into an interactive mindtool rather than just an input/output device.

Access: For a copy of the *Mindware* catalogue ($2) write to: Mindware, 1803 Mission St., Suite 414, Santa Cruz, CA 95060. Phone: (800) 447-0477.

INPUTTING SIGMUND

To give you an idea of how psychological software works, the following is an analysis of Sigmund Freud, as presented by the MindViewer computer program. (MindViewer is similar to programs called Mind Prober and Dr. Shrink.) You enter the name, sex, and age of the person you want analyzed. The program then asks you to agree or disagree with a series of adjectives—"trustworthy," "very cheerful," "calculating," etc.—on a scale of 1 (strongly agree) to 4 (strongly disagree). MindViewer then generates a personality profile of the target. In this case, we didn't know Sigmund Freud personally, but we described him according to biographical information and his own writings. Of course, the software didn't know we were inputting Freud, only that we wanted a profile of a middle-aged man named Sigmund. What we got was the following. We have abbreviated and rewritten the actual report in parts. Of most interest is the section entitled, "How to Make Friends with Sigmund."

Sigmund Freud and his future wife, Martha Bernays, 1885

SIGMUND'S PUBLIC SELF

Many people mistakenly perceive Sigmund as somewhat angry. But he is not necessarily the aggressive sort. His public persona tends to be a front that is carefully calculated to keep certain people at bay. This can be very effective. After all, who wants to be around someone with a bad temper?

SIGMUND'S PRIVATE SELF

Although Sigmund may appear friendly enough, underneath the surface is a person who is not at ease around other people. His ego tends to be fragile and his self-esteem is subject to ups and downs. He sometimes feels different from everyone else. He prefers to search out an isolated niche for himself.

WHAT HE HATES

Sigmund hates to be dressed up. Formal attire does not fit with his self-image of a member of the counterculture. Give him a new set of clothes and you could cause him real pain.

WHAT HE LOVES

Deep down Sigmund loves to do things that cause him problems in the long run. He sometimes gets himself into difficult situations in which the emotional consequences are too much for him to handle. Then he wonders how the whole mess got started in the first place.

SIGMUND'S TOP-SECRET SEX FANTASIES

Unless under the influence of some chemical, Sigmund is likely to have difficulty trusting his partner enough to share his secret desires or sexual fantasies. He insists on his independence and only establishes relationships on his own terms. This may frustrate those who want to be his lovers, but he isn't one to care.

HOW TO MAKE FRIENDS WITH SIGMUND

You have to get the ball rolling if you want to make friends with Sigmund. Approach him in a relaxed fashion and ask open-ended questions to get him talking. Don't expect more than one- or two-sentence answers. There may also be silences, and worst of all, an occasional uncomfortable pause while he is in midthought.

HOW TO INFLUENCE SIGMUND

People like Sigmund are among the hardest individuals to influence. They don't like being persuaded and they especially don't like being seen by others as being persuadable. Make it clear to him that there is little work involved in the decision process and that the results of the decision are insignificant. Personal ease is crucial to Sigmund in reducing his anxieties to the point where he can make a decision, so make the process as simple as possible.

TIMOTHY LEARY—NOW ON DISKETTE:

TURNING ON THE SCREEN GENERATION

Timothy Leary

Timothy Leary has turned his skilled hand to many professions: Harvard professor, LSD prophet, author, fugitive. Now he's a software publisher. His best-known program is Mind Mirror, which helps you see yourself more clearly by constructing mind maps of yourself and your friends. (See "Mind Mirror," page 151.)

We asked Leary how he got into software. "How could you not?" he shot back. Software, explained Leary, is key to the new education. One of his latest programs, Inter-Com, is being tested presently at Pennsylvania State University. "All the studies have shown," says Leary, "that learning best takes place in small groups with high interaction." Inter-Com sets up high-speed staccato-like responses between a teacher (the computer) and students. Leary calls it "an ongoing exam." For example, the opening eight lines of *Huckleberry Finn* might appear on the screen, followed by the image of a professor who starts pitching questions. The students' responses would then be immediately scored and tabulated for accuracy and insight. The computer would also determine whether the students' answers were a "bluff" or a "wimp." The whole idea, says Leary, is to keep the classroom "fast moving, exciting, competitive." Ideally, Inter-Com would be used in a group setting, with a computer terminal for each student and a larger screen in the room so all the students could see how others were progressing.

"Our present system is guaranteed to fail," says the former Harvard professor. "A professor drones on in front of the class for six weeks, the students read some books on their own, then they take a test." Leary pauses a few seconds. "No, no, let me correct that. The system succeeds in producing what it wants to produce: a generation of clones inspired by greed and fear."

Leary predicts that soon "eighty percent of our education will be accomplished through a screen." That screen might be attached to a computer or a television, but nevertheless our education will be screen oriented. Or, he says, the screen may be replaced by a pair of goggles on which we'll receive TV, movies, computer readouts, virtual realities, and telephone. "How is a fourteen-year-old going to sort out all that information on her goggles?" That's why, he submits, we need better software to massage all this information.

Yeah, but what about drugs? Has Mr. Psychedelic forsaken drugs for video screens? Has LSD been replaced by VDT? No, says Leary, they're inextricably connected. Television arrived in the 1950s, he points out, readying kids of that era for the next revolution: the drug explosion of the 1960s. Psychedelic trippers, he points out, reacted like couch potatoes, watching the pretty pictures flash by on their mind screens. Then came video games and computers. The TV-LSD-video game generation was psychologically tuned into moving flashy, electronic, digital information around a screen. It's no accident, Leary has pointed out, that many of the early designers and marketers of computers and software were adept in the use of psychedelics. "Young Americans who had been tuning TV screens since infancy and turning on their brains with psychedelics," he has written, "could handle accelerated thought-processing, multilevel realities, and instantaneous chains of digital logic much better than their staid, buttoned-up MBA rivals at IBM."

For a view of the future: "Go read *Vineland* by Thomas Pynchon," Leary suggests. "It's about being taken over by the tube and drugs." Software, though, not drugs, is the key. Leary wants software that will let us manipulate, edit, and enhance movies, TV programs, and computer information, to let us create our own realities. Cut up Coppolla and Kubrick, he says, stick them together and make your own movies. "Mass media is irrelevant," says Leary. "It's personal media I'm interested in."

WOULD THE BUDDHA USE A MODEM?

You approach the electronic temple—or, really, a series of temples within temples inside the abstract space of your computer screen—with some trepidation. You've never worshiped in a computerized church before. But the gateway, called "Openings" on the menu, sets you at ease:

WELCOME TO OPENINGS! IN THIS PLACE THERE ARE MANY DOORS. EACH OPENS INTO A NEW, FAMILIAR REALM OF THE HEART.

You have just logged on to the Awaken Virtual Learning Community, the creation of computer-conferencing pioneers Trudy and Peter Johnson-Lenz of Lake Oswego, Oregon. After setting up an "electronic chapel" on the EIES (Electronic Information Exchange System) network several years ago, they became convinced that a computer system is a natural place to "create a sacred space together." For Awaken they have created rituals that you can enact on your computer screen with people you'll never meet in the flesh. That is, you're hooked up, via telephone modem, to other like-minded computer users around the country (or the world).

Let's say it's December. You can join a Circle of Light and ritually celebrate "the return and rebirth of the light" in honor of the Winter Solstice, Hanukkah, and Christmas. The computer asks you, "Are you relaxed and centered?" If you answer no, it leads you through a brief meditation. Then the four directions are displayed on your screen. EAST = GRANDFATHER FIRE. SOUTH = MOTHER EARTH. WEST = GRANDMOTHER OCEAN. NORTH = FATHER SKY. To cast the circle, you touch each direction in turn by pressing your hand against the computer screen before pushing <return>. (Pressing the screen doesn't physically do anything; it's a symbolic gesture.) The names of all the participants then appear on the screen in a circle. A verse appears:

THE FOUR DIRECTIONS BLESS THIS SPACE
THE LIVING CENTER'S FULL OF GRACE
WE ARE NOW SURROUNDED WITH WHITE LIGHT
OUR CIRCLE'S CAST, OUR HEARTS SHINE BRIGHT.

From here you can can enter any of the following "rooms": "Stories and Touchstones of the Season"; "Letting Go to Make Room"; "What Wants to Be Born"; and "Endings and Beginnings."

The circle format is incorporated into all the on-line workshops and rituals. "In a typical computer conference one or two people end up dominating the discussion," says Trudy. "With the circle format each person gets a chance to speak in turn." (If two people want to continue a discussion, they can step aside into a separate "sharing space" to carry on their conversation.)

There is an ongoing on-line Healing Circle and an ongoing Dream Group, where you can share your dreams and help fellow dreamers decipher perplexing symbols in theirs. You can also sign up for month-long workshops that include "weekly experiential exercises and processes" on such topics as "Right Livelihood," "Ways of Knowing," and "Personal Mythology." In an advanced dream workshop, you can work on such skills as "dreaming the same dream from several points of view," "dreaming someone else's dream," and "understanding parallels between your personal dream and larger community or societal issues."

"Imagine that you're at the end of your life," the computer asks you, guiding you through an introspective process on the subject of Right Livelihood. "What would you most want to be able to say about the life you have lived?" The Johnson-Lenzes see these "virtual learning systems" as prototypes of a spiritual-expert system, a transpersonal version of the computer-expert systems used in medicine and other fields.

Someday you may be able to log on to Awaken and take an electronic shamanic journey (Will reading "BOOM-BOOM-BOOM" on the screen really serve the same function as the shaman's deerskin drum and rattles?) or engage in on-line experiments in assuming multiple identities. At least, these are two of Peter's current fantasies. Perhaps Awaken will evolve into an on-line spiritual community, a sort of geographically dispersed electronic ashram. Perhaps the spiritual expert system will even become a sort of spiritual master. "It won't have the awareness of an Awakened Teacher," says Peter, "but it might be able to provide some useful mirrors for you." And, lacking the awareness of an Awakened Teacher, the on-screen guru will never start collecting Rolls-Royces or lapse into twenty years of silence.

Access: Awakening Technology, 695 Fifth, Lake Oswego, OR 97034. Phone: (503) 635-2615. To link up with Awaken all you need is a pure heart and (1) a personal computer; (2) a modem (300, 1200 or 2400 baud); and (3) telecommunications software with VT100 terminal emulation. Community membership costs $35 per month, $75 for three months, or $275 for a year. Call or write for a free catalogue of online workshops and other activities, which range from $25 to $65 each (in addition to the basic membership fee). If you are connecting from outside the Portland, Oregon, area, contact PC Pursuit (1-800-835-3638) and Galaxy's StarLink (505-881-6988) which offer low-cost alternatives to long distance.

Trudy and Peter Johnson-Lenz

INSTANT · NIRVANA: ENLIGHTENMENT IN · AN · IMPATIENT · AGE

•

In the old days getting enlightened was a long, tedious process. You might be forced to meditate on the same silly koan ("Does the cow have a Buddha nature?") for twenty or thirty years, all the while suffering blows to the head from your irascible Zen master. Or you'd have to hand over your karma and your bank account to some smarmy, Cadillac-driving perfect master, and even then you couldn't be sure you were really enlightened or just in a hypoglycemic state brought on by a steady diet of curried dhal and weak tea.

Now all that has changed.

"Technology has sped up, and the evolution of consciousness is speeding up equally," says Allessyn Moore, of New York City, who teaches workshops in something called the Hemi Sync process (about which you'll hear more later). "Why not cut the enlightenment process by twenty or forty years, so you'll have twenty or forty years to be in that state?" Why not indeed? Most of us don't have the time to imitate St. Simeon the Stylite, one of the Desert Fathers, who spent thirty years perched atop a pillar. Moreover, the dharma may not be so easily transmitted to minds that have been shaped by the Shopping Channel and MTV. It is difficult during the best of times to "concentrate on the letter 'hum' and rouse the Kundalini, piercing the center of the Svayambhu-linga," and next to impossible during the morning rush hour. No, what we need is E-Z Zen, a state of grace for people who aren't ready to give up their condos.

The traditional quick nirvana, the E-Z Zen of the West, has been drugs, of course. Yes, yes, drugs are BAD, but the fact is that many of our great religious philosophers, from William James (nitrous oxide) to Aldous Huxley (mescaline) and Ram Dass (LSD), were introduced to mysticism by illicit substances, perhaps because Nancy Reagan was not around to advise them otherwise. Huxley's trip, which took place one May morning in 1953 in the Los Angeles hills, became the cornerstone of his manifesto *The Doors of Perception*. As the hallucinogen seeped into his brain, Huxley exulted, "I was not looking now at an unusual flower arrangement. I was seeing what Adam had seen on the morning of his creation—the miracle, moment by moment, of creation." Marveling that a small change in brain chemistry could bring about a mystical experience similar to the ecstasies of the world's great saints, he came to the following hypothesis: For practical reasons, the human nervous system normally filters out most of the overwhelming barrage of messages from the universe and reduces consciousness to a "measly trickle . . . that will help us stay alive on the surface of this particular planet." What mescaline had done, he theorized, was to temporarily bypass the brain's "reducing valve."

Psychologists now agree with Huxley that our "normal" state of mind is only one of many possible states. The tidy plot of consciousness that our culture calls home is merely "consensus reality," to use a favorite term of psychologist Charles Tart. The study of altered states of consciousness has shown that certain mental states are useful for, say, double-entry bookkeeping while other, quite different states are conducive to composing a poem or understanding the creation/destruction cycle of the universe. A mind that can operate in only one mode is like a television set stuck perpetually on channel two. To be psychologically flexible is to be capable of tuning in to several different channels at will—from the five o'clock news to Pee Wee Herman—*without* ingesting illegal drugs.

How do you learn to tune in to different frequencies and still keep your urine clean? The traditional route, as we've said, is a lengthy, rigorous spiritual practice such as meditation, chanting, yoga asanas, devotion to a guru, fasting, monastic isolation, wearing saffron robes, and handing out garishly illustrated pamphlets in airports. "We are still following techniques that are ten thousand years old, and then we wonder why they don't work," says Brother Charles, a former Vedic monk who has created a line of high-tech meditation audiocassette tapes. (See "*Of Course* the Buddha Would Wear a Walkman!," page 170.) If there is such a thing as McMeditation, this may be it: Brother Charles claims his technique accelerates the spiritual process by 75 percent and that "we've got the cave experience of fifty years

down to twelve—that's a big breakthrough!" Perhaps if the Buddha had had a pair of headphones and Brother Charles's "holodynamic sound process," he would not have had to spend so many years sitting under the Bodhi tree obsessing about the Four Noble Truths.

For today's busy spiritual go-getter there is a whole bazaar of interesting new psychospiritual technologies around. Many of them combine the spiritual sophistication of the East with the technological know-how of the West and promise everything from inner peace to enlightenment in a few sessions, a weekend, or less. Using a special EEG machine called Mind Mirror (see "Brain Waves of the Gods," page 171), the seeker can learn to imitate the brain waves, and presumably the consciousness, of a "fully awakened" yogi in several sessions. The Hemi Sync sound process, invented by out-of-body acrobat Robert Monroe, is said to speed up the enlightenment process by some twenty years, and once again this is accomplished with state-of-the-art audio engineering. (See "Ticket to the Astral Plane," page 174.) Now it is even possible to become an avatar, which is to say, an incarnation of a god, in five days instead of spending scores of disappointing lifetimes being buffeted by the wheel of karma and ending up a spiritual zero. (See "Be a God—or Just Look Like One," page 173.)

The era of the all-knowing guru has been replaced by a do-it-yourself era of cassette tapes, channeling kits, past-life recall kits, "three-minute meditation" courses, and astral-projection manuals. The Zen/Protestant work ethic—chopping wood and carrying water for fifty years—is passé. Sometimes all you need to reach nirvana is to hang around a certain sacred vortex in Arizona and "take responsibility for your own reality." This is, in the main, an inoffensive trend and even a healthy alternative to surrendering to someone called Love-and-bliss-ananda, but it can lead to unforeseen social problems. Has anyone really thought about what will happen when *everybody* gets enlightened? What if the planet becomes overpopulated with headphone-wearing bodhisattvas and New-Age–music-appreciating arhats? Will there be any regular, unenlightened proles left to man our nation's insurance agencies and compose our government forms? That's one thing we're worried about. The other thing is a phenomenon we'll call the Allisonization of consciousness.

While doing our research for this chapter we discovered that at least 50 percent of people involved in contemporary spiritual endeavors are named Allison or some hard-to-spell variant, like Allyson or Allessyn, and many of them have a penchant for signing their letters or concluding their answering machine messages with the universal nineties salutation, "Light and Love." Don't get us wrong; the New Age Allisons are very nice, but the Allisonization of the soul seems to go hand in hand with a Pollyannaish spiritual optimism, a belief that every day in every way we are getting better and better. Even the little green men in spaceships pause from their interstellar mapping expeditions to lecture us about "clearing away old, limiting patterns of beliefs." Okay, but let's not lose sight of the fact that we're in the latter years of the Kali Yuga, a Leona Helmsley-esque Dark Age of unbridled greed, spiritual darkness, and materialism, which is scheduled to last until about A.D. 4,000, according to the Hindus. Neither Nostradamus nor the ancient Hopis foresaw anything very pleasant coming down the pike (or out of the sky) in the near future. Edgar Cayce did say that an enlightened New Age would begin around 1999, but not before large chunks of the seacoast fall into the ocean, causing great havoc in the real-estate market in Malibu. Hey, and what about the ozone layer, Bhopal, and the Salvadoran death squads?

But if every Golden Age has a dark lining, that's all the more reason to experience altered states now and again. In this we can borrow a few tools from other cultures that are more sophisticated about nonordinary states than we. "Many 'primitive' people believe that almost every normal adult has the ability to go into a trance state and be possessed by a god," notes Tart in the introduction to his landmark volume *Altered States of Consciousness*. "The adult who cannot do this is a psychological cripple." (Of course, that was written in 1970, before the average American adult acquired the ability to go into a trance state and be possessed by a long-winded discarnate spirit.) Just as the Eskimos have several dozen words for snow and Americans have hundreds of words for breakfast cereals, metaphysically oriented cultures have many terms to describe refined states of mind beyond our ordinary K mart consciousness. Sanskrit, for example, is said to have at least twenty different nouns for "consciousness" or "mind."

What is an altered state, anyway? In a classic study, psychiatrist Arnold M. Ludwig determined that an altered state of consciousness (or ASC) had many of the following characteristics: distorted time perception, usually a sense of timelessness; "depersonalization," or loss of the sense of self; lowered inhibitions; ineffability (meaning you can't describe it, which may explain why the world is still waiting for the Great Acid Novel); a tendency to link thoughts associatively and metaphorically rather than logically; heightened empathy; and synesthesia (a cross-wiring of the senses so that you might hear colors or taste sounds). Altered states can be induced by either sensory deprivation (the monotony of winter in Antarctica, a total body cast, a flotation tank) or sensory overload (chanting, percussive sound, whirling-dervish dancing, Fillmore West).

According to a survey by an Ohio State University anthropologist, Erica Bourguignon, 90 percent of the world's cultures engage in some kind of semiofficial altered-state-inducing ritual: rain dances, chants, sweat-lodge ceremonies, All Saints' Day parades, etc. We even have a few ourselves, if you count Super Bowl Fever, rap music, and the Jerry Lewis telethon. "The fact that they are universal," says Bourguignon, "must mean that these states are very important to human beings." For one thing, we all need a mental vacation now and then, an occasional foray into the Galápagos and the Tierra del Fuego of our soul. Altered states also contain much valuable psychological information if we can but retrieve it (remember the ineffability gap). After all, most religions began in an altered state: Think of Mohammed's dream or St. Paul's vision on the road to Damascus.

"Altered states remind us that we're more than we think we are," Charles Tart tells us. "There is tremendous human suffering because we've banished them. We live so immersed in our ongoing psychological processes that we're in a kind of waking trance. And it is 'normal'; everyone is in it."

To avoid the heartache of normality, you can try out some of the mind trips, consciousness-altering tools, and parallel realities listed in this chapter:

THE NIRVANA MERCHANTS

WHAT A LONG, STRANGE TRIP IT'S BEEN
•

"If you see me stop breathing, can you touch my left shoulder?" your partner asks. "Sure," you say, relieved, at least, that for the first session you will be a "sitter" (that is, a helper) and not a "breather." You're even more relieved when the speakers begin to blare screechy, dissonant music composed by heavy-metal aliens, and some people start to moan and writhe on the floor.

You've heard that Holotropic ("moving-toward-the-whole") Breathwork is the "best nondrug high in America." And you figure that the inventor of the process, psychiatrist Stanislav Grof, ought to know a thing or two about altered states. Originally a doctrinaire Freudian, Grof had his paradigms shifted in the early 1960s when he became a pioneer of LSD psychotherapy. At the Psychiatric Research Institute in his native Prague, and later at the Maryland Psychiatric Research Center, he guided some 4,000 subjects through LSD sessions and came up with a revolutionary new map (he called it a "cartography") of the human psyche. The inner journeys he charted convinced him that the birth experience (or, rather, the "perinatal experience," including fetal existence) was *the* crucial psychic issue. "Until you have processed the feeling matrix of the most fundamental experience of your life—birth—and faced and overcome your fear of dying, you will be held an emotional hostage," he explains. The prototypical trip transports the seeker back to the birth experience, according to Grof, and often beyond it to a rich transpersonal domain of ancestral "memories," mythological angels and demons, gods, guides, and spirits.

"This is *therapeutic?*" you wonder, as strange Balinese monkey chants are broadcast from the speakers. On the mats your fellow participants look like inmates in an ancient lunatic asylum or figures in a Hieronymus Bosch painting. A woman arches her back as if in the throes of some purgatorial torture; another lies in a deep, trancelike slumber, dead to the world. A man jumps up and begins to dance feverishly, a St. Vitus's dance from a fifteenth-century lifetime. You hand a Kleenex to your "breather" when she begins to cry like a newborn baby ripped prematurely from the womb. Soon your time will come.

When some of his patients became "stuck" in parts of the LSD trip, Grof taught them a method of hyperventilation to help them break through "blocks" and complete and resolve the experience. To his surprise, he found that the breathing itself had psychedelic effects, triggering profound altered states, waking dreams, flashbacks, birth memories, past-life memories, and encounters with spiritual beings. Today, Grof, his wife, Christina, and various colleagues are teaching the "holotrophic breathwork" *sans* drugs—the active ingredients are breathing, music, movement, and the permission to experience unusual states of consciousness—and people are getting stoned out of their minds.

After the breathing, the participants use crayons and pastels to sketch mandalas expressing their experiences. There are blissful and wrathful deities, a host of interstellar beings, some creation scenes, and at least one crucifixion. During the verbal rehash, many people report that they have relived and resolved childhood traumas such as sexual abuse and beatings. Others describe the suffocating torment of squeezing through the birth canal, the anguish of an abortion attempt while they were fetuses, or the joyous liberation of being born. Several recall past lives. One woman, whose life had been plagued by encounters with violent, abusive men, suddenly saw herself as man in a past life, walking down a road a hundred years ago, en route to rape a series of women. "I was *him*," she gasps. Not a few people met spiritual guides, remote ancestors, and beings from beyond the solar system.

"All we can say," writes Grof, "is that somewhere in the process of perinatal unfolding a strange . . . leap seems to occur, in which deep self-exploration in the individual unconscious turns into a process of experiential adventures in the universe at large, which involves what best can be described as cosmic consciousness or the superconscious mind."

Access: Grof Transpersonal Training, 20 Sunnyside Ave., A-314, Mill Valley, CA 94941. Phone: (415) 453-5860. Stanislav and Christina Grof's latest (1990) book is *The Stormy Search for Self*, published by Jeremy P. Tarcher; hardcover $19.95.

OF COURSE THE BUDDHA WOULD WEAR A WALKMAN!
•

Some of the headphone-wearing people you see walking around malls in the San Fernando Valley are not listening to Guns 'n Roses; they're tuned in to the godhead. You can spot them by their beatific smiles. "*It* meditates *you*," is how one satisfied user describes Brother Charles's meditation cassettes. As personal assistant to the late Swami Muktananda, Brother Charles—né Charles Cannon—spent years in an ashram performing orthodox Vedic rituals, meditating, chanting, and studying the Upanishads. Then he discovered a shortcut to nirvana: "contemporary high-tech meditation" in the form of audiotapes. "After all," he says, "we are Americans. We have created McDonald's. If we can create fast foods, can we not create fast enlightenment?"

How does it work? Well, imagine monks chanting mantras and playing droning instruments in Himalayan caves. Reverberating off the cave walls, these chants tune the monks' brains to frequencies conducive to higher states of consciousness. Brother Charles claims that he can pack the same mind-altering sound effects into a cassette tape. "There is not a single tone but the interaction of many tones, producing a vibrato effect when they interact," he explains. "The interval between the bottom and top in a vibrating tone can be adjusted in cycles per second to the frequency range of brain waves: beta, alpha, theta, and delta." These mystical frequencies are embedded in surf sounds, wind chimes, and ethereal chants, and their effect, according to Brother Charles, is to "synchronize" the right and left hemispheres of the brain.

Some psychologists have started prescribing Brother Charles's instant meditation for stressed-out clients, even though, as one acknowledges, "This will put us out of business." That's because all the subconscious memories that make up your brain's "program" are stored in the alpha, theta, and delta frequency ranges, according to Brother Charles. "If you've meditated over fifty years in a cave," he explains, "you were using your mantra to rescript your data bank. That was called enlightenment. Now we can go into that alpha range and keep ourselves there at the flip of a switch. Whatever data is around is going in. So, okay, let's program it." Bingo, you've reprogrammed your brain.

One type of tape, the Alpha Experience series, is designed for light meditation, stress release, and relaxation. The Genesis Experience series is intended for deeper, theta-wave meditation. Another, industrial-strength series transports

the user to the deeper delta state, in which the uninitiated go to sleep but seasoned meditators can remain awake and experience transcendental "witness consciousness," according to Brother Charles. These heavy-duty tapes can be obtained only by participating in the Recognitions Program, a spiritual correspondence course operated by Brother Charles's organization, Multidimensional Synchronicity through Holodynamics (MSH). Participants meditate regularly with the tapes, keep a daily journal, and send in detailed reports every two weeks, which are fed into the MSH data bank. A meditator may phone in to ask, "I'm twitching. What have you got in the data bank about that?" According to Brother Charles, "documented research" has shown that his high-tech program accelerates spiritual growth by 75 percent over traditional techniques. Now you can become a fully enlightened Buddha in twelve years instead of fifty.

Access: For information about the tapes, the Recognitions Program, or MSH retreats contact: MSH Association, Route 1, Box 192-B, Faber, VA 22938. Phone: (804) 361-2323. For product orders call: (800) 962-2033.

BRAIN WAVES OF THE GODS
•

Some years ago, C. Maxwell Cade, a British psychophysiologist, wired up a number of "fully awakened" Indian yogis and studied their brain waves. He found that the brains of these holy men exhibited a characteristic EEG pattern, which he dubbed the Awakened Mind pattern. He went on to invent a machine, the Mind Mirror (not to be confused with Timothy Leary's software of the same name), to display these enlightened brain waves in a graphic form and train others to imitate them. After Cade's death, his top student, Anna Wise, took over the Mind Mirror research. The device paints a detailed picture of the brain's electrical activity that you can use as biofeedback. Electrodes lead from your scalp to a briefcase-sized machine that displays a pattern of lights on a split screen, representing your EEG activity in both brain hemispheres. Using meditation, visualization, or breath-control techniques, you train your brain to match the Awakened Mind pattern (which resembles the bosomy, ample-hipped, wasp-waisted torso of a forties movie queen). Users soon learn to recognize the "feeling tone" of this pattern, press a "hold button" to freeze the screen, and see how close they come.

At the Anna Wise Center in San Francisco, Wise and her associates use Mind Mirror to identify clients' brain-wave patterns and then teach them to move to higher states of consciousness. This is accomplished with various levels of instruction, from basic visualization to advanced Tantric, Kundalini, and Zen practices. At many new-wave brain parlors, where Mind Mirrors are part of the equipment, aficionados use them to take readings of their mental state before and after a Synchro Energizer session or a float in the isolation tank, say. Or you could use Mind Mirror to assess how your meditation is progressing.

Recently Wise has found other desirable brain-wave patterns besides the yogic one. As Director of Human Tech-

Brother Charles

The Mind Mirror

nology for the consulting firm The Stanford Associates (TSA), she helps businesses apply consciousness testing and training to managerial goals. Would a comptroller's brain waves resemble those of a dhoti-clad swami? One of Wise's present projects is matching occupations to brain-wave patterns—for example, determining the ideal Marketing Director EEG pattern, which may differ markedly from the Personnel Director's. Sometimes she maps a company's collective "brain wave" by overlaying the EEG patterns of individual employees. One such client, a stressed-out Wall Street technology firm, was told it needed to "relax its corporate body."

Access: The Anna Wise Center offers various courses in "Mind Mirror Biofeedback & Consciousness Training," including basic and advanced Awakened Mind classes, professional certification training in the Mind Mirror, and corporate consciousness-training programs. If you want to actually purchase a Mind Mirror, the machine will run you about $4,000. Workshops at the center range from $25 (for a single evening) to $250 (for a weekend). For information, or to be included on the mailing list, contact: The Anna Wise Center, 475 Gate Five Rd., Suite 213, Sausalito, CA 94965. Phone: (415) 331-2651. The center can refer you to a trained Mind Mirror operator in another part of the country. Mind Mirror can also be experienced as part of Michael Hutchison's Megabrain Workshops (see page 27).

A COURSE IN MIRACLES
●

Over a six-month period in 1965, Helen Schucman, a fifty-six-year-old Columbia Medical Center psychologist, the daughter of a bourgeois German-Jewish family, an atheist, and a confirmed Freudian, had a series of highly symbolic dreams. At the end of them, she was awakened by a voice that announced, "This is a course in miracles. Please take notes." Being a psychologist, her first thought was that she was going crazy. (Being ex-students, our first thought would have been, "Is this going to be on the exam?") But the voice wouldn't go away.

Schucman called her boss, Bill Thetford, who advised her to take notes. Every night she took dictation from the voice, which, to her dismay, announced itself as Jesus. And every morning Thetford typed out her notes. Schucman still didn't like the whole business (she never did) but continued for seven years. The result was the three-volume *The Course in Miracles,* which you'll probably never see anyone reading on the subway or the beach. Although it's a channeled work, *The Course in Miracles* has little in common with Ramtha or Agartha. Volume I is a 622-page textbook presenting a highly intellectual mystical philosophy. Volume II is a 365-page "workbook" containing a meditative lesson for each day of the year. Volume III is a slim "manual for teachers" consisting of a glossary and answers to many commonly asked questions.

Upon completing their transcription, Schucman and Thetford asked the voice what to do and were told to put the manuscript aside until the right person came along to publish it. Schucman, who knew that announcing she had just spent seven years taking dictation from Jesus would not be a smart career move, was happy not to publicize her experience. Yet, six months later, Judith Skutch, who had just established a nonprofit institution and had heard about the text, contacted Schucman and Thetford and eventually became the publisher. The books were published in 1976. By 1989 half a million sets had been sold.

"The Course asks that people take total responsibility for their own reality," explains Claire Baird Ludlow, president of the Harmonie Institute in Amherst, Massachusetts, which is dedicated to teaching the course. "We can make the world either heaven or hell." That sounds a lot like Seth, but the Course in Miracles is more mystical, rigorous, and comprehensive than Seth's philosophy, and Jesus seems to be the better writer. This is not a preachy, catechism-style Jesus with a beard, halo, and sky-blue robes; the underlying philosophy of The Course—notably the concept that the phenomenal world is illusory—is more esoteric, Eastern, or gnostic than mainstream Christian.

The interesting thing is that The Course really *is* a course—rather as if Plotinus or Meister Eckhart had come back to teach a continuing-education class at your local community college. Because the material is so demanding, Ludlow suggests starting with the workbook of exercises rather than the textbook and studying with a group rather than alone. The workbook's daily lessons, she says, are structured to help the reader gradually gain a different perception of reality. Each one-to-three-page lesson offers a phrase, such as "I am never upset for the reason that I think," to repeat at certain periods during the day. The number of daily mantralike repetitions is increased as you work your way through the book.

Access: *The Course in Miracles* ($25 for 3 volumes in soft cover) is sold in spiritual and esoteric bookstores. Or you can obtain copies from The Foundation for Inner Peace, Box 635, Tiburon, CA 94929. (If you can't afford the price, write and explain your situation, and the books will be sent to you free.) To find a Course in Miracles group in your area write Miracles Distribution Center, 1141 East Ash Ave., Fullerton, CA 92631.

BE A GOD—OR JUST LOOK LIKE ONE
•

A few years ago we got a call from a California acquaintance with extensive New Age connections. "Have you heard about Avatar?" she asked. "Everybody's doing it." Then she mentioned some human-potential heavies. We had to admit we were so out of it that (1) we hadn't heard about it, and (2) we thought about an avatar more or less along the lines of Webster's definition, that is, as "a god's coming down in bodily form, an incarnation of a god." As in Krishna or Jesus. We'd always assumed we probably didn't know any avatars personally and that anyone who aspired to be one would have had to prepare many lifetimes ago, be born with blue skin or a halo, or at least be preceded by a line of prophets. We learned, however, that if you can lay down your old belief systems and $2,000, you can become an avatar in five days.

It took a former scientologist, Harry Palmer, of Elmira, New York, to discover the quick way to godhead while floating in an isolation tank in 1986. He then spent another two months perfecting procedures to "discreate" unpleasant realities. "The tools of Avatar are actually as ancient as the Vedas," he explains in a promotional tape. An avatar, in his terms, is "a being who has descended to an earth plane but still has the choice of going back to the original state he was in." Getting back to that original state involves thirty to forty hours of training in the "body-handling process," the "creation-handling process" and other technocratic-sounding procedures. The grand climax comes when the teachers/Avatar Masters—they got to be Masters by paying an additional $3,000 to take a nine-day Master's Course—unveil the Ultimate Process. We have no idea what that is, avatarship being a highly secretive and giddy state not unlike the Brownies' "fly up" ceremony. But at the end of it you "reenter the world and create the reality you wish to experience." (We hope one of these newly hatched avatars will not neglect to create a reality with an intact ozone layer.)

If you happen to meet an avatar, he or she will probably look like a regular guy or gal. At least the gushy, hugging avatars featured in the pages of the *Avatar Journal* look no different from other mortals you might meet at Safeway. But avatars know that they are "cocreators with God." They believe they chose their parents and every detail of this present life and all past ones. They have also recognized that planetary disasters are the product of repressed mass wishes, and they may use the "universe-handling process" to help other people at a distance—which will surely come as a great relief to flood victims in Sri Lanka.

Access: The Avatar Course (tuition $2,000) is "delivered" by local Avatar Masters. For the Master nearest you, contact Star's Edge International, 900 Markham Woods Rd., Longwood, FL 32779. Phone: (407) 788-3090. (Advanced courses get progressively more pricey.) Also available from Star's Edge: an introductory tape by Harry Palmer ($5), a subscription to *Avatar Journal* ($8 a year), and the recently declassified *Creativism Workbook* ($12.95), which imparts the first lessons in Avatarship.

LOOK, MA, NO BODY!

TICKET TO THE ASTRAL PLANE
•

That morning, having lost interest in holding the solar system in my hands (can't believe I just said that!) as the tape had directed me to do, I visualized the Focus 15 blue "door." Finding nothing there, I proceeded through red, yellow, pink, green, purple, and finally into white. Using white as "level 21," I continued to "26." . . .

Bob Monroe

Gateway Voyage participants on an outdoor "break"

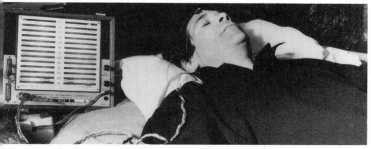

Subject at the Monroe Institute

The Explorer has left his body back there in a darkened, soundproof chamber at the Monroe Institute in rural Virginia, but, thanks to a system of microphones, loudspeakers and electrodes, his astral travels are being carefully plotted by Bob Monroe, who is acting as Monitor. If things get too heavy out there on the fringes of the cosmos, the Explorer can signal for help, and Monroe's reassuring, all-American, air-traffic-controller voice will guide him back to Focus 10 (mind awake, body asleep), tell him to wiggle his toes and circle in for a safe landing in the CHEC (controlled holistic environmental chamber) unit. Monroe knows how to do it, having left his body thousands of times.

Robert A. Monroe, a successful radio executive who directed, wrote, and composed music for more than 400 radio programs in the forties, quite unexpectedly began having out-of-body experiences (OBEs or OOBEs) in 1958. He found that it was easy to "unhook" from his body at night, and, clad only in his astral body, pass through walls, cruise down the streets of his neighborhood, spy on friends and neighbors, occasionally pinching someone and leaving black-and-blue marks as evidence. Naturally, he often doubted his sanity and did not go public with his unusual hobby until 1971, when his out-of-body classic *Journeys Out of the Body* (Doubleday) was published. Before publishing the book he voluntarily submitted himself to in-depth psychiatric and psychological tests, which found him to be quite sane.

Convinced that most people separate from their bodies during sleep and can be trained to have fully conscious OBEs—visiting friends 3,000 miles away, exploring the moon (which Monroe Institute Explorers find barren and boring), or entering other "reality systems"—Monroe began looking into ways of mass-producing the experience. He felt sure that OBEs were related to particular brain-wave frequencies. So he set out to determine which brain frequency, measured in cycles per second, or hz, was conducive to which OBE, then recreate that frequency with sound waves. The brain, he found, naturally resonates to a frequency of sound—a phenomenon Monroe, always prone to techy terms, dubbed the "frequency following response" (FFR). The problem, though, is that while most brain waves are less than 16 hz, the human ear cannot hear anything lower than 30 hz. Fortunately, Monroe determined, if you introduce separate sounds to each ear with headphones, the brain will, in effect, subtract the difference and resonate to the inaudible beat. If you pipe sound of 100 hz to one ear and 104 hz to the other ear, the brain will "hear" ghostly beats at 4 hz—a theta/delta frequency on the border of sleep and waking that may launch an astral trip.

Hemi Sync recording

A high-tech consciousness center

A typical CHEC unit

Devising a digital counter, I sailed backward through darkness as the counter flashed numbers faster than I could read them. Somewhere near where I perceived to be one hundred (ninety-eight?), I stopped and saw many people milling around: They looked like holograms, but conveyed the message of being "live." Some ignored me, some moved away, but several approached me with great joy. I sensed that the latter felt that they were stranded and thought that I was there to guide them back.

The Monroe Institute of Applied Sciences, founded in 1973, immediately began attracting volunteer astral travelers, who would lie for hours in Pullman-car-type isolation booths, wired to the gills, testing out particular combinations of sound frequencies. They soon discovered that Focus 10, a state in which the body is asleep but the brain is alert, was an excellent launching pad to the nonmaterial world. Mon-

roe found he could trigger OBEs by first inducing sleep and then, just as a person is losing consciousness, jolt the mind awake with some high-frequency beta signals. The resulting sound cocktail became known as hemispheric synchronization, or Hemi Sync, and was patented in 1975. The technique is supposed to produce a state of consciousness in which both brain hemispheres automatically work together.

Nowadays, at six-day OBE training sessions known as the Gateways Voyage, would-be astral travelers hole up in CHEC units and, using the prepared tapes, glide to Focus 3, 10, 12, 15 and beyond to the otherwordly Focus 21, known as "Other Energy Systems." Other energy systems usually means extraterrestrial intelligences, who have been contacting hard-core Explorers lately, including Monroe himself, and dictating information about the structure of the universe. One enthusiastic fan, Dr. Elizabeth Kübler-Ross, of death-and-dying fame, visited the Institute in the hopes of experiencing what it felt like to "die." She left more than satisfied, having had an OBE during one session and a "peak experience" during another. But not all participants achieve lift-off and not all are wildly enthusiastic. S. Keith Harary, himself a gifted OBE subject, underwent an earlier version of the current program and reports, "If Monroe's procedures work at all, they're still not necessary to have an OBE." In fact, the Monroe Institute touts the program for many purposes besides out-of-body travel: meditative states, healing, pain control, psychological exploration, concentration, retrieving buried memories, etc.

Access: The Monroe Institute, Route 1, Box 175, Faber, VA 22938. Phone: (804) 361-1252. The six-day Gateways Voyage, held several times a year at the institute, costs $650 plus $545 lodging and meals. If you can't get your physical body to Virginia, the institute can refer you to a qualified person in your area who conducts two-day Hemi Sync–guided Excursion Workshops, which will take you up to Focus 12 (Expanded Awareness). You can also buy a rich variety of Hemi Sync tapes for relaxation, concentration, meditation, catnapping, overcoming addictions, stroke recovery, and other purposes, including playing golf. For a catalogue or to place orders: Interstate Industries, Inc., P.O. Box 130, Nellysford, VA 22958. Phone: (804) 361-1500. Robert Monroe's books—including his latest, *Far Journeys* (Doubleday/Dolphin, $9.95)—are also available through Interstate Industries. "Interstate," by the way, refers to the ability to "unhook from local traffic and travel the interstate," as Monroe puts it.

Flight control at the Monroe Institute

NO DATE ON SATURDAY NIGHT? WHY NOT LEAVE YOUR BODY!

•

There are as many ways to leave your body as there are get-rich-quick schemes. But which ways work? As an aspirant astral traveler you have many questions: Should I remove my jewelry? Should I lie down with my body on a north-south axis? Should I envision a trapdoor at the top of my head? Should I eat raw eggs? *Leaving the Body: A Complete Guide to Astral Projection,* by well-known paranormalist D. Scott Rogo, covers the terrain in detail, from the Monroe technique and methods practiced by British occultist Aleister Crowley to dietary restriction, dream control, and remote viewing experiments. Rogo, a veteran OBE-er himself, is a good source of information about "research" in this vertiginous field.

To astral travel coach Rich Stack of New York City, out-of-body adventures are as simple as one-two-three and as upbeat as a Disney movie. In fact, you can master the basics in just a month if you take Stack's classes or study his book *Out-of-Body Adventures: 30 Days to the Most Exciting Experience of Your Life.* A Seth devotee, Stack regards the physical universe you and I call home as a dull backwater, a spiritual Guam. He tells you how to set aside fears and limiting beliefs ("Are you at all uneasy about leaving your body because you think you might wind up not coming back?") so that you can visit more glamorous parallel realities. Learn such tricks of the trade as "Floating out from

the Hypnogogic States," as well as tips on lucid dreams, visualization, and "Things to Do in the Astral World" (like meeting friends, flying to the moon, meeting yourself in another lifetime, and "astral sex").

Another primer on the subject, *The Traveller's Guide to the Astral Plane,* by British astral-projection artist Steve Richards, has an occultish, Theosophical tone and offers curious tales about Swedenborg, Edgar Allen Poe, and Indian fakirs in suspended animation. If you're like us, you'll feel less inclined to experiment with astral projection—the old terminology for OBEs—after reading about some of the hellish journeys recounted in this volume.

Access: *Leaving the Body: A Complete Guide to Astral Projection* by D. Scott Rogo is published by Prentice-Hall Press. Paper $7.95.

Rick Stack teaches ongoing six-session courses in out-of-body experiences (as well as classes in the Seth material) in New York City, and periodically gives courses in Boston, Chicago, and Cincinnati. For information write: Rick Stack, P.O. Box 1506, Gracie Station, New York, NY 10028. His book *Out-of-Body Adventures: 30 Days to the Most Exciting Experience of Your Life* is published by Contemporary Books, 180 North Michigan Ave., Chicago, IL 60501. Paper $7.95.

The Traveller's Guide to the Astral Plane by Steve Richards is published by The Aquarian Press, Wellingborough, Northamptonshire, NN8 2RQ, England. Paper $7.99 (plus shipping) from Pyramid Books and the New Age Collection, P.O. Box 4546, 35 Congress St., Salem, MA 01970-0902. Phone: (508) 744-6261.

OUT-OF-BODY ADVENTURES
30 Days to the Most Exciting Experience of Your Life
RICK STACK

HOW TO GET HIGH AND STILL KEEP YOUR URINE CLEAN

SAILING THE SEVEN SENSES
•

Five scalp electrodes linked me (J.H.) to Les Fehmi's biofeedback machine. I was trying to get the gizmo to blink a light and beep softly at me, its way of praising me for producing alpha brain waves. All the while, a very calm, tape-recorded voice was asking me questions like, "Can you imagine what it would be like to experience your thumbs, the three-dimensional presence of your thumbs, intimately and subtly?" Now, this is the sort of question that might get a little weird if posed in the context of *The Story of O,* but I knew the tape had only honorable intentions, even when it urged me to picture the "space between" my internal organs. I was doing the Open Focus Training, the brainchild of psychologist Lester Fehmi.

As a young assistant professor of psychology in the late 1960s, Fehmi hooked up his brain to a homemade biofeedback machine and tried to produce more alpha waves. "I tried all the common things," he recalls, "relaxation procedures, music, incense—all with minimal effect." It was only when he pondered spatial questions like "Can you imagine the space between your eyelids?" that the amount and amplitude (strength) of his alpha waves went up. He also found that he could get his brain to produce more alpha only by *not trying to*—a phenomenon known as passive volition.

Today Fehmi's Open Focus Training is considered the crème de la crème of brain-wave-biofeedback techniques. At his Princeton Biofeedback Clinic, he uses an EEG machine to measure "brain-wave synchrony" a condition in which all parts of the brain produce the same kinds of brain waves simultaneously. With the EEG providing feedback, he trains clients to perform visualization exercises that help them "spread attention evenly over the seven senses" (that's the usual five plus "thinking" and the "sense of the time"). This training is necessary, says Fehmi, because the stresses of modern life force us into a chronic Type-A "fight or flight" mode. In this mental state of emergency, a person's consciousness contracts into a "narrow focus" condition—much like trying to squeeze through the revolving doors at Grand Central at rush hour. The result is a whole spectrum of stress-related ailments. (Fehmi has catalogued some seventy stress symptoms, from teeth grinding to hypertension and loss of sex drive, and says his patients often check off fifty of them on a first visit.)

The Open Focus Training aims to reverse this process. After a period of training, adepts can forgo the biofeedback machine and practice Open Focus consciousness while making megadeals or driving down the San Bernadino Freeway. Many Open Focus veterans report interesting, even transcendent, altered states. "Can you imagine," says the tape-recorded voice, "that all experiences exist in the same space, a space witnessed by a cloud of awareness floating in space, permeated by space. . . ." At the time, believe it or not, I could.

Access: Open Focus Training costs $165 for an initial session, $95 for subsequent visits. (The sessions are generally covered by medical insurance.) About 5,000 biofeedback practitioners in the U.S. offer some form of the training. For information contact: Princeton Biofeedback Clinic, 317 Mt. Lucas Rd., Princeton, NJ 08540. Phone: (609) 924-0782. New York office: 30 Lincoln Plaza, New York, NY 10023. Phone: (212) 265-1983. The Clinic also provides audio- and videotapes and other stress-management aids.

RAINBOW CRYSTAL SPIRIT VIBRATIONS FROM ATLANTIS
•

In India and Tibet, they have mantras, or sacred sounds, designed to have profound effects on the brain and nervous system. In America we have Muzak, which induces a mild trance and causes supermarket shoppers to buy more Charmin. And now we have New Age music and music therapy.

Unlike Jimi Hendrix, Tone-Lōc, or the Beastie Boys, much New Age music is deliberately therapeutic—as long as you aren't operating heavy machinery while you're listening to it. No one ever called "Purple Haze" therapeutic, let alone the bad vibes at Altamont, but, on the other hand, has anyone ever really gotten down and boogied to amplified raindrop sounds, swoosh-swooshing surf, and long, languid piano and synthesizer compositions entitled "Crystal Earth Heartthrobs"? Never mind—New Age record covers typically carry raves not from *Rolling Stone* or *Spin,* but from pain-control clinics.

"Tribal cultures used music to help invoke deities, effect healings, and create altered states of consciousness," notes Jonathan S. Goldman, director of the Sound Healers Association of Boulder, Colorado. (Goldman used to be a Jimi Hendrix–style hard-rock guitarist before he looked out into the audience one day and noticed everyone was *angry.*) "Today's New Age musicians are essentially striving to use sound in the same way." The compositions of New Age music king Steven Halpern are reportedly based on laboratory studies of galvanic skin responses, EEG studies, and Kirlian photography. Sam McLellan's "The Music of the Five Elements" has been touted as an "acoustic acupressure session," while Don Campbell's "Crystal Meditations" is supposed to slow down the listener's brain waves, inducing deep meditation. The pieces often incorporate mind-altering techniques borrowed from shamanic singing, the ancient mystery schools of Greece and Egypt, and the harmonics of Gregorian chants. Campbell and his colleagues at the Institute for Music, Health, and Education in Boulder, Colorado, can quote you state-of-the-art research on audiological curves, psychoacoustics, and the effects of certain frequencies on body tissues.

But you can enjoy music therapy without listening to synthesized Atlantean dolphin chants. The eminent music therapist Helen Bonny considers New Age music a form of musical junk food, preferring to use Brahms, Beethoven,

Don Campbell

and Mozart in her "guided imagery and music" work. As an LSD/altered-states researcher from 1969 to 1975, she concluded that music, unlike unpredictable psychedelics, was a "safe trip." In her music therapy, she plays selected classical music while guiding the client through an imaginary journey—such as flying through the clouds or walking through a primeval rain forest.

Access: The Institute for Music, Health, and Education—P.O. Box 1244, Boulder, CO 80306. Phone: (303) 443-8484—offers courses by telephone, tape, and correspondence as well as in person, and gives intensive four-day training programs in music and healing at different locations around the U.S. every summer. The Institute's director, Don Campbell, has a new book *The Roar of Silence* (paper $9.98; available from the Institute) that includes exercises, meditations, and images to help readers work with music. Or you can take one of his eight albums/tapes of transforming music with you to K mart to cancel out the Muzak.

The Sound Healers Association, directed by Jonathan Goldman, can be reached at P.O. Box 2240, Boulder, CO 90306.

To keep abreast of New Age music: *The Heartsong Review,* published semiannually, carries reviews of current "spiritually conscious" music from traditional Native American chants and New Age instrumentals to children's folk songs and "electronic and space music." A year's subscription costs $6, two years, $10. A book on the subject, *A New Age Record Guide* by P. J. Birosik, is published by Macmillan Publishing Company. Paper $12.95.

To find a certified music therapist in your area contact: American Association of Music Therapy, P.O. Box 359, Springfield, NJ 07081.

To contact Helen Bonny: The Bonny Foundation: An Institute for Music Centered Therapies, 418 Charles St., Salina, KA 67401. Phone: (913) 827-1497. *Music and Your Mind,* by Helen Bonny and Louis Savary, is published by Station Hill Press, Barrytown, NY 12506. Paper $10.95.

NINE HUNDRED YOUS
•

You step into a tiny chamber, take a seat, and greet 900 people who look exactly like you! In fact, they *are* you. The Star Chamber is part isolation tank, part light-and-sound machine, part kinky boutique changing room, where mirrors set at ingenious angles bounce your image around, creating 900 doppelgängers, all with your split ends and mild overbite. When a meditator focuses on a mandala, the myriad shapes and colors eventually coalesce into a single image, and that's what is supposed to occur with the Star Chamber's replications of your body. "You are impressing on your mind what you are," explains Katie Gooden, a spokesperson for Reflections, the company that makes the Star Chamber. "Your mind can't tolerate all the input and integrates it into one image."

At the same time, the Star Chamber hits you with a synchronized sound-and-light show, much like the Synchro Energizer or the D.A.V.I.D., except that the sound is transmitted by standard speakers rather than headphones and the lights are at the top of the chamber rather than in goggles. In front of you is a keyboard you can use to change the frequencies, dim the lights, and control the sound. And then you hear the soothing taped voice of the Star Chamber's inventor, Cliff Cowles, a Carmel Valley, California, psychologist. "Imagine you are not here," it says. "Imagine your right brain as a balloon. Let your right brain become a huge basket of popping corn. Feel your right brain being eaten by friendly dwarfs, thousands of them." See, there's a self-improvement angle to this science-fiction experience. Cowles has produced twenty-five self-help tapes to be used with the Star Chamber, on subjects ranging from "Brain Integration" to "Retuning Relationships."

As of this writing, there are over 150 Star Chambers in mind gyms and meditation spas nationwide. "It's the next health-spa idea," Cowles predicts. "You'll see them in the mall. You'll pay ten dollars, get your brain tuned up, and go home." Accompanied by a thousand popcorn-munching dwarfs? No thanks! We can't even remember the names of the original seven.

The Star Chamber

Access: Reflections, P.O. Box 1249, Carmel Valley, CA 93924. Phone: (408) 659-4799. There are two models. The Professional model goes for $4,500 and has a birchwood exterior. The Executive model costs $2,945 and is made of vinyl pressboard. The main difference is that the Professional can be disassembled by two people in ten minutes; the Executive, which is pegged and doweled, takes two hours to take apart. If you don't want to buy a unit, Reflections can refer you to a facility in your area that has a Star Chamber. The company itself conducts Star Chamber workshops, and the self-improvement tapes can be used without a unit.

ISOLATION A-GO-GO
•

Sure, isolation tanking is nice, but it's so wet. And so . . . isolated! For people who prefer their floats dry—and maybe not quite so isolated—a Colorado firm has created the Super Space relaxer. It's a dark, soundproof box where the "float" is achieved not with actual immersion in saltwater but with a floppy waterbed covered with a velvetized skin. "The inside of the Super Space relaxer," the brochure explains, "is a warm, modern cave where you may come to know yourself. The noise, dust, visual distractions and even the touch of the outer world float away as you recline in the quiet, heavenly comfort. . . ." So you can float without getting wet or worrying about whose germs might be floating in there with you, and, in case you should get bored, there's a Pulsating Water Massage and video and audio to enhance your trip.

This must be an idea whose time has come, because about a year or two ago, we found a Detroit float center with a Flotation Entertainment Center, complete with hydromassage, a 19″ color monitor, an eight-speaker audio system, a choice of wet or dry float, *and* ample room for a fellow floater to share your, um, isolation. "Only a small percentage of people really want to turn everything off," explained the device's creator, Pete Panelli, a longtime floater and former Mr. Michigan. "When you watch *Star Wars* in there you feel like you're floating through space." This may seem a bit like joining a gossipy Trappist order, and indeed when we tried to track down Tranquil Visions again it had vanished from the directory-assistance universe. But in the nineties, it seems, you *can* have it all. "Relaxers represent a quantum leap in sensory-isolation technology," explains the Super Space brochure. "They are truly sensory-enrichment environments." We see. According to the company's literature, these new, improved sensory deprivation—whoops, enrichment—tanks induce a theta brain-wave state conducive to "quality meditation, calmness, integration of various aspects of personality, intuition, creativity, dreamlike visual imagery, childhood memories, and insight from unconscious sources."

Access: Relaxation Dynamics offers four different models of the dry tank: Super Space, InnerSea, PrivateSea, and Think Tank. If you're a well-heeled isolation/enrichment buff you can buy or lease-purchase one; the tanks range from $5,000 to $22,000. Otherwise, you can rent time at a facility offering sessions. For information contact Relaxation

Dynamics, 3000 Broadway, Suite 9, Boulder, CO 80304. Phone: (303) 440-4535. We could not track down the Flotation Entertainment Center, its inventor, or its host center, the Tranquil Visions Float Center in Detroit. (Maybe you know where they've gone?)

DOING THE RHYTHMS
•

"I was raised on rock 'n' roll, fast food, and subways," writes Gabrielle Roth in her book *Maps to Ecstasy: Teachings of an Urban Shaman*. "I've never been on any trips to exotic cultures or studied tribal techniques. I read the papers, go to the movies, worry about what to fix for dinner, and go to work like most people. Only for me, going to work is going on a journey—a journey to an ecstatic level of consciousness." I wish we could say we felt the same way, but it's hard to reach an ecstatic level of consciousness while looking out for unclear antecedents. Roth, on the other hand, is artistic director of her dance/theater/music company, The Moving Center, and probably has someone else proofread her manuscripts. In her workshops she introduces participants to a vigorous, cathartic form of ecstatic dance, and helps them identify their own basic rhythms, ritualize their own dances, and thereby initiate an intense personal dialogue between the body and the spirit. If you can't dance with Roth you can read her highly original book, wherein you'll meet the "five rhythms"—flowing, staccato, chaotic, lyrical, and still—and learn to "do the rhythms" as a pathway to ecstasy and self-knowledge. A series of practical exercises and shamanic tasks bring to life the "five powers"—the power of being, the power of loving, the power of knowing, the power of seeing, and the power of healing.

Access: For information about Gabrielle Roth's workshops, training programs, and tapes contact The Moving Center, P.O. Box 2034, Red Bank, NJ 07701. Phone: (212) 505-7928. *Maps to Ecstasy: Teachings of an Urban Shaman* by Gabrielle Roth is published by New World Library. Paper $8.95.

KUNDALINI CITY, U.S.A.

DOWN AND OUT IN THE MULHADARA CHAKRA
•

Hindu sacred texts depict kundalini as a coiled serpent sleeping at the base of the spine. When this spiritual energy awakens, they say, it rises up the spinal column, through the chakras (the body's seven energy centers) and explodes as a great burst of light in the head. Kundalini rising may bring enlightenment, but it can also be a real bummer.

The kundalini phenomenon became known to the West through Gopi Krishna, a teacher and administrator in Kashmir who had a sudden, spontaneous kundalini experience in 1937 at the age of thirty-four, leading eventually to the experience of *samadhi*, or cosmic consciousness. In his 1971 memoir, *Kundalini: The Evolutionary Energy in Man,* he describes this rapture—the blissful stream of *soma,* or divine nectar, coursing up the spinal column and filling his brain with radiant light—as well as the physical and mental tortures he endured along the way. At times he felt as if he were being burned alive. In the dark he noticed a reddish glow around his body. He suffered from insomnia, severe back pains, weakness, and stark terror. He often thought he was dying or going mad. Despite all the hardships, Gopi Krishna decided that kundalini "is the real cause of all the so-called spiritual and psychic phenomena, the biological basis of evolution and the development of personality, the secret origin of all esoteric and occult doctrines, the master key to the unsolved mystery of creation . . . ," etc.

Maybe you think you don't have to worry about this sort of thing if you live in Cleveland and have never heard of a chakra or a *shushumna* (the subtle energy channel in the spinal column) but cognoscenti say that kundalini is on the rise (sorry!) in the West. "Today kundalini awakenings occur more frequently, with and without training," observes Lee Sannella, M.D. Sannella, a psychiatrist and ophthalmologist with more than a passing interest in spiritual practices, has treated numerous cases of kundalini rising among ordinary, suburban-bred, Wonder Bread–eating Americans. (Okay, well, most of them were doing some kind of meditation or yoga and probably ate pita bread, not Wonder Bread.) In his book *The Kundalini Experience: Psychosis or Transcendence?* he reviews some fascinating case histories, categorizes the major kundalini symptoms—from strange optical and auditory phenomena and sensations of intense heat and cold to "single seeing" and out-of-body experiences—and attempts to construct a scientific model. The fact that he doesn't entirely succeed is less his fault than that of our present rudimentary understanding of the human brain. But after reading his book you will not dismiss kundalini as a bizarre psychotic episode.

For a more scholarly view of the phenomenon, check out *Kundalini: The Arousal of the Inner Energy* by Eastern-art scholar Ajit Mookerjee. Here you'll find discussions of the rays of *tattvas* (subtle elements) from original manuscript sources, lovely illustrations of chakras with diminutive de-

Gopi Krishna

ities perched on them, and detailed maps of the planes of existence up to Mahabindu (the Absolute Void).

Access: *Kundalini: The Evolutionary Energy in Man* by Gopi Krishna is published by Shambhala Publications, Inc., P.O. Box 308, Boston, MA 02117. Paper $9.95. The revised and expanded 1987 edition of *The Kundalini Experience: Psychosis or Transcendence?* by Lee Sannella, M.D., is published by Integral Publishing, P.O. Box 1030, Lower Lake, CA 95457. Paper $9.95. *Kundalini: The Arousal of the Inner Energy* by Akit Mookerjee is published by Destiny Books, Park St., Rochester, VT 05767. Paper $12.95.

Several organizations are currently studying the kundalini phenomenon. The Kundalini Research Foundation carries out the work of Gopi Krishna in the West: P.O. Box 22248, Darien, CT 06820. Phone: (203) 348-5351. The Academy for Religion and Psychical Research recently held the first conference on kundalini in North America: P.O. Box 614, Bloomfield, CT 06002. Phone: (203) 242-4593. The Spiritual Emergence Network, which has worked extensively with victims of the kundalini experience, is covered under "Spiritual Emergencies," below.

SPIRITUAL EMERGENCIES
•

Bothered by a buzzing sensation in your crown chakra? Not sure if those vivid mandala patterns you see in Italian restaurants are acid flashbacks or a side effect of all that hatha yoga you've been doing? Now there's a place to call for advice: The Spiritual Emergence Network in Menlo Park, California.

Originally centered at the Esalen Institute and called the Spiritual Emergency Network, SEN was founded in 1980 by psychiatrist Stanislav Grof and his wife, Christina. (See

"What a Long, Strange Trip It's Been," page 170.) In 1968 Christina underwent a startling spiritual awakening during childbirth, followed by years of often harrowing visions of birth and death, auditory hallucinations of chanting and choral music, haunting coincidences, and strange bodily sensations. Her former teacher and mentor, myth mogul Joseph Campbell, sent her to Esalen to meet Stan Grof. Finally she was able to recognize her bewildering experience as the classic "kundalini awakening" phenomenon. Knowing that

people troubled by painful vibrations in the heart chakra aren't likely to find a sympathetic ear at the local mental-health clinic, she founded a twenty-four-hour hotline for spiritual freak-outs.

"A Christian housewife with two toddlers just called," says a SEN volunteer. "She'd been trying to figure out the numbers for the lottery, and her hand just took off for hours—automatic writing. When she finally asked the beings who were channeling through her for help, they told her to look on a page in a book where our number was listed." Had she been directed to another number, she might have ended up in a hospital emergency room being sedated with Thorazine, but at SEN she could talk to someone familiar with kundalini crises, accidental channeling, shamanic illnesses, out-of-body experiences, and other symptoms of spiritual emergence. If necessary, she could be referred to one of the "helpers" in SEN's database, including psychiatrists, psychologists, healers, yoga teachers, bodyworkers, parapsychologists, spiritual teachers, and spiritual communities throughout the U.S. and in eighteen foreign countries.

The typical caller, according to Jeaneane Prevatt and Russ Park, SEN coordinator and intern, respectively, "is a forty-year-old female (60 percent) experiencing some form of kundalini awakening (24 percent)." But some callers may be troubled by encounters with space beings, sudden episodes of clairvoyance or channeling, eruptions of past-life memories from Mesopotamia, or terrifying visions of dismemberment in a shamanic Lower World. The Grofs have identified ten different forms of spiritual emergency: (1) the shamanic crisis; (2) the awakening of kundalini; (3) episodes of unitive consciousness (peak experiences); (4) Jungian "psychological renewal through return to the center"; (5) a crisis of psychic opening; (6) past-life experiences; (7) communications with spirit guides and "channeling"; (8) near-death experiences; (9) close encounters with UFOs; and (10) possession states.

Access: The Spiritual Emergence Network, c/o Institute of Transpersonal Therapy, 250 Oak Grove Ave., Menlo Park,

CA 94025. Phone: (415) 327-2776. For further reading: *Spiritual Emergency: When Personal Transformation Becomes a Crisis,* edited by Stanislav Grof, M.D., and Christina Grof, includes interesting contributions by R.D. Laing, Lee Sannella, Ram Dass, Hoger Kalweit and others on shamanic, kundalini, Jungian, transpersonal, and other aspects of spiritual crisis. Published by Jeremy P. Tarcher; paper $12.95. *A Sourcebook for Helping People in Spiritual Emergency* by Emma Bragdon, Ph.D., a Grof protégée who did much of her fieldwork at SEN, is written for "helpers" but contains some good guidelines for coping with spiritual crises as well as an appendix of referrals. (Lightening Up Press, 855 No. San Antonio Rd., Suite R, Los Altos, CA 94022. Paper $11.95.)

KUNDALINI AND ME

After the publication of the first edition of *The Kundalini Experience,* Lee Sannella, M.D., received a letter from a young woman who had unwittingly triggered a kundalini experience in 1970 by taking LSD. At the time she had never heard of kundalini and was quite distressed by her symptoms. Following is a portion of her account, included in the 1987 edition of his book:

"In 1970, at the age of eighteen, I took three trips on LSD. The first two trips were beautiful and 'spiritual'—during the second I experienced what was probably a form of 'satori.' During the third I experienced what I now call 'kundalini.'

"Preceding the kundalini was an awareness of my capacity to turn off my mind and self—to annihilate my individuality without physical death. (Right now this is meaningless to me, but it was my experience.) Shortly thereafter I felt a rush—a roar—of white light shoot up from the base of my spine through and out the top of my head. I was terrified, panicked, and thought I was dying. I 'yanked' down the rush of light energy. It occurred again and again, with seconds or minutes in between. I kept yanking it down. I went to an emergency room and was given Thorazine. I saw a psychiatrist for six weeks. He was not very helpful but served as an anchor in my confusion.

"The roar and rush of white light continued. We called this LSD flashbacks. At first it occurred several times a day. At times I would jump up from a sound sleep with the white roar. During this time I was mostly preoccupied with the certainty that I was either dying or going crazy. I was not particularly interested in the experience itself, only in stopping it. After six months of anxiety, palpitations, weight loss, and diarrhea, I went to the hospital (medical, not psychiatric) for a week of tests, and rest and recuperation. The first night I was there I closed my eyes to go to sleep and felt a light touch between my eyebrows and felt that things would now get better. . . .

"The next two years were difficult, even though I became more adept at controlling the energy rushes. I learned to stop the rushes at the base of my skull. At times my head and neck would shake from the effort of holding back the energy. I didn't always feel in synch with my body. Often my body was in a slightly different position from the one I subjectively experienced. . . .

"From the age of twenty-five to twenty-seven I no longer experienced fear regarding my kundalini experiences. When I felt the beginnings of the shaking and vibrating I would go to where I could be alone. I sometimes put my body into positions it wanted to assume. . . . Sometimes I made sounds. . . .

TIME TRAVEL WITHOUT TEARS

"I began meditating—in my own style: I would relax and allow/cause a certain feeling to saturate my body. I realized since reading your book that the feeling spreads approximately in the order you mentioned, beginning with the feet. The feeling is a sweet porous emptiness and is not just on the surface. The switch makes my body feel as if it were all one substance/energy. Then something happens in my eyes. There is a pressure in my eyes directed to a point behind and between them. Then, sometimes, something switches there, and I experience a vast dark clearness, and I am a point in it. Occasionally somewhere along the line my body feels like it is floating and moving.

"During the last couple of years I have been frightened only once. I felt as if I (my subjective energy-self) were growing bigger and bigger (around eighteen feet), and I was afraid that I would vanish. The vibrating has occurred only twice that I recall. . . . I welcome the vibrating and go along with it, and the result is increased joy. . . .

"The floating feelings during meditation have increased and are exactly the same feeling as flying in dreams. One morning in bed, before waking, I realized that I would have to 'move in' a few more inches before I could wake up because I was not quite in synch with my body. So I moved in and promptly woke up. This was not a thought but an experience of my senses. Another new thing that has happened a few times is that I will be asleep but completely conscious . . . and I can see with my eyes closed. I just lie there in bed and look around the room with my eyes closed and see in incredible detail. This is very unlike dreams. It is exactly like vision.

"I recently had a physical-sensation dream of 'merging'—the word for it was given in the dream. I merged with another person. First the porous, empty, sweet feeling occurred, then our trunks merged, then we had to pull our straying arms into synch.

"I am telling you about these dreams because I know that they are the further workings of kundalini. It is the same energy, becoming more and more refined. And it is the same whether I am waking or sleeping or meditating."

—Reprinted from *The Kundalini Experience: Psychosis or Transcendence?* by Lee Sannella, M.D.; with permission from Integral Publishing, Lower Lake, California.

BACK TO THE FUTURE
●

Dr. G: Where are you?
Harry: I'm reporting to the termination room.
Dr. G: Are you still in the pyramid?
Harry: Yes.
Dr. G: Why are you in the termination room?
Harry: It's my turn to change units.

It had to happen. In the course of regressing a man to his previous lives, Dr. Bruce Goldberg, a dentist–turned–past-life therapist, was astonished to hear broadcasts from the future. It seemed that his client, a Baltimore TV personality, was speeding up the space-time turnpike *in the future direction*. Eventually he began describing lifetimes in 2135, 2271, and 2273 in vivid detail, from his home in a glass pyramid to his "molecular reassembly" job at the plant. Realizing that he was dealing with *progression* and not *regression*, Goldberg went on to guide other clients into the future—a future that makes you want to scream, "Beam me up, Scotty!" Now, you may ask, how can people "remember" the future? If you weren't stuck in these stupid conventions about past and future, you'd understand that "by leaving the earth plane or entering into a hypnotic trance you can read the past or future without the restrictions that occur in the waking . . . state." If you're interested in what goes on in the termination room or what a typical dwelling looks like in the middle of the next century, you can read all about this in Goldberg's book *Past Lives, Future Lives*.

If you have the urge to travel into the future *yourself* you can pick up some tips in *Your Future Lives* by Brad Steiger, et al. (We hope the other six authors will forgive us for not listing their names; we're tired of typing names like "Kelynda" with no surname.) "The awareness of a future life has permitted many troubled men and women to free themselves of the anguish and anxiety of their present lives and to progress into the productive and positive aspects of their future lives without undergoing the transition of physical death," explains Steiger, a veteran of many beyond-the-beyond adventures. Naturally, we *were* eager to free ourselves from the anguish of our present life, so we perked up when the book assured us that we really didn't have to go on living a life of "negative programming." We were all set to try a series of exercises designed to launch our consciousness into the future, when we read the warning: "You will not be distressed if new coastlines have formed . . . if new mountain ranges have appeared . . . if cities have gone underground. You will not be disturbed even if alien species should now walk among us. . . ." Well, we felt we might be a *tad* disconcerted by such drastic sociogeological changes, so we've decided to confine our attention to the immediate future—no more than three weeks from next Monday.

Access: *Past Lives, Future Lives: Accounts of Regressions and Progressions through Hypnosis* by Dr. Bruce Goldberg is published by Newcastle Publishing Company, P.O. Box 7589, Van Nuys, CA 91409. Paper $6.95. *Your Future Lives* by Brad Steiger, et al. is published by Whitford Press, 1469 Morstein Rd., West Chester, PA 19380. Paper $12.95.

THE PALACE WHERE WISHES COME TRUE
●

As his time travelers lie in a circle, Joe Hart's easy-does-it Arkansas twang guides them to a forest clearing, where they ascend an obelisk to the year 2137. Strolling through the Museum of the Past, they can view their own (present) lives on exhibit. (Look, Mabel, over there by the Eisenhower golf club! Isn't that my hula hoop?) Later, they can drop by the Palace Where Wishes Come True. Many time tourists have had compelling visions: A businessman visited a distant planet, a transparent world of crystal cities. A couple landed in a world composed entirely of music. A woman was transported through air and sea on the back of a flying porpoise. Another traveled to a universe in which every inhabitant was dressed in Nancy Reagan's borrowed Adolfo clothes. (Just kidding.)

Why 2137? At first, Hart, a retired University of Arkansas associate dean, had people project themselves only twenty years ahead, but "I was getting a lot of stuff out of *Star Wars* or science fiction, and people couldn't get past their own deaths." He found that traveling *far* into the future freed up their creativity. "Time travel helps people look at problems and resources in ways they never did before," he explains. "The experience of accomplishing goals in the future and understanding what steps were taken to achieve those goals helps end defeatist cycles." Corporations have used future travel sessions as part of those trendy motivational retreats that get executives' profit-making juices flowing, and in Little Rock, Arkansas, the chiefs of all the city's operating divisions have taken trips to the future. (When you're next in Little Rock watch out for city comptrollers wielding laser guns.)

Access: For information about Hart's workshops write him at: 2717 Breckenridge, Little Rock, AK 72007. For $10.95 you can order a tape that will permit you to try time travel on your own.

KARMA KIT
●

Your past lives are all back there somewhere . . . but how to get at them? Now ARE, the Edgar Cayce organization, offers a learn-at-home course to help you recover those wild and wacky times on the lost continent of Mu. The "Beyond Past Lives" kit includes six "practical lessons" on three cassette tapes, a karma questionnaire, affirmations, quotes from the Cayce readings, and exercises to help you identify karmic "hot spots" in your own life. The course is supposed to help you recognize your "karmic patterns" and use the "law of grace" to keep from building up more bad karma in this life.

Access: "Beyond Past Lives: The Dynamics of Karma and Grace" by Lynn Sparrow can be ordered from: ARE Press, 67th St. and Atlantic Ave., P.O. Box 595, Virginia Beach, VA 23451. For Visa and MasterCard orders call toll free (800) 368-2727. Price $29.95 plus postage and handling.

WHEN IN ROME BELCH LOUDLY AFTER EVERY MEAL
●

Sure, you want to master time travel, but have you thought about all the embarrassing problems you could encounter with medieval hygiene, ancient cuisine, and Roman orgy etiquette? Do you know the right kind of hip boots to pack when you take the kids to the Jurassic age to see brontosaurus and stegosaurus? No? Well, be sure to pack a copy of *The Complete Time Traveler: A Tourist's Guide to the Fourth Dimension* by Howard J. Blumenthal, Dorothy F. Curley, and Brad Williams. This tongue-in-cheek Baedeker for time tourists addresses the nitty-gritty issues of temporal vacationing: How to handle chamber pots in London in 1600. The best buys at the Agora marketplace in Athens. What those dried-up-looking things are on your plate in your tour of the Old Testament (toasted locusts). How women should dress for time travel (as men). Which is the best seat in a stagecoach. Why Sparta is a great burg for single gals. What to wear when touring King Arthur's England. Why the Children's Crusade of 1212 is not a good idea for a family vacation. The guidebook also offers tips for operating a wide variety of time machines and Time Travel Viewing (TTV) software, handling immunization requirements for visiting the 1800s, avoiding hassles with the Time Patrol, and many other practical details.

Access: *The Complete Time Traveler: A Tourist's Guide to the Fourth Dimension* by Howard J. Blumenthal, Dorothy F. Curley, and Brad Williams is published by Ten Speed Press, P.O. Box 7123, Berkeley, CA 94707. Paper $13.95.

MEDITATION À LA MODE

SPIRITUAL SAMPLER
•

Sure, you'd like to meditate but you don't know a Zen koan from a sushi bar, Vipassana from Hare Krishna. An audiotape called "Five Classic Meditations," by Shinzen Young, an ordained Buddhist monk and director of the Community Meditation Center in Los Angeles, guides the seeker through five different meditation techniques. The first is a mantra (repetitive-sound) meditation, using the traditional Buddhist mantra *Om mani padme hum,* which, loosely translated, means "Hail to the jewel in the lotus." (This was our favorite technique of the five, but that may be because we've had previous mantra experience.) The second meditation is from the Vipassana tradition, the earliest and simplest Buddhist meditative tradition, and is designed to focus attention on the moment-to-moment flow of awareness. (Your neighbors may overhear you mumbling, "Knees... shoulders... thinking... whole body... toes..." and assume that you are talking along with "Sesame Street.") The other three meditations are a Loving Kindness Meditation; a Karma Yoga Meditation to make your daily work into a meditation practice (I wish we could say we were doing it now, but our line of work tends to build up negative karma rather than work it off); and a Kabbalah Meditation on the forces of creation, from the Jewish mystical tradition. The starter meditations on the tape are intended only as introduction; if you find something you like, Young encourages you to seek further instruction from a teacher or group.

Access: The sixty-minute audiocassette tape "Five Classic Meditations" is available from Audio Renaissance Tapes, Inc., 5858 Wilshire Blvd., Suite 205, Los Angeles, CA 90036. $9.95.

THE GANGES IN YOUR KITCHEN
•

If you're tired of squeamish meditators who are always worrying about being exposed to "low vibrations," you'll appreciate the down-to-earth, nondogmatic approach of *The Fine Arts of Relaxation, Concentration, and Meditation* by Joel Levey. This little jewel of a meditation handbook allows you to browse and sample various meditative practices drawn from Zen, humanistic psychology, Tibetan Buddhism, Sufism, Christianity, Judaism, and other systems. In practical, easy-to-follow steps you can master the basics of sleeping meditation, hollow-body meditation, meditation on the four elements, two-domains-of-reality meditation, self-remembering, Zen breathing, creative visualization, kitchen-yogi meditation, drop-in-the-ocean meditation, and many other excellent techniques—all without shaving your head or handing out silly tracts on street corners. There are also interesting discussions of biofeedback, meditation research, sports as "Western yoga," and the psychophysiology of stress control.

Access: *The Fine Arts of Relaxation, Concentration, and Meditation: Ancient Skills for Modern Minds* by Joel Levey is published by Wisdom Publications, London. (U.S. address: 45 Water St., Newburyport, MA 01950.) Paper $14.95. Wisdom Publications' catalogue carries the world's largest selection of books on Buddhism and Tibet. For orders call (808) 272-4050.

THE VARIETIES OF MEDITATIVE EXPERIENCE
•

Do you gravitate to zazen, the Russian orthodox "Jesus Prayer," the Kabbalistic Tree of Life, or Gurdjieff's "self-remembering" techniques? Would you rather chant *la ilaha illa 'lla* ("There is no god but God") with the Sufis, or practice *maithuna,* "the arousal of *shakti*—kundalini energy—through controlled, ritual sexual intercourse" with the Tantric Buddhists? (This turns out not to be as much fun as it sounds.) To make an informed decision about your spiritual path, you may want to consult *The Meditative Mind: The Varieties of Meditative Experience* by Daniel Goleman, a longtime student of Eastern meditative traditions and a behavioral science reporter for *The New York Times.* Beginning meditators and old India hands alike will enjoy the excellent, to-the-point summaries of the world's major meditative traditions from Hindu Bhakti, Indian Tantra, Kundalini meditation, Zen, and Jewish Kabbalah, to Tibetan Buddhism, Krishnamurti's Choiceless Awareness, Gurdjieff's Fourth

KITCHEN YOGI MEDITATION

The technique that follows was inspired by the insight that all of life's daily activities can be transformed into meditations, even the most mundane and ordinary activities such as washing and chopping vegetables. The key to this transformation lies in the art of paying close attention to whatever is happening in the present moment. We all spend much of our lives doing routine and mechanical chores. Experiment with these guidelines to see how you can transform whatever you are doing into an experience of wakefulness.

1. Begin by grounding yourself. Feel the contact between the two soles of your feet and the floor. Note the feeling of your feet touching the ground and sense that the floor beneath connects to the earth

2. Knees slightly bent, feel your legs growing down into the earth. Hips, thighs, legs growing down into the earth.

3. Move your awareness next into your navel center, your center of power.

4. Now allow the upper part of your body to open and become alive. As you exhale allow your shoulders to drop. With each exhalation let your eyes be soft and your jaw be loose and soft.

5. With each exhalation come back to your body. Sense your body posture.

6. Be receptive. Allow the visual sensation of the vegetables to come to you as you chop with the knife.

7. There is nothing to do but feel the sensation of the knife in your hand. Feel its hardness. Become aware of the sensation of contact, the touch of your hand on the knife. Are you squeezing more than you need to as you chop? Soften your grip.

8. Allow the feeling of the vegetable you are holding to come to you. Note the quality of its sensations.

9. Feet touching the floor.

10. Knees slightly bent.

11. Moving from the center.

12. Be aware of the breath.

13. Eyes soft.

14. Receive. . . .

15. Stay in touch with sensations.

16. Attend to every moment as if it were your last.

17. Soft and alert. Relaxed and precise.

18. Mindfulness moving from moment to moment.

—from *The Fine Arts of Relaxation, Concentration, and Meditation: Ancient Skills for Modern Minds* by Joel Levey; reprinted with permission of Wisdom Publications.

Way, and Maharishi Mahesh Yogi's Transcendental Meditation. (The latter, Goleman points out accurately, is really a traditional Hindu practice in a Westernized package.) The author does an admirable job of analyzing the "psychology of meditation" both in the East and the West and of summarizing recent psychophysiological research.

Access: *The Meditative Mind: The Varieties of Meditative Experience* by Daniel Goleman is published by Jeremy P. Tarcher, Inc. Paper $8.95.

THE THREE-MINUTE MEDITATOR
●

Although *The Three-Minute Meditator* by David Harp inexplicably carries an endorsement from Ben & Jerry, the ice-cream people, and the typesetting and copyediting looks as if it were done by ice-cream vendors on a sugar high, it delivers exactly what it promises: a number of excellent mini-meditations you could pace with an egg timer. There are eating meditations, "conscious-driving" meditations, thought-counting meditations, an "Ooh/Aah" meditation, a sneezing meditation, a "taming the Rambo mind" meditation, even a hot-pepper meditation and a cold-shower meditation. The message here is that daily life, with all its traffic gridlocks and late-night phone calls from your mom, is a spiritual exercise if we "live in the now."

Access: *The Three-Minute Meditator* by David Harp is published by mind's i press, P.O. Box 460908, San Francisco, CA 94146-0908. Paper $6.95. If you send in a stamped, self-addressed envelope, the author will help you start a Three-Minute Meditation group in your area.

THINGS THAT GO BUMP IN THE NIGHT

DESPERATELY SEEKING LEONARD
●

Kathlyn Rhea has been called "the body finder" because of her reputation for using her psychic powers to help police detectives solve crimes. Now the Bethesda, Maryland, psychic has put together a workbook, *Mind Sense,* the bulk of which consists of black-and-white photographs of people (none of whom look like escaped killers, we're glad to say) on whom you're supposed to exercise your ESP. When we tested our psychic abilities on "Leonard," we correctly guessed his age (60–69), hair color (gray), eye color (hazel), build (tall, medium-boned), and race (Caucasian). We also intuited rightly that he was a widower. By this time, we were pretty impressed with ourselves and started to dial the *National Enquirer* to unveil our psychic forecasts for the 1990s (Elvis will still be dead, and extraterrestrials will still be communicating miracle arthritis cures) when our psi suddenly plummeted. We were *sure* that Leonard lived in a condo, but his residence turned out to be a one-story stucco house. We had him pegged as a semiretired term–life insurance salesman, when he is actually a lawyer. We guessed he kept lovebirds, but he has a German shepherd for a pet. His hobbies, which we reckoned were military history, commemorative coin collecting, and skeet shooting, turned out to be gardening, inspirational writing, tennis, track, baseball, basketball, and fishing. Well, we blew it, but what can you expect from people who once scored "significantly below chance" in a parapsychology experiment?

Access: *Mind Sense* by Kathlyn Rhea is published by Celestial Arts, P.O. Box 7123, Berkeley, CA 94707. Paper $12.95.

INTUITION SCHOOL
●

By the time you've completed Nancy Rosanoff's eleven-week course, *Intuition Workout,* you may think the order to "sit down and make yourself comfortable" is the key to becoming the next Jeanne Dixon. Most of the visualization exercises in this course begin with that admonition. After getting comfortable and breathing deeply, you'll do things like "present your Intuition with your desire, the thing or event you really want in your life." We were stymied early on by an exercise requiring us to visualize five barometers indicating our well-being on various planes from the physical to the spiritual, and all we could see was an ominous low-pressure front coming in from Cleveland. But maybe you'll do better.

Access: Nancy Rosanoff gives private workshops and group courses on intuition. For information: 131 E. 95th St.,

New York, NY 10128. Phone: (212) 860-7164. Her book *Intuition Workout: A Practical Guide to Discovering and Developing Your Inner Knowing* is published by Aslan Publishing; paper $9.95. A set of three audiotapes by Rosanoff called *Intuition Workout* and another three-tape set, *Introduction to the Chakras,* are also available for $29.95 each from Aslan Publishing, 310 Blue Ridge Dr., Boulder Creek, CA 95006. Phone: (408) 338-7504.

PRECOGNITION MACHINE
•

For high-tech psychics there's the Perceptron, an electronic ESP tutor developed by parapsychology notables Russell Targ and Keith Harvey. Basically, the device is a random-number generator (a staple of parapsychology labs) capable of making 100,000 decisions a second. Your mission is to foresee which of four colors the machine will choose, and you can play in three modes: Clairvoyance, Telepathic (with a partner), and Psychic Puzzle (whatever that is). According to the manufacturer, the machine will "enhance your ability to recognize your intuitive impressions and can bring you to a level of intuitive awareness unlike anything you've experienced before."

Access: The Perceptron is available for $39.95 from JS & A, 3100 Dundee Rd., Suite 801, Northbrook, IL 60062. Phone: (800) 323-6400.

NIRVANA MARKETPLACE: TOOLS FOR ENLIGHTENMENT

FAR-OUT FRACTALS
•

Fractals are the acid rock of higher mathematics, the just-say-no generation's answer to Altamont and the Summer of Love, and now you can watch them unfold right on your VCR. Fractals are computer-graphic representations of the hip new mathematics of chaos. The equations that generate them describe complex, unpredictable, chaotic events in nature, such as fluid turbulence and the weather, but you don't have to have a Ph.D. to appreciate the video version. Watching a fractal video is a bit like watching a time-lapse photo of a surreal flower coming into bloom, and connoisseurs swear that these undulating, rococo shapes—set to music in the videos—bring back the good old days of the Haight circa 1967. When we played the video at a party, we found a crowd gathered around the set saying, "Oh, wow!" You might also use fractals as a high-tech meditation.

Access: A "Fractal Fantasy" videotape is available from Media Magic, P.O. Box 2069, Mill Valley, CA 94942. Phone: (415) 381-4224. $30 plus shipping. (A catalogue is available.)

MYSTICAL SECRETS OF THE MASTERS—ON TV
•

The Movements

If you know any Gurdjieff buffs you've probably heard about the Movements. Gurdjieff supposedly learned them from one of the secret brotherhoods he hung out with and passed them on to selected disciples, who in turn passed them on to others under various conditions of secrecy or schism, so that by now there are a zillion Gurdjieff splinter groups who disagree about everything, including the proper way to do the Movements. In any case, the Movements are a top-secret spiritual dance form, the mystical equivalent of a classified document. And now, for just $129, even spiritual clods and lowlifes can get their hands on them, thanks to the miracles of modern video technology. Mystical oddity E. J. Gold, the author of numerous eccentric spiritual books, has videotaped the sequences for the first time "in his private studios" and is marketing them as a two-videotape Movement series. (Wait till the secret brotherhoods find out about this!)

Access: The Movements videotapes are available from: Gateways Books & Tapes, P.O. Box 370, Nevada City, CA 95959. Phone: (916) 477-1116. Tape One costs $69.95; Tape Two, $79.95; the two may be purchased together for $129.

THERE'S A PARTY IN MY PANTS
•

If you're like many people, you probably worry about your *ch'i.* Being low on *ch'i,* or spiritual energy, is like having iron-poor blood, only worse. Fortunately, there's something you can do about it. Laurence Ostrow, a movement-therapy teacher from Santa Cruz, California, can sell you some ChiPants. Instead of the usual seam where the legs meet the crotch, these trousers have a flap of cloth called a gusset. "These pants allow you to express your *ch'i,* your energy, with greater comfort and freedom of movement," Ostrow explains. And there's more. The gusset is cut in a crystal shape and for an extra five bucks you can have a genuine crystal sewn into the pants' back seam. "We make no claims about the effect of the crystals," says Ostrow, "but I will tell you that a chiropractor from L.A. called to tell us he had a device that measured his *ch'i*. After wearing my crystal pants for two weeks, it went up forty points." A friend of ours, who ordered a pair sans crystals, reports that the ChiPants are very comfortable, but lacking a *ch'i*-measuring machine, he hasn't actually been able to measure his *ch'i*.

Access: To order ChiPants or a free catalogue contact: Ch'i Concepts, Inc., 125 Walnut Ave., Santa Cruz, CA 95060. Phone: (800) 331-2681. Prices run from $25 to $49.

PERSONAL APOCALYPSE
●

You've probably heard that the world is about to end. After all, we're nearing the final crunch of the millennium. Any day now, you'll be cruising down the New York State Thruway in your Ford Fairlane when along comes the Rapture, and all good fundamentalist Christians will be whisked up into heaven out of harm's way, while you and your secular humanist friends will be stuck in a horrible global disaster-movie scenario known as the Tribulation. Then won't you be sorry you didn't take the time to talk scripture with those nice, clean-cut young men hawking the *Watchtower*? Not to worry. The Apocalypse, with all its beasts and angels, whores of Babylon, Armageddons, Antichrists, and Heavenly Kingdoms, will actually take place *inside you*. So maintains psychotherapist Peter Roche de Coppens in his manifesto *Apocalypse Now: The Challenges of Our Times*. If you read this book, you'll learn that in the last two decades of the twentieth century, humanity—and that includes you!—is being given a major "test," an "initiation." How do you cram for this exam and pass unscathed through your "personal Apocalypse"? Buy this book, of course, and learn how to do impressive tricks with astral planes, chakras, the law of etherealization, etc. If you're not too annoyed by the high density of capital letters (as in Higher Self) and reminiscences of the author's dramatic mood shifts, you can find some interesting psychospiritual exercises here. At least it's better than worrying about the Antichrist.

Access: *Apocalypse Now: The Challenge of Our Times* by Peter Roche de Coppens is published by Llewellyn Publications, P.O. Box 64383-Dept. 677, St. Paul, MN 55164-0383. Paper $9.95.

SPIRITUAL DISNEYWORLDS
●

Instead of revisiting Disneyworld on your next vacation, why not take the Winnebago to a sacred site? On second thought, better leave the Winnebago at home; the Hopis won't appreciate it, and neither will the unseen spirits. "If we are lucky, and we are finally able to visit our 'personal' sacred site," explains Natasha Peterson, sacred-sites connoisseur and author of *Sacred Sites*, "there is sometimes a sense of déjà vu, that indeed we have been to this place before." On the other hand, if you're like us, you may have a sense of *jamais vu*, that you are lost in a remote Arizona canyon, far from AAA, and not really sure if you're in an

ancient ceremonial spot or a sleazy tourist trap. Which is why you need this guidebook.

Sacred Sites provides clear driving directions to the best power places and sacred sites in the U.S.: The ancient megaliths of Mystery Hill, New Hampshire ("America's Stonehenge"). The Great Serpent Mound in Ohio (a relic of an ancient serpent faith). Enchanted Rock in Texas (a primo holy mountain and vision-quest site). The Big Horn Medicine Wheel in Wyoming. Chaco Canyon in New Mexico. (You know it's good because Jose Arguelles, organizer of the Harmonic Convergence, spent that fateful day of August 16, 1987 there.) Sedona, Arizona (land of many vortexes). California's Mt. Shasta (sacred mountain, UFO landing pad, and motherland to a hundred cults). And, of course, Hopiland in Arizona. (Good luck, paleface. A sign on the road to the ancient Hopi village of Old Oraibe reads: "Warning: No outside white visitors allowed because of your failure to obey the laws of our tribe as well as your own.") Once you locate a sacred site and avoid offending the locals, *Sacred Sites* fills you in on its history and cosmic significance and offers useful advice about what to do there: e.g., meditate, get permission from the park ranger to hold a sun dance or solstice ceremony, or make your own medicine wheel. This is a useful book for sacred tourists, and just reading it will make you feel as if you were already in communication with the great spirits of the land.

Access: *Sacred Sites: A Traveler's Guide to North America's Most Powerful, Mystical Landmarks* by Natasha Peterson is published by Contemporary Books, 180 North Michigan Ave., Chicago, IL 60501. Paper $9.95.

CHANNELING KIT
●

Tired of sitting home by the karmic phone waiting for Seth, or Ramtha, or somebody else's spiritual guide to ring you up from across the eons? Now a New Age organization, Stillpoint of New Hampshire, can teach you how to channel all by yourself. The Co-Creation Course I, "Applying Universal Principles for Self-Empowerment," is a home-study program of six lessons and six audiotapes to guide you toward channelhood. You start with an exercise for "inviting your nonphysical teacher into your life" (you'll need a "golden cord of energy" for this) and a channeling aptitude test. You'll progress to techniques for charting your "natural cycles," your "power seasons," and your own personal Wheel of Life, finally reaching your goal in lesson six: "nothing but oneness." All of this is supervised by a discarnate spirit guide called Mentor, channeled by Meredith Lady Young, who sounds like a writer of romantic fiction but who is, in fact, the author of *Agartha: A Journey to the Stars*. Hey, wait. If the entity is Mentor, who or what is Agartha? Well, don't ask us.

Access: Stillpoint International, Inc., Box 640, Walpole, NH 03608. Phone: (800) 847-4014 (603-756-9281 foreign and N.H.). Cost of the course: $89.95. Stillpoint also offers

HOW TO MAKE YOUR OWN MEDICINE WHEEL

Medicine Wheel National Landmark/Satellite Wheel

The Bighorn Medicine Wheel in Wyoming is a stone circle about ninety feet in diameter surrounding a central cairn, or rock pile. The stone points of the circle line up exactly with the rising and setting sun of the summer solstice. It appears that the Medicine Wheel is at least 200 years old, and may be up to 700. At these sacred places, ancient forefathers celebrated through their rituals where they were, how they were, and what they were. Parts of the medicine wheel represent all these things.

It is quite easy to make your own medicine wheel. One must approach the process, however, with the utmost sincerity. An earnest willingness to get to know yourself and connect with a sacred site is what is most important.

Create the four directions in this order: south, north, west, and finally east. . . . These four directions represent aspects of ourselves. South, the first stop on the medicine wheel, symbolizes our raw self, our feelings, emotions, and gut reactions. North represents wisdom and intellect, the rational mind. West signifies death of form and matter and its transformation. Everything in the universe, from stars and planets to plants, animals, and you and I, must die. In the east is that which does not die. The east symbolizes the spirit, life eternal, evolution, and illumination. It is the goal of the medicine wheel.

With a compass in hand, you can take these concepts and connect with a sacred site. Always move clockwise.

Start with the south. Face in that direction and make a small offering if you like. (Native Americans used raw tobacco.) Then ask: Who am I? Plumb the depths of your emotions. You know the answer already, although at first you may think you do not. Once you have the answer, give sincere thanks to the Spirit of the South.

Turn to the north. Ask: Why am I here? For what purpose have I been given this life? What is my goal? After you are clear about the answer, give sincere thanks to the Spirit of the North.

Now face west. Think of the day that dies in the west. As west represents death, contemplate what it is that must die inside of you in order for you to reach your goal. It might be a vice or a particular attitude. What is it? Once you know, give sincere thanks to the Spirit of the West.

Finally, turn to the east. You're on your way home. Meditate on what you've learned. Once you're focused on what that is, you've reached illumination. You've become part of the medicine wheel. Give thanks.

—Reprinted from *Sacred Sites* by Natasha Peterson. Published by Contemporary Books, Inc., Chicago. Copyright © 1988 by RGA Publishing Group, Inc.

a Co-Creation Course II, an Agartha Program, and lots of other empowering stuff. For $15 you can get a Power Thought, a three-line personal message "channeled specifically for you or your loved one by a Universal Teacher, Mentor or Genesis." (Who's Genesis?)

EXTRATERRESTRIAL NEWSLETTER
•

You've read the book; you've seen the mother ship; now you can subscribe to *The Communion Letter*. It's a quarterly newsletter "written and edited by witnesses" (though not, apparently, by the bug-eyed "Visitors" themselves) to keep you up to date on the activities of *Communion* author Whitley Strieber, other "witnesses," and their interdimensional pals. The letter has a fairly stolid appearance and the ads promise, "No rumor mongering. No hysteria. Just good solid reporting."

Access: *The Communion Letter*, P.O. Box 10235, San Antonio, TX 78210-0235. $20 for four quarterly issues.

WANTED: TRANSCENDENTAL TYPIST
•

"What sets Darryl Anka apart from numerous other California channelers who communicate with spirit guides is that Anka claims to be in touch with Bashar, an extraterrestrial from the Orion constellation." This is the sort of information you can pick up from Robin Westen's *Channelers: A New Age Directory*. In addition to a history of channeling, the directory includes biographies of all the major channelers in the U.S., from Jach Purcel (Lazaris) and J. Z. Knight (Ramtha) to Tam Mossman (James) and Pat Rogedast (Emmanuel). A New Age Directory in the back provides a state-by-state listing of channelers across the U.S., as well as entity-oriented seminars, newsletters, and bookstores; psychic/astrological cruises; and "transcendental typing" services specializing in channeled transcripts. You'll find that, just as you might expect, there is a high population density of spirit guides in Sedona, Arizona, and only a handful in the entire state of Mississippi.

Access: *Channelers: A New Age Directory* by Robin Westen is published by the Putnam Publishing Group/Perigee. Paper $9.95.

EVERYBODY SPEAKS
•

A couple of years ago, if you wanted to know what Seth or Orion or Matraiya was up to, you could read *Metapsychology*, a surprisingly literate and scholarly quarterly devoted to "discarnate intelligences." Edited by Tam Mossman, who edited the Seth material, it was crammed with channeled material—"anything where mind or personality can exist outside a physical nervous system," in Mossman's words. Alas, it is no longer being published, but you can order back issues through the Austin Seth Center in Texas and be enlightened by articles such as "ORION on Homosexuality," "Telepathic Communication with a Dolphin," and "The Moon-Phase Wheel of William Butler Yeats." If you're only interested in Seth's opinions, you can subscribe to *Reality Change*, "a magazine for people who want to change their lives."

Access: Back issues of *Metapsychology* ($6.50 each) and current and back issues of *Reality Change* (four issues, $18; single copy, $5.95) can be ordered from: Austin Seth Center, P.O. Box 7786, Austin, TX 78713-7786. Phone: (512) 479-8909.

THESE ARE A FEW OF MY FAVORITE HIGHS

In the early seventies, when getting high was still an acceptable alternative to obsessing about real estate, Ed Rosenfeld started researching altered states of consciousness. There were, he discovered, an awful lot of ways to get high without drugs—about 250 different ways, as a matter of fact. He traveled around the transpersonal scene experimenting with some highs and learning about others too exotic to try, and finally put them all together in the 1973 classic *The Book of Highs: 250 Methods for Altering Your Consciousness Without Drugs* (Quadrangle/New York Times Books).

The book is now out of print and difficult to track down. But we tracked Ed down one day and took him out to breakfast at a New York City coffee-shop to pick his brain. We found him in an unrelated line of work (he publishes a newsletter, *Intelligence,* about neural nets and artificial intelligence) but willing to reminisce about some of his favorite highs. "People always used to ask me what was the most unusual high I'd encountered," he told us, "and I used to say 'kayak disease.' " Kayak disease is an unpleasant hallucinatory state experienced by the Greenland Eskimos after spending three days at sea in a kayak, and Ed doesn't recommend it for novices. We told him we weren't really interested in any of the "negative" altered states catalogued in the *Book of Highs,* such as paranoia, narcotic withdrawal, demonic possession, sleep deprivation, and self-flagellation; we can get enough paranoia by receiving letters from the New York State Department of Taxation and Finance. We also explained that we were interested mainly in cheap, do-it-yourself highs requiring a modicum of equipment—which meant that prolonged radar screen observation, electrical stimulation of the mastoid, and "breakoff" (something that happens to high-altitude jet pilots) were out of the question. Ed was kind enough to oblige us with a description of the following pleasant, relatively easy-to-assemble, do-at-home highs

REPETITION TAPES

These are loop tapes that repeat the same sound, word, or phrase endlessly, like a mantra. Rosenfeld was introduced to one by scientist John Lilly, the noted dolphin man and inner-space explorer. Lilly played a tape with the word COGITATE repeated over and over to a roomful of a hundred people. "After a few minutes I became tense and nervous," recalls Ed, "I was tired of listening to the same word over and over. Suddenly the tape changed. It said, "MELT INTO IT." After the tape was over, Ed turned to a friend to compare notes. "Tape changed, didn't it?" he said. "It sure did," said his friend, "It changed from saying 'COGITATE' to 'COUNT TO TEN.' It turned out that everyone in the room heard the tape change to a different word or phrase, and all were convinced that the change was actually on the tape and not in their brains. However, the tape had never actually said anything other than "COGITATE." These auditory hallucinations are the brain's natural response to a boring, repetitive stimulus, according to Lilly.

Access: The Cogitate Tape by John Lilly is available for $9.98 plus shipping from: Gateways, P.O. Box 370, Nevada City, CA 95959. Phone: (916) 477-1116. Or make your own repetition tape.

FINNEGANS WAKE

You may have a copy of Joyce's dense, stream-of-consciousness opus on your bookshelf, but you've never actually read it, have you? Of course not; no one has. Yet, according to Ed, it's a consciousness-altering text. "You have to read it *aloud,*" he tells us. "When you read *Finnegans Wake* aloud you get into Joyce's world, which is an aural world, a 'surround.' It is meant to be read out loud, to be shouted, to be sung, to be laughed. I find it helps to affect a brogue." Ed says that Joyce's multilayered puns and metaphors are intended to break through our cultural indoctrination and our linear modes of thought, and that a major theme in the book is the fluctuation between linear and nonlinear forms of information-processing. He said a lot more, too, but we had trouble information-processing it. So just read the book aloud, okay?

HYPNOGOGIC PHENOMENA (DROWSINESS BEFORE SLEEP)

The hypnogogic state is that reverie state you're in as you're drifting off to sleep. In this limbo between sleep and waking your mind fills spontaneously with images, visions, conversations, and half-dreams. Many artists, inventors, and scientists claim they get their best material in this natural altered state. Ed tells us that you can tap into it with a simple method devised by psychologist Charles Tart: Lie on your back and let yourself drift off into the hypnogogic state. But keep your arm in the air by bending it at the elbow. This way, when you start to really fall asleep, the muscles of your arm will relax and your arm will fall, waking you up. Then you can begin the exercise again. With a little practice you'll be able to recall everything that happens during the hypnogogic state. "You might find some revealing images, or see your experiences in a new perspective, or arrive at the solution to a problem that has been bothering you," explains Ed. Another high is to explore the hypnopompic state, that dreamy state you're in when you're not quite awake in the morning.

COMPRESSED TIME
•

This is a dramatic way of altering the subjective experience of time, but you may need someone else to help you do it. The pioneering work in the field was done by Linn Cooper and Milton Erickson, who experimented with time distortion in hypnosis. And Stewart (*Whole Earth Catalogue*) Brand led an interesting compressed-time workshop at Esalen in 1969. Ed quotes from the course description: "Multiply time by one twelfth. An hour passes every five minutes. It's mealtime every half hour or so. Night is brief and oddly restful. Altogether it's an unboring, unhurried experience in which more (and different) accomplishments are possible than in normal clock time."

ZEN MORNING LAUGH
•

"This technique was taught to me by [Zen authority] Alan Watts, who learned it from a Japanese Zen master in California," says Ed. "The Zen master does it every morning as a form of meditation." Get out of bed and stand up. Place your hands on the back of your hips, palms upward. Now laugh and keep laughing, letting your laughter build and

rush through your body. Laugh fully for a few minutes, then turn on Willard Scott.

THE PRISONER'S CINEMA
•

"If you let a light shower beat on your eyelids, you're going to start to see visions—a full-color light show—right on your eyes," says Ed. This is a method of evoking phosphenes, the stars you see when you rub your eyes. (The stars are actually in your brain.) With a light stream of water, you can see mandalas, according to Ed; if you turn up the pressure you see spiderweb patterns. It's called the Prisoner's Cinema because it's something prisoners traditionally do to get high.

PSYCHEDELIC BATHTUB
•

This was the invention of Harry Herman, an altered-states researcher of the sixties. "He had all these ways of getting people blasted out of their minds, and one of them was the psychedelic bathtub," Ed tells us. The bathroom was outfitted with various light-and-sound fixtures like color wheels, strobe lights, and a revolving mirrored ball, and the walls were covered with moving moiré patterns and colored lights. In this ambience the subject would step into a bath filled with luminescent bubble bath and get high on the moving lights, the shimmering and revolving moiré patterns, the flickering strobes, and the beams of rainbow light from the mirrored ball. Sometimes chants or electronic music were added for good measure. (There is no research we know of on the effects of a psychedelic bathroom on the resale value of a house.)

THANATOLOGICAL AWARENESS
•

Thanatos is Greek for death, and thanatological awareness means "awareness of death." It may strike us as ghoulish, but thanatological awareness was a major hobby of the ancient Tibetans and Egyptians. Both cultures made elaborate preparations for death, setting aside tools for the dead and coaching individuals in the fine etiquette of dying and traveling on to the next world. In our culture most of us would rather watch the Super Bowl than spend our time studying afterdeath guidebooks like the *Tibetan Book of the Dead,* but we can cultivate thanatological awareness in small ways. "Gurdjieff used to tell his students to live every moment as if it were their last," Ed tells us. "The point is that death has a positive side. Near-death experiences, life-threatening experiences, or the death of someone close to you can bring about an acute sense of what it is to be alive."

STAINED GLASS
●

"People go to church for a variety of reasons," notes Ed, "many having to do with the alteration of consciousness." While many of the old rituals have lost their mind-altering power, stained glass remains a "profound experience," he notes. "It was the ultimate expression of light for an epoch of history." A good trip is to sit in church for a day and watch this solar-powered light show—an ever-changing play of colors, shadows, intensities, and patterns. If you feel moved to pray, so much the better, because "fervent prayer" is also a high, according to Ed.

SEMANTIC AWARENESS
●

Another strange trip is to pay strict attention to the messages encoded in words. One experiment Ed recommends is the following: "Set aside a day for taking everything said to you exactly at face value. Even when people are kidding you, respond as if they are giving a sermon. If someone says something sarcastic or facetious, treat it as though he has shared his most profound insight with you. The point is to show that people almost always say exactly what they mean, even when they conceal it in sarcasm or facetiousness."

N O U V E A U · C H E O P S :
EAST MEETS WEST
M E E T S · A M A Z O N · B A S I N

•

A famous Tibetan prophecy, attributed to Guru Rinpoche, who brought Buddhism to Tibet

in the eighth century, says: "When the iron bird flies, and horses run on wheels, the

Tibetan people will scatter like ants across the world and the Dharma [the sacred teachings]

will come to the land of the red man." (In some versions this is abbreviated to, "When

the iron bird flies, the Dharma will come to the West.") Well, the iron bird has flown,

and, thanks to the Chinese invasion of 1959, Tibetan lamas, tulkus, and rinpoches are

scattered all over the world. And the Dharma has landed in the New World.

But this chapter is not  about Tibet. Think of
Tibet as a symbol of the planet's higher soul,
rather like the mythical Mt. Meru of Eastern
philosophy. Just as the Tibetan Dharma—or a
piece of it—is now avail- able at any number of
places from California to Boulder to New York

City, so is the planetary, collective "Dharma," the wisdom of the ages. We're talking about the secret teachings of Osiris and Isis, ancient Gnostic eucharist ceremonies, the Sky World of South American shamans, the myths of Quetzalcoatl, Native American vision quests, Tibetan mandala work, and the carving of sixth-century rune staves. Today, without unduly disrupting your routines of lawn care or spackling the bathroom, you can take classes in Egyptology, runes, Mayan prophecies, Jewish Kabbalah, and psychic transport as taught by the ancient Mystery Schools. You can sign up with a metaphysical travel agency for a vision quest in Death Valley, a tour of "interplanetary grids" in Peru, or an audience with the Dalai Lama. You can learn how to set up a small altar to the Great Goddess in your den and how to select the proper *athame* (ritual knife) for magic.

As we were writing the above, a magazine called *Gnosis* fell open on the desk next to us. A small display ad caught our eye—"Alchemical Mercury: Pure Intelligence in Motion," an item that is "available for the first time publicly in the Western world." On the same page we spotted a classified ad for "The Essene Book of Days 1990," a daily journal "based on the teachings found in the Dead Sea Scrolls." We learned that we could also order Stone Age ceremonial blades with neolithic designs, an Emerald Tablet of Hermes Trismegistus, and a video of Inanna, a 4,000-year-old Sumerian goddess. For one dreamlike, existentially uncertain moment, we wondered, "What century are we in?"

Notwithstanding ubiquitous slavery, low life expectancy, human sacrifice, and the lack of aspirin or other over-the-counter analgesics, many people today seem to wish they'd been born in, say, 3000 B.C. or A.D. 700. Take Lisa Peschel, author of *A Practical Guide to Runes*. "It is truly unfortunate for our studies that we are born in the twentieth century instead of, say, the sixth," she laments. "Were we living in the sixth century we could have been taught orally by our village shaman." On the bright side, of course, we can learn about runes from a paperback book and avoid being gored by an aurochs. But Lisa Peschel has a point. Where is our village shaman when we need him? Where, come to think of it, is our *village*? Where are our elders, our sages, our bards; our harvest festivals and our coming-of-age rites?

"We are in an age that has severed itself from nature and magic," observe Jamie Sams and David Carson, creators of the Medicine Cards, a kind of tarot based on traditional oral Native American teachings. "The Medicine Cards are a method of remedying that dissociation." They do so by transporting us to a timeless neolithic village, a tribal land where the earth, the four directions, the late-summer corn, and the phases of the moon are still sacred. "Picture, if you can, a roaring Council fire and six elders sitting in the North under a new crescent moon," the Medicine Cards tell us. "The crescent moon is drawn on the Earth in corn pollen. Three elder men sit on the left as you approach from the south, and three elder men sit on the right. . . ."

A similar Earth Magic is practiced by the 15,000 or more priests and priestesses of the Goddess. On a night of the full moon, in the hills of Berkeley, California, for instance, you may hear them chanting:

All-dewy, sky-sailing, pregnant moon,
Who shines for All,
Who flows through all . . .
Aradia, Diana, Cybele, Mah . . .

Who is the Goddess? Well, She has many names—Inanna, Cybele, Hecate, Ishtar, Astarte, Spider Woman, Yemaya, Kore, Diana, Demeter, Isis—but let's just call her the Great Goddess, the mother of the universe. The Goddess was worshiped long before our Episcopalian god, and She is definitely back—perhaps to save the world from ozone depletion and nonbiodegradable Pampers, perhaps to cure us of our modern alienation. (See "Back to the Goddess," page 207.) Goddess worshipers have revived ancient pagan holidays like Candlemas, Beltane, and Samhain (Hallow's Eve); they celebrate the seasons, the waxing and waning of the moon, draw pentagrams, and cast spells. Why? "Life is more than a job," writes the Hungarian-born "mother of the Goddess movement" Zsuzsanna E. Budapest. "Now, as we approach the turn of the century, we must relearn our ancient heritage, begin to get in touch with old celebrations, stage more festivals, enrich our lives with guiltless power. . . ."

Now, you may ask, why do we need a Goddess? What's wrong with good old God? Nothing, of course, but we must ask, *"Which* God?" In some early Christian Gnostic texts—banned from the Bible by the Church Fathers—God is worshiped as both Father and Mother and the whole universe is said to be created by a false god called a Demiurge, which makes the world we see around us no more authentic than a TV-simulated "reenactment" of the news. (See "Where Have All the Gnostics Gone?" page 212.) To some people God is Hunab K'u, the Mayan creator god; to others it's an adventurous Norse/Germanic divinity called Woden.

"It is clear," writes the author of a recent scholarly article on the Northern Mystery School tradition, "that Woden is alive, perhaps more so than any ancient God." At first glance this seems an odd statement to make about a defunct deity—even though the Woden archetype fascinated Jung (as well as the Nazis, though that's not Woden's fault). Then it struck us that Woden fans may know something we don't. Perhaps deities are like Elvis; they linger on in the collective unconscious for hundreds or thousands of years. And perhaps they are capable of resurrection. In fact, the Virgin Mary has been appearing more frequently in recent years, according to philosopher Michael Grosso, an expert in Marian visions. "The most spectacular case was the Marian apparition in Zeitoun, Egypt, in 1961, when thousands of people of all religious persuasions witnessed extremely dazzling apparitions of a goddess figure." What's the Blessed Virgin Mary doing in our skies, alongside weather satellites and supersonic jets? Gross thinks that Marian apparitions, like UFO sightings, may be a case of "collective psychokinesis" brought on by millennial anxiety and the overall "destructive potential facing our planet."

Consider: As a species, we've spent a hundred-thousand years in a tribal, hunter-gatherer lifestyle and maybe five years dealing with modems, faxes, and such. You personally may not have done much tracking of caribou or worshiping the Milky Way in your lifetime, but your ancestors did, and your brain was shaped by the sum total of their experiences. Ask anthropologist/shaman Michael Harner, who spends his time beating a deerskin drum and guiding ordinary middle Americans on a shamanic journey to the luminous Lower World and Upper World known to South American medicine men, Laplanders, Australian aboriginals, etc. (See "How I Spent My Weekend in the Lower World," below.) Though it may seem a strange way for insurance claims adjusters, dental hygienists, and CPAs to spend the weekend, Harner insists that shamanism comes naturally, because "our ancestors have been practicing these techniques for forty-thousand years." When criticized for giving "crash courses" in a complex psychospiritual discipline, Harner replied—in the wake of the Chernobyl disaster of 1986—that "if the nation states of the world are working day and night on a crash course of their own for our mutual annihilation, we cannot afford to be any slower in our work in the opposite direction. The leisurely teaching that was possible in ancient tribal cultures is no longer appropriate. . . . People need to be awakened or they may sleep forever."

If the Goddess, Quetzalcoatl, Woden, et al. are returning, it must be because we need them. The Hopis say that we're in a time of *koyaanisqatsi,* or "world out of balance," and that the present world will end soon and none too pleasantly. The ancient Mayan calendar identifies 2012 or 2013 as the end of the present age and the beginning of a new one, which we cannot be absolutely sure will contain either ourselves or remote-control television. (See "Waiting for Kukulkan, Quetzalcoatl, Koyaanisqatsi, et al.," page 218.) Gnosticism is enjoying a renaissance today, and Gnosticism is fundamentally a theology of apocalypse, of the "last things." Writing about "The Dark Side of Gnosis" in *Gnosis* magazine, Erik Davis points out, "The Gnostics' negation of the body and their disbelief of sensual data prepare us for the modern world of media events and simulation. Their paranoia is ours, and their weapons should be, too." He proceeds to advocate a kind of high-tech Gnostic anarchism. "Jam signals, disrupt communications, bring the noise, listen to interference patterns, the dynamic chaotic mind of decay. . . ."

(Oh, chill out, Erik! Still, we can't deny that we seem to be on the verge of many possible apocalypses, nor can we reject out of hand the Gnostic premise that the entire world might be the result of a cosmic screw-up by a Demiurge.)

In any case, we need all the wisdom—all the Dharma— we can get. In this chapter we've listed spiritual practices, sacred teachings, tools, and techniques that have come from all over the world (and from all centuries) to arrive on our doorstep.

SHAMANS WITH CREDIT CARDS

HOW I SPENT MY WEEKEND IN THE LOWER WORLD
●

You lie on the floor, shivering under your blanket. The steady *boom-boom-boom* of the deerskin drum drives you deeper into the world of the spirits. As the fabulous flora and fauna of the Lower World unfold before your inner eyes, you forget that you're physically in Manhattan, surrounded by arbitrageurs and Crazy Eddies. A jaguar runs by with a message for you.

Your guide for this journey is Michael Harner, anthropologist-turned-shaman. In 1961, while doing fieldwork among the Conibo Indians of the Peruvian Amazon, he became curious about the phantasmagoric "journeys" of the local shamans ("witch doctors" or "medicine men" to the unenlightened). One day, under the influence of *ayahuasca,* a potent plant hallucinogen sometimes known as the "soul vine," he made an unforgettable odyssey himself—and this at a time when, in his words, "Timothy Leary was just popping his first mushroom." Three years later, under the tutelage of the Jivaro Indians of the Ecuadoran Andes, he underwent an even more powerful initiation into the spirit world. He has been making spirit journeys ever since.

What is a shaman, anyway? To be a shaman, according to the comparative religion scholar Mircea Eliade, one must *make a journey* in an altered state of consciousness. Rhythmic drumming or some other type of percussive sound is the usual means of trance induction, though in some cultures hallucinatory plants are used. In a tribal society, the shaman journeys to diagnose or treat illness, to perform divination or prophecy, to make contact with spirits, guardians, "power animals," or superhuman guides or teachers. Though the word shaman comes from the language of the Tungus tribe of Siberia, Harner points out that all of us are the descendants of shamans. Many so-called witches were actually making shamanic journeys on their proverbial broomsticks, and old St. Nick, with his flying reindeer and his ritual trip down the chimney, is a shaman par excellence. But the Church was not friendly to shamanism; so in the West shamanism was exterminated or driven underground by the Inquisition. It survives intact among North and South American Indians, Africans, Australian aboriginals, Siberian Eskimos, and Laplanders, among others.

It was not until the late 1960s and early 1970s that Harner came out of the closet about his curious hobby. One day, while giving a lecture at Esalen he tried out a quick group shamanic practice and found that it worked surprisingly well. He also stumbled on two key facts: (1) drumming— or monotonous percussive sound—was as powerful a portal to the unseen world as hallucinogenic drugs were; and (2) almost anyone, from the little old lady from Dubuque to a finance officer at Citibank, could become a shaman. And very quickly, too. Harner managed to distill the magic of the shamanic journey into a two-day workshop, held periodically at many locations around the world. Drums and rattles, shamanic songs, and other shamanic techniques are used to induce what Harner calls "the shamanic state of consciousness." Then the participants take off into "nonordinary reality," which is divided into two realms known as the Lower World and the Upper World. In the former, they discover their own "power animal," in the latter, a teacher/guide. They may be befriended by a brown bear, meet a race of elfin beings in a luminous world inside a waterfall, ride on the back of a giant fish with a pig's snout, climb a sacred mountain, or enter the kingdom of the Sun God.

However peculiar it may seem to talk to coyotes and oak trees, Harner insists that shamanism "is really just getting back to our common human nature and reconnecting with the plants and animals and the planet itself."

Access: For information about Harner's workshops and training courses contact: The Foundation for Shamanic Studies, Box 670, Belden Station, Norwalk, CT 06852. Phone: (203) 454-2827. The cost of the weekend-long Basic Workshop is about $155. The foundation also sells several audiocassettes to induce a shamanic journey: drumming, Australian didgeridoo (ancient hollow drone) sounds, shamanic singing, and Tibetan bowl sounds. ($13 each.) For further reading: *The Way of the Shaman* by Michael Harner is published by Bantam Books. Paper $4.50.

AT LAST, A LIFESTYLE MAGAZINE FOR SHAMANS
●

Shaman's Drum is a lavishly illustrated quarterly "journal of experiential shamanism." Its readers are evidently the type who look down on the Easy Listening shamanism of Carlos Castaneda and Lynn Andrews and want to stay au courant on the Greenland Inuit, Siberian drum séances, shamanic practices among the Jingpo, and Tibetan magical rituals. Contributors include Stanley Krippner, Ralph Metzner, Alberto Villoldo, Frank Waters, Jeanne Achterberg, and Gary Snyder.

Access: *Shaman's Drum*, P.O. Box 2636, Berkeley, CA 94702. A year's subscription (4 issues) is $15; eight issues, $28.

THE SHAMAN'S MEDICINE BAG
●

Shaman's Path, compiled and edited by Gary Doore, is a splendid anthology of writings on many facets of shamanism from Native American medicine rituals to sacred sites, holotropic breathing, and shamanic techniques used in a hospital pain clinic. The list of contributors is a who's who in neoshamanism: Michael Harner, Stanley Krippner, Stanislav Grof, Felicitas Goodman, Joan Halifax, Jeanne Achterberg, and Brooke Medicine Eagle, among others. You may not be a shaman after reading this book, but you'll want to be.

Access: *Shaman's Path*, compiled and edited by Gary Doore, is published by Shambhala Publications, Inc., Horticultural Hall, 300 Massachusetts Ave., Boston, MA 02115. Paper $10.95.

I WAS AN AZTEC CORN GODDESS
●

The Aztec Corn Goddess, depicted in Mesoamerican art, is a kneeling woman sitting gracefully on her heels, her outstretched hands placed palms down on her thighs. One day, Felicitas D. Goodman, Ph.D., a professor emeritus of anthropology and linguistics at Denison University in Ohio, imitated the goddess's pose. "I was startled when gradually, as if under a master sculptor's hands, my face became elongated into a snout and my buttocks turned into sinewy haunches," she recalls. "Then, as if this were not bad enough, to my utter embarrassment a tail began to grow at the end of my spine!" The Corn Goddess posture turned out to be a ritual posture for changing shape—for metamorphosis.

Goodman was as surprised as anyone. She had begun her research into religious trances by studying glossolalia, or "speaking in tongues," among members of a Pentecostal church. Then, in the early 1970s, she conducted trance experiments with graduate students using a gourd and rattle and found that their experiences were utterly unpredictable.

By chance she came across some meditation research by a Canadian psychologist who reported the queer fact that meditators' belief systems changed according to *what body posture they assumed for meditation*. That gave Goodman an idea.

Starting in 1977, she gathered a group of Ohio State University graduate students and taught them to assume selected postures from aboriginal art. One of the first came from a Pacific Northwest Indian carving of a small shaman being embraced by a huge bear. The ecstatic expression on the shaman's face tipped Goodman off. She had her students study a photograph of the carving and copy the posture, shook her rattle for fifteen minutes, and then recorded what they said. Many reported that during the trance their bodies or heads "would split open, as if to receive a substance, a flow of energy. . . ." Goodman had expected that the postures would produce a change in mood; instead, they triggered changes in *perception*. When one posture launched a subject on a spirit journey to the Sky World, she realized she was dealing with something profoundly sacred.

Carving of a small shaman being embraced by a huge bear

So far Goodman has culled thirty-one trance-inducing postures from primitive art and anthropological photographs and has catalogued them according to function. There are postures for healing, for divining, for attracting game, for traveling to the Sky World, for journeying to the Lower World to meet the spirits of the dead. The Bear Spirit posture, which has turned up in more than 100 different locales around the world, is a universal healing posture. Another

ancient posture, the Feathered Serpent, leads to a profound experience of death and rebirth. Then there's the Olmec Prince, an early Mesoamerican figurine in an ornate headdress who sits cross-legged, head propped up by his fists, his tongue protruding between his lips, and his eyes rolled upward. When people copied this posture, they found themselves undergoing remarkable metamorphoses. During one metamorphosis exercise, a Swiss schoolteacher with an intense dislike of snakes found himself becoming a snake. "I didn't realize how delicate and vulnerable they were," he said. "I was continually afraid that someone might step on me and break my spine." Another man turned into a tree and experienced having his bark gnawed by bears. Goodman does not interpret these experiences as symbolic dreams but as literal events that occur in another reality. For example, she thinks that one posture, known as The Man of Cuatla, transports subjects to a scene described in the *Popol Vuh*, the Mayan creation saga.

Access: For information about Felicitas Goodman's work contact her c/o Cuyamungue Institute, Rt. 5, P.O. Box 358-C, Santa Fe, NM 87501. Phone: (505) 455-2749. *Where the Spirits Ride the Wind* by Felicitas Goodman, Ph.D., is published by Indiana University Press. Hardcover $35; paper $12.95.

Dr Felicitas D. Goodman

YOU ARE ALL SHAMANS

AN INTERVIEW WITH MICHAEL HARNER

Michael Harner

Q: Where does shamanism come from?
Harner: Shamanism is neither East nor West. In human history shamanism came first—before priesthoods. Our ancestors have been testing these techniques for about 40,000 years. There is some-

thing about shamanism that is just going home; that's the way people feel about it. One problem nowadays is that almost anything that involves feathers and drums is considered shamanism. But every medicine man is not a shaman. Many of the medicine men and women of the Plains Indians are more like priests than shamans. They make sacrifices, offer prayers, and perform formal rituals. One difference between a shaman and a priest is that the shaman freaks out in the middle of the so-called ritual. In other words, a change of consciousness occurs and the shaman is no longer there.

Q: What is the difference between a medium and a shaman?

Harner: A medium is a person through whom spirits speak, either through automatic writing or through the voice. The shaman is the person who journeys to visit the spirits and interacts with them just as you and I would interact if we were meeting in a room.

Q: Can ordinary Americans really become shamans?

Harner: Well, I've trained many thousands in shamanism so far, and they seem to be doing just fine. The ones who have trouble with journeying are people who don't visualize well—lawyers, accountants, the so-called left-brain types. They usually can be trained in mediumship.

Q: Is shamanism a religion?

Harner: No, and there is no place for a guru in shamanism. It teaches people techniques in a ridiculously short period of time, and then they interact directly with the same sources that Moses and so on were working with.

Q: Can you describe the "shamanic state of consciousness"?

Harner: It is a disciplined altered state of consciousness in which you enter another reality where you can obtain help and information. The information you get is perfectly designed for you. If an Australian aboriginal journeyed to the Upper World and met an Italian-style Virgin Mary, it wouldn't mean the same thing to the aboriginal as it would to an Italian.

Q: Is the journey ever dangerous?

Harner: When I started this work a lot of people warned me it would be dangerous. But I've trained many thousands and I haven't found these dangers yet. You cannot journey on the drum the way you would on LSD. You have to maintain your own concentration and discipline to keep journeying.

Q: Your shamanic initiation in the Amazon involved *ayahuasca,* a very potent psychedelic. Can people really achieve the same effects without drugs?

Harner: My first experience was in 1961. Hardly anyone was into altered states then, so I had no frame of reference. I was just doing what the natives said I had to do to learn what I wanted. But drugs are not necessary. A minority of shamanism societies use psychedelics. In our workshops people who have had experience with psychedelics are pleasantly surprised at the effects they get from drumming. When properly used, drumming is a superb way of entering this other reality.

Q: In tribal cultures the shaman is a healer. Is healing fundamental to shamanism?

Harner: Shamanism is good for solving any problems you have in daily life. Where can I find a job? Where are the caribou? People often take a journey to organize their workweek.

Q: Are the shamanic realities—the Lower World and the Upper World and so on—in the shaman's mind? Or are they really out there in the universe somewhere?

Harner: No one knows the answer to that question. Many people *assume* they know the answer, and some of these people are called psychologists. My own position is that the human brain is not necessarily the biggest thing in the universe. When you do this work long enough, many micromiracles occur that cannot be explained in terms of the solitary mind. But people need to try out the shamanic methods and decide for themselves.

INSIDE MR. MCGREGOR'S GARDEN:
A (BRIEF) SHAMANIC JOURNEY

My first mission is to get to the Lower World, a feat accomplished by dropping down through a hole in the ground like Alice in Wonderland. (I've since learned that Alice, like the protagonists of many children's stories and fairy tales, is actually a shamanic heroine.) Any kind of hole will do—a well, a spring, a rabbit hole. One city dweller made her descent through a manhole, though a natural entry point is recommended.

"Does anyone ever fail?" I ask.

"I had two clients who failed to make a journey," says John Ford, my guide for this forty-five-minute shamanic journey. A retired engineer with a trim salt-and-pepper beard and the nonjudgmental air of people who have spent a lot of time in the human-potential movement, Ford is trained in the Harner method of "shamanic counseling." This is not counseling in the usual sense. Ford does not worry about whether I am neurotic, psychotic, or riddled with phobias; he simply guides me into a shamanic parallel world where I will receive guidance from my own unconscious or transpersonal sources.

"One lady was very kinesthetic," Ford tells me. "She *became* things. She didn't walk along and have a visual-audial journey like most people; she became a tree and didn't know what she was. She saw things but she wasn't moving. Another person was suffering from anxiety attacks. She got into a tunnel and just kept going down. She saw all sorts of interesting things on the walls but she never hit bottom. It frightened her and she never came back."

Well, I've picked my entry point: the bottom of a lake. When the tap-tap-tap of the drum (on Ford's tape) starts, I dive in and promptly hit bottom. For a minute I expect to be stuck upside down with my head in the sand, so I'm relieved to find myself slipping right through the lake floor, as if the molecules composing me were dissolving. ("In the Lower World the ordinary rules of reality aren't with us anymore," Ford had explained. "Time is a variable; space is a variable; shape is a variable. You can't get hurt because you can't hurt a spirit. And in the shamanic reality anything you see you can talk to—an animal, a tree, a rock, even light.") Now I am in the prototypical shamanic tunnel. On the way down I reach out and touch the tunnel walls, which are wet, cool, and carpeted with a rich, velvety moss. I could just hang out here, tripping on the humid, slippery cave walls, but the drumbeat in my ears nags me to get on with the journey.

Finally, a clearing. I end up in a sunny meadow with the emotional texture of childhood. There is a buzzing, a sense of tiny, unseen, dancing creatures. The place feels like Mr. McGregor's garden. Reaching the tall grass at the edge, I notice I am quite small. Giant cornstalks tower above me like redwoods, and there is a little brown bunny, just my size, noisily chewing an ear of corn. Feeling absurd—surely it would be classier to receive messages from an eagle, a tiger, or a jaguar!—I ask this little Beatrix Potter creature, "Are you my power animal?"

The answer seems to be yes, and the bunny takes off down a path, zigzagging as bunnies do. I follow him as he hops along a stand of mournful eucalypti bordering a riverbed.

A series of events follow (I won't bother the reader with all the details) and I end up in an underground chamber looking at a circular sand painting in mauves, pinks, corals, and lavenders. I meet a "teacher," who remains hooded and laconic, ignoring me as he labors on the sand painting. It is divided into eight sections, each of which is an exquisitely detailed scene, like the intricate biblical stories in bas-relief carved on Gothic cathedral doors. "This is the story of your life," says a voice in my head. Unfortunately, I can't decipher any details. Remembering my mission to ask the teacher a question, I ask the first thing that pops into my mind. "Is my son happy?"

It may seem an odd question to ask about an eight month old, my son's age at the time of this journey. He really isn't old enough to have any serious complexes; his interests are those of a puppy or a kitten: chasing balls, biting stuffed animals, and dropping spoons from his high chair to test whether the law of gravity really works every time. But lately, perhaps because of an ear infection, antibiotics, or the simultaneous cutting of four front teeth, he had seemed a bit of an alien, and my attempts to make meaningful contact with his preverbal mind seemed to fail.

The answer to my question *seems* to be yes. (Simple yeses or nos don't seem to be the rule in *my* shamanic universe.) Whereupon I levitate through the roof to another series of ascending activities, like climbing a spiral staircase made of clouds. I scale a beanstalk-like tree full of birds' nests and understand somehow that I am supposed to bring back an egg. Stepping inside a tree trunk, I find a tiny dwelling complete with miniature cupboards filled with tiny plates, cups, and saucers. I am in the home of small, Munchkin-like characters with squeaky voices. "We are the People of the Lake," they inform me. Everywhere I go I seem to find the trappings of a fairy tale, as if my subconscious harbored a hundred Brothers Grimm manqué.

Finally, I hear the return signal—an insistent tat-tat-tat—and I scurry back up through the tunnel to the Real World, where John Ford and I spend another thirty to forty minutes playing back my tape and discussing it. (Following the usual practice in shamanic counseling, I had narrated my journey while experiencing it.)

There is, after all, some coherence to this universe. In my encounters with bunnies, little people, beanstalks, Mr. McGregor's garden, and such, I seem to be symbolically entering my son's inner world. Communicating wordlessly with the bunny, I am in a sort of primal Eden, a preverbal state where men and beasts (or adults and babies) understand one another perfectly. An analyst might say that the bunny was a veiled image of my son, or that when I shrank to bunny proportions myself I was regressing to my own infancy. In any case, in some way that I can't fully explain, I feel restored to myself.

—J.H.

SCHOOL FOR KABBALAH

AND YOU DON'T EVEN HAVE TO BE JEWISH
●

The Kabbalah, the Jewish mystical path, is the polar opposite of Zen "no-mind"; it's mind, mind, mind, and more mind. This is not for the Shirley MacLaine–inspired casual mystic—or the superficial writer of post–New Age catalogues. Its hierarchically arranged, interpenetrating, unpronounceable Worlds—*Azilut, Beri'ah, Yetzirah,* and *Asiyyah*—too closely resemble those unfathomable textbook diagrams of chemical bonds for our tastes. Furthermore, it's a real pain to put apostrophes in all those Hebrew words. And, of course, a serious Kabbalist should have a good working knowledge of Hebrew, the Torah and Jewish law, Kabbalistic doctrine and cosmology; and if you did, you wouldn't be reading this book, would you? No, you'd have something better to do, like help redirect all created things back to the Divine.

But if the Kabbalah really is the secret wisdom of God, passed down to Adam and Moses, and then passed on orally from teacher to student, it ought to be accessible to all human beings, even Torah-ignorant slobs like ourselves. British Kabbalah scholar Z'ev ben Shimon Halevi (whose secular name is Warren Kenton) evidently thinks so. At his Kabbalah workshops he emphasizes that the Tree of Life is really a detailed manual for spiritual transformation as well as a map of creation. He leads participants through a series of mental exercises designed to show them that the Four Worlds reside within themselves. First, they explore the First World of the body, *Asiyyah;* then *Yetzirah,* the Second World, the domain of the psyche; then the sky-blue stratosphere of the Third World, *Beri'ah,* the abode of the True Self. While some students linger there, others ascend like angels to the Fourth World, *Azilut,* the realm of divinity. "Man contains all that is above in heaven and below on earth," Halevi reminds the class, adding that students can observe this themselves by practicing the "shift in worlds." After prepping in the school of *Yesod,* or ego, the students visualize themselves perfecting various skills in the great university of *Tiferet,* the Self. Then they are led into the Upper Halls of the Kabbalah, where many have radiant visions. Halevi tells them of the great beings who dwell in these halls beyond the self and adds, somewhat mysteriously, that their teachings are still being transmitted by secret esoteric schools.

Halevi is the author of eight books on the Kabbalah, two of which are how-tos. *The Work of the Kabbalist* relates the Tree of Life to depth psychology and imparts practical techniques and rituals that the student can apply to daily life. *School of Kabbalah,* his most recent book, sets forth guidelines for group work. Whether your Kabbalistic group meets for a few weeks and disbands, or, like the sixteenth-century groups that met in Safed, spawns a whole new Kabbalistic lineage, its overall purpose is "the training and tuning of consciousness," according to Halevi. A major portion of the book chronicles the life cycle of a Kabbalistic group.

Access: For information about workshops and classes write: Warren Kenton, 30-A Greencroft, London, England NW6 3LT. *The Work of the Kabbalist* (paper $9.95) and *School of Kabbalah* (paper $8.95), both by Z'ev ben Shimon Halevi, are published by Samuel Weiser, Inc., Box 612, York Beach, ME 03910.

KABBALAH THERAPY
●

Traditionally, Hasidic rebbes were part-time shrinks—transpersonal shrinks, that is. Their spiritual counseling included imagery work, dream analysis, storytelling, "mental shock," and advice, according to New York psychologist/Kabbalah authority Edward Hoffman, Ph.D. They sometimes advised the seeker to travel to an unfamiliar town and "there you will find an answer to your question," and they employed oracular methods such as Torah divination and "soul reading" in a trance state. In his own psychological practice, Hoffman does not exactly employ Torah divination, but he does adapt passages from age-old Kabbalistic texts to help clients through a difficult period. He also trains them in Kabbalistic meditative techniques for developing the "Higher Will" and the imagination. "I have found the Kabbalistic emphasis on storytelling and on training the Higher Will to be quite effective in helping people to find their pathway to divine purpose," he explains.

Access: For information contact Edward Hoffman, Ph.D., Four Worlds Center, P.O. Box 540, East Meadow, NY 11554. Phone: (516) 864-1912. Hoffman also sells a thirty-minute Kabbalistic meditation on (VHS) videotape, "A Mystical Journey through the Hebrew Alphabet," for $29.95. His books on Kabbalah include *The Heavenly Ladder* (Harper & Row, paper $8.95) and *Father, Teacher, Leader,* (Simon & Schuster, $19.95).

MAIL-ORDER QABALA
●

The *goyische* version of the Kabbalah is usually spelled Qabbalah, or Qabala. The people who are into it are unfa-

"MAIDEN, MOTHER, CRONE, THE WEAVER, THE GREEN ONE . . ."

●

It is the winter solstice, but the goddess worshipers are shedding their clothes and plunging naked into the frigid Pacific. Afterward, all the devotees circle the bonfire and a priestess leads the Tree of Life meditation. Facing east, she takes out a Swiss army knife and casts a circle to create a sacred space within the profane world. Reverently, she calls on the guardians of the east, Aradia and Nuit. Next she traces her knife to the south, north, and west, in turn, with an invocation for each direction. Then comes the chant to the Great Goddess.

"Isis, Astarte, Ishtar, Aradia, Diana, Cybele . . . ," the gathering chants. "Come into us! Touch us! Change us!"

The Goddess (also known as the Great Goddess) is the happening deity of the nineties. Unlike Yahweh or Allah, the Goddess is *immanent* in the world; which is to say, she doesn't hole up in heaven, aloof from creation, issuing commandments and curses; she is right here *in* human beings, animals, the moon, pear trees, rocks, perhaps even double-strength freezer wrap (well, okay, maybe not in freezer wrap). For Goddess worshipers—devotees of the Old Religion that predated Judaism and Christianity—there is no such thing as original sin and no split between spirit and nature. The rites of the Goddess are linked to the seasons, vegetation cycles, the phases of the moon, the alternation of light and dark in the Wheel of the Year. "She is the shared circle of birth, maturation, death, and regeneration of all life, the changing of the seasons, the waxing, full, and waning moon, the daily tides, and the rising-setting sun," writes Diane Stein, a practicing priestess of the Goddess. "She is childhood joy, first periods, falling in love and giving birth, motherhood and menopause, aging, and death until being reborn."

The Goddess revival owes something to a British amateur folklorist and witch named Gerald Gardner, who in the 1950s claimed to have found secret, Goddess-worshiping, Wiccan (traditional witchcraft) covens in Britain. Gardner's "research" has since been questioned, even by his spiritual descendants, but it did serve to fuel a quiet pagan renaissance. It was not until the 1970s and 1980s, however, that the Goddess really went public. Margot Adler, who published her influential study of pagan groups in 1976 as *Drawing Down the Moon,* estimates that there are at least 15,000 practicing Goddess worshipers. Many are feminists who, alienated by patriarchal religious traditions, find in the Goddess a compassionate mother god, a

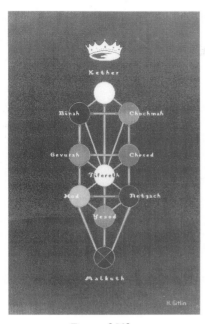

Tree of Life

miliar with names like Schlomo or Schmuel; they may call themselves Trismegistus, Moondragon, or Morning Glory and refer to themselves as pagans, alchemists, or Gnostics. Basic to Qabala is a method called Pathworking, powerful meditations that take the seeker on an inner journey through the Tree of Life. You can find numerous how-to books on Qabala on the shelves of your local esoteric bookstore. Or you can learn about Pathworking and other Qabalistic techniques through a correspondence course offered by a Seattle organization called Cinnabar. The thirty-six lessons, designed for serious students, explore in detail the ten Spheres and twenty-two Paths of the Tree of Life. Techniques include "the use of divine Names, vibration, the Middle Pillar exercise, out-of-body experience, and the invocation of the Higher Self." A Cinnabar spokesman points out, "As a mystical system developed within our Western culture, the Qabala is more suited to Westerners than are traditions imported from the Orient."

Access: Cinnabar, P.O. Box 95674, Seattle, WA 98145. The fee for the course is $19.50 per lesson, or $630 for the entire course. The Cinnabar people claim you can get lots of individual attention from their staff.

deity who would never launch a bloody crusade or an auto-da-fé. "The images of the Goddess," writes Starhawk, a San Francisco–area witch, "inspires women to see ourselves as divine, our bodies as sacred, the changing phases of our lives as holy. . . ."

Goddess worshipers usually refer to themselves as pagans, and many are practitioners of Wicca, or witchcraft. Some Goddess worshipers are eco-feminist social crusaders like Starhawk, a minister of the Covenant of the Goddess. She and her fellow witches have barricaded the roads leading to the controversial Diablo Canyon Nuclear Power Plant, spent weekends in jail, and woven symbolic spiderwebs outside San Francisco's males-only Bohemian Club (to mock the club's Shakespearean motto, "Weaving spiders come not here," and perhaps discomfit famous, non-Goddess-worshiping Bohemians like Henry Kissinger and Ronald Reagan). Most Goddess worshipers, however, "lead ordinary lives in the regular world, as secretaries, doctors, or policewomen," according to Margot Adler.

The Goddess is worshiped in her three essential aspects of Maiden, Mother, and Crone, corresponding to different parts of the year. Goddess buffs may invoke many different goddesses, from the Greek Athena to the earthy, cronelike Ceridwen, Celtic goddess of the cauldron of life and death, but all are seen as aspects of one Great Goddess. "The Goddess might be named Kore in the spring,

after the Maiden aspect of the Greek Goddess," explains Starhawk. "A Witch of Jewish heritage might call on the ancient Hebrew goddess as Ashimah or Ahserah; an Afro-American Witch might prefer Kemaja, the West African Goddess of the sea and love. In most traditions of the Craft [witchcraft], the inner name of the Goddess is recognized to embody great power, and so is kept secret, revealed only to initiates. The other names most commonly used are Diana, for the Goddess of the moon, and Aradia, her daughter. . . ."

Goddess worshipers often gravitate to midwifery, homeopathy, meditation, aura and crystal healing; they read tarot and runes, study the Qabalistic Tree of Life, and rummage through herbalist shops for mugwort or ground mountain ash leaves. They may gather to "draw down the moon" on the night of the Full Moon, and cast spells for such occasions as finding a job or even a parking place. But do not think that devotees of the Old Religion are ultra-ultra-reactionaries who would rather be living in an ancient Near East hunter-gatherer culture. Starhawk, for one, envisions the Goddess religion as a "religion of the future, firmly grounded in science." She writes, "In future or contemporary Goddess religion, a photograph of the earth as seen from space might well be our mandala. We might meditate on the structure of the atom as well as icons of ancient Goddesses; and see the years Jane Goodall spent observing chimpanzees in the light of a spiritual discipline."

KABBALAH FOR DAILY LIFE:
THE LAMED-VOVNIKS (THIRTY-SIX HIDDEN SAINTS)

One of the oldest and most profound Jewish legends is that of the thirty-six just men, known in Yiddish as the *Lamed-vovniks* (*lamed-vov* means "thirty-six" in Hebrew). Tradition has taught that in every generation the world itself is sustained by these secret saints. As the Talmud records the evocative words of the fourth-century Babylonian Jew Abaye, these exalted personages "daily receive the Divine Countenance."

In some intriguing tales that have come down through the centuries it is told that each of these holy figures knows the identity of all the others. In this way, they form a hidden network—a cabal—that spans the continents. In other stories, it is said that no member is even aware of his own supernal role, let alone that of his peers. But common to all variants of the legend is the notion that these mighty saints are outwardly quite ordinary, engaged in the most mundane occupations—a cobbler, a water-carrier, a teacher of small children. Yet the simplest act of the *Lamed-vovnik* is seen to exert incalculable effects on others.

For instance, it is said that a certain village tanner in the early Hasidic era was a *Lamed-vovnik;* after his death this apparently ignorant fellow was discovered to have composed secret and sophisticated Kabbalistic treatises. Two seemingly uneducated ritual slaughterers in another tiny Eastern European shtetl were likewise found after their deaths to have written—unbeknownst to their neighbors—erudite metaphysical texts that only the most learned could comprehend. Released from the conceit that accompanies fame, such exalted persons are in this manner able to carry out most effectively their sacred mission.

Perhaps you have already encountered some or even all of these thirty-six "hidden just men." Possibly you have even suspected that an individual whom you met was far more than he—or she—appeared to be at the time.

In this exercise, think back over the course of your life and identify those people who, through the kindness, simplicity, and quiet serenity displayed to you and others may have been secret *Lamed-vovniks*. Focus on your present circumstances and look for possibilities. Remember that flamboyance has never been their style; you may therefore have to stimulate your memory and awareness a bit. You may not be able to list all thirty-six—yet—but name as many as you can.

You may also wish to assume that, at all times, there is at least one *Lamed-vovnik* secretly operating in your life. If so, who is he or she right now?

—from *The Heavenly Ladder*, by Edward Hoffman, Ph.D. (Harper & Row, 1985). Reprinted by permission.

BACK TO THE GODDESS

WHEN GOD WAS A WOMAN

The story of the most ancient of religions, the religion of the Goddess, and the role this ancient worship played in Judeo-Christian attitudes toward women.

MERLIN STONE

A HARVEST/HBJ BOOK

WHEN GOD WAS A WOMAN
●

"Blessed art thou, O Lord our God, that thou has not made me a woman." So goes the morning prayer of devout Jews. But long before Yahweh/Jehovah ran the shop, God *was* a woman. In her landmark book *When God Was a Woman,* Merlin Stone tells the story of the primal Great Goddess whose religion flourished in the Near and Middle East for thousands of years before the macho deities of Israel, classical Greece, and Christianity turned the universe into a men's club. She appears as Ishtar, Astarte, Ashtoreth, Isis, Inanna; she is called the Queen of Heaven, Lady of the High Place, Celestial Ruler, Lady of the Universe, Her Holiness; she pops up as the Greek Demeter, the Egyptian Nut, the Celtic Ceridwen. We may even recognize her in the Christian Mary, Queen of Heaven. Dismissed by archeologists and scholars as a big-hipped "fertility goddess" and idol of a minor "fertility cult," the Goddess was actually the supreme creator of the universe, a warrior, huntress, lawmaker, prophetess, and healer. When the patriarchal religions supplanted the old religion, the Great Goddess was depicted as wanton and depraved—a Whore of Babylon, a graven idol, a cosmic chippy. She has been belittled or ignored even by archeologists and religion scholars. Now Stone has set the record straight, and her book is one of the bibles of the current goddess revival.

Access: *When God Was a Woman* by Merlin Stone is published by Harvest/Harcourt Brace Jovanovich. Paper $7.95.

OUT OF THE BROOM CLOSET
●

If you want to slip into the world "between the worlds," into the "That-Which-Cannot-Be-Told" of Wicca, *The Spiral Dance,* by Starhawk, witch superstar and political activist, is your passport. Specifically, you'll find yourself kibitzing at trendy ecoactivist Bay Area covens where the witches have names like Honeysuckle Amber and are heavy into recycling and Gestalt. Entranced, you'll observe witches casting circles, raising the cone of power, drawing down the moon, celebrating the eight Sabbats of the Wheel of the Year, and calling on the Goddess, Lady of Many Names:

The earth is rent
& Persephone
the Maimed Whose name may not be spoken
is swallowed by the land of the dead. . . .

Part poetry, part manifesto, part incantatory guidebook, *The Spiral Dance* shows us how witches use magic (which occultist Dion Fortune called "the art of changing consciousness at will") to build symbolic bridges between the unseen world and the mundane. Amid slices of Wiccan life, ceremonial poems and chants, and reflections on the Goddess, there are lessons in "banishing," quartering the circle, trance work, candle gazing, astral vision, and scrying (concentrating on an object, such as a crystal ball, in order to induce psychic vision). There are depictions of rituals for the major pagan holy days, recipes for a wide variety of spells and herbal charms, psychological and consciousness-altering exercises, and suggestions for finding or working with a coven. (Starhawk's own coven is based on the Faery Tradition, which harks back to the Little People of Stone Age Britain.)

Access: *The Spiral Dance: A Rebirth of the Ancient Religion of the Great Goddess* by Starhawk is published by Harper & Row. Paper $12.95. Another book by Starhawk, *Dreaming the Dark* (Beacon Press), is a manifesto on feminism, paganism, and politics. You can write to Starhawk c/o Harmony Network, P.O. Box 2550, Guerneville, CA 95446-2550.

WHAT ARE *YOU* DOING FOR VENERALIA?
●

As I (J.H.) write this, I learn that today, April 1, is Veneralia, an ancient Roman holiday that sounds suspiciously like a sexually transmitted disease. Consulting *The Grandmother of Time,* by Zsuzsanna E. Budapest, I read: "This is the holiday of Venus (Aphrodite to the Greeks), the goddess of love and death, of orchards and sexuality, of the waters of the world. This celebration appears to be a practice peculiar to women, who washed the image of the Goddess in rivers and lakes before again adorning her with her precious jewels and new long robe." I am not sure how to celebrate Veneralia on such short notice with no image of the Goddess handy, so I guess I will just ignore it and wait for Megalisia—the Phrygian/Roman festival of Cybele—on April 3 and 4, when men who aspired to be the Goddess's priests tradi-

tionally castrated themselves in Her honor. Well, maybe I'll pass on that too.

But I must say I loved *The Grandmother of Time,* a pagan calendar of rituals, spells, holy days, and stories of the Goddess for every month of the year. It's a funny, earthy, festive neopagan memoir/datebook/self-help book whose author brings from her native Hungary memories of actual rural pagan rituals, spells, enchantments, maypole dances, and so on. Budapest, often described as the "mother of the Goddess movement," fled Hungary during the revolution of 1956. After a conventional married life in Chicago (well, fairly conventional; she did practice worship of the Goddess at an altar in her backyard), she ended up in California, founding the first feminist coven, the Susan B. Anthony Coven Number 1, in 1971. In 1975 she became the first witch in 300 years to go on trial for her beliefs (she was arrested for reading tarot cards for an undercover policewoman). Fortunately, she was not put into a sack and drowned like her sixteenth-century predecessors, so we can learn from her about Veneralia, Beltane, and the festival of Kore; as well as directions for holding puberty rites, "crowning rituals" for middle age, blessings of newborns, rites to honor the dead, and a whole smorgasbord of spells.

Access: Zsuzsanna E. Budapest (known as "Z") is director of the Women's Spirituality Forum, which sponsors Goddess lectures, retreats, and annual spiral dances on Halloween in the San Francisco Bay Area. Contact: Women's Spirituality Forum, P.O. Box 11363, Oakland, CA 94611. Phone: (415) 444-7724. *The Grandmother of Time* is published by Harper & Row. Paper $13.95.

NAME THAT GODDESS
•

One sign that the Goddess has returned is that hundreds of women are asking themselves, "Which goddess am I?" or "Which goddess am I *today?*" Athena in a mannish, dress-for-success suit taking a deposition? A Persephone, "queen of the underworld," drawn to the occult arts and dark poetry?

A suburban Demeter in a maternity dress from Sears?

If the role models come from the seven major goddesses of the ancient Greek pantheon—Artemis, Athena, Aphrodite, Demeter, Persephone, Hestia, and Hera—that has a lot to do with Jungian analyst Jean Shinoda Bolen, M.D., and her book *Goddesses in Everywoman.* Before she started doing official goddess work, Dr. Bolen noticed in her therapy practice that the myth of Hera could help bring insight to a jilted woman in the throes of jealousy, or that a woman tangled in confusion over a dissertation could profit from Psyche's example. Soon she was seeing "goddesses in every woman," noticing, for example, that Patty Hearst, the abducted daughter of rich, Olympian parents, was a modern version of Persephone, abducted by the god of the underworld. Bolen's book and her workshops are a good guide to finding the goddess inside you—or the goddesses, rather. Bolen has observed that "as a woman 'shifts gears' . . . she can shift from one goddess pattern to another: in one setting, for example, she is an extroverted, logical Athena who pays attention to details; in another situation, she is an introverted hearth-keeping Hestia for whom 'still waters run deep.' "

A somewhat complex picture of the Greek goddesses emerges in the work of Jennifer Barker Woolger and Roger J. Woolger, a husband-and-wife Jungian team who hold goddess workshops, seminars, and festivals. Even as they wrote the different chapters of their book, *The Goddess Within,* the authors reported being possessed by different goddesses. "It was not easy to write about the goddess Athena as solely the principle of wisdom, for example. We found ourselves arguing endlessly about our text until we realized that Athena is a warrior goddess who loves competitiveness and fights. . . . When we wrote about Demeter, the mother goddess, we found ourselves quieter and more placid—but we both found we were tending to overeat." (As for us, when we *read* the chapter about Artemis we started ordering bows and arrows from sporting-goods catalogues.) By goddesses, the Woolgers mean the archetypes, of course, and they understand Athena, Demeter, Hestia, Hera, et al. as different aspects of the Great Goddess. If you're planning on throwing

a goddess festival or fertility ritual at your house, you can get some good game ideas from the book's final chapter, "Games Goddesses Play," a collection of individual and group exercises such as "Find Your Missing Goddess" and "Planning the Goddess Rituals."

Access: Jean Shinoda Bolen, M.D., gives frequent lectures, workshops, and seminars. For information or a workshop schedule contact Betty Karr, P.O. Box 1828, Sonoma, CA 95476. Phone: (707) 996-8823. *Goddesses in Everywoman* by Jean Shinoda Bolen, M.D., is published by Harper & Row. Paper $7.95. The masculine counterpart, *Gods in Everyman,* also published by Harper & Row, profiles the male deities: Ares, Zeus, Poseidon, etc. Hardcover $18.95.

Jennifer and Roger Woolger offer seminars, workshops, lectures, and festivals to the goddesses. For information write: Laughing Bear Productions, 5 River Rd., New Paltz, NY 12561. *The Goddess Within: A Guide to the Eternal Myths that Shape Women's Lives* by Jennifer Barker Woolger and Roger J. Woolger is published by Fawcett Columbine/Ballantine. Paper $12.95.

BOOK OF SHADOWS
•

Do you know how to Draw Down the Moon? How to recognize a familiar? How to contact the departed? How to deal with a psychic attack? You will if you follow the guidelines set forth in *Earth Magic: A Dianic Book of Shadows* by Marion Weinstein, a practical Wiccan manual that covers everything from choosing the proper *athame* (ritual knife) and "forming the alignments" to working moon magic and contacting spirit guides. "We live in two worlds: the World of Form and the Invisible World," writes Weinstein. "In this case, the World of Form is manifest as our planet, Earth. The Invisible World includes 'Everywhere' else. The witch's magic is done with the conscious use of Both Worlds. But our goal is to move and to live perfectly and easily between the Worlds—always." This handbook is an excellent, straightforward introduction to the major Wiccan deities and powers (Diana, Selene, Hecate, Kerumnos, and Pan); the significance of the pentagram; the tools of the trade; the activities of a typical coven (a group of thirteen witches who meet on the eight Sabbats, or holidays, as well as during different phases of the moon); and much more.

Access: *Earth Magic: A Dianic Book of Shadows* is published by Phoenix Publishing Inc., Portal Way, P.O. Box 10, Custer, WA 98240. Paper $7.95.

THE WITCHES TAROT
•

The Witches Tarot, created by Ellen Cannon Reed, is described as the "perfect tarot for the Pagan, Witch, or Qabalist." The Devil, the Hierophant, and the Hermit of the Major Arcana have been replaced by a Horned One, a High Priest, and a Seeker, which is understandable. What we don't understand is why the Princesses of the various suits look as if they had emerged from the cover of a romance novel. Why is the eight of Pentacles a bodybuilder? Why does The

Universe (number twenty-one of the Major Arcana) have the shape of a *Playboy* centerfold? And why has the Hanged Man, whom we'd always pictured as wan and wasted, been pumping iron? The deck can be used with any tarot layout you like. If you get Reed's companion book, *The Witches Tarot,* you can learn how to use the cards as keys to "Pathworking," astral journeys through the Qabalistic Tree of Life.

Access: "The Witches Tarot" by Ellen Cannon Reed is available for $12.95 from Llewellyn Publications, P.O. Box 64383-669, St. Paul, MN 55164-0383. *The Witches Tarot* book is available for $9.95, paper.

THE EMPEROR IS DEAD; LONG LIVE THE GODDESS
•

Gone is the stern, patriarchal *I Ching* of fathers, emperors, and government officials; banished are misogynist messages like "To bear with fools in kindliness brings good fortune./ To know how to take women/Brings good fortune." *The Kwan Yin Book of Changes* by Diane Stein, a priestess of the Goddess religion, is named for Kwan Yin, the Chinese goddess of mercy. "Grounded in a Goddess matriarchy," this new incarnation of the oracle dishes out a rich stew of insights from Wicca, the Chinese calendar, the zodiac, the tarot, and Hopi religion. It is intended as a "Wheel of the Year meditation cycle" as well as an oracle, and an appendix connects the Chinese months to the Western zodiac, the Wiccan Sabbat calendars, and the Hopi Road of Life. In fact, *The Kwan Yin Book of Changes* seems rather like an egg roll that has metamorphosed into a tortilla; we're not altogether sure it's still the *I Ching*. But it's a nice, poetic oracle, nonetheless. We threw the coins and got hexagram #20, Kuan (Contemplation), which reads, in part: *Kuan is the time of the Crone, of Demeter refusing life while Persephone is gone. Samhain is past, the night when the dead and unborn touch the presently living, and when Hopi Kachinas leave earth for the underworld. In the death and end of the year lie the seeds of her new beginnings; the Spiritual Woman contemplates the cycle.*

Access: *The Kwan Yin Book of Changes* by Diane Stein is published by Llewellyn Publications, P.O. Box 64383, St. Paul, MN 55164-0383. Paper $9.95. Stein also gives workshops on Kwan Yin; a Kwan Yin workshop tape is available from Llewellyn for $7.95.

NETWORK OF PAGANS
•

Are you a practicing Wiccan, Neopagan, Goddess Worshiper, Shaman, Druid, Seer, Ecofeminist, Native American, Medicine Person, Norse Religionist, Gnostic, Mystic, Hermetic Magician, or Pantheist who would like to network with other Wiccans, Neopagans, Goddess Worshipers, etc? Check out Circle Network, of Mt. Horeb, Wisconsin, an international information exchange and contact service for people who are heavily into the Earth with a capital E. It is coordinated by Circle, a Wiccan church and, according to its

A NEOPAGAN DATEBOOK

DECEMBER 22   WINTER SOLSTICE, YULE

The longest night of the year, the point of deepest winter. Rebirth. The Great Goddess gives birth to the Divine Sun Child; Tammuz and Persephone are born. Priestesses play the role of midwives to the infant year. Proper ritual ambience: an altar decorated with holly, evergreen, and mistletoe.

FEBRUARY 2   CANDLEMAS, BRIGID

Dedicated to Brigid, goddess of fire and inspiration. The feast of the returning light, a time of new beginnings. The sun child born at the solstice is nurtured; negativity, winter, and death are cleansed away. Good for all types of "seedlings," including creative projects. Proper ritual ambience: a cauldron filled with earth.

MARCH 21–23   VERNAL EQUINOX, EASTER

Spring's return, the seed time. A time of balance, when light and dark are equal. Kore/Persephone returns from the Land of the Dead. Goddess and consort, Ishtar and Tammuz, dance together. Proper ritual ambience: spring flowers, painted eggs, the Wheel of Light.

MAY 1   BELTANE, OR MAY EVE

The child born at the Equinox becomes a young woman; the flowering and fertility of the Goddess. A festival of desire, courtship, playful sexuality. Proper ritual ambience: a maypole.

JUNE 21   SUMMER SOLSTICE, OR LITHA

The longest day of the year, the triumph of light. The Horned God is at the peak of his power. The Sun King embraces the Queen of Summer. The Mother Goddess's mature reign. A season of mystery, sex magic, of entrances into the unknown; the fulfillment of wishes. Proper ritual ambience: an altar decorated with roses and other summer flowers, a bonfire in the center of the circle.

AUGUST 1   LAMMAS, OR THE GREEN CORN FESTIVAL

The Sabbat of the first fruits and green corn, the end of summer, the waning of the light. The goddess as reaper and taker of life. The Sun King is dead in the underworld, his body turned to grain; Persephone has entered the labyrinth. Proper ritual ambience: sheafs of wheat, corn, grains.

SEPTEMBER 22   FALL EQUINOX, MABON

The second harvest; the witches' thanksgiving. What has been reaped will sustain us through the season of barrenness. Day and night, light and dark, are in perfect balance. The Sun King has sailed west to become the Lord of Shadows. The goddess (Ishtar, Demeter) mourns for her consort/child. Proper ritual ambience: fall fruits, flowers, and grains.

OCTOBER 31   SAMHAIN, HALLOWMAS

The Witches' New Year. The night when the veil between the worlds is thin, the gates of death are open, the dead walk. The time of the dark moon and Hecate's rule, the descent into winter. The Lord of Death is honored. The Sun Child (Tammuz, Persephone) is conceived. The triumph of eternal life over physical death. One who would understand light must understand darkness. Proper ritual ambience: apples, pomegranates, mirrors, late-fall vegetables.

literature, "one of the few Wiccan groups in the world that has legal recognition as a church on state and federal levels of government." (We didn't think pagans would care to be recognized on state and federal levels of government, but what would we know?) The quarterly *Circle Network News* ($9 for a year's subscription) carries articles on rituals, invocations, herbal recipes, reviews, and news. You can also order books, recordings, herbs, and ritual tools (contact Circle for a free catalogue) and for $11 you can obtain a copy of *Circle Guide to Pagan Resources*, a 153-page book of "Wiccan, Pagan, and other Magickal listings." Every summer Circle founder Selena Fox runs a week-long School for Priestesses for women and another week-long training program in Wiccan Shamanism. She and her husband and Circle cofounder Dennis Carpenter travel around the U.S. and Canada every year putting on lectures, workshops, and seminars on topics such as Magic Craft, Neopagan Culture, Herbcraft, and Past-Life Recall.

Access: Circle, P.O. Box 219, Mt. Horeb, WI 53572. Phone: (608) 924-2216.

PAGAN SUMMER CAMP
•

Want to experience the good pagan life as if there were no microwaves, nuclear reactors, and Presbyterians in the world? Every June, just before the summer solstice, hundreds of pagans, Wiccans, goddess worshipers, shamans, Druids, and wizards descend on southwestern Wisconsin for the Pagan Spirit Gathering. Sponsored by Circle, PSG is touted as a "chance to live a holistic pagan lifestyle in a totally pagan space." Most pagans camp out in tents, and clothing is optional. Activities include a Mother Earth Ritual, a Power Animals Dance, Sweatlodge rituals, various rites of passage, chanting, drumming, bardic circles, and a bonfire dance.

Access: PSG, Circle, P.O. Box 219, Mt. Horeb, WI 53572. Phone: (608) 924-2216. Registration is $65 for adults.

WITCHES' SEMINARY
•

We thought only comic-book witches had names like Wanda or Sabrina, but the high priestess of Our Lady of Enchantment, a Wiccan church in New Hampshire, calls herself Lady Sabrina (and she has appeared on both "Donahue" and "Geraldo"). OLE's Seminary of Wicca, founded in 1981, offers workshops, home-study programs, weekly worship services, and a library of 6,000 occult volumes. For $119 you can take an eight-lesson Wicca home-study course, which covers making your tools, working within a magick circle, candle magick, cord magick, healing magick, Full Moon and Sabbat ceremonies, and other witchy stuff. There are also home-study courses in sorcery, Egyptian magic, herbalism, and prophecy. The organization publishes a bimonthly newsletter, *Outer Court Communications* (annual subscription $12).

Access: Our Lady of Enchantment, P.O. Box 1366, Nashua, NH 03061. Phone: (603) 880-7237.

A MOON-VOW, FOR THE LOSS OF WEIGHT

When the Moon shows cold and slender,
Stand beneath her starved light,
Wearing only white and silver—
Say, to whet her appetite,

I make my Vow to fast until
This crescent Moon shines round and full;
While she waxes let me wane:
I must lose, that she may gain.

While she grows, take silver wine,
Silver water, silver milk,
And bread like snow or linen fine,
And fish as clear as ice or silk—
But only these, and less of all
Than you would wish, to feed her well.

—Reprinted with permission from *The Crone's Book of Words* by Valerie Worth; published by Llewellyn Publications, P.O. Box 64383, St. Paul, MN 55164-0383. Paperback $6.95.

WHERE HAVE ALL THE GNOSTICS GONE?

THE GNOSTIC GOSPELS
●

In 1945, an Arab peasant named Mohammad 'Ali al-Samman found a jar in a cave near the Egyptian town of Naj 'Hammadi. Inside it were numerous leatherbound papyri, which for the next thirty years would be stolen, traded on the black market, and hidden away, like an expensive art heist in a Hitchcock film. The "Gnostic Gospels," fifty-two sacred books of one of the earliest Christian sects, did not emerge into the wide world of academic scholarship until 1975–1980. Among the first to study them was Harvard religion scholar Elaine Pagels. Out of her long hours squinting at Coptic script in an obscure annex of the Egyptian museum in Cairo came, in 1979, a highly acclaimed book, *The Gnostic Gospels*.

By about A.D. 200 Christianity was standardized into the orthodoxy we know today and the contents of the New Testament (the Gospels of Matthew, Mark, Luke, and John, the

A GNOSTIC SAMPLER

THE RAISING OF ADAM FROM THE MUD BY EVE (*FROM* "ON THE ORIGIN OF THE WORLD")

After the day of rest, Sophia [Wisdom] sent Zoe, her daughter, who is called "Eve [of life]," as an instructor to raise up Adam, in whom there was no soul, so that those whom he would beget might become vessels of the light. When Eve saw her colikeness cast down, she pitied him, and she said, "Adam, live! Rise up on earth!" Immediately, her word became a deed. For when Adam rose up, immediately he opened his eyes. When he saw her, he said, "You will be called 'the mother of the living' because you are the one who gave me life."

THE REVELATIONS OF ADAM'S ORIGIN AS TOLD TO HIS SON SETH (*FROM* THE APOCALYPSE OF ADAM)

The revelation which Adam taught his son Seth in the seven-hundredth year, saying, "Listen to my words, my son Seth. When God had created me out of the earth along with Eve, your mother, I went about with her in a glory which she had seen in the Aeon from which we had come forth. She taught me a word of knowledge of the eternal God. And we resembled the great eternal angels, for we were higher than God who had created us and the powers with him, whom we did not know.

"Then God, the ruler of the Aeons and the powers, divided us in wrath. Then we became two Aeons. And the glory in our hearts left us, me and your mother Eve, along with the first knowledge that breathed within us. . . . Since that time we learned about dead things, like men. Then we recognized the God who had created us. For we were not strangers to his powers. And we served him in fear and slavery. And after those events we became darkened in our hearts."

FROM THE GOSPEL OF PHILIP

And the companion of the Savior is Mary Magdalene. But Christ loved her more than all the disciples and used to kiss her on the mouth. The rest of the disciples were offended by it and expressed disapproval. They said to him, "Why do you love her more than all of us?" The Savior answered and said to them, "Why do I not love you like her? When a blind man and one who sees are both together in darkness, they are no different from each other. When the light comes, then he who sees will see the light, and he who is blind will remain in the darkness."

FROM THE SETHIAN-OPHITES

When he was led to his death, the Christ and Sophia departed to the Imperishable Aeon, while Jesus was crucified. Christ did not forget what was his own, but from above sent into him a certain power which raised him in a body which was both psychic and spiritual; the worldly elements remained in the world. When the disciples saw that the transformed Jesus had risen again, they did not recognize him. . . . And the greatest error of the disciples was this, that they thought he rose in a worldly body, and did not know that "flesh and blood do not attain to the kingdom of God." . . .

Some of them say that the serpent was Sophia herself; for this reason it was opposed to the maker of Adam and gave knowledge to men, and therefore is called the wisest of all. And the position of our intestines through which food is taken in, and their shape, shows that the hidden Mother of the shape of the serpent is a substance within us.

Epistles of Paul, etc.) were etched in stone. But before that time, according to Pagels, "numerous gospels circulated among various Christian groups, ranging from those of the New Testament . . . to such writings as the Gospel of Thomas, the Gospel of Philip, and the Gospel of Truth, as well as many other secret teachings, myths, and poems attributed to Jesus or his disciples." Some Gnostic texts describe multiple heavens, with a magic password for each. Some hold that Jesus did not suffer on the cross and was not literally resurrected. Some revere God as both father and mother. Some identify Mary Magdalene as Jesus' closest disciple and chosen successor. In general, the Gnostic texts contain secret, esoteric teachings aimed not at the hoi polloi (who would become the flock of Catholic Christianity) but at "the few," those evolved souls capable of *gnosis,* or knowledge. Gnosis is not rational knowledge but "an intuitive process of knowing oneself." Like Buddhists, many Gnostics insisted that ignorance, not sin, is the cause of suffering, and that divinity could be understood only by diving deep within the self. "For Gnostics," Pagels writes, "exploring the psyche became explicitly what it is for many people today implicitly—a religious quest."

Access: *The Gnostic Gospels* by Elaine Pagels is published by Vintage Books/Random House. Paper $6.95. A subsequent book by Pagels, *Adam, Eve, and the Serpent* (Vintage Books/Random House; paper, $8.95), tells how the Genesis story was perverted into a tale of original sin. (According to the Gnostics, Adam and Eve were heroes for eating from the tree of knowledge and defying a jealous, hostile creator.)

GNOSTIC CHURCH
•

According to some traditions (including the Gospels of Mark and John), Mary Magdalene, not the apostle Peter, was the first person to see the risen Christ. Therefore, the reformed prostitute should have been the first pope of the Christian church. That is not how it worked out, of course; if we'd had pontiffs named Mary, Michelle, or Stephanie, history might have been rather different. But there is a secret Christian lineage that recognizes Mary Magdalene as the favored disciple, and its line of succession has reportedly continued unbroken from Mary herself right up to the Most Reverend Rosa Miller, Presiding Bishop of the Ecclesia Gnostica Mysteriorum (Gnostic Church) in Palo Alto, California. "I was contacted over twenty years ago by the Hierophant-Bishop of the Order [of Mary Magdalene] and ordained and consecrated as the successor of the Lady," Bishop Miller explains. "I also embraced the oaths of secrecy, but there was one clause: When the time came, I was to lift the veil of secrecy. . . ." That time has come, although the Mary Magdalene Lineage "remains an esoteric order and time only will tell if our relics and records can sometime be made public."

What has been made public are certain formerly secret sacraments, such as a Gnostic Eucharist celebrated as a *hieros gamos,* or sacred marriage, of Sophia, the Mother of the World, and her consort, the Christ. "Come enter the Bridal chamber and receive the most holy mystery of the Three-in-One," says the priest in the Gnostic Church in Palo Alto, holding a chalice covered by a veil of white lace. "As the Logos and the Holy Spirit are united in the Father, so may ye attain to this divine union." (Why do we think Cardinal O'Connor and Jerry Falwell would not appreciate this symbolism?) There are no creeds to parrot in the Gnostic church; no references to sin or guilt. Considering "all beliefs to be transitory," in Bishop Miller's words, the church may take its scriptures from the Bible, the Gnostic Gospels, or the Bhagavad Gita. The teachings and rituals derive chiefly from the mystery teachings of the early Gnostics and the Kabbalah. "We use myth and symbol, not theology and dogma," she points out.

Access: The Ecclesia Gnostica Mysteriorum (Church of the Gnosis), 3437 Alma, No. 23, Palo Alto, CA 94306. Phone: (415) 494-7412. Reverend June Mikkelson, Rector. A Eucharist is celebrated every Sunday at 10:30 A.M. The church publishes a newsletter, *The Gnostic.*

A MAGAZINE FOR THE GRAILLESS LANDS
•

Gnosis magazine is not a lifestyle magazine for cave-dwelling early Christian Gnostics. It calls itself a "journal of the Western Inner Traditions," and that includes Sufism, Germanic runes, the grail legends of the British Mystery tradition, witchcraft and neopaganism, goddess worship, transpersonal psychology, the Kabbalah, the Cathar heresy, Rosicrucianism, Druids, alchemy, the esoteric teachings of Rudolf Steiner, etc. The articles are written by authorities in the field and tend to be in-depth and scholarly. More Old-Old Age than New Age, *Gnosis* has attracted more than 5,000 subscribers who are apparently endlessly nostalgic for the good old days of A.D. 700, when the grail legends were fresh and Woden was in Valhalla, gazing out over the many worlds. It also has the most rarefied classifieds we've seen. Here's the place to look for alchemical manuals, information about "Aquarian Mysteries and Rites of the Rose and Cross," journals of "pagan Celtic mythopoetic reality," ancient Latvian folk poems to the Goddess, as well as the usual lost teachings of Jesus.

Access: *Gnosis,* P.O. Box 14217, San Francisco, CA 94114. Published quarterly; a year's subscription is $15.

ARE THE FOUR NOBLE TRUTHS GOOD FOR YOUR MENTAL HEALTH?

•

Instead of weeping all over your therapist's Laura Ashley prints every Wednesday at four o'clock and popping Valiums for your anxiety attacks, you could let the Dalai Lama handle your neuroses. Not His Holiness himself, of course, but someone else with his worldview. "Buddhist psychology is reaching a state of semirespectability in the West," according to Dr. Lobsang Rapgay, a Tibetan physician with a Ph.D. in Buddhist psychology. "So many psychologists are using it in one form or another." And why not? Aren't the Buddha's Four Noble Truths ("Life is suffering," etc.) the most eloquent summation of the human condition? The fact is, Buddhists have been carefully scrutinizing the psyche since about 500 B.C. and have evolved an astute and intricate psychology. Their science of mind is based on the idea that the fundamental mental disease is delusion, specifically, the fiction of a real, autonomous self. While Western psychology views the person as an ego, Eastern psychology tries to treat the real patient, consciousness itself.

According to the original Buddhist psychology text, a section of the Pali Canon called the *Abhidhamma,* the personality is not made up of structures—like id, ego, and superego—but of a series of ever-fluctuating mental states. Therapy consists of the painstaking study of these mental states by means of meditation and introspection. The Vipassana school of Buddhism carries the technique of introspection—the moment-to-moment monitoring of one's mental states—to a high art. Be forewarned, however, that a Buddhist psychotherapist may not be concerned with building you a high-performance ego for a world of leveraged buyouts and rising mortgage rates. The process of meditation can even exacerbate your demons for a time. In fact, the symptoms of enlightenment can be similar to the symptoms of insanity. "To live each moment as it happens and as though it had never happened before is typical of the psychotic, who doesn't have a cohesive sense of self," Jack Engler, a clinical psychologist at the Harvard Medical School and a Vipassana meditation teacher, pointed out at a recent conference on Buddhism and psychotherapy. "But it is also the goal of meditation."

Access: For information about Vipassana meditation, contact Insight Meditation Society, Pleasant St., Barre, MA 01005.

LET THE DALAI LAMA HANDLE YOUR NEUROSES

THE DHARMA COMES TO THE COUCH

•

Since about the eighth century, when the *Gyu-zhi,* the Tibetan medical/psychiatric manual, came into being, Tibetan Buddhist lamas, yogis, and physicians have been practicing a unique form of psychotherapy. A Tibetan "therapist" approaches your hang-ups with a complex blend of spiritual, magical, and medicinal procedures. He'll perform an analysis of your urine (considered by Tibetan medicine to be a perfect mirror of the body's internal state), do a special kind of pulse diagnosis, and take down your history. After determining whether you suffer from a "hot" or a "cold" disease, he'll check for an imbalance of the three "humors," wind, bile, or phlegm. Tibetans say that wind (*rLung*) disorders are especially apt to cause mental symptoms such as excitability, anxiety, insomnia, and manic depression. If your mental illness is of a karmic nature, no medicine can help you, and a lama will have to be called in. A lama or teacher may be needed in any case, for much of Tibetan psychotherapy consists of "Dharma medicine," religious practices designed to transform consciousness.

If a *gdon,* or "ghost," is causing your obsession or depression, tantric practices such as mantras, mandala meditations, or visualizations of certain deities will be prescribed—usually in tandem with herbs, dietary and behavior changes, acupuncture, moxibustion, or other physical treatments. We Westerners think ghosts are silly, of course, but Tibetan ghosts—or demons or spirits—are not like *Fate* magazine ghosts. *Gdons* are flamboyant personifications of our mental projections; they are the dark psychic forces that cannot be admitted into consciousness, or they may be the imprints of deeply lodged mental habits and thought patterns. Who doesn't have a few *gdons* in the attic? At bottom, of course, Tibetan "shrinks" believe that all mental suffering is the result of clinging to the false notion of an ego, an independent identity. The ultimate cure for psychological problems is enlightenment, which can take many sessions.

Access: For information about Buddhist or Tibetan Buddhist psychology contact:

•Dr. Will Roth, 1270 Ruffner Rd., Schenectady, NY 12309. Phone: (518) 374-1792. Dr. Roth may be able to refer you to a practicing Buddhist psychologist in your area; he recently organized a major conference in New York City on Buddhism and psychotherapy, sponsored by the Karma Kagyu Institute of Woodstock, NY. (The address of the institute and the affiliated Karma Triyana Dharmachakra Monastery is: 352 Meads Mountain Rd., Woodstock, NY 12498. Phone: (914) 679-5906.)

•Dr. Lobsang Rapgay, Institute for Tibetan Medicine and Buddhist Psychology, P.O. Box 56196, Los Angeles, CA

90056. Phone: (213) 477-3877. (See "Tibetan Personality Test," below.)

•The Office of Tibet, 107 East 31st St., New York, NY 10016. Phone: (212) 213-5010.

•Tibetan Medical Institute, Khara Danda Rd., Dharamsala, Dist. Kangra H.P., India 176215.

For a comprehensive overview of Tibetan medicine/psychology, consult *Tibetan Buddhist Medicine and Psychiatry* by Terry Clifford. The book boasts a forward by the Dalai Lama as well as an original translation of three psychiatric chapters from the *Gyu-zhi*. Published by Samuel Weiser, Inc., Box 612, York Beach, ME. Paper $12.95.

ME AND MY DAKINIS
•

Tsultrim Allione

In 1970, a nineteen-year-old American college dropout named Joan Ewing was ordained as a Tibetan Buddhist nun and given the name Karma Tsultrim Chodron, which means "Discipline Torch of Dharma in the Lineage of Karmapa." She took a vow of celibacy and silence and lived alone in a cave in northern India. Three years later she renounced her vows, moved to the States, got married twice, and had four children, but Tsultrim Allione, as she now calls herself, did not exactly turn into a Material Girl. Fulfilling a mission given her by her own teacher, a Tibetan lama, she now instructs Western women in the ancient tantric science of the dakinis.

A dakini may appear as a human being or a goddess, either peaceful or wrathful, but essentially a dakini "is the energy of the undomesticated feminine," says Allione. "The dakinis are the energy that isn't defined, the energy that moves and influences you. It manifests through people, and maybe there are people who are in the dakini energy all the time." In her dakini workshops Allione guides twenty to thirty women through a "form of Buddhist psychotherapy" combining traditional tantric practices with Gestalt techniques. In tantric Buddhism there are five major dakinis, repre-

senting the five "passions" of anger, ignorance, pride, passion, and jealousy. During deep meditation, certain dakinis—such as the fierce, lion-faced dakini—manifest themselves to Allione's students. "The dakini appears and guides them through their life and shows them all the instances of anger." Later the students explore the significance of the dakini with various Gestalt techniques, including movement, dialogues, and constructing a mask to express the dakini vision.

Some Buddhists are critical of the dakini classes, objecting that the teachings Allione inherited from her lama are less Buddhist than Bon (the pre-Buddhist shamanic religion of Tibet). Others think that the Dharma should not be mixed up with worldly objectives like getting a better job, especially since tradition holds that any person who misuses the Dharma for material gain will end up in a hell realm with a bunch of scary Tibetan demons. A friend of ours who took a weekend workshop tells us, "It was a fast-food approach. It was just like a regular Gestalt weekend—lots of crying, making these masks with fur and feathers, and stuff. I thought it was tacky." But others evidently like it. Allione says, "The feedback I've had is that there's been an incredible transformation in people's lives—not only in a spiritual way, but in a material way as well."

Access: Tsultrim Allione's workshops, usually held at country-retreat settings, range from two to twelve days. For information contact Tsultrim Allione, 361 Old Mill Rd., Valley Cottage, NY 10989. Phone: (914) 268-3050. For further reading: *Women of Wisdom* by Tsultrim Allione tells the story of six Tibetan female mystics and of the author's own pilgrimage. Published by Routledge & Kegan Paul of London (American address: 9 Park St., Boston, MA 02108). Paper $8.95. A new book is expected out in 1990 or 1991.

TIBETAN PERSONALITY TEST
•

The Tibetan humors aren't just quaint medieval fluids; they too have a symbolic side, being physical/psychical manifestations of the three basic mental afflictions of desire, hatred, and ignorance. Is a wind disease any less scientific than a diagnosis of schizophrenia, which literally means "splitting apart" and for which there is no cure? One of the most prominent Tibetan "therapists," Dr. Lobsang Rapgay, a Tibetan physician with a Ph.D. in Buddhist psychology, has developed a Tibetan personality test based on the theory of humors. Using a questionnaire covering nineteen areas, he can diagnose patients as belonging to one of seven personality types: wind-bile, bile-phlegm, and so on. Intrigued by the test, two Philadelphia scientists are using twenty-nine volunteers typed by Dr. Rapgay to test their hunch that the humors correspond to specific neurotransmitters (serotonin, dopamine, etc.). Perhaps someday the Dharma will come to the couch, and we'll be able to consult Biological-Dharmic psychiatrists who specialize in bipolar phlegmatic depressions and schizobilious disorders.

Access: Dr. Lobsang Rapgay, Institute for Tibetan Medicine and Buddhist Psychology, P.O. Box 56196, Los Angeles, CA 90056. Phone: (213) 477-3877.

EXCUSE ME, IS THIS THE HUNGRY-GHOST REALM?

•

The late Chögyam Trungpa Rinpoche once predicted that Buddhism would come to the West as a psychology. Indeed, Trungpa himself, an incarnate lama of the Kagyu and Nyingma lineages who fled Tibet in 1959, has given the West a new breed of Buddhist therapists, trained in contemplative psychotherapy at Trungpa's Naropa Institute in Boulder, Colorado. Contemplative therapists do many of the same things ordinary therapists do—like counsel disturbed adolescents, drug addicts, and antisocial personalities—but they tend to view psychosis as an extreme journey through the "six realms of existence." The six realms, according to Trungpa's model of consciousness, include the realm of the gods (ruled by self-absorption); the realm of the jealous gods (paranoia); the human realm (passion); the animal realm (stupidity); the realm of the hungry ghosts (poverty); and the hell realm (anger). Even a sane mind regularly transits all the realms, from the god realm to the hell realm of anger and aggression. To gain a direct experience of this phenomenon, psychology students at Naropa undergo a classic Tibetan practice called *maitri*, or space-awareness meditation, spending hours and whole days in special rooms whose different shapes and colors reflect the different realms and intensify the corresponding emotions.

Access: For information about the Naropa Institute's two-and-a-half-year master's program in contemplative psychology (as well as other institute programs) contact: Director of Admissions, The Naropa Institute, 2130 Arapahoe Ave., Boulder, CO 80302. Phone: (303) 444-0202.

Naropa Institute meditation practice

Contemplative dance/movement class at the Naropa Institute

WYRDER AND WYRDER:
NORTHERN MYSTERY SCHOOLS

WYRD ACTORS
•

Several years ago, British psychologist Brian Bates discovered a thousand-year-old Anglo-Saxon manuscript hidden away in the bowels of the British Museum. It was a list of healing spells and incantations called *Lacnunga,* and it revealed to Bates the existence of a pre-Christian shamanic tradition in Britain during the Middle Ages. This path goes by the term "The Way of Wyrd"—"wyrd" is pronounced like "weird"—and means, essentially, "the meaning of life." Medieval shamans were selected at an early age for their sensitivity to psychic/psychological forces and their ability to embody these forces in stories, according to Bates. Who does that remind you of? Bates was reminded of actors, whose ability to portray psychological states, he thinks, is the modern counterpart of wyrd magic. With an interdisciplinary team at Sussex University in England, he has gone on to elaborate a "Middle Earth" psychology, combining techniques like psychodrama with the symbols of medieval Anglo-Saxon shamanism. And he has developed a special workshop for actors.

"Fire melted the ice engulfing the earth and created life," Bates yells, as his students (who have included the likes of Glenda Jackson and Liv Ullman) act out a Dark Age legend of the beginning of the world. The fire actors scream and cackle, while the ice actors moan soulfully. "Get up ice!" Bates orders, and the ice "giants from the underworld" lumber toward the fire people, shivering, lurching, arms extended mummy-style. They hiss as they fall into the fire. Later the actors will practice other rituals such as connecting

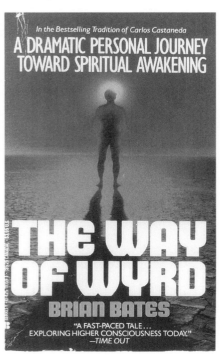

In the Bestselling Tradition of Carlos Castaneda

A DRAMATIC PERSONAL JOURNEY TOWARD SPIRITUAL AWAKENING

THE WAY OF WYRD

BRIAN BATES

"A FAST-PACED TALE... EXPLORING HIGHER CONSCIOUSNESS TODAY." —TIME OUT

with one another through special fibers that "smithing dwarves" have made for their bodies. "Society says that actors are neurotic, self-serving outsiders," says Bates, "but actors are the heirs of the shamans."

Access: Brian Bates, Sussex University, Falmer, Brighton, Sussex, England BN1 9QN. His book, *The Way of Wyrd,* is published by Berkley Books, 200 Madison Ave., New York, NY 10016.

PLEASE PASS THE URUZ
•

Before they became an alphabet, used by the Germanic and Norse people of Northern Europe, runes were a magical system of pictographs representing natural forces and objects. Many runes look like something a psychotic killer would scratch on a wall, and some, like *Uruz,* the rune for aurochs, would not seem to have a lot of modern significance. Nevertheless, runes are making a big comeback.

The dean of runes is Edred Thorsson, author of *At the Well of Wyrd: A Handbook of Runic Divination* and several other runic texts. A Northern Mystery scholar and aficionado of a rather intense Germanic deity named Woden (or Odhinn), Thorsson clearly does not approve of using runes as a parlor game. In his book he guides the would-be runecaster through a series of traditional rituals such as (1) cutting and scoring of staves; (2) calling on the norns (other gods and entities); (3) casting the staves; (4) calling on the gods, etc., etc. If you follow his directions you will find yourself facing north with your right index finger in the air, saying, "Hammer in the North, hallow and hold this holy stead." After you cast and interpret your runes, you will be out in your backyard scanning the sky for omens—dark-colored birds mean yes; light-colored birds mean no. (When the neighbors stare, just pretend you're an avid ornithologist.) If you can pronounce words like "Ljossalfheimr" and "Svartalfheimr," this may be for you.

For the neophyte—i.e., someone who can't spell Ljossalfheimr—*A Practical Guide to Runes* by Lisa Peschel might be a bit easier to handle. Written by a Wiccan pagan, this clear, down-to-earth rune handbook contains lucid interpretations of the twenty-five runes of the elder FUTHARK alphabet (used between the third century B.C. and the eighth century A.D.) and several sample divinatory layouts.

Access: *At the Well of Wyrd: A Handbook of Runic Divination* by Edred Thorsson is published by Samuel Weiser, Inc., Box 612, York Beach, ME 03910. Paper $7.95. *A Practical Guide to the Runes* by Lisa Peschel is published by Llewellyn Publications, P.O. Box 64383, St. Paul, MN 55164-0383. Paper $3.95. For information about seminars and workshops on runes contact Lisa Peschel, c/o The Llewellyn New Times, P.O. Box 64383-593, St. Paul, MN 55164-0383.

WAITING FOR KULKULKAN, QUETZALCOATL, KOYAANISQATSI, ET AL.

MAYANS R US

•

The ancient Maya traced their ancestry to star beings from the Pleiades and developed an astronomy so advanced they correctly calculated the length of a year (364.2422 days) when Europeans were still chucking spears at wild bisons. Their sacred 260-day calendar, the *Tzolk'in,* was not just a supremely accurate timekeeping system based on the cycles of Earth and Venus; it was also a window on a vast cosmos, measuring out a succession of "worlds" of 5,200 years, embedded within longer, 26,000-year ages. In case you wondered, we are in the latter days of the Fifth World, which began in 3113 B.C. and ends in A.D. 2011, 2012, or 2013 (depending on whom you listen to). That date will also mark the end of a 26,000-year cycle that began around the time Cro-Magnon man started fooling around with crude tools. Then the Sixth World will be born.

If you are a non-Mayan you may ask, "So what am I supposed to do about it? *I* didn't invent that rain-god–infested calendar." Or perhaps you'll wonder, "Will I be able to get take-out sushi in the Sixth World?"

Perhaps not, but you can get your affairs in order for the coming "Itza Age," the Mayan-style Age of Aquarius that will begin in 2013, according to Hunbatz Men. A native Mayan "daykeeper"—an authority on Mayan history, calendrics, and cosmology—Men is among the first to travel outside his country and seek a wider audience for his spiritual message. "The great calendar . . . of 26,000 years is completing its cycle now," he has announced. "This is the time to learn about cosmic truths, and HUNAB K'U [the supreme creator god] is awakening our conscious and our unconscious selves because it is time to enter our new heaven." To ease the transition, Men is leading groups to the ancient Maya ceremonial centers to be initiated into Mayan esoteric knowledge. In 1989 over a hundred pilgrims journeyed to

the Yucatan centers of Nah Chan, Etz Nah, Uxmal, Kabah, Lol Tun, and Chichen Itza, enacting rites that had been dormant for over 500 years. "All the participants had experiences that caused them to remember aspects of past lives," reports Men. "Many experienced the sensation of regressing time. The ancient Maya created the sacred centers so the good spirits could live forever in these eternal places and assist those who returned seeking the knowledge." In 1990 Men plans to lead a multicultural group to the Guatemalan sites of Tik'al (where the "cycles of cosmic time remain registered" and where ancient Mayans "worked with the kundalini in order to awaken the sacred serpent of wisdom"), Quilighua (home of the "wisdom of the Southern Cross"), and Copan, birthplace of the Tzolk'in. The initiates who journey to the initiation centers will become "teachers in the new solar age," according to Men.

Access: Hunbatz Men can be reached through: Indigenous Mayan Community, Apdo Postal 7-013, Merida 7, Yucatan, Mexico. For information about Men's pilgrimages to the Mayan ceremonial sites contact TimeWindow Tours, P.O. Box 2685, Santa Fe, NM 87504. Phone: (505) 988-3735. *Secrets of Mayan Science/Religion* by Hunbatz Men, paper $9.95—published by Bear & Company, P.O. Drawer 2860, Santa Fe, NM 87504—is a poetic, albeit recondite, introduction to Mayan esoteric wisdom.

WHAT ARE YOU DOING *AFTER* THE APOCALYPSE?

•

Remember the Harmonic Convergence on August 16–17, 1987? The world didn't end then, but thousands of people did rush off to sacred sites ranging from the Great Pyramid of Cheops to Mt. Shasta and the power places of Sedona, Arizona, to be photographed in silly poses by *Time* magazine. They were observing the date that the Mesoamerican prophecies identify as the end of nine cycles of hell beginning in 1519 (when Hernando Cortez landed in the New World) and the beginning of thirteen cycles of heaven. But you ain't seen nothing yet. Just wait till A.D. 2012. The mastermind of the Convergence was art historian/pop eschatologist Jose Arguelles, whose New Age interpretation of the Tzolk'in—which some academic Mayanists have criticized, but let's not get into that—predicts that the world as we know it will end in A.D. 2012. Well, not end exactly. It will either change into a postindustrial, utopian Solar Age, in which we'll all live harmoniously alongside the returned Mayan masters, or it will be Apocalypse City. The choice is up to us. We'd better hurry, because we have just about twenty years left to shape up, during which time there will surely be more apocalyptic festivals to attend.

Access: Jose Arguelles, P.O. Box 1709, Makawao, HI 96769. Several books by Jose Arguelles, including *The Mayan Factor* (paper $12.95), are published by Bear & Company. P.O. Drawer 2860, Santa Fe, NM 87504.

THE KOYAANISQATSI SYNDROME
●

To the Hopis, the "people of peace" who live on the edge of Arizona's painted desert, this is a time of *koyaanisqatsi,* or "world out of balance." *Very* out of balance. The Hopis say we are living in the final days of the "fourth world," which will be destroyed in a war between the U.S. and "those who possessed the first light of wisdom—China, Palestine, India, Africa." According to Hopi legend, the United States will be devastated by "gourds of ashes" which will fall from the sky and boil the rivers, scorch the earth, and cause an incurable disease. Most commentators believe the reference is to nuclear bombs, and that the prophecies will be fulfilled any day now. Very soon afterward, Pahana, a messianic figure related to the Mesoamerican Quetzalcoatl (Kulkulkan in Mayan) and known as the "lost white brother," will return to usher in the new Fifth World, which probably will not contain microwave ovens or "Wall Street Week." There may not be much you can do about this, unless you're a Hopi. Hopi prophecy has it that only those who follow the ancient teachings, and they don't mean Lutheran or Southern Baptist, will survive. But you can learn more about it by reading Frank Waters's fascinating book, *The Book of the Hopi.*

Access: *The Book of the Hopi* (paper $8.95) by Frank Waters is published by Penguin Books.

CHEROKEE MILLENNIALISM
●

Like the Mayans, the Tsalagi (Cherokee) people claim to be the great-great-great-grandchildren of interstellar tourists from the Pleiades. And they use essentially the same calendar as the Mayan/Aztec, according to which the Fifth World is on the verge of destruction and the Sixth World about to emerge from the wreckage. We learned this from *Voices of Our Ancestors: Cherokee Teachings from the Wisdom Fire* by Dhyani Ywahoo, the twenty-seventh-generation caretaker of the Ywahoo lineage. She is also founder and director of the Sunray Meditation Society in Vermont, an international spiritual society devoted to planetary peacekeeping and the diffusion of the teachings of traditional Native elders. The book imparts lessons in Native American forms of kundalini work, lucid dreaming, crystal meditation, visualization, and other psychospiritual practices.

Access: Sunray Meditation Society, P.O. Box 308, Bristol, VT 05443. *Voices of Our Ancestors* by Dhyani Ywahoo is published by Shambhala Publications, Inc., Horticultural Hall, 300 Massachusetts Ave., Boston, MA 02115. Paper $12.95.

The Aztec Circle of Destiny
Astrology & Divination from the Ancient Aztec World
Bruce Scofield & Angela Cordova

THE AZTEC CIRCLE OF DESTINY
●

The *Tonalpouhalli,* the Aztec version of the ancient Mesoamerican calendar, was a system of divination as well as a record of days. Now Bruce Scofield and Angela Cordova have reincarnated it as the Aztec Circle of Destiny, complete with a twenty-card deck of the Aztec days, a cloth bag containing thirteen wooden chips decorated with the ancient number glyphs, and a 240-page guidebook. The latter fills you in on the history of the calendar stone and offers sample card layouts, readings, and lists of associations for the 260 days of the calendar. You can use it to answer questions, cast horoscopes, and "journey with expert guides through ancient Mexico" in the company of gods named Tezcatlipoca, Cozcacuauhtli, and Tlazolteotl. You can also impress your dates with knowing comments like, "You know, you remind me of Chalchihuitlicue, the beautiful young goddess of storms."

Access: "The Aztec Circle of Destiny" by Bruce Scofield and Angela Cordova is available from Llewellyn Publications, P.O. Box 64383-669, St. Paul, MN 55164. $19.95.

NOUVEAU MYSTERY SCHOOLS

100 THINGS TO DO WITH A KA
●

About twenty-five years ago, Robert Masters, a well-known consciousness researcher, went into a series of telepathic trance states in Karnak in front of a statue of Sekhmet, a lion-headed Egyptian goddess of austere aspect, and was taught the contents of the lost sacred Books of Sekhmet. He went on to initiate many other people, including Edgar Mitchell, the astronaut, and the late Margaret Mead, in the goddess's program, called the Way of the Five Bodies, or the Fifth Way. Now he has made these channeled ancient Mystery School practices available to the public in a weirdly compelling book, *The Goddess Sekhmet: The Way of the Five Bodies*.

Dr. Robert Masters

According to the ancient Egyptian mystery schools—as interpreted by Masters—human beings have five different bodies, each of which moves in a different dimension of reality: SAFU, the spiritual body, KHU, the magical body, HADIT, the "shadow," KA, the "double," and AUFU, the physical body. Most of us spend all our time taking AUFU to the gym for low-impact aerobics or shoring it up with expensive tummy tucks, while neglecting the health and well-being of the vastly more important KA, HADIT, et al. The Way of the Five Bodies teaches you how to work out all your bodies.

I (J.H.) followed the directions for one of the book's psychospiritual exercises while riding the bus to my dentist.

The Goddess Sekhmet

Silently and, I hope, unobtrusively, I began to intone all 100 or so names of the goddess: "MOTHER OF THE GODS . . . THE ONE WHO WAS BEFORE THE GODS WERE . . . LADY OF THE PLACE OF THE BEGINNING OF TIME . . . EYE OF HORUS . . . ROAMER OF DESERTS . . . AWAKENER . . . LADY OF ENCHANTMENTS . . . LADY OF MANY FACES . . . GIVER OF ECSTASIES . . . RULER OF SERPENTS AND DRAGONS . . . SUBLIME ONE . . ." Fortunately, all my fellow passengers were typical New Yorkers and were too absorbed in their own trance states to notice that I was falling into an ancient Egyptian trance. Other dental appointments and deadlines interrupted my Fifth Way studies before I had time to practice the other interesting techniques in Masters's book, and I never even came close to creating an Imaginal Body or projecting a Double, a mirror-image body I could use to travel in other dimensions. In a Double, Masters points out, you can even meet up with other advanced souls wearing *their* Doubles, but you must be very careful. If you do bad things with your Double, "you will be damaged in future incarnations as well as in this one, and the higher and subtler the body that commits the offense, the more incarnations the penalties extend through." All in all, Fifth Way work sounds pretty heavy. Masters warns the reader at the outset that his book has the power "to alter your reality more or less extremely. If it leads deeply into the Fifth Way, then you will awaken to recognize that you have been living in a kind of demented dream, close to the edges of both madness and death."

Access: For more information on instruction in Egyptian (and Hawaiian) magic, write: Robert Masters, P.O. Box 3300, Pomona, NY 10970. *The Goddess Sekhmet: The Way of the Five Bodies*, first published by Amity House, is scheduled to be reissued in late 1990 by Llewellyn Publications, P.O. Box 64383, St. Paul, MN 55164-0383.

NEO-PLATONISTS IN HOT TUBS
•

They don't exactly *look* like neo-Platonists, Gnostics, Orphic ecstatics, or alchemists; they look like well-heeled, Volvo-driving housewives, psychologists, and bank presidents. But they are initiates in an ancient mystery school. "We've synthesized some very ancient methods of transformation in a modern form. We call it Nine Gates: a modern mystery school program," explains Gay Luce, a consciousness pioneer who lives in Marin County, California. You might see the school as a reincarnation of a reincarnation: an updated, highly eclectic version of the mystery schools of the Hellenistic world, which, in turn, had their roots in the Mysteries of ancient Greece and Egypt.

The curriculum of the ancient mystery schools included astrology, astronomy, mathematics, philosophy, cosmology, and psychic transport, but the fundamental lesson was transcendence. Luce explains that psychic energy can vibrate at many different frequencies just as electromagnetic energy does. In our ordinary Burger King consciousness we use only a fraction of these potential frequencies, but we can gain access to the entire range by activating the subtle "energy centers" where our energy field is focused and "tuned." The Nine Gates refer to these nine energy centers—"Actually, there are more than nine but nine is a nice mystical number," says Luce—and spiritual techniques of different mystery schools are employed for each "gate." To activate energy centers in the feet, for instance, Luce has used the maze from the floor of Chartres Cathedral, which is based on a Druid maze. "The centers of the feet tap into the energy which comes from earth. The Celtic Druids believed the creator was the goddess of the earth, and that you could hear the earth through the feet. They walked the maze as a meditation."

The mystery schools of the Hellenistic world mixed sacred teachings of the Orphic and Dionysiac mystery cults of ancient Greece, ancient Egyptian and Mesopotamian religions, and innumerable Gnostic, neo-Platonist, Hermetic, and Christian contemplative sects. Similarly, the Nine Gates program mixes teachings from Hawaiian Kahuna, African shamanism, Sufism, Tibetan Buddhism, Native American shamanism, Basque ritual, and Christian mysticism. "We do initiations," says Luce. "It's not the kind of school where you listen to lectures and talk. *You* are the program." Some participants develop telepathic powers, she says, but that is not the point. "The mystery schools are about the honing of character."

Access: The Nine Gates program consists of two separate ten-day sessions and costs $3,500. Contact: Nine Gates, 220 Redwood Highway, Suite 61, Mill Valley, CA 94941. Phone: (415) 927-1677.

COSMIC TOURISTS

The new travel trend of the nineties is the *spiritual* vacation. Perhaps because of the imminence of the millennium, the pilgrimage, which had been steadily declining in popularity since the late Middle Ages, is back in style, and this time there are special travel agencies to handle the details.

The very best place for a spiritual vacation is a sacred site, a mysterious locus in the earth's grid where the material world thins out and otherworldly energies loom large. Lourdes, Delphi, Lascaux, Mecca, Machu Picchu, Benares, Stonehenge, and the pyramids of Egypt are all sacred places, as are various sacred vortices in Arizona and Mt. Shasta, power spots in Bali and Indonesia, cairns and fairy mounds in the British Isles, and any place ever visited by Atlanteans or UFOs. "The idea of a sacred place, where the walls and laws of the temporal world dissolve to reveal wonder, is apparently as old as the human race," writes Jim Swan in his essay "Sacred Places in Nature," published in *Shaman's Path*, edited by Gary Doore. He has collected "hundreds of case histories of people who have felt drawn to certain special places where they have undergone transformative experiences." Here are some of the options:

DEATH VALLEY VISIONS
•

Some people's idea of a good time is a four-star restaurant in Paris; for others it's three days and nights alone on a mountain in California's Death Valley, fasting, calling to Spirit for a medicine name, and praying for a vision. Tourists

Bird Brother and Sedonia Cahill

of the latter persuasion may be found on one of the ten-day Great Round Vision Quests into Death Valley and the high desert of the Inyo Mountains. "The quests are designed after the traditional quests of the Native Americans but are tailored to meet the needs of contemporary people," according to guide Sedonia Cahill and "dream facilitator" Bird Brother. "The Medicine Wheel teachings form the foundation for these journeys into Self and Spirit. The ten days are spent in circle clarifying intentions, receiving Medicine teachings, dancing, singing, weaving a personal, mythic heroine/hero's journey, sharing ceremony"—all culminating in three days and nights alone on a mountain.

Access: Sedonia Cahill and Bird Brother, The Great Round Vision Quests, P.O. Box 201, Bodega, CA 94922. Write for a brochure or call (707) 874-2736. Eight vision quests are offered each year, and there is also a year-long apprentice program for qualified questers.

ENGLAND BEFORE PRINCESS DI
•

Stonehenge

Urquhart Castle, Loch Ness

If your taste runs to cairns, dolmens, enchanted forests, castles, Druids, fairy mounds, solstice ceremonies, and whatever crawls out of Loch Ness, Wilson & Lake International offers several "metaphysical/sacred sites" tours of England, Scotland, and Ireland. With guides who are knowledgeable about the ancient earth religions and the "centers

of light"—like Peter Caddy, cofounder of the Findhorn Community in Scotland—you embark on pilgrimages to Stonehenge, Glastonbury (known in ancient times as Avalon), Loch Ness, Iona, the Orkney Islands, and other ancient sacred spots. On one tour, you'll experience the midsummer solstice in Avalon; on another you'll learn about the Great Goddess and our "Atlantean heritage" at Stonehenge. "Participants on past tours have had unique and joyous experiences, which have made profound changes in their lives," the company claims.

Access: Wilson & Lake International, 330 York St., Ashland, OR 97520. Phone: (503) 488-3350.

Earthwatch volunteers at work

TALK TO A DOLPHIN
•

Since 1979 Louis Herman and his coworkers at the Kewalo Basin Marine Mammal Laboratory in Honolulu have been teaching language to two twelve-year-old female dolphins, Phoenix and Akeakamai. Each of the "girls," as they're known, reportedly understands well over 600 sentences, more than many free-lance writers we know. By joining an Earthwatch expedition, you can spend two to four weeks with these intelligent, sociable marine mammals who have never been known to nuke a neighbor or launch a television ministry. You'll help with tank cleaning, feeding, and recording data; if you stay till week four, you might get to try some hand signals. Earthwatch, a nonprofit institution that funds field research by finding paying volunteers (that's you!), sponsors 120 projects around the world. By paying $1,000 to $3,000, you can lend a hand at an Amazonian rain forest conservation project, save bald eagles in Missouri or cranes in Vietnam, investigate the mysterious pollution near the Arctic Circle, study the nutrient cycles of Siberia's Lake Baikal, and many other admirable things. Better not bring any aerosol sprays along, though.

Access: Earthwatch, 680 Mount Auburn St., Box 403N, Watertown, MA 02272. Phone: (617) 926-8200. Two weeks with the dolphins costs $1,950; four weeks, $2,600.

VACATION WITH A VORTEX
●

In 1981 the entity "Albion" reportedly channeled information about sacred energy vortices, or power spots, around Sedona, Arizona, and now you can tour the best of them with Sedona Red Rock Jeep Tours' Vortex Tour, also known as the Sacred Earth Tour. During the three-hour tour you'll visit some of the major vortices, work with crystals, learn to "smudge and walk in balance" (whatever that is) and other New Age/Native American activities.

Taking the Vortex tour

Access: Red Rock Jeep Tours, P.O. Box 10305, Sedona, AZ 86336. Phone: 1-800-848-7728. The tour is $45 per person for one or two people; $40 for three to nine people.

BUT WHAT IF THE PHARAOH SEES US?
●

Want to hang out in the Great Pyramid by yourself—well, actually, by yourself with your fellow tour members? Wander into hidden chambers, and even stand between the paws of the Sphinx? You can—on Power Places Tours' "Inside Secret Egypt" expedition. Power Places' director, Dr. Toby Weiss, who has a Ph.D. in the History of Consciousness, is the "foremost international authority on power places and

The Great Pyramid

ancient healing sites," so the locales of the tours are not chosen randomly. Other Power Places expeditions are to the Amazon, Bali, the Hawaiian island of Moloka'i, Peru (highlights: summer solstice at Machu Picchu and a side trip to the fabled UFO landing site at Lake Titicaca), and Tibet (with tour leader Gary Wintz, the first Westerner to live in Tibet in modern times). Ask about special UFO conferences in Peru and millennium gatherings in Egypt.

Access: Power Places Tours, Dr. Toby Weiss, 28802 Alta Laguna Blvd., Laguna Beach, CA 92651. Phone (714) 497-5138.

DON'T STEP ON INTERPLANETARY GRIDS
●

If you went on an ordinary tour to Peru, you'd probably come home with a few phony pre-Columbian trinkets, but if you went on a Visions Travel pilgrimage you might come home with a snapshot of the space brothers near Lake Titicaca. Visions Travel specializes in "spiritual metaphysical tours" to the sacred places of the world, and its Star People Tour of Peru, led by UFO aficionados Sherry and Brad Steiger, expressly focuses on UFO activity in the Andes. On the other hand, if you visit the Andean sacred sites with channel Shyla Kamil and her entities, Abraham and Malaya, you'll "connect with the interplanetary healing grids that lead us to etheric doorways." The tours of Egypt, India, Nepal, Greece, Hawaii, the Amazon, Indonesia, and Bali are equally cosmic and are led by well-known psychics, swamis, channels, or metaphysicians. For example, the tour of India and Nepal is led by Swami Virato, whose credentials include having written for Penthouse *Forum* magazine, and features instruction in Tantric sexual philosophy, "accentuated by a special diet of Indian delicacies designed to enhance passion, romance, and the ecstasy of knowing our own love nature. . . ."

Access: Visions Travel & Tours, Inc., 9841 Airport Blvd., Suite 520, Los Angeles, CA 90045. Phone: (213) 568-0138; (800) 888-5509.

MILLENNIAL STUDIES IN BALI
•

Instead of carping about the local currency with Ethel and Murray Potemkin from Cleveland, you can discuss chakras with leading lights of the human-potential movement in Bali, where the Millennium Institute for Holistic Studies offers a wide array of "adventures in growth and transformation." You can learn shamanic ecstatic rituals and healing techniques from psychologist Alberto Villoldo, Ph.D., who was initiated into the shamanism of the Incas in the Amazon and the Andes. With Zen Master Richard Baker Roshi, founder of California's Tassajara Zen Mountain Center, you can take a side trip to the Tantric Buddhist monument of Borobudur on Java and meditate among carvings representing the worlds of desire, form, and formlessness. You can contemplate the Enneagram with Helen Palmer, explore dreams with Stanley Krippner, or master the "teaching of the shields" with modern shaman Joan Halifax.

The institute offers "Millennium Journeys and Expeditions" to other parts of the world, as well. In Brazil, Alberto Villoldo will take you to a community of healers called the Valley of the Dawn, a secluded psychic-surgery center, and a candomblé priestess knowledgeable about Afro-Brazilian ecstatic trance traditions. If you go to the Sacred Lands of India and Tibet, you'll get an audience with the Dalai Lama at his monastery in Dharamsala and a visit with Satya Sai Baba, "India's living saint," as well as a pilgrimage to the burning ghats on the Ganges and a three-day vision quest near Kathmandu. On a "Myths of the Millennium" tour of Egypt and Greece with New Age personality Patricia Sun, you'll aim to "build bridges between our ancient myths and those of the next millennium" as you experience the full moon at the pyramids of Giza and Sakara.

Access: For information contact the Millennium Institute for Holistic Studies, P.O. Box 935, Palo Alto, CA 94301. Phone: (415) 321-2169. The programs in Bali cost between $2310 and $3,275, depending on your point of departure. Journeys and Expeditions cost about $3,000.

EAST/WEST BAZAAR: WHERE TO BUY A USED BARDO

AMERICAN BOOK OF THE DEAD
•

Everyone loves the *Bardo Thodol*, or *Tibetan Book of the Dead*. But how are people who have spent their entire lives surrounded by computerized sprinkler systems and self-defrosting refrigerators supposed to relate to the "greenish-black Ghasmari, who stirs the skull-bowl with a vajra" when it comes time to "drop the physical," as they say? We could all use an updated, Westernized version of the classic Tibetan dying manual to guide us to the right afterlife bardos, and now there's *The American Book of the Dead* by E. J. Gold. Gold, who appears inexplicably familiar with the between-life states, refers to the bardos as the "macrodimensions" and to the body as the "biological machine." His book (the fruit of "the direct teachings of the guides—perhaps you think of them as teachers, sufis, arhats, bodhisattvas") is rather hypnotic, but we are not sure that during our final moments of Earth we want to listen to a well-meaning friend read us passages like the following: *If I start smelling something very sweet, really sickeningly sweet, then I'm about to be born as a horsefly in a pile of dung. Whatever it looks like, if it smells sweet or looks foggy or cloudy, I won't get near it. I'll back off, using the power of revulsion and disgust, and choose another womb entrance instead.*

Access: *The American Book of the Dead* by E. J. Gold can be ordered from Gateways, P.O. Box 370, Nevada City, CA 95959. Phone: (916) 477-1116. Paper $12.50 plus $1.50 shipping.

FROM ABAASY TO ZVORUNA
•

Sure, you know all about Zeus and Yahweh, but how much do you know about Huracan, the Mayan god of summer storms, or the Roman funeral goddess Nimitra, not to mention hundreds of obscure but nonetheless demanding deities from Latvia, Assyria, and the Caroline Islands? *A Comprehensive Dictionary of the Gods* by Anne S. Baumgartner can help you learn to avoid offending the gods by confusing a Walpurgisnacht with a Ragnarok (as we've been known to do) or making the mistake of dancing with a skeleton during a *danse macabre*. If you flip through this lighthearted volume, you'll learn that ophiolatry is serpent worship; that dwarfs excell at metal work because of their sharp eyesight; that if you are not a Lacandon Maya, you are not a real person; that the first sea serpent was spotted by Norse sailors in Scandinavian waters; that the first of all living creatures was the great spider Sussistinnako; that trolls vary greatly in size, some of them being too large, in fact, to crouch under bridges.

Access: *A Comprehensive Dictionary of the Gods: From Abaasy to Zvoruna* by Anne S. Baumgartner is published by University Books, A Division of Lyle Stuart Inc., 120 Enterprise Ave., Secaucus, NJ 07094. Paper $9.95.

THE SEVEN AFRICAN POWERS
•

Do you know which saint is claiming your head? The identity of your guardian angel? Your destiny within the religion of Santeria, the Cuban or Puerto Rican version of neo-African voodoo? For just $5.25 you can get a consultation with the Orishas (the seven African powers) at the Universal Life Church of the Seven African Powers in Miami. If you can't get to Miami, you can take a sixteen-lesson correspondence course ($5 per lesson or $55 for the entire course) from the church. Each lesson deals with a specific Orisha and contains certain ebbos, or spells, that will "improve the quality of life for the student." The Church is also preparing a catalogue of magical substances used in the spells of Santeria.

Access: The Universal Life Church of the Seven African Powers, Temple of Oddua, P.O. Box 453336, Miami, FL 33245-3336.

MEDICINE CARDS
•

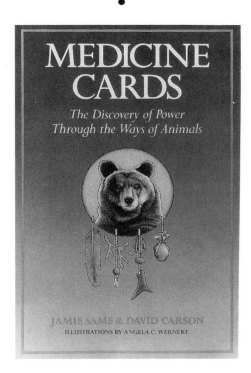

By "medicine" Native Americans don't mean Excedrin or Ex-lax, of course; they mean "anything that improves one's connection to the Great Mystery and to all life." The Medicine Cards draw their wisdom from "teachings . . . handed down from many elders in the Choctaw, Lakota, Seneca, Aztec, Yaqui, Cheyenne, Cherokee, Iroquois, and Mayan traditions," according to the cards' creators, Jamie Sams and David Carson of New Mexico. The fifty-four handsomely illustrated Medicine Cards—forty-four power animal cards and nine blank shield cards for personal use (you can sketch your own totems or gods on them)—come with a very nice companion book. It explains the concepts of the nine totem animals, the medicine wheel, and the medicine shield and gives instructions on six different divinatory spreads: a Pathway Spread, Sun Lodge Spread, Father Sky/Mother Earth Spread, a Medicine Wheel Spread, Moon Lodge Spread, and Butterfly Spread.

Most of the text is devoted to an explanation of the symbolism of each of the forty-four power animals. "When you call upon the power of an animal," the authors explain, "you are asking to be drawn into complete harmony with the spirit of that creature's essence." If you have pulled the Crow card, for example, you learn that, "Crow can bend the laws of the physical universe and 'shape shift,' " and that, "Crow is an omen of change. Crow lives in the void and has no sense of time. The Ancient Chiefs tell us that Crow sees simultaneously the three fates—past, present, and future. Crow merges light and darkness, seeing both inner and outer reality."

Access: "The Medicine Cards: The Discovery of Power through the Ways of Animals" by Jamie Sams and David Carson (illustrations by Angela C. Werneke) are published by Bear & Company, P.O. Drawer 2860, Santa Fe, NM 87504. $26.95.

THE OTHER BIBLE
•

Okay, here's all the good stuff that they threw out of the Old and New Testaments. Read about dozens of alternative creation and Eden myths! Meet divine and demonic beings you've never dreamed of! Wonder at new versions of Exodus, the deluge, and the infancy of Christ! Thrill to the account of the war in heaven *before* the creation! Learn how the demiurges screwed up and created a world that would eventually contain Las Vegas and twenty-four-hour wedding chapels! The book is *The Other Bible*, and its selections are drawn from the Jewish Pseudepigraphia, early Kabbalah, Haggadah, Midrash, Christian Apocrypha, and Gnostic scriptures. It includes the writings of Hermes Trismegistus, Plotinus, Ptolemaeus, Marcion, Mani, and Pseudo-Dionysus, as well as works attributed to Enoch, Solomon, Isaiah, John, James, Peter, Paul, and Augustine. Copious appendices, notes, and glossaries help you find your way through this intriguing Judeo-Christian looking-glass world and explain why the texts were excluded from the "real" Bible. A great gift idea for your Gnostic, Kabbalistic, Hermetic, or just plain esoteric friends, but bear in mind that it's very heavy (literally).

Access: *The Other Bible*, edited by Willis Barnstone, is published by Harper & Row. Paper $16.95.

THE WAY OF CARTOUCHE
•

This system of divination takes its name from the oval or oblong figures found on Egyptian monuments and papyri. The nicely illustrated nine major cards in the deck correspond to the nine major gods of the ancient Egyptian pantheon—Osiris, Isis, Horus, Thoth, et al.—and the remaining sixteen cards depict symbols such as the ankh, the lotus, the pyramid, and the scarab beetle. According to its creator, Murry Hope, this new oracle "encapsulates those archetypal energies . . . known and understood by the ancient Egyptians" and displays them in a form the Aquarian-age psyche will recognize, especially if it has spent several incarnations in Middle Egypt. In the companion hardcover book, he explores the spiritual and psychological symbolism of the cards and suggests methods of using them for self-knowledge, divination, meditation, healing, talismanic purposes, and getting in touch with past lives.

Access: "The Way of Cartouche: An Oracle of Ancient Egyptian Magic" by Murry Hope is published by St. Martin's Press, 175 Fifth Ave., New York, NY 10010. A set, including cards and book, costs $22.95.

A SHORT COURSE IN FAERY MANNERS
•

When entering Faery, the dwelling place of the Fairies, you must (1) take an iron implement (usually a knife); (2) refrain from partaking of food or drink; and (3) behave courteously among the inhabitants. That way, you'll be allowed to go home again. This is the sort of information you can pick up from John and Caitlin Matthews's *The Aquarian Guide to British and Irish Mythology,* an A-to-Z guide covering lots of interesting stuff about Arthur and The Round Table, Lady Godiva, Yggdrasil, Morgan Le Fay, Ceridwen, as well as more obscure figures with hard-to-pronounce names.

Access: *The Aquarian Guide to British and Irish Mythology* by John and Caitlin Matthews is published by The Aquarian Press, Thorsons Publishing Group, Wellingborough, Northhamptonshire, NN8 2RQ, England. Paper $12.95 plus shipping from Pyramid Books and the New Age Collection, P.O. Box 4546, 35 Congress St., Salem, MA 01970-0902. Phone: (508) 744-6261.

THE SECRET DAKINI ORACLE
•

A few years ago we were visiting friends who spent all their time sitting cross-legged on the floor consulting the Secret Dakini Oracle deck. Before long, we were hooked, too, and muttering things like, "Oh God, I got Mt. Meru *again!*" We can't explain why, but the Dakinis *know everything* about you. Maybe that's because they are archetypal "guardians of the inner mysteries of the self," according to Nik Douglas and Penny Slinger. Douglas, a Sanskrit and Tibetan scholar, immersed himself in the stone carvings of

53 TREE SPIRIT / YAKSHI

48 WHITE LADY / MOTHER OF PEARL

59 PEARLS BEFORE SWINE

Cards from the Secret Dakini Oracle deck

sixty-four Dakinis—embodiments of the female principle of wisdom—in the Ranipur Jharial Temple of Orissa, India, before creating this system of tantric divination. Collage artist Penny Slinger created the sixty-five surrealistic full-color collage cards, which depict archetypal images drawn from Eastern mystical teachings: Mercury, Puja/Purification, Maya/How She Spins, Waves of Bliss, etc. Twenty-two of the designs correspond to the twenty-two Major Arcana of the tarot, and the cards can read according to traditional spreads such as the Tree of Life and the Celtic Cross. Both the illustrations and accompanying text convey a hip, Western, épater-les-bourgeois version of Tantric mysticism, and, wow, is the goddess Kali ever "mean and heavy."

Access: "The Secret Dakini Oracle: A Tantric Divination Deck" by Nik Douglas and Penny Slinger is available from U.S. Games Systems, Inc., 179 Ludlow St., Stamford, CT 06902. The Oracle deck costs $15; the book, $8.95.

"YOU ARE NOW READY TO GO TO BED"
•

Whew! It's about time! You've already taken a bath, massaged your partner with perfumed oil, put on a red robe, concentrated on the Muladhara chakra, contemplated the creative union between the two cosmic elements, filled your wineglasses, repeated the names of Shiva and Parvati, eaten some meat, refilled your glasses, eaten fish, meditated on the Kundalini, rinsed your mouths with water and eaten the cardamom seed to sweeten your breath, after first meditating on how the outer husk of the seed hides the two halves of the kernel . . . This is Tantric foreplay, as described in *The Eastern Way of Love* by Kamala Devi, who has adapted for Westerners a sexual yoga she discovered in Calcutta and Kathmandu. You'd better have a lot of time on your hands because there's a lot more cardamom chewing and Kundalini contemplating before you even get to third base. But maybe it's worth it, because at the climax a "shuddering flash pierced by awareness should seize you in a moment filled with overpowering brilliance. . . . The moment is beyond the senses, as if there has been an immediate and profound contact with the truth." Then can you turn on Johnny Carson?

Access: *The Eastern Way of Love* by Kamala Devi is published by Simon & Schuster/Fireside; paper $11.95.

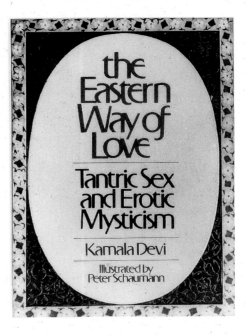

the Eastern Way of Love

Tantric Sex and Erotic Mysticism

Kamala Devi

Illustrated by Peter Schaumann

THE · THINKING · MAN'S
GUIDE TO BRAIN
RENOVATION · AND · REPAIR

·

The world of brain science was turned upside down in 1973. That was the year neuro-

scientists Candace Pert and Solomon Snyder, working at Johns Hopkins University in

Baltimore, startled the scientific community with their discovery of the opiate receptor. A

receptor is a site where a molecule of a drug or a naturally produced chemical fits into a

cell like a key in a lock. The opiate receptor was the first receptor ever found in the brain,

and its existence had enormous implications. Why, for example, would the human brain—

which has remained structurally unaltered for at least 40,000 years—possess receptors

for modern drugs such as morphine and heroin? The obvious answer is that our brains make their own versions of these substances, and in fact they do. Two years after Pert and Snyder brought off their coup, two Scottish scientists, John Hughes and Hans Kosterlitz, dis-

covered the endorphins, the brain's own morphine.

Endorphins are powerful chemicals. Rats who are allowed to activate their own endorphins in the laboratory do so to the point of exhaustion. "Opiates are about pleasure," explains Candace Pert, "and now we know the molecular structure of pleasure." Research with endorphins may one day lead to techniques for controlling pain, improving the immune response, and conquering diseases such as hypertension and Alzheimer's.

With the discovery of the opiate receptor, a new era in brain science was born. Today, over forty receptors have been isolated in the brain. They play key roles in anxiety and calm, attentiveness, euphoria, sensation-seeking, introversion and extroversion, sleep and wakefulness, convulsions, and muscle relaxation. There is even a receptor for the street drug angel dust, though no one knows for sure what this receptor is doing in the brain. Researchers have found that even a slight change in the density of certain receptors changes how food tastes, whether a concerto excites you, or even whether you can stand up to an obnoxious boss.

Why should you care? Because by carefully studying receptors in the lab, scientists have created a new technology for modulating our inner life. Most of these new substances are still in laboratory development, but in this final chapter we want to give you a glimpse of things to come in the arena of consciousness expansion.

Pharmacologists are now designing magic bullets for the brain, "cleaned-up" drugs that travel directly to the desired receptors to produce a specific effect—to wake you up, put you to sleep, make you stop eating, or make you amorous— while bypassing other receptors. Present drugs do in fact react with receptors to create their effects. Unfortunately, they also set off inappropriate receptors along the way, creating undesirable side effects. It's like painting your toenails by sloshing a can of paint over your feet. Barbiturates are a good example. Yes, they help you get to sleep, but they also make you dull and stuporous, deprive you of rapid-eye-movement sleep (the dream stage of sleep), and also turn you into an addict. Drugs that make you less nervous might also make you drowsy or slur your speech. "All our old drugs were discovered through one accident after another," explains Solomon Snyder. "After we already had the drugs we went back and figured out how they worked. Now we have the molecular tools to design a whole new line of drugs." Many of those drugs are profiled in this chapter.

Receptor technology may also become the basis of psychotherapy in the future. Candace Pert sees the eventuality of the "total receptor work-up." According to Pert, when you go in for a psychiatric exam in the year 2000, the doctor will make a PET scan (a diagnostic "photograph") of your brain. "We'll drop in a very selective drug with a radioactive isotope," says Pert, "which will 'light up' the brain, and then we'll be able to get a three-dimensional look at the receptors—which areas are okay, which need tuning. We're going to have computerized maps of the brain—all of the different substances we know of and some we haven't yet discovered. The data come out in the form of light gradients, and those are transformed into numbers by the computer. One day we'll have each neurotransmitter on a separate floppy disk.

We'll know the different distributions in the brain and we'll find out a lot about what goes wrong. Then maybe the patient will be given a highly specific dose of, say, ten drugs that will straighten things out."

In short, when it comes to enhancing the brain and consciousness, it appears the primary hope for the future will be better living through chemistry. But there are more drastic measures.

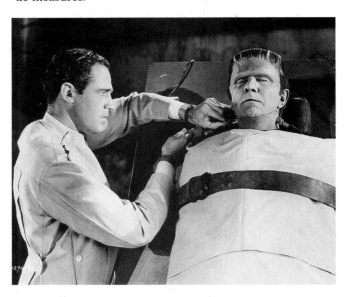

One of these drastic measures first appeared in 1982 in Stockholm, Sweden, where surgeons at Karolinska Hospital performed the first "brain transplant" on a man with Parkinson's disease. Brain transplants, as they're commonly called, are not Frankensteinian procedures in which an entire brain from one human being is dropped into the skull of another. The proper term is "brain implant," and in this case a section of dopamine-rich tissue from the patient's adrenal gland was grafted to his brain. Parkinson's disease is caused by a breakdown in production by dopamine-producing cells in the brain, and it was hoped that adrenal implants would alleviate the problem. Those first brave attempts apparently failed, the patients displaying almost no improvement. In 1985, however, a Mexican team led by Ignacio Madrazo began performing the same basic operation in a different fashion on 100 Parkinson's patients and reported astounding results in the *New England Journal of Medicine* in 1987. Madrazo's group reported that its patients went home virtually cured. They didn't even need medication. Some American scientists have been very skeptical of the "Mexican miracle," claiming that little or no follow-up was performed and that some Mexican patients showed up at U.S. hospitals sicker than reported.

On the other hand, American patients now receiving adrenal implants have shown some improvement. According to Dr. Harold Klawans of Rush Medical Center in Chicago, his implant patients have less "off time" (when they're immobile and nonfunctional), though they still require medical management. Recently, doctors in Sweden, Mexico, and England have had success implanting brain cells from aborted fetuses in Parkinson's patients. Most scientists concur that implanting fetal cells rather than adrenal cells is a better *scientific* idea: Embryonic cells, which are still dividing, should have a better chance of hooking up to neurons in the patient's brain—and, in fact, fibers can actually be seen growing out of the implant to their proper target in the brain in animal studies. However, socially and legally, fetal implants are not such a great idea. Sacrificing the unborn to treat the aged is not a politically safe alternative. The safest bet is to use tissue from spontaneous miscarriages, but there are approximately a million Parkinson's victims in the U.S., and not that many spontaneous abortions. And the possibilities of abuse are enormous: A black market in aborted fetuses in which the poor and unborn are purchased by the rich and aged.

The real hope may come from animal tissue. Using genetic engineering and molecular biology, scientists are attempting to remodel pig brain tissue so that it can be used to patch up ailing human brains. At the present, there is little outrage over dead pig fetuses, though that may come.

If all the problems of brain transplants can be solved, then a multitude of renovation jobs can be performed on us all. Besides the obvious problems of Parkinson's and Alzheimer's, brain grafts may one day be used to treat stroke, spinal injuries, Huntington's chorea, chronic pain, some forms of obesity, head injury, multiple sclerosis, depression, schizophrenia, and even brain-based fertility and potency problems.

We hate to be too optimistic. There are always side effects. Don't ever let anyone tell you there aren't any. For example, at Rush Medical Center in Chicago, adrenal-implant patients experienced some strange sensations. One woman, lying in her hospital bed, thought she was fishing in a lake. Another patient became convinced that salesmen were roaming from room to room in the hospital, pressuring patients to buy major household appliances. Six of Rush's seven patients had delusions. The symptoms passed after a few days and don't appear to be harmful, but no one can explain them. Doctors at other U.S. hospitals noticed similar phenomena among their implantees. One theory is that the adrenal implant is packed with a variety of mind-altering neurotransmitters, including endorphins. But Rush researchers have failed to find these chemicals in their patients' spinal fluid.

On the following pages you'll read about some of the brain-renovating, mind-improving "products" predicted for the very near future. But whether they're receptor-technology drugs, brainstorming devices, or neurological procedures, keep in mind that when you tamper with the brain, you're playing with something no one really understands. And side effects are inevitable.

Probably the best example of misguided brain tampering in this century is the bizarre story of Egas Moniz, a Portuguese psychiatrist who discovered that by banging a pick into a person's frontal cortex and cutting the nerve fibers that run to the rest of the brain, one can relieve many forms of mental illness, including aggression and hyperemotional states. The operation was called a prefrontal lobotomy, and became so popular that 40,000 were performed in the United States during the 1940s and '50s. Moniz won the Nobel Prize for medicine in 1949 for his invention of the lobotomy. Upon the occasion, *The New York Times* stated: "Surgeons now think no more of operating on the brain than they do of removing an appendix. [Moniz and his colaureates] taught us to look with less awe on the brain. It is just a big organ . . . and no more sacred than the liver." Of course, we now know that a lobotomy turns one into a virtual zombie, and anyone today who would make a statement like the one above would have to have a brain no more complex than his liver.

Some of the following may turn out to be the endorphins, penicillins, or polio vaccines of the 1990s and beyond. Others may end up being twenty-first-century versions of the prefrontal lobotomy. Which are which? It would be nice to know.

SUPERCAFFEINE
●

"Caffeine is one of the best drugs there is," says Solomon Snyder, M.D., of Johns Hopkins. "It makes you alert, gives you a little jolt of energy, and fights drowsiness." But, of course, there are drawbacks to caffeine, says Snyder, one of the country's leading pharmacologists. "Caffeine can cause jitters, wakefulness, and occasional heart palpitations. It would be nice to eliminate some of caffeine's unwanted effects and make a new form that only improves awareness."

What Dr. Snyder and his colleagues are trying to do is to make a "cleaned-up" caffeine. His team has traced caffeine's alertness effect to the way it binds to sites in the brain called adenosine receptors. The next step is to develop compounds to react more cleanly with these receptors. The result could be a substance more powerful than the rarest espresso, but without the side effects. Snyder thinks this ultracaffeine could be available within the next five years.

SKYDIVING PILLS, WIMP PILLS
●

Always wanted to sky dive, but were too cowardly? Or are you the type whose idea of a good time is playing Russian roulette with five loaded chambers and one empty? Oddly enough, there may soon be pills for both of these conditions, opposite as they are. Odder still, both pills, if they are ever created, will be based on the same chemical substance. This magical elixir is called serotonin, a chemical messenger that is the key to two very different personality types: the compulsive daredevil and the wimp with a paralytic fear of bodily harm.

Serotonin evidently acts differently in different parts of the brain, according to Timothy Walsh, M.D., of the New York State Psychiatric Institute. "A person with an abnormality in serotonin activity in one part of the brain might have a chronic urge to race motorcycles, but the rest of his brain would be quite normal. It's like having one loose connection in a television set that's otherwise okay."

What Walsh envisions are serotonin-manipulating compounds that act like guided missiles. Each molecule of the drug would be wrapped in chemicals that would keep the drug inactive until it reaches its target in the brain. In this way, one pill could turn Milquetoasts into heroes while another would put the brakes on the Evel Knievels of the world.

RUSSIAN MIND-CONTROL MACHINE
●

For decades there has been a rumor circulating that the Russians have a machine that acts on people's brains via radio waves. Well, it's not a rumor. It's true, though the machine cannot really "control" the brain with any specificity.

It's called the Lida, and in the 1970s Russian scientists sent us a model as part of a Soviet-American scientific exchange. The Lida turned out to be a crude machine made of vacuum tubes and other components of World War II vintage. But it worked. U.S. scientists placed a nervous cat in a metal cage and positioned the Lida next to it. When the machine began to hum and broadcast radio waves in the frequency of deep-sleep EEGs, the cat went into a trance. W. Ross Adey, of the Pettis Memorial Veterans Administration Hospital in Loma Linda, California, the scientist to whom the Russians loaned the Lida, comments: "Instead of taking a Valium to relax yourself, it looks as if a similar result could be achieved with a radio field." The Soviets claim they have successfully used the Lida to treat insomnia, hypertension, anxiety, and neurotic disturbances. And there are the usual rumors of a more sophisticated machine that controls minds from a distance. Most scientists pooh-pooh this notion. On the other hand, in recent years considerable evidence has been amassed to indicate that the weak electromagnetic fields produced by radar installations, microwaves, video-display terminals, and power lines can affect the brain. Is the day too far away when we can focus this energy for beneficial purposes?

MODERATE MANIA
●

Manic-depressives oscillate between breathtaking mania and the depths of despair. There is, however, a mild, expansive high that manic-depressives often experience between these wild mood swings. It's called hypomania, and Dr. Mogens Schou, the Danish psychiatrist who developed lithium treatment for manic depression, believes that further research into lithium and other compounds will soon lead to a chemical understanding of this pleasant, "golden mean" state. Dr. Schou, who won the prestigious Lasker Award for his lithium treatment, describes "a life in a light chronic mania, subjectively more attractive than even the most pleasant hashish or alcohol euphoria" when science develops a drug that turns on hypomania at will.

ST. TERESA'S ECSTASY . . . IN A HELMET
●

The young man floated toward a strange glow in the forest, whereupon an alien entity gave him an "extremely meaningful message." But this was no UFO encounter. The young man was wearing an experimental helmet fitted with magnets that beamed a low-level magnetic field at his temporal lobes, brain areas associated with time distortions, dream states, and assorted odd psychic phenomena. The helmet is the invention of neuroscientist Michael Persinger, of Laurentian University in Sudbury, Ontario, and Persinger's fifty test subjects routinely spend half an hour immersed in ecstatic, mystical, visionary experiences while clad in his motorcycle-helmet-like apparatus.

"The deep structures of the temporal lobe are electrically unstable and sensitive to all sorts of things, including the biochemistry of stress, psychological distress, insufficient oxygen, and fasting," says Persinger. "That could explain why, when mystics go through self-induced stressful rituals and yogis go to high mountaintops and fast, they report transcendental events." Persinger says that electrical activity within the temporal lobe is associated with such mystical experiences, so he uses his electric helmet to sort of jump start his subjects into a transcendental experience.

Persinger's subjects report feelings of floating, leaving their bodies, and a sense of "great meaningfulness." Does this mean St. Teresa, Buddha, and Muhammad had oddly wired temporal lobes? And can we all become prophets by donning Persinger's helmet? Perhaps. The researcher's goal is to use his device to trigger transcendental experiences in nonreligious people faced with the fear of death.

YOU'VE-HAD-ENOUGH DRUG
●

Do you have trouble backing away from the bar or buffet? Help may be on the way in the form of fluoxetine hydrochloride. Fluoxetine increases your brain's concentrations of serotonin, a neurotransmitter that—among its many other duties—controls appetite and mood. Claudio Naranjo, of the Addictions Research Foundation, gave the drug to heavy drinkers, who then cut their alcohol consumption by 20 percent. "It wasn't that they no longer got high or that alcohol now made them sick," explains Naranjo. "Their desire to consume alcohol simply decreased." The new drug may help overweight people eat less, but has no effect on smokers, says Naranjo. "This suggests that different parts of the brain are involved in controlling abnormal consuming behaviors."

Fluoxetine is actually not that futuristic. The drug itself already exists, marketed by Eli Lilly under the name Prozac, an antidepressant. However, Naranjo emphasizes that more research is needed before Prozac can be prescribed as an antidrinking or antibinging drug.

STIMULATE THOSE BABIES
●

Want to keep your brain young? The secret may be to lead a more exciting infancy. In a pioneer cradle-to-grave study of rats by Stanford University neuroscientist Robert Sapolsky, it was found that if the rodents were handled often as infants, they preserved their mental faculties—and their brain cells—well into old age. The rats were given a brief period of extra attention during the first three weeks of their life. After that they received no special treatment. At age two and a half, positively geriatric for a rat, the scientists found that these animals ran their mazes far more competently than control rats. Autopsies also revealed that their brains exhibited little of the usual age-related cell loss in the hippocampus, a key area for learning and memory.

Sapolsky says that cells in the hippocampus are destroyed by stress hormones, and he believes that the stimulated rats can better adjust to stress and thus avoid these harmful hormones (called glucocorticoids). We don't know yet whether the same trick will work on human babies, but just to be safe, why not fondle your next newborn a little bit more avidly during those critical early weeks?

AROMA DRUGS
●

Someday the cockpit of a Boeing 747, the control room of Three Mile Island, and the driver's seat of your Suburu may all smell like peppermint. Smells can affect performance, and researchers at International Flavors and Fragrances, one of the world's largest manufacturers of scents and flavors, hope one day to come up with the right combination of smells to keep tired pilots from flying their passengers into the Empire State Building or nuclear power plant operators from inadvertently exposing the reactor core.

Early results from an experiment at the University of Cincinnati show that peppermint is a likely candidate as a vigilance enhancer. "Typically, in vigilance experiments," says psychologist William Dember, one of the Cincinnati scientists, "performance declines over time. And afterward people report feeling kind of cranky, irritable, and uncomfortable. They may even complain of eyestrain or sore shoulders." To find out whether the proper scent would make a difference, Dember and his colleague Joel Warm subjected people to a monotonous task: They had their subjects watch a video

screen for fifty minutes; their job was to detect the occurrence of an infrequent and unpredictable signal. Through oxygen masks they received whiffs of various scent pellets, pumped from an adjacent room by a fish-tank pump. Some subjects got peppermint; others muguet, a floral scent that smells like lily of the valley. The control group got only unscented fresh air through their masks.

The performance of all three groups declined over time, but the scented subjects declined less. The peppermint and muguet groups also perceived the task as less demanding. Both fragrances appeared to be equally effective, and, concludes Dember, "It may very well be that the introduction of any fragrance will prove to have a beneficial effect." Long-married couples take note: Perhaps someday you'll take an oxygen mask and peppermint pellets to bed with you to help stem the tedium of lovemaking.

THE FIREFOX PHENOMENON
●

Firefox was perhaps one of the worst movies ever made, but it was based on an interesting idea. The main character, played by Clint Eastwood, pilots a Soviet plane that responds directly to his thoughts. No, neither the Soviets nor the U.S. Air Force has such a device just yet, but the essential technology it would be based upon is already in development.

Clint Eastwood in *Firefox*

Various researchers are working on silicon chips to be implanted in the middle of a human nerve. So far, experiments have already been carried out on monkeys and rats. The idea is that nerve fibers grow through microscopic holes in the chip, and brain signals traveling down the nerve can be shunted off to a radio receiver and transmitter. The radio, in turn, transmits the brain's orders to an external computer, which controls the machine of your choice: a jet, car, boat, or your toaster oven. Of course, the first uses of such technology will be more practical applications. Dr. Joseph Rosen, a Stanford University plastic surgeon who conceived of the idea, says the chip would be used to restore nerve-damaged fingers, hands, arms, and legs. But Greg Kovacs, the primary designer of the project, points out that "eventually, it could open an entire world of new possibilities by allowing our own nervous systems to motivate machines."

MEMORY TRANSPLANTS

Picture this: You're not getting along with your spouse. Certainly you've both tried to work things out, even gone to a marriage counselor. But bad memories keep resurfacing, reminding you both of what a mess it's been. She keeps bringing up that time you spent the mortgage money on a new shotgun. You're still haunted by the image of her in bed astride the electrician. So your marriage counselor has sent you to the Mnemo Unit of the hospital. Here, the bad old memories will be extracted, and nice new ones will take their place. A memory of a happy marriage is the best prescription for a future happy marriage.

Sounds bizarre, but someday it may happen. Memory transplants are based on the pioneering work of Elizabeth Loftus, a University of Washington psychologist who discovered through some interesting experiments that many of the memories we carry with us to the grave are falsely optimistic ones. Moreover, it's a good thing. Pleasant memories, even if inaccurate, may be one key to a happy life. Loftus's work has convinced her that human memory can be tampered with and falsified, like an embezzler's books, and that all of us are walking around with minds full of counterfeit remembrances.

This comes as a blow to psychology. While there are about fifty different theories on memory, most experts cherish the belief that there is a permanent, if not always accessible, memory. But Loftus's work destroys this concept.

In one experiment, a subject is shown a "murder suspect" with straight hair. Later, the subject is purposely led to overhear a conversation in which someone describes the suspect's hair as curly. Invariably, subjects in this experiment will "remember" a frizzy-haired perpetrator. Once implanted, says Loftus, a phony memory is so strong it can become the "truth." A witness can even pass a lie-detector test.

As for more mundane events, Loftus's research indicates that we all wear rose-colored glasses as we travel down memory lane. We remember voting more often, being promoted more often, taking more plane trips, sleeping with more members of the Dallas Cowgirls than the records indicate. "Why are we wired up this way? Why does our past acquire this kind of prestige-enhancing glow?" she asks. "I think this helps us live happier lives."

Conversely, depressed patients often have painful memories. Successful therapy tends to make these memories fade away. What Loftus suggests is that we replace bleak memories on purpose, implanting rosy remembrances in their place. Hypnotist-psychiatrist Milton Erickson, for example, once used hypnotic suggestion to implant happy childhood memories in a depressed patient, whose depression subsequently lifted.

Loftus suggests, perhaps tongue in cheek, that memory-improving clinics might be set up. Imagine a clinic where doctors could treat bigots by supplanting their racial prejudices with pleasant memories of the ethnic group in question. Or let's say your marriage is on the rocks. Perhaps (falsely) romantic memories of your husband can replace all those forgotten anniversaries. Or why not extend it to entire populations? Perhaps collective memory transplants could expunge national feuds. Frenchmen could be hypnotized into "remembering" wonderful times with their good friends, the Germans.

Seriously, in the future people need not be the passive victims of their infantile traumas, their parents' mistakes, their past heartbreaks and failures. Once we gain access to the brain's storage and retrieval mechanisms, the mind can be reprogrammed at will

TIRED OF WASHING YOUR HANDS?
●

Obsessive-compulsive disorder wreaks havoc upon the lives of its victims. A student never makes it to school because he's too busy driving back and forth over the same stretch of road, constantly stopping to make sure that each bump isn't a body under his tires. A mother rewashes clothes all day long, taking them from the dryer and putting them back into the washer because she's convinced that germs have contaminated them the instant they leave the dryer. The classic case, of course, is that of the person who must wash his hands over and over.

Henrietta Leonard, of the National Institute of Mental Health, estimates that about 3 percent of the adult population suffer from obsessive-compulsive disorder. The disease, once considered a psychological problem, is now believed to be chemically based, caused by a biochemical imbalance in nerves deep in the brain. And now there's a drug for it. Clomipramine has shown promise in trials with 578 obsessive-compulsives, in whom it reduced symptoms by 40 percent. No one is sure why it works, but it may enhance the action of serotonin. Phillip Ninan, a psychiatrist at Emory University, claims that 80 percent of his subjects improved after taking clomipramine, which is marketed by Ciba-Geigy under the name Anafranil. Ninan says that before treatment, one of his subjects virtually lived in the bathroom. "Because she was worried that urine would touch her clothes," explains Ninan, "she would wipe herself for hours and then recruit her mother and husband to wipe her. After treatment, she's out of the bathroom in minutes."

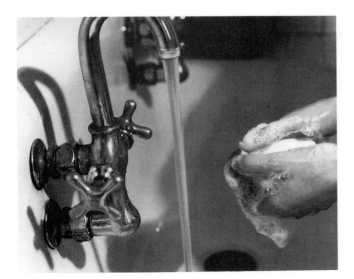

FEAR OF WRITING IN PUBLIC . . . AND OTHER PHOBIAS
●

Phobias may seem silly to the casual observer, but they can be disabling to the victim. "A person with a fear of eating in public, for instance," points out psychiatrist Thomas Uhde, "might not be able to date. He or she would be continually making excuses to avoid eating in a restaurant." Uhde is a researcher at the National Institute of Mental Health where he has met some interesting subjects. "We had one patient with a fear of writing in public who couldn't take her children to the doctor because she might have to fill out a medical form in front of other people. Others would turn down promotions or quit their jobs if a situation came up that required them to speak in public."

Fortunately, Uhde may have an antidote, a drug called phenelzine. Phenelzine, a type of antidepressant drug called an MAO inhibitor, along with several other treatments, was tested on sixty-five subjects with overwhelming fears of writing, eating, or speaking in public; using public bathrooms; or interacting socially at all. Phenelzine reportedly worked as well as weeks of standard psychological therapy.

A PRESCRIPTION APHRODISIAC?
●

A drug with the catchy name of LY163502 may become the first prescription aphrodisiac. "For the first time we have a molecule literally designed for that purpose," says psychologist Leonard Derogatis, director of the Medical Psychology Division at Hahnemann University in Philadelphia. The drug works on the dopamine receptor in the brain that is involved in the stimulation and maintenance of sexual arousal. Oddly, LY163502 developed serendipitously out of research into Parkinson's disease, which normally afflicts the aged. When doctors were testing the drug L-Dopa on Parkinson's patients in the late 1960s, they noticed that the drug had an unusual side effect. "Little old guys who hadn't had sex in thirty years were chasing nurses down the hall," says Derogatis. "Since L-Dopa is the precursor to the neurotransmitter dopamine, it gave us a hunch that dopamine must be involved in the sexual behavior system."

LY163502 is being tested on over 600 subjects, ranging in age from the thirties to over seventy. These are people with actual sexual dysfunction, with problems involving desire, arousal, or orgasm. A woman in her midthirties, for example, who lost her desire after childbirth reported that she and her husband were behaving "like honeymooners" after she took the drug. Derogatis predicts that a prescription version of LY163502 (under a catchier name, we hope) could be available in a couple years.

MEASURING SAMADHI

One of the first steps to creating transcendence on demand—in the lab or with a pill—is to figure out exactly what it is. But how does one scientifically quantify rarefied states of mind such as those described in Tibetan sacred texts like the *Bardo Thodol (Tibetan Book of the Dead)*? It seems impossible, but Dr. Daniel Brown of the Harvard Medical School wanted to give it a try.

He and his team traveled to Dharamsala, India, in the Himalayan foothills, where they set up shop in a small hotel. The Dalai Lama provided the subjects: advanced Tibetan Buddhist meditators handpicked by His Holiness himself. What Brown and his colleagues asked themselves was this: What happens to perception during the deep meditative state called *samadhi*, when the meditator's mind is said to merge with the universe? The Harvard team had the monks view the letters s, x, and z through an apparatus called a tachistoscope that exposes images for a fraction of a second. What happened is a real eye-opener. The monks called out the fleeting letters with an 80 percent accuracy rate while not meditating. But when subjected to the same exercise during meditation, every holy man scored zero. The meditators had "stopped the mind," seeing nothing with their eyes wide open.

Interestingly, earlier studies found the opposite: Subjects' visual acuity had actually increased during meditation. But these experiments were done with less skilled meditators, and Brown suspects that shallow meditation increases visual perception while profound meditation cuts off the physical world.

The Dalai Lama

In any case, Brown et al. have brought us a hair closer to understanding the physiology of enlightenment. Similar efforts in the past have harvested some important fruits. Biofeedback and the "relaxation response," for example, developed out of studies of yogis' phenomenal control over their bodies. But such benefits are merely spin-offs of a greater accomplishment: enlightenment. Says Brown: "The goal of meditation is to overcome the limits of ordinary perception by totally changing one's perception. The outcome is a state of enlightenment in which you simply do not experience the kind of suffering built into everyday life."

THE LIVING COMPUTER

HOW ABOUT A BIOCHIP FOR YOUR BRAIN?

Rather than being like a computer, tomorrow's brain may actually *be* a computer—if James McAlear has his way. McAlear is one of several scientists who are trying to make a biochip, a computer chip made of organic molecules. The wonderful thing about a molecular chip is that, being tiny and three-dimensional, it could pack a million times the computing power of its solid-state equivalent. McAlear has patented a technique for making a conductor out of a protein molecule, and founded a company, EMV Associates, Inc., in Rockville, Maryland, to develop a biochip. The ultimate goal is to create a VSD, or Very Small Device, that could actually be implanted in a brain.

What McAlear and his colleague John Wehrung have in mind is artificial vision. A miniature television camera mounted on eyeglasses would serve as the "eyes." The camera's signals would be converted to pulses and sent to an array of miniature electrodes implanted in the brain. That part isn't revolutionary. But McAlear's electrodes would be coated with cultured embryonic nerve cells, which would actually hook up with nerve cells of the visual cortex.

But the biocomputer of McAlear's dreams is a godlike instrument of thought, marrying the number-crunching power of electrons to the reasoning talents of neurons. An entire molecular computer will set up symbiotic residence in your brain, sending out shoots of nerve fibers to grow into brain cells. It will have a double-helix structure so it can replicate itself. You will be able to store any sort of information on your biochips. For example, you might choose to etch the contents of the Library of Congress in its circuits. Then by thought alone, your neurons could access the information on demand. Uniting your nervous tissue with circuit switches 100 million times faster than organic synapses, the implant will become a "superior, omnipotent being," according to McAlear. Furthermore, he thinks, the being of the user will live on in the biocomputer rather than in the central nervous system. When you die, the implant—storing your personal record and all your knowledge—could be implanted in a fresh host. "That pretty much fits the specifications for an immortal soul," notes McAlear. Convenient, too. Just think: If the sales manager for your southwest territory drops dead on you in a Dunkin' Donuts, don't bury all of him. Remove his biochip to implant in a low-priced replacement. The chip will contain all his contacts and his knowledge of the field.

Of course, biochip researchers are still trying to work out the bugs, but who knows?

EUPHORIA: A NEW SMART DRUG?

•

Euphoria (n-methyl aminorex), an Ecstasy-like drug that appeared mysteriously in the neopsychedelic underground a few years ago, is now being touted as a smart pill as well as a light hallucinogen. As one experimenter reported, "Approximately forty-five minutes to an hour after ingesting a full dose of Euphoria, you have the sensation that the clouds are parting in your brain and the sun is coming out. In this burst of clarified mentation, solutions to intellectual problems seem obvious, and neurosis virtually disappears."

While Euphoria is reportedly good for helping you to focus on your inner life, it can also be used as a tool for focused creativity and organized work. Some users have reported they get a lot done while on the drug. Perhaps this is because Euphoria is distantly related to speed (methamphetamine), and appears to act on the brain, as speed does, by stimulating the release of dopamine and noradrenaline. Yet Euphoria does not cause burnout as speed does. Be forewarned, however, that taking Euphoria every day can make you jittery and anxious and cause other amphetamine-like side effects. In truth Euphoria is not a very futuristic drug. It exists right now. But it may be a while before you can get it easily. Euphoria has been scheduled by the DEA (Drug Enforcement Administration); that is, it's now illegal.

BOOST YOUR SAT SCORES: TAKE A PILL!

•

If you're one of those people who break into a cold sweat at the sight of an exam blue book, there may now be a drug to ease you through your next test. It's called propanolol, and according to Dr. Harris Faigel of Brandeis University, twenty-five extremely anxious students took it an hour before they dove into the all-important Scholastic Aptitude Test (SAT). The result: The subjects boosted their scores by as much as 120 points, reports Dr. Faigel, who said he was "flabbergasted" by the findings. How do you get it? Propanolol is a very common high-blood-pressure drug, and you'd have to convince your physician that you have a medical need for it before exams. Or it could be the basis of antianxiety drugs of the future. Our question is: Will it do anything for a blind date?

ANGEL DUST FOR BRAIN DAMAGE?

•

As a recreational drug, PCP (angel dust) has little to recommend it. It can cause violence and seizures. People high on angel dust are often brought to hospital emergency rooms in a violent and incoherent state, sometimes exhibiting symptoms virtually identical to schizophrenia. In the future, however, PCP may actually become a staple item in emergency rooms. Doctors may end up saving patients with angel dust rather than saving them from it.

As it turns out, PCP may be beneficial for victims of stroke or other incidents such as near-drownings in which oxygen is cut off to the brain. It appears angel dust may prevent permanent brain damage in such patients, according to the Department of Health and Human Services' Alcohol, Drug Abuse, and Mental Health Administration. In tests on animals, a single dose of PCP within eight to ten hours prevented—and sometimes even reversed—brain damage wrought by a stoppage of oxygen-carrying blood to the brain. Such brain damage often leaves patients with impairment of speech and movement.

This good side to PCP was discovered accidentally by a group of doctors studying the effects of drug abuse on the brain. Angel dust appears to prevent neurons from producing toxicity when deprived of oxygen. Doris Clouet of the National Institute of Drug Abuse says the Institute is developing several "clean" versions of PCP. These angel-dust mimics would save the brains of stroke victims yet lack PCP's distressing side effects.

"THE SILICON CHIP INSIDE HER HEAD . . ."

•

In a glass dish in Washington, D.C., a clump of living brain cells from a rat fetus grow directly onto an electronic computer chip. According to the National Institutes of Health's neurobiologist Richard Wyatt, the computer chip is "eavesdropping" on the electrical conversations that take place among brain cells. Object: to learn the language of the brain. Once that is accomplished, the chip could act as a bridge between brain cells, acting as a kind of switchboard. A manmade "communications center" could have broad applications. Patients with Parkinson's and Alzheimer's disease as well as accident and stroke victims could have their brains repaired with the new implant. And, predicts Wyatt, cells-on-a-chip could one day correct congenital brain damage and mental retardation.

NATURAL PAINKILLER

•

As mentioned, in 1973 pharmacologists Candace Pert and Solomon Snyder isolated the famous opiate receptor in the brain. A receptor is a site in tissue that reacts with a specific chemical, just as a lock reacts to a specific key. The earth-shattering discovery of the opiate receptor demonstrated that the brain must be manufacturing its own opiates to fit in this receptor. It does, of course, and these opiates turned out to be the famous endorphins, those neurotransmitters that make us feel so good.

Now Solomon Snyder has uncovered a new receptor that makes us feel less good. Snyder and his team at the Johns Hopkins Medical Institutions have found receptors for the molecule bradykinin on nerve pathways activated by pain. Bradykinin, or BK, it turns out, is what makes us hurt. Scientists have long suspected BK's role in pain, because tissues release it during injury, and when you inject BK into blood vessels or other tissue it causes severe pain. "Other molecules are released and can cause pain," says Snyder, "yet this is the first real evidence that bradykinin is the key one in the body's mechanism for registering pain."

The next step is to develop a class of drugs that block the BK receptors and thus prevent pain. Already there's been some progress. Scientists at Nova Pharmaceutical Corporation exposed animal smooth muscle tissue, which contains BK receptors, to a number of synthetic chemicals. These chemicals, called BK antagonists, differ only slightly from basic BK structure; they block the receptors without stimulating them. The blocked tissues then fail to contract as they do when exposed to BK. Another series of tests was conducted on live animals. Researchers used antagonists to block the BK receptors in rats' paws. Then they "stimulated the paws with pressure," but the rats failed to react, demonstrating that the BK antagonists fended off pain. (The wonderful euphemism "stimulated the paws with pressure" is the phrase used in the Johns Hopkins literature; what this means exactly is something we don't like to think about.) In any case, the research so far has been so positive that Nova hopes to conduct clinical trials soon in humans. Let's just hope they don't stimulate their paws with pressure.

SEXY DIET DRUG
●

Endorphins are those magic brain opiates that seem to play a role in pain relief, euphoria, learning, and have even been linked to "runner's high" and that tingling feeling you get down your spine when you hear your favorite musical passages. But endorphins have their black side—especially for people with eating problems. For endorphins also play a key role in appetite. But anything endorphins can do, the opiate-blocking drug naltrexone can turn off. And this includes appetite.

Researchers have known for some time that naltrexone makes animals eat less, but evidence for its effectiveness in humans has been sketchy. But recently, Allen Levine, at the Veterans Administration Medical Center in Minneapolis, used a naltrexone-like drug to stem the appetite of an obese, brain-damaged patient who ate uncontrollably. Levine believes this research may lead to a commercially available diet drug in the near future. Present amphetamine-based diet drugs affect heart rate, blood pressure, and a whole range of other body functions.

Naltrexone, unlike these compounds, is not addictive, and, according to Levine, "it may not have any serious side effects, except that people may feel a little manic."

There is one unusual finding, however. "We would expect that an opiate blocker would decrease sexuality," says Levine. "But in animals it [naltrexone] actually seems to heighten sex drive, and it may well prove to have the same effect on people."

DREAM PILL
●

Researchers at the National Institute of Mental Health have succeeded in increasing people's dreams—or at least the dream recall—by giving them the drug physostigmine. Physostigmine increases the action of the brain chemical acetylcholine, and by so doing induces rapid-eye-movement (REM) sleep when administered to sleeping subjects.

Seventeen volunteers were given the drug intravenously after they had fallen asleep, while others were given a placebo. Researchers then woke up the subjects during REM or non-REM periods and asked them about their dreams. Physostigmine-injected subjects were far more likely to report dreams in the REM state (89 percent of the awakenings), though the drug did not increase dream recall in the non-REM state. REM sleep and dreaming are not synonymous, but there is better recall when in the REM state and the subject matter of recalled dreams tends to be more bizarre than that experienced under non-REM sleep. For those with an impoverished dreamlife—or those who simply can't remember their dreams—physostigmine may be the dream enhancer of the future.

DROWNED RATS AND MEMORY ENHANCERS
●

Memory, like most everything else in the brain, is chemical, and scientists are closing in on the biochemical mechanisms that shift into gear whenever we remember something—or forget. Researchers now believe that the brain activates memory pathways during learning. Some of these pathways stay in place for years, others for only seconds. The key to setting up these pathways are NMDA receptors, or at least that's the theory of Gary Lynch and Michel Baudry at the University of California at Irvine.

To prove this, three separate drug companies developed drugs that block NMDA receptors and tested these substances on swimming rats. Normal rats trapped in a water maze swam their way to safety. But other rats, treated with NMDA blockers, didn't make it. The task for the future is to be able to run the experiment in reverse, developing drugs that stimulate rather than annihilate memory.

HEART OF A LION, MEMORY OF AN ELEPHANT (OR VICE VERSA)
●

French scientists have succeeded in transplanting segments of embryonic quail brains into the brains of chick embryos. When the birds finally hatched, five of the six chickens crowed like quail.

When the scientists dissected the brains of the birds, they found that the part of the brain that controls bird vocalization in the chicks was entirely of quail origin. The chickens walked, pecked, ate, and generally acted pretty much like normal chickens, though none reached maturity. (If you crowed like a quail, you might be slow to mature also.) This bizarre experiment was conducted at the Institute for Cellular and Molecular Embryology Research in Nogent-sur-Marne in France. Eric Balaban, of the Rockefeller University Field Research Center in Millbrook, New York, who collaborated on the project, emphasized: "This is purely a research

DESIGNER DRUGS

THE NEW PSYCHEDELICS

Most of the drugs mentioned in this chapter have "socially redeeming" value. That is, they have been developed specifically to treat a disease or a problem or to make us more productive or thinner or smarter or a little bit less crazy. But what about pills that make us happier, even if we're not sick or crazy or lazy? Well, the National Institutes of Health were not set up to make us happy. Fortunately, not every developer of designer drugs is a lab-coated scientist working for the government. A variety of psychedelic chemists are using state-of-the-art technology to bring us a new generation of mood-altering drugs, some legal, some not.

One of the most newsworthy of these substances is MDMA, or Ecstasy. Now illegal, in the mid-1980s it was the hottest of the new designer psychedelics. MDMA is sometimes called "a beginner's LSD." It provides a much shorter trip than LSD, but without the risk of phantasmagoric hallucinations. In essence, what these chemists are doing is designing new, improved psychedelics, drugs with more specific and more predictable effects.

To design a new drug, a chemist takes a known compound and makes a series of analogs, adding side chains to the molecule, replacing a hydroxyl group with a methoxyl group, and so on. It's the same procedure used to design "magic bullets" for high blood pressure or diabetes, but in the psychedelic realm every slight chemical modification produces a different state of mind. The difference, for example, between Ecstasy (MDMA) and Eve (MDE) is just a carbon atom, yet as you can see from the descriptions below the drugs are quite different in their effects. "There are over two hundred known psychedelic compounds, and for every one today there will be ten tomorrow." That was the statement of chemist extraordinaire Alexander Shulgin—and he made this announcement back in 1983. Today, there are indeed legions of designer mind drugs. Following are some of the better-known ones. Some of these drugs are ex-

otic—creatures of the lab. A graduate chemistry student, for instance, makes up a batch for his friends. Don't expect to find all of these on the street. Are they legal? In most cases, no. But this is a tricky area. All designer drugs were in fact legal at one time. But the federal Drug Enforcement Administration (DEA) has a tendency to "schedule" them (make them illegal), or at least limit their use severely. So err on the side of safety. Assume any neopsychedelic you run into is illegal until proven otherwise. We present the following information not as a consumer guide for the present, but as an indication of the kinds of mood-altering drugs that may be available in the future on a safe and legal basis.

MDA: This is the grandfather of a family of compounds favored by the neopsychedelic underground. On a chemical basis, MDA is a cross between mescaline and amphetamine (speed). It's popular as a love drug, providing colorful hallucinations. It also provides a long, physically debilitating trip.

MDMA (a.k.a. XTC, Ecstasy, Adam): In its legal heyday, this was the premier neopsychedelic. A milder analog (chemical cousin) of MDA, connoisseurs call it an empathogen: It is said to enhance communication, trust, and empathy. It has been popular among psychotherapists, used as a means of "opening the heart," allowing patients to be more emotionally forthcoming in treatment. Provides a trip lasting three to six hours.

MDE (a.k.a. Eve): As mentioned above, this drug is chemically close to MDMA. Subjectively, however, it is quite different. As one user puts it, MDE is "strictly intellectual—no feeling tone whatsoever." It's a good drug to take before negotiating with your landlord or your boss.

2-CB (a.k.a. CBR): Another MDMA analog, praised as an aphrodisiac. It's much more visual and hallucinogenic than XTC, and some find it frightening. Praised as an aphrodisiac, 2-CB is called an "MDMA for the senses" and "the ultimate in telepathic communication."

tool, with no immediate applications to human medicine, but it may prove helpful in explaining why the immune system rejects some transplants." True, the work may have no application at present. But think of it: If you can implant a quail brain into a chicken, perhaps one day we'll be able to implant a chicken brain into Dan Quayle.

DOET: Has different effects at different dosages. Visual, pretty, and psychedelic at high doses; said to foster creativity and remove writer's block at low doses.

2CT2: Said to produce dark, earthy visual patterns similar to those evoked by psilocybin (magic mushroom). 2CT2 is chemically related to 2-CB.

Most of the new psychedelics are formed by tinkering with the mescaline molecule. "The nature of our reality is determined by the way we process sensory information, so in principle any aspect of reality could be altered by a drug," says David Nichols, a Purdue University medicinal chemist and one of our generation's best tinkers. Nichols is working on second- and third-generation drugs for minor psychiatric ills: neuroses, phobias, communication barriers, anomie. Unlike some of his predecessors in the 1960s, Nichols has avoided considerable controversy by testing his compounds on mashed rat brains rather than sophomores' worldviews. He has brewed a promising substance with "the same empathetic properties as MDMA but less of a high," which he hopes will be more palatable to the establishment.

Of course, there are dangers. One member of the phenethylamine family (MDA, mescaline, etc.) leaked out into the underground in the late 1960s as STP, causing legendary freak-outs at a be-in. DOB, a megahallucinogen 400 times more potent than mescaline, also turned up in the street, with disastrous results. "DOB is a compound I made when I was a graduate student," explains Nichols. "I heard a couple of people took too much of it, developed gangrene, and lost their legs. I feel bad about it, but, you know, you publish your data. I just hope some good comes out of all this."

How precisely can a particular molecule tap into a particular compartment of the mind? Can psychedelic chemists transmute base consciousness into gold? A highly respected chemist tells about a compound he made whose sole effect is to distort the perception of music. Sometimes anything seems possible: nirvana drugs, Freudian drugs, Jungian drugs, empathy drugs, age-regression drugs, telepathy drugs, drugs that erase traumatic memories, unblock writer's block, or slow the perception of time. "One day," says one chemist, "they'll come up with a drug where you hear the first three bars of *Eine Kleine Nachtmusik* and that's it."

NEW BRAINS FROM CELL BANKS
•

NGF, or nerve growth factor, is one of the great hopes for treating degenerative brain diseases such as Alzheimer's and Parkinson's. Recently neuroscientist Fred Gage, of the University of California at San Diego, injected NGF through ultrathin tubes into the brains of aged, learning-disabled rats. The rats' memories improved and some of the neurons in their brain enlarged over their previous shrunken state. The immediate hope for humans is to infuse NGF into the brains of human Alzheimer's patients in order to improve their learning and memory and retard the disease. However, the vision of living human brains bristling with refillable tubes isn't a pretty one. So Gage offers a more elegant method for the future: "You can take cells from a patient's own body, perhaps from the skin, insert factor-producing genes into these cells, and then graft them to the brain."

This method, called neurografting, may one day be replaced by something even more futuristic: brain-cell replacement. Patients with degenerative diseases could have their faulty brain cells replaced with fresh cells from future "cell banks." Ira Black, director of the Division of Developmental Neurology at Cornell University Medical Center is cultivating rat brain cells in culture. In his New York City lab, Black is growing cells from the basal forebrain that degenerate in Alzheimer's and cells from the substantia nigra that degenerate in Parkinson's. He then probes these cultured cells with fresh combinations of genetic material in order to identify new nerve growth factors. Black has succeeded in getting embryonic nerve cells to continue to divide in a test tube, thus making cell banks a possible reality for the year 2000. "We hope that by understanding the factors that regulate nerve cell division in culture," says Black, "we may someday be able to induce the mature cells in the mammalian brain to begin dividing and thus heal themselves after illness or injury. But this is far in the future."

THE 2 A.M.—WOW CHAMBER
•

The 2 A.M. wow is a phrase coined by Michael Persinger of Laurentian University in Sudbury, Ontario (see "St. Teresa's Ecstasy . . . in a Helmet," page 232). It's that rush you get when you've been up all night meditating, reading, or just thinking all by yourself, and suddenly you're overcome with the profound conviction that you're at one with the universe. (Unless you're Woody Allen, who often feels "at two" with the universe.)

Psychologists Persinger and Katherine Makarec have created a special chamber that induces the 2 A.M. wow almost at will; it has worked on more than 200 subjects. Persinger and Makarec place their subjects in a quiet, dimly lit room, play them a recording of soothing astral sounds, and bathe them with a gently flickering strobe light. About one of every fifteen subjects reported experiences of "intense meaningfulness" (whatever that is), and one even saw a figure of Christ outlined in the strobe light. Persinger and Makarec have analyzed the special brain-wave patterns of the 2 A.M. wow, and speculate that the phenomenon is stimulated by a drop in the brain's production of the chemical messenger serotonin. Persinger calls these events "microseizures" and says they may also be responsible for the imagery that drives artists and poets.

INDEX

Photo/illustration credits:

Pages 8 (top), 23, 45: Courtesy of Psych Research, Inc.

Pages 8 (bottom), 28 (both right): Courtesy of Synchro-Tech

Pages 9 (top), 33: Courtesy of Profit Technology

Pages 9 (bottom 2), 18, 24 (both), 25 (both): Courtesy of Synetic Systems

Page 13: Pamela Ticoulat

Pages 14, 15, 16, 17, 19, 21, 22, 34, 80, 167, 170: Peter Menzel

Page 27 (both): Courtesy of Michael Hutchison/Megabrain

Page 28 (left): Courtesy of Light and Sound Research Corporation

Page 29 (left): Courtesy of Megabrain

Page 29 (right): Karen Shirey/Courtesy of Megabrain

Page 31: John Griffin/Courtesy of Synchro Energize

Page 32: Courtesy of The Downing Institute

Page 36: Courtesy of Dimensional Sciences, Inc.

Page 37: (both) Courtesy off Somasonics, Inc.

Page 38 (left): Courtesy of Tranquilite Times

Page 38 (right): Courtesy of Theta Technologies

Pages 39 (both), 42 (right), 43, 47 (right): Courtesy of Inner Technologies

Page 42 (left): Courtesy of Transformation Technologies

Page 47 (left): Courtesy of Yoshiro NakaMats

Pages 49, 51, 59, 66, 67, 73 (right), 75 (left), 84 (top), 86, 89, 91 (both), 92 (all), 93 (left), 94, 117, 118, 119, 136 (left): Penny Slinger

Pages 51, 65 (right), 121, 122, 162: Bettmann Archive

Page 55: Nancy Margulies

Page 60: Bonnie Schiffman/Brain Ed Center

Pages 64, 123, 130 (top), 132, 136 (right), 229, 230, 233: Movie Still Archives

Pages 65, 70, 100 (bottom), 114, 120, 124 (left), 137, 138 (all), 185, 231, 235: Olga Spiegel

Page 68: Courtesy of Memory Assessment Clinic

Page 69 (top): Konstantin/Courtesy of Jon Keith

Pages 73 (left), 83, 84 (bottom), 85 (both), 87, 88, 93 (both right column illustrations), 95 (right), 96, 97, 108, 113: Jim Harter

Page 74: Judith Hooper

Page 75 (right): Mankind Unlimited, Inc.

Pages 76, 116: Marika Moosbrugger

Page 77 (top): Courtesy of Biofeedback Systems

Page 77 (bottom): Courtesy of New Product Development

Pages 78, 226 (all): Courtesy of U.S. Games Systems, Inc.

Page 79: Bob Sasson/Ingo Swann

Page 95 (left): Photo by Susan Buirge/Courtesy of Barbara Shor

Page 100 (top): Stephen LaBerge

Page 104: Lotte Jacobi/Courtesy of Saybrook Institute

Page 105 (left): Michael Jang/Courtesy of The Delaney and Flowers Center for the Study of Dreams

Page 106 (left): Courtesy of Healing Arts Assoc.

Page 106 (right): Courtesy of White Dove Farm

Page 124 (right): Common Boundary

Page 125 (right): Judy Tart

Page 126, 182, 193: Paintings by Alex Grey

Page 127: Painting by Rene Magritte

Page 129: Courtesy of Hakomi Institute

Page 130 (bottom): Wide World Photos

Page 135 (left): Courtesy of Inner Links

Page 135 (right): Courtesy of Hilbar Enterprises

Pages 141, 154: Courtesy of Thought Technology Ltd.

Page 144 (left): Courtesy of Xpercome

Pages 144 (right), 153 (right), 155: Courtesy of Psychological Psoftware Company

Page 145: Fisher Idea Systems, Inc.

Page 146 (all): Courtesy of MaxThink, Inc.

Pages 147 (both), 148 (right), 149, 150, 151 (both), 152 (both), 153 (left): Courtesy of Mindware

Page 148 (left): Experience in Software

Page 163: Alice Springs

Page 165: Photo copyright © Ron Karten, Courtesy Awakening Technology

Page 171: MSH Assoc.

Page 172: Photo by John Bradford Schwartz/Courtesy Anna Wise Center

Page 174 (top): Nancy Conran Photography/The Monroe Institute

Page 174 (bottom two photos), 175 (top and bottom left photos): The Monroe Institute

Page 175 (middle left and right): *Richmond Times-Dispatch*/ The Monroe Institute

Page 178 (left): Courtesy of The Institute for Music, Health, and Education

Page 178 (right): Reflection

Page 180: Photo by Chuck Robinson/Courtesy of Kundalini Research Foundation, Ltd.

Pages 181, 202: Paintings by Vaclav Vaca

Page 188: Courtesy of Gateway Books and Tapes

Page 190: Erwin and Peggy Bauer/Bruce Coleman

Pages 195, 218: Charles Bensinger

Page 199 (right): Focus, Wein

Page 199 (left): Courtesy of Cuyamungue Institute

Page 200: Courtesy of Michael Harner

Page 205: Computer graphic/Harvey Gitlin

Page 215: Tsultrim Allione

Page 216 (top): Courtesy of The Naropa Institute

Page 216 (bottom): Courtesy of The Naropa Institute/Photo by Steve Olshansky

Page 220 (both): Robert Masters

Page 221: Julie Finn, Courtesy of Great Round Vision Quests

Page 222 (photos in right column): Earthwatch

Page 222 (photos in left column): Courtesy of Wilson and Lake International

Page 223 (right): Power Places Tours

Page 223 (left): Courtesy Sedona Red Rock Jeep Tours, Inc.

Page 236: Tom Stoddart-Spooner/Gamma-Liaison

ABOUT THE AUTHORS

Judith Hooper is the author of *The Three-Pound Universe* and the founder of the *Omni Whole Mind Newsletter*. Born in San Francisco, she was the editor of two California newspapers before coming to New York as an editor for *Esquire, Good Housekeeping,* and *Omni*. Her articles have appeared in *Psychology Today, American Health, Cosmopolitan, Penthouse, New Age Journal,* and *The New York Times*. A graduate of Smith College, Hooper holds a masters degree in comparative literature from the University of California at Berkeley. She lives in Amherst, Massachusetts.

Dick Teresi is the author of several books on science and technology. He is also the former director of new magazine development for Omni Publications International, where he was instrumental in launching both *Omni* and *Longevity* magazines. He has written for *Lear's, Cosmopolitan, Savvy, Good Housekeeping, The New York Times, The Washington Post, Newsday, Penthouse,* and *The Lutheran*. A graduate of Northwestern University's Medill School of Journalism, he lives in Amherst, Massachusetts.